RIVERSIDE COMMUNITY COLLEGE
1916

D0407648

Crowell's Handbook of
Contemporary American Poetry

Crowell's Handbook of Contemporary American Poetry

By KARL MALKOFF

Thomas Y. Crowell Company
New York   Established 1834

Copyright © 1973 by Karl Malkoff

Designed by Ingrid Beckman

Manufactured in the United States of America

ISBN 0-690-22625-X

2   3   4   5   6   7   8   9   10

Library of Congress Cataloging in Publication Data

Malkoff, Karl.
    Crowell's handbook of contemporary American poetry.

    Includes bibliographies.
    1. American poetry—20th century—History and criti-
cism. I. Title.
PS323.5.M3   811'.5'409   73-14787
ISBN 0-690-22625-X

for *Jason* and *Scott*

Preface

Although this handbook contains biographical and bibliographical information, it is not primarily a compilation of facts. It is intended rather as a guide to the actual process of reading contemporary American poetry, a body of work that presents special problems even for the student of literature.

Not very long ago, the study of contemporary literature was considered unnecessary. Earlier periods were studied for the very reason that their aesthetic assumptions were often alien, their frames of reference obscure. The assumptions of contemporary writing were considered common cultural property, accessible to the intelligent, educated man. In the twentieth century, however, modernist literature, the work of writers like James Joyce, Ezra Pound, and T. S. Eliot, made complacency with regard to contemporary literature impossible. The perspectives with which they viewed the world seemed in themselves attacks on commonsense reality. The ability to understand the most important writing of one's age was no longer something one absorbed; it had to be learned. Since the Second World War, however—and it is on this relatively unexplored period that this handbook concentrates—the problem of understanding has been complicated. It is no longer simply a question of a different perspective; there are a multiplicity of perspectives, most of them unfamiliar.

In fact, there has probably never before been more confusion, not simply as to what constitutes good poetry, but also as to what constitutes a poem at all. Consequently, many readers, although perfectly at ease reading fiction or more conventional poetry, are at a loss when confronted by contemporary poetry. The intention of this book is to give those readers their bearings, to enable them to understand what the poets are trying to do.

The Introduction traces the development of the aesthetic theories of major schools (or movements) in contemporary American poetry; it explores the assumptions underlying the poets' methods, with the hope of understanding the vision of reality implicit in those methods; and it identifies the poets most commonly associated with those movements. This is not an attempt at rigid categorization, always a tricky, misleading business. Poets do not fit neatly into place; even the originators of particular poetic schools do not consistently follow their own principles. But these are the ideas that have informed much of contemporary American poetry, and an awareness of them renders intelligible a good deal of what seems hopelessly out of reach. The introduction is supplemented by alphabetical entries on particular movements, more historically oriented, for those who want quick factual information.

However, although contemporary poetics provides a framework for the study of the poetry, each poet has his own vision of reality, creates his own universe. There are more than seventy essays on individual poets. These essays contain brief biographical statements (longer in the case of major figures, or where biography is crucial to an understanding of the work), and, more important, a description of the poet's principal themes and methods. In most cases, the poet's development is traced and, when appropriate, his work is linked with his poetic school, so that the reader can turn to a fuller discussion of underlying theory. In almost every instance, there is close reading of specific poems, so that the broader principles are given concrete application. Each entry concludes with a bibliography of the poet's work.

It has been my intention to explain rather than to evaluate. But in addition to conscious discriminations made within the body of a particular poet's work, the very structure of this kind of handbook is inherently evaluatory: in the amount of space alotted to each poet and, of course, in the selection of poets. With regard to length of entries, while it is obvious that a ten-page entry designates a poet of greater importance than one given a one-page entry, I had no intention of making this a precise measure. For example, the fact that the essay on Robert Lowell is longer than the essay on Theodore Roethke does not mean that I consider Lowell the more important or better poet; it simply took me more space to write about him.

Some of the criteria for inclusion were arbitrary—necessarily so. The book is limited to American poets who have not commercially published books of poetry before 1940. This year, sandwiched by the deaths of Yeats (in 1939) and Joyce (in 1941), is as accurate in dating the end of the modernist movement as an artificial boundary can be. Although previously established poets continued to write after this date, most of the forces peculiar to contemporary American poetry make themselves felt in the work of the newer poets. The most important exception to this is Projectivist poetry, which is a clear extension of Ezra Pound's Imagism and William Carlos Williams' Objectivism. While there are no individual entries on Pound and Williams, considerable space in the Introduction has been devoted to an examination of the development of this tradition, and to the *Cantos* and *Paterson*, both of which are crucial to that development. Finally, while I may regret the omission of entries about certain poets made necessary by this temporal criterion, one or two exceptions would lead to an endless number; and these omissions do not significantly distort one's conception of the poetic energies at work in the post-modernist period.

Then there is the question of taste, a question that is complicated by the very reasons that make a handbook of this sort so necessary. With so many poetic theories available, uniform standards cannot be defined. It is extremely difficult to compare the relatively formal verse of Anthony Hecht with the open poetry of Charles Olson or the more communal, politically oriented work of Imamu Amiri Baraka. In any case, my purpose in writing this book has been to enable readers to make judgments rather than to make judgments for them. More than half the poets included unquestionably belong here either because of intrinsic merit (that is, what they were trying to do they did well) or because of their importance to other poets. Beyond that point, taste becomes more individual. And the immense quantity of poetry being written does not make the process of selection easier. I will simply add that I have made a conscious effort to be representative in my selections, and I hope that even poets and critics who disagree with particular choices will feel that I have presented on the whole a reasonable picture of contemporary American poetry.

The fact that this is a handbook of contemporary poetry presents still another special problem. Most of the poets considered are alive and writing; and posthumous volumes of recently dead poets continue to appear. An attempt has been made to keep biographical and bibliographical information up to date and, in the case of significant books by important writers, briefly to relate the new poetry to the existing body of work. But, in these cases, detailed critical study has been impossible, except where reconsideration of a poet's methods or stature was demanded.

Although I have not relied heavily on secondary sources and have attempted to cite those sources when appropriate, I must acknowledge a general debt to the critics of contemporary American poetry whose work preceded mine and whose insights have contributed to my own understanding of the work of the poets. I am equally in debt to my colleagues at the City College of New York, especially to Edward Quinn and Edmond Volpe, who read portions of the manuscript, and to my students.

Karl Malkoff
City College of New York

Contents

Crowell's Handbook of
Contemporary American Poetry

Introduction

A SHORT HISTORY OF
CONTEMPORARY AMERICAN POETRY

I: Contexts

It is no accident that the history of a given period becomes clearer and less complicated in proportion to its removal in time. The historical imagination is a necessary violation of experience, a selective mode of vision that is blind, whenever possible, to more complex aspects of reality. As years pass, blindness confirms blindness, until finally only minor contradictions remain. And so the shape and substance of established literary traditions are relatively well defined, with no more than an occasional ripple of uneasiness, or a still rarer revolution of taste whose attacks on the literary establishment succeed chiefly in confirming the establishment's underlying assumptions while challenging less crucial conclusions. The writing of the history of a *contemporary* period brings home emphatically the poverty of critical criteria deprived of the friendly support of habit. Some periods of literary history are particularly lacking in a common ground on which even controversy can take place. Allowing for the fallacy that insists that our own world is the most sophisticated and complex of all, we are now in the middle of one of these periods.

At the end of the fifties, it was possible for two anthologies representing the best in modern American poetry (*New Poets of England and America,* edited by Donald Hall, Robert Pack, Louis Simpson, 1957; *The New American Poetry,* edited by Donald M. Allen, 1960) to be published without a single poet being represented in both books. (The Second Selection of *New Poets of England and America,* 1962, improved slightly on this record by including one poet from Allen's book, Denise Levertov.) What is especially striking is the number of recent anthologies that have found it necessary to include statements on poetics by writers represented. Rarely before has there been so much disagreement not simply on how to write good poetry, but on what actually constitutes a poem.

This confusion of means and ends is partially the result of a common literary phenomenon: the conflict of opposing factions. The two anthologies

1

mentioned above, for example, are good instances of academic judgment versus the antiestablishment establishment, of a commitment to relatively tight poetic forms versus a belief in open poetry. The state of the criticism of poetry in this country since the Second World War has encouraged this and all other divisions. Reviewers and critics of poetry tend overwhelmingly to be poets themselves, associated however vaguely with one group or another; with some admirable exceptions, their comments are thoroughly predictable, closer to manifesto than objective analysis. This, as I have suggested, is a normal state of affairs. It is possible, however, that the multiplicity of perspective we encounter today is also linked to changes in the very nature of consciousness, which profoundly affect, among other things, the writing of verse.

The impact of the First World War on the Western world can hardly be overestimated; in some respects, it was far greater than that of the Second World War, if for no other reason than that the first had led the way into a nightmare of brutality and terror. The large-scale destruction of civilian armies was accomplished then with the assistance of modern technology, killing more and quicker—but much of the slaughter took place at close quarters. The more recent detachment between the instrument of destruction and the man controlling it, and the further detachment between instrument and victim, which led to poems such as James Dickey's "The Firebombing," was not yet fully developed. The emphasis in World War I poems, as in "Strange Meeting" by the British poet Wilfred Owen, was on the face-to-face violation of common bonds of humanity, or, as in section 4 of Ezra Pound's *Hugh Selwyn Mauberley*, the repudiation of civilized values. With all sense of order lost, the need to discover order that might not be apparent, but that existed nonetheless, became the dominant literary concern between world wars.

The word "discover" is crucial; the artist does not impose order upon reality, he finds it there. This is what the Odysseus figure of Pound's *Cantos* seeks, this is the object of Yeats's *A Vision* and of much of his poetry, of Eliot's commitment to classicism, monarchy, and the Anglican Church. And it is this obsession with order that led these writers, the greatest of a larger group, to flirt with law-and-order-loving fascism or, in Pound's case, to full support of Mussolini during the Second World War.

By the end of the Second World War, the quest for order was no longer dominant. Perhaps it is a matter of exhaustion. A quarter-century of elaboration of any theme may be sufficient. It may also be that with the rise of powerful totalitarian states, and with stifling bureaucracies and power complexes in the "democratic" nations, order was no longer the desired object but the enemy. Order was the concentration camps; it was a suppression of freedom so final that even chaos held fewer terrors. The threat to the very existence of individual identity supersedes the absence of a coherent system within which the individual can effectively function. The concern with public worlds, inevitable in a classical revival, began once more to shift to the private. The communal experience was still important; maybe it was more important than it had ever been in modern history. But the road to communal experience was through the self.

I do not mean to suggest that post–World War I poetry was monolithic. It is no truer that every writer had a passion for order than that every writer was a fascist. This was, after all, the period of great experimentation in the arts. The point is, there was an almost universal concern with order, if only to repudiate it. The termination of this obsession had many consequences. One of the most interesting, for our purposes, was the freeing of the poet's perceptual energies, which had been devoted to the discovery of a humanistically ordered universe, to explore the act of perceiving itself. In other words, there was a shift from ethics to epistemology. For the first time, poetry felt the full effects of a new model of the physical universe, effects which had been anticipated to be sure, but which had been somewhat blunted by systems transcending perceptual experience.

Today faith in the solidity of the material world has finally been shaken; commonsense reality no longer has firm claims on us. Newton and Euclid did not, we have learned, formulate universal laws; their principles apply only to special cases and collapse thoroughly when the scale becomes too large or too small. We have learned about the relativity of time and space, that all measurements are meaningful only in relation to a specified point of reference, that properties are meaningful only in terms of a specific observer. There are principles of indeterminancy, built-in limitations to the knowable universe. And this universe, governed by entropy, is itself apparently expanding toward diffusion and exhaustion.

As belief in the absolute existence of an objectively knowable reality diminishes, exploration of specific points of reference should logically increase. This is precisely what has happened. To some extent, this explains the current diversity of poetic modes. The implicit threat of chaos was, of course, confronted by the great innovators of the first half of the twentieth century, by Joyce, Proust, Pound; but its implications were contained by the cycles of the eighteenth-century philosopher Vico, by loops of time, by economic messiahs. Modern literature has moved from Joyce to Beckett, from Proust to Borges, from Pound to Charles Olson; it has moved from the devotion to order to a vision of reality that defines experience as not even being absurd, since to call the universe absurd is to imply at least the possibility of one that is not; and that is beyond conception.

Contemporary American poetry can be understood as a series of attempts to reinterpret the relation of man's inner world to the perceptual universe: the effort to expunge the subjective ego and concentrate on the object perceived, which led from IMAGISM to OBJECTIVISM to PROJECTIVE VERSE; the superficially opposite (but actually quite complementary) attempt of CONFESSIONAL POETRY to establish the legitimacy of not only private but often unconscious alogical experience, as an expression of communal consciousness; the mystic search for the oneness of being that cuts across most allegiances; and the seemingly endless variations on these basic themes.

The writers who constitute these "movements" are, of course, vastly different from one another; but they hold in common, for the most part, an important characteristic: they have little use for the subjective ego that conventionally passes for the self in the Western world. Norman O. Brown, Marshall McLuhan, and Frantz Fanon have told us in one way or another that the domination of one area of experience over another (the genitals over the rest of the polymorphously perverse body, sight over the other senses), or of one people over another, has had its day; they apocalyptically foresee the end of the Western, humanistic conception of individuality, in short, the death of the ego. Our poets, without, for the most part, talking about the cataclysm, seem most decisively to be experiencing it.

It remains to be said, before beginning a more detailed study of the writers concerned, that many poets writing today—many fine poets, I should add—do not at all fit into the categories outlined above. For some, as a matter of fact, the shift has not been from ethics to epistemology, but almost the opposite. The concern for morality in art, in some cases a clear vestige of an earlier sensibility, has been infused with new life by the black writers; the battle of the thirties between the notion of art if not for its own sake, at least for the individual's sake, and art in the service of social justice may well have to be fought again. And there are still other writers for whom the threat to the self leads not to new modes of expression, but rather to a firm defense of existing forms.

In any case, there is an excitement in contemporary American poetry, as well as a diversity, that has had few parallels. Certainly American literary history knows no other comparably large group of poets so thoroughly masters of their craft, and in THEODORE ROETHKE and ROBERT LOWELL, the postwar period has at least two poets of the first rank.

II: From Imagism to Projectivism

It is by now a critical commonplace to speak of the orthodoxy imposed earlier in this century upon American verse by Ezra Pound and T. S. Eliot, from which only since the Second World War—possibly because of some of the reasons sketched above—have poets begun to escape. A line of tough, witty, often ironic poetry, steeped in awareness of great traditions and enduring mythic patterns, has certainly had its period of thorough domination and is far from being totally extinct. Overlooked, sometimes, is the fact that if the Pound-Eliot line provided the establishment, Pound is also at the root of an equally enduring poetic perspective evolving through William Carlos Williams and Charles Olson. This perspective, which emerged from IMAG-ISM, has provided much of the energy used to depose the former literary dictatorship.

One of the earliest Imagist manifestos centered on three precepts:

1. Direct treatment of the "thing" whether subjective or objective.

2. To use absolutely no word that did not contribute to the presentation.

3. As regarding rhythm: to compose in the sequence of the musical phrase, not in sequence of a metronome.

The first two points must be taken together. They are both reactions to what Pound and his friend and mentor T. E. Hulme, whose essay "Romanticism and Classicism" is one of the central documents in modern British and American poetry, would have called the excesses of romanticism: the preoccupation with the infinite, and therefore the abstract, at the expense of the concrete, the physically perceptible; the flood of talk and speculation about experience in place of the attempt to communicate experience directly. What Pound suggests, in his essay "A Retrospect," as a means of this direct communication is the Image:

> An "Image" is that which presents an intellectual and emotional complex in an instant of time. I use the term "complex" rather in the technical sense employed by the newer psychologists, such as Hart, though we might not agree absolutely in our application.
>
> It is the presentation of such a "complex" instantaneously which gives that sense of sudden liberation; that sense of freedom from time limits and space limits; that sense of sudden growth, which we experience in the presence of the greatest works of art.

Of at least as much importance as what an Image is, is what it is not. It is not, for example, mere description. It is not, in fact, description at all, although many who used the term took for granted that it was. "Don't be descriptive," Pound warned in "A Retrospect," "remember that the painter can describe a landscape much better than you can, and that he has to know a deal more about it." If an Image, which originally meant a visual perception but finally came to refer to any of the senses, is not description, what then is it?

Here is Pound's classic example:

In a Station of the Metro

The apparition of these faces in the crowd;
Petals on a wet, black bough.

The purpose of this poem, obviously influenced in spirit if not in precise form by the Japanese *haiku*, is not at all to describe the faces in the crowd; physical details of those faces are almost entirely missing. Pound relies for his effect on the juxtaposition of two images to form his Image: the "intellectual and emotional complex in an instant of time." Significance resides neither in one image or the other, but in the tension between the two. It is not a simple metaphor. The faces remind the poet of petals on a wet, black bough, but the contrast between images, between the faces emerging from the crowded metro and the natural vitality of the petals on a bough wet with life, is at least as important as the resemblance that evoked the Image to begin with. The "meaning" of the poem, then, lies not in what is said but in what is implied. And the reader, in whose mind the images are brought together, in whose consciousness the "energy-discharge" (to use Charles Olson's phrase) takes place, becomes an active participant in the creative process.

It must strike many readers that Pound's definition of Image comes very close to what is now commonly accepted as a definition of a literary symbol: something concrete and definite used to represent something abstract and indefinite. And yet Pound himself was often critical of symbolism. The confusion is probably a matter of vocabulary. For Pound a symbol was what might more properly be called a sign—a definite one-to-one relationship; the natural symbol, or the Image, corresponds to the current conception of symbol:

> I believe that the proper and perfect symbol is the natural object, that if a man use "symbols" he must so use them that their symbolic function does not obtrude; so that a sense, and the poetic quality of the passage, is not lost to those who do not understand the symbol as such, to whom, for instance, a hawk is a hawk.

("A Retrospect")

The third Imagist dictum, addressing itself to rhythm, is an appeal for free verse. Free verse did already exist, as far back as Milton, on as large a scale as Whitman, as recently as Stephen Crane. But the Imagists were here establishing it—or, if we question their power or that of any other individual or group so to determine the course of literary history, announcing it—as the prevalent "metrical" form of the modern age. Although free verse involves a certain amount of liberation and places fewer obstacles between the poet and what he wants to say, it plunges him into new difficulties: first, it is possible that in metrical poetry the obstacles themselves are essential to the poetic process, that only by working his own feelings or ideas against them can the poet formally realize his vision; second, free verse removes the expectation of a consistent meter from the reader's mind, and thereby deprives the poet of an important source of poetic tension; and finally, it raises the question of where the appropriate rhythm is to be found now that the arbitrary framework of meter no longer exists. On the first two points, Pound would no doubt concede that the writing of free verse is especially difficult, requiring above all firm self-discipline. Quoting Eliot, Pound pointed out, "No vers is libre for the man who wants to do a good job." On the last matter, he said: "I believe in 'absolute rhythm,' a rhythm, that is, in poetry which corresponds exactly to the emotion or shade of emotion to be expressed."

Now this is a quasi-mystical proposition, although some contemporary heirs of Pound, such as Olson, Robert Duncan, and Robert Creeley, have rationalized it by rooting rhythms in biology and man's connections with the natural world. In fact, the entire notion of the Image freeing the reader from limits of time and space has a remarkable transcendental quality for an aesthetic grounded so firmly in concrete reality. The Image, or the symbol, then, is ahistorical; it shifts man's attention to aspects of his experience that are independent of time and place. It does not deny subjective experience, though in truth it de-emphasizes it, but it begins to treat the inner world as if it were a manifestation of the outer.

Not too long after Pound had published his "A Few Don'ts by an *Imagiste*" (*Poetry* 1, March 1913), the movement fragmented. Amy Lowell and her followers practiced what Pound called "Amygism"; they emphasized the pictorial aspects of Imagism and for them the term seemed finally to encompass almost any short poem in free verse. To dissociate himself from the Amygists, Pound formed his own school, Vorticism, whose principles were expressed in the two issues of its sponsoring magazine, *BLAST*. In his essay "Vorticism," written for the *Fortnightly Review* in 1914, Pound summed up: "The image is not an idea. It is a radiant node or cluster; it is what I can, and must perforce, call a vortex, from which, and through which, and into which ideas are constantly rushing." In the same chapter, Pound commented on his "Metro" poem: "In a poem of this sort one is trying to record the precise instant when a thing outward and objective transforms itself, or darts into a thing inward and subjective." Imagism, or Vorticism, for Pound was not a matter of picture; it was a question of energy, of tension between inner and outer worlds.

The next formal attempt to prevent good Imagism from being driven out by bad Amygism was made by Ezra Pound's close friend, William Carlos Williams. In the early 1930s Williams, along with George Oppen and Charles Reznikoff, founded the Objectivist Press (which published three or four books before folding), with the avowed purpose of rescuing Imagism from its lack of formal necessity. In his *Autiobiography*, Williams defined Objectivism's purposes:

> . . . the poem, like every other form of art, is an object, an object that in itself formally presents its case and its meaning by the very form it assumes. Therefore, being an object, it should be so treated and controlled—but not as in the past. For past objects have about them past necessities—like the sonnet—which have conditioned them and from which, as a form itself, they cannot be freed.
>
> The poem being an object (like a symphony or cubist painting) it must be the purpose of the poet to make of his words a new form: to invent, that is, an object consonant with his day. This was what we wished to imply by Objectivism, an antidote, in a sense, to the bare image haphazardly presented in loose verse.

The most important extension of Pound's theory is barely recognizable in this passage, but it is there: the idea that the poem is an object in itself, a reality in itself, and not simply an imitation of reality. This concept had been central to Williams' notion of poetry years before the Objectivist Press came into its brief existence. In *Spring and All* (1922), Williams wrote:

> Imagination is not to avoid reality, nor is it description nor an evocation of objects or situations, it is to say that poetry does not tamper

with the world but moves it—It affirms reality most powerfully and therefore, since reality needs no personal support but exists free from human action, as proven by science in the indestructibility of matter and of force, it creates a new object, a play, a dance which is not a mirror up to nature but—

> As birds' wings beat the solid air without which none could fly so words freed by the imagination affirm reality by their flight.

Nature, Williams says, is important to us "because it possesses the quality of independent existence, of reality which we feel in ourselves. It is not opposed to art but apposed to it."

It is never easy to separate the obvious from the revolutionary. The idea that the poem is a "closed system," a universe in itself, governed by its own logic, its own rules, certainly did not originate with Williams, although he did anticipate the NEW CRITICISM, which, beginning in the thirties and forties, made this an assumption for generations of students of poetry. But that a poem should interest us not for what it says about *the* real world, but because it is *a* real world, may be, if not truly innovative, the principle's most forceful shape in our age. We can learn more about the nature of being by studying a complete system than by analyzing in great detail a fragment of a more complex system. Just as our universe consists of a variety of particles held together in tension by gravitational, magnetic, and nuclear attraction, so the poem is a field of energy held together by the powers of imagination.

For Williams, as for Pound, the final purpose of art was liberation from conventional worlds of perception, the transcending of the ego by experiencing the ways in which the self participates in the universal—not necessarily through mysticism, but by seeing man himself as an object in the natural universe. And, like Pound, Williams is most interested in that moment of tension and interaction between inner and outer worlds:

> The inevitable flux of the seeing eye toward measuring itself by the world it inhabits can only result in . . . crushing humiliation unless the individual raise [himself] to some approximate co-extension with the universe. This is possible by aid of the imagination. Only through the agency of this force can a man feel himself moved largely with sympathetic pulses at work—. . . .
>
> In the composition, the artist does exactly what every eye must do with life, fix the particular with the universality of his own personality . . .
>
> *(Spring and All)*

This reverses the usual assigning of attributes; here, the objective world is not universal but particular, the private world is not particular but universal. The self is universal insofar as it is in touch with "sympathetic pulses." What these pulses are, except that they seem linked to rhythms of the natural universe, is not completely explained by Williams. For that we must turn to Charles Olson and Robert Duncan, but not before examining an-

other implication of the passage quoted above. The artist does in his composition, says Williams, what every eye does with life. The business of the
artist, then, does not necessarily isolate him from the common body of men.
If, as modern science tells us, there is no absolute model of the universe, if
the "real" world lies neither totally within the sensory system of the observer nor within the material properties of the object observed but in an
interaction between the two, then each individual is in a very real sense the
creator of his own universe. The artist is different chiefly in that he accepts
responsibility for his creation rather than contending it is simply there.
Thus, when the poet talks about the poetic process, as many contemporary
poets do almost exclusively, he is not engaged in shop talk, but is addressing himself to universal conditions of existence.

The poetry and poetics of Wallace Stevens are not generally thought of
as being in the tradition of Pound and Williams; in many respects, they are
not. But like the others, Stevens was at the start of his career an Imagist poet.
Like them, he realized the limitations of Imagism and moved beyond it.
The direction he took at that point clearly serves to distinguish him; he relied too much on wit, irony, and the French Symbolists to utilize open
verse. His original preoccupations, however, were as involved with problems of perception as those of the contemporary Projectivist poets. The famous early poem "Thirteen Ways of Looking at a Blackbird" is one of the
chief examples in our literature of the poet encountering not the commonsense reality of the materialist but the very limits of the sensible universe.
Section 9 of that poem is especially suggestive:

> When the blackbird flew out of sight,
> It marked the edge
> Of one of many circles.

It seems analogous in some respects to attempts to measure position, mass,
or velocity of electrons indirectly; it is the point of the bird's disappearance,
not its presence, that marks the edge of the circle. Further, the circle is not
only the path of the bird, but the horizon beyond which it descends. What
is striking about the image is its potentiality. There are many circles—many
paths the blackbird could take, many positions of the horizon of the rotating
earth. The circle also is the shifting boundary between visible and invisible
worlds, possibly between intellectual and material realities as well. It is
surely the line between imagination and reality. Poetry, Stevens said, is "an
interdependence of imagination and reality as equals." Although Pound and
Williams might have stressed independence rather than interdependence,
was not Stevens echoing Pound's interest in "the precise instant when a
thing outward and objective transforms itself, or darts into a thing inward
and subjective"? As a gloss to section IX, we could ask for nothing better
than Pound's remark.

When his essay "Projective Verse" appeared in *Poetry New York* (No. 3)
in 1950, CHARLES OLSON, soon to become the new rector of Black Moun-

tain College (see BLACK MOUNTAIN POETS), was little known to the reading public or the academic community. With that essay, which William Carlos Williams considered important enough to reprint in part in his *Autobiography*, Olson became the principal spokesman for a sizable group of young poets who, rejecting the wit, irony, and decorum of Eliot and Stevens, saw Pound and Williams as the true masters of modern American poetry. Olson's essay became a frequently cited central manifesto for the movement. Years before Marshall McLuhan had become part of popular culture, Olson, supporting open, or Projective, verse, attacked closed verse,

> *that verse which print bred and which is pretty much what we have had, in English & American, and have still got, despite the work of Pound & Williams.*

Projective verse takes us back to the ear, probably more emphatically than Pound or Williams.

Olson has three precepts that give shape to his general movement. First, "COMPOSITION BY FIELD." He defines the poem as, "at all points . . . a high energy-construct and, at all points, an energy-discharge." This formulation, which has disturbed many critics, becomes less troublesome if we remember Pound's early poems held together by the tension between juxtaposed images, and Williams' description of imagination as a force, an electricity, that puts man in touch with the largely sympathetic pulses of the natural world.

Olson's second principle, phrased by Robert Creeley, states that "FORM IS NEVER MORE THAN AN EXTENSION OF CONTENT." As Williams had put it, the poem is "an object that in itself formally presents its case and its meaning by the very form it assumes." Williams, Olson, and Creeley all extended Pound's belief in absolute rhythm to the total formal structure of the poem.

The third precept insists "ONE PERCEPTION MUST IMMEDIATELY AND DIRECTLY LEAD TO A FURTHER PERCEPTION. . . . MOVE, INSTANTER, ON ANOTHER!" Like his predecessors, Olson has no use for the talky, the speculative. The experience itself, in high tension with sequent experiences—that is what he is after. And like Pound ("Don't be descriptive") and Williams ("Imagination is not . . . description nor an evocation of objects or situations . . . it creates a new object"), Olson equally abhors the simple painting of pictures:

> The descriptive functions generally have to be watched, every second, in projective verse, because of their easiness, and thus their drain on the energy which composition by field allows into a poem. . . . Observation of any kind is, like argument in prose, properly previous to the act of the poem, and, if allowed in, must be so juxtaposed, apposed, set in, that it does not, for an instant, sap the going energy of the content toward its form.

To this point, Olson's essay has been little more than the extension of Pound's and Williams' poetics. Olson picks up Williams' almost cryptic suggestion that man's perception of the phenomenal world is doomed to frustration "unless the individual raise [himself] to some approximate co-extension with the universe," and develops it into his central statement about the nature of poetry and the nature of reality:

> Objectism is the getting rid of the lyrical interference of the individual as ego, of the "subject" and his soul, that peculiar presumption by which western man has interposed himself between what he is as a creature of nature . . . and those other creations of nature which we may, with no derogation, call objects. . . .
>
>   . . . If [man] sprawl, he shall find little to sing but himself, and shall sing, nature has such paradoxical ways, by way of artificial forms outside himself. But if he stays inside himself, if he is contained within his nature as he is participant in the larger force, he will be able to listen, and his hearing through himself will give him secrets objects share.

Western man has traditionally—almost, by now, instinctively—identified his self with his ego, with that part of him that acts as mediator between the unconscious and the demands of others, of society. But man has other modes of being other than consciousness. He is made of blood and bone, nerve and flesh, all bound together by innate natural rhythms. He is a collection of atoms and molecules, filled with electrically organized energy. It is only self-consciousness that separates man from the rest of existence; yet even here he is filled with longing, with the longing to be reunited with his material reality, to participate again in something greater than the single self. According to Olson, poetry fulfills this longing.

Not at all uncomfortable with the mystical (or so he confesses in his May 1959 "Letter to Elaine Feinstein"), Olson nonetheless locates the source of Pound's absolute rhythm, and of Williams' form inherent in the object, in human biology, in man's own existence as object:

> the HEAD, by way of the EAR, to the SYLLABLE
> the HEART, by way of the BREATH, to the LINE

This is, in some respects, almost simplistic. It is, however, a legitimate attempt to reestablish by means of the poem the unity of mind and body, lost before the seventeenth century's dissociation of sensibility, even before the Cartesian severing of spirit and matter.

ROBERT DUNCAN, a teacher at Black Mountain College and disciple of Charles Olson, has followed up the suggestion that the line's rhythm comes from bodily sources. In "Notes on Poetics Regarding Olson's 'Maximus,'" an important but largely unnoticed essay (published in the *Black Mountain Review* in January 1964), Duncan expands the notion of muscular, rather than visual, poetry as the dominant mode in contemporary verse:

> Starting with the image, and so with Ezra Pound (but I mean this as beyond imagism—the vision he makes clear in the Cavalcanti piece) embodied in the language, a speech in which the eye works, and moving by means of the embodying in the language of the "act" toward the act—in taking hold. "I grasp what you mean." Hence,

the "Cantos" are central, as active; and the "Wasteland" or "Four Quartets," beside the point, as dramatic.

Duncan goes on to redefine Pound's "three kinds of poetry." Melopoeia, he agrees with the master, has to do with the ear, with the musical quality of the poem. It has also, he adds, to do with the breath, blood, with natural rhythms. Phanopoeia has to do with the eye, the visual imagination. Duncan characterizes this as the quality of focusing. In Logopoeia, Duncan goes far beyond Pound's "the dance of the intellect among words." This is, he suggests, the function of the locomotor muscular system, the final source of organization for the poem.

The theories of Olson and Duncan, and of ROBERT CREELEY, who has acted as apologist for the group, with some ideas of his own, have been roundly attacked by critics with academic allegiances. Since the Projectivists trace the origins of their aesthetic to the writings of Pound and Williams, the hostility of some critics illustrates how alien to the academic mind Pound and Williams, although acknowledged as giants of some sort or another, really are. However, ironically enough, the Projectivist line has recently found firm and convincing support in the hands of a poet, critic, and scholar whose academic credentials are beyond reproach—and who probably would not want to be identified with the Projectivist school anyway. I am referring to Stanley Burnshaw, whose *The Seamless Web* (1970), which deals with Pound infrequently, Williams once, Olson and his followers not at all, is possibly the most important book on aesthetics for the next few decades.

Burnshaw's thesis is essentially this: poetry is concerned with creature knowledge rather than cultural knowledge. The latter pertains to the ego, to history, to the products of man's consciousness of himself; the former has to do with man's fundamental bonds with the natural world, and as such is beyond time and history, reason and philosophy. Burnshaw draws heavily on biology and psychology to show that biological rhythms are crucial to man's life whether he chooses to acknowledge them or not, that there is even a basic electrical rhythm of the brain to which the entire organism wishes to return when disturbed by crisis. Poetry is then the product of this entire organism, expressing its totality of being, rather than of the ego, of the conscious portion. It is, in fact, the aspect of the poem as a creation of the total organism that holds such great fascination for the human mind. As for the question of who writes the poem, Burnshaw denies—offering much evidence for his denial—that it is simply the product of the conscious mind, but argues that the poem is, to a great degree, done *to* the poet, written by *means* of him rather than *by* him. Ego and consciousness are instruments of divisiveness, of individuation, of separation; poetry, whose prime characteristic is to note similarities among things apparently distinct, reestablishes a sense of primal harmony.

There is hardly space here to examine Burnshaw's propositions—which are to aesthetics what Norman O. Brown's were to psychology, Marshall McLuhan's to communications, Frantz Fanon's to sociology—in appropriate detail; and it is precisely in detail that the strength of his arguments lie. But it is interesting to note where he concurs with at least some of Projectivist dogma. The notion of poetic field, for example, often attacked as meaningless jargon intended to hide an absence of thought, is given theoretical support in *The Seamless Web:*

> Hence a poem is not only a grand, all-encompassing image "composed" by individual images but a self-containing field of reciprocal forces in which each element is suffused with and suffuses metaphoric influence. This condition bears witness to the transformation that occurs within what is seen from outside as a framed-in universe of an extraordinary sort.

Burnshaw also supports Duncan's conception of muscular poetry (though Duncan is not specifically alluded to, possibly not at all in mind or even read):

> But words are also biology. Except for a handful of poets and scholars, nobody has taken time to consider the feeling of verbal sounds in the physical organism. Even today . . . the muscular sensation of words is virtually ignored by all but poets who know how much the body is engaged by a poem. That words are physical events for the organism, even when experienced in silence, others will of course quickly acknowledge. Indeed, it is obvious and, taking it for granted, they "naturally" pass it by.

An important distinction, however, must be made between the theories of Stanley Burnshaw and those of the Projectivists. While Burnshaw is interested in formulating an aesthetic that will encompass all of poetry, the Projectivist theorists are concerned with stimulating the writing of a specific kind of poetry. And it is ultimately by the poetry rather than the theories that the Projectivists must be judged. A school of writers, of which Olson, Duncan, and Creeley form the core, certainly exists to be judged. The historical survey made by Donald M. Allen in his preface to *The New American Poetry,* though now more than ten years old, still serves as a good guide to the heart of the movement.

Olson, Duncan, and Creeley were teachers at Black Mountain College in the early fifties. Edward Dorn and Joel Oppenheimer studied there. Paul Blackburn, Paul Carroll, and Denise Levertov, all are associated with the original group by publication in *Origin* and the *Black Mountain Review.* Duncan forms a link with the poets of the San Francisco Renaissance, a movement that had developed there in the late forties, with Brother Antoninus and Lawrence Ferlinghetti, among others. Gary Snyder, Michael McClure, and LeRoi Jones (Imamu Baraka) are some of the other relatively well-known poets who became associated with the movement, as did the Beat Generation and the New York Poets, who are discussed separately below. Donald Allen warns that the separation of these poets into distinct categories is largely a matter of historical accident and arbitrary order; he could have added that the uniting of all these poets in one large category is a similar oversimplification. Nevertheless, whatever their differences, it is clear that their poetry is rooted chiefly in the Pound-Williams-Olson tradition. We cannot pretend to have placed the contemporary period in its proper context without considering, however briefly, the three great monuments of that tradition: Pound's *Cantos*, Williams' *Paterson*, and Olson's *Maximus* poems.

III: Three Major Poems

For all its importance to modern poetry, the Imagist movement led to a dead end. Almost every poet of stature involved in it was forced to transcend Imagism, though all profited by the association. T. S. Eliot and Wallace Stevens, in different ways, turned the Image into the Symbol, buttressed by a surface of wit and irony. Ezra Pound and William Carlos Williams, however, moved beyond Imagism through its own dynamics, through the tensions created by juxtaposed images.

If the poem is to be limited to a single perception, to a single intellectual or emotional complex, it is clear that although the poem's image may be resonant, it cannot carry the full weight of a comprehensive view of reality; it can, to be sure, suggest that view, but it cannot give it concrete form. Pound's early Imagist poems, however, had tested the possibilities of images in juxtaposition. Perceptions placed in sequence would enrich those surrounding them; the reader, in whose mind the final context for the poem resided, would participate directly in the creative process. The problem was that on the one hand a series of images without organizing principles would be chaotic and meaningless, while on the other a strongly related series of images would amount to a narrative. The *Cantos*, accordingly, make use of certain archetypal patterns, for example, a complex of quest myths, especially those involving descent into the underworld. Taking advantage of the cyclical, repetitive nature of history, however, and taking very literally the notion that insight into the nature of things, escape from time to' the perspectives of eternity, involves a transformation, a metamorphosis, Pound assembled an endless stream of characters, situations, even modes of reality. These were set off, one against the other, so that the reader could "find" for himself in the apparently random flux of experience underlying pattern. The creation of form out of flux is precisely the central theme of the *Cantos*.

The tension between order and chaos is at the heart of all confrontations; as I have suggested, this tension is also the form of the poem. A selection from the beginning of Canto II will illustrate how Pound uses that tension to hold the poem together:

> Hang it all, Robert Browning,
> there can be but the one "Sordello."
> But Sordello, and my Sordello?
> Lo Sordels si fo di Mantovana.
> So-shu churned in the sea.

> Seal sports in the spray-whited circles of cliff-wash,
> Sleek head, daughter of Lir,
>   eyes of Picasso
> Under black fur-hood, lithe daughter of Ocean;
> And the wave runs in the beach-groove:
> "Eleanor, ἐλέναυς and ἐλέπτολις !"

In the space of eleven lines, Pound has referred to a great Victorian poet, one of his poems, the subject of that poem, Sordello, as a historical personage in his own right, an Italian biographical note in which the troubadour Sordello is identified, a Chinese poet or philosopher, the daughter of an Irish sea-god, the contemporary Spanish artist, and Eleanor (Helen of Troy), destroyer of ships and cities. The images do not tell a consistent story—and this has been one of the principal causes of frustration in readers of the *Cantos*—but they are not completely unrelated. Browning's poem "Sordello," here the prototype of the artist's interpretation of history, or man giving historical form to a sequence of actions, is juxtaposed with other possible Sordellos, and with the actual historical document in which the facts of his life are recorded. Which of these is the real Sordello? Clearly, the "biography" is no more real than Browning's version, or, possibly, than Pound's own. Raw events require a formal intelligence, and it is neither more nor less than that which the poet supplies. The entire complex of images is further complicated by the fact that Sordello, subject of Browning's poem, is himself a poet, so that we end with a poet (Pound) looking at a poet (Browning) looking at a poet (Sordello), refracting experience at each remove (and these removes may easily be increased by adding the author of the *vita*, Dante, in whose *Commedia* Sordello appears, as well as various *personae* from the *Cantos*, to the series).

Yet so far the images have all related to Sordello. This unity is broken with the reference to So-shu, who has been identified with the Chinese poet Li Po or with the Chinese philosopher Chuang Tzu. Although this ambiguity may prevent precision of interpretation, it is an instance of a cultural hero involved in giving form to experience, churning the sea, that is, the flux of reality. This tension of form and flux, crystallized in the formation of the "GREAT CRYSTAL," and in the birth of Venus from the waves later in the *Cantos*, is crucial. It is also significant that the contrasting culture in this case is Eastern. So-shu stands in contrast to Sordello-Browning-Pound as representatives of opposing visions of reality, but the underlying unity of the creative imagination is perhaps more important. The daughter of the Irish sea-god Mamannan mac Lir appears in the next lines, associated both with the change and turbulence of the ocean, and with the clear form of beauty in its midst; in short, she is an early version of the birth-of-Venus motif. Picasso, still another image of the artist, may suggest the fragmentation out of which wholeness must be achieved.

The final line introduces Helen of Troy, one of Pound's heroines, almost interchangeable, it would seem at many points in the poem, with Aphrodite herself. Here, as elsewhere, Pound sees Beauty as a destructive force (cf.

"Your eyen two wol sleye me sodenly/I may the beauté of hem nat sus-
teyne" from Chaucer's "Merciles Beauté" in Canto LXXXI); but we must
keep in mind the kind of world that beauty destroys. It is essentially the
complacent, philistine, bourgeois existence that Beauty unbalances. And for
Pound, who saw his own political role in large terms, the cataclysmic effect
of Beauty on the course of human history could not be thoroughly negative.
Form and flux; art and history. These are the tensions holding together the
lines quoted above. And it is by means of these and similar tensions that
each Canto is held together, and the poem itself.

William Carlos Williams needed *Paterson* much in the same way Pound
needed the *Cantos*. In Williams, however, there is even more emphasis on
the metaphysical corollary to the formal difficulties of writing Imagist verse
on a large scale; going even further than Pound in his wish to accentuate
the object at the expense of subject, Williams' dominant rule became, "Say
it, no ideas but in things." To deal with the abstract rather than concrete
reality was simply too great a violation of experience for Williams to en-
dorse.

Although the logical conclusion of Williams' method leads to an assem-
blage of concrete fragments very much in the manner of Pound, there are
differences of sensibility as well as theory between the two that result in
distinct poetic textures. We cannot, for example, examine the dynamics that
hold Williams' poem together by quoting a passage several lines long. The
units of Williams' imagery tend to be much greater than Pound's; a summary of several pages is required to achieve a similar analysis.

In the section at the beginning of *Paterson* entitled "The Delineaments of
the Giants," we first see the giant Paterson (who will be identified with the
New Jersey city, a doctor practicing in that city, and everyman) stretched
out under the Passaic Falls, very much the way H. C. E. is stretched out
across Dublin in *Finnegans Wake* (to which book Williams is as indebted as
he is to the *Cantos*). Then comes the famous exhortation, "no ideas but in
things," followed by a description of the river crashing from the gorge "in a
recoil of spray and rainbow mists." Next, a parenthetical remark about reading the language of the rocks and river, and a linking of man and city.

To this point, although there has been a certain fragmentation in flow of
thought, paralleling the flow of the river and marked by alternating inden-
tations of verse, the poem moves almost conventionally; but the next passage is radically different. It is prose, a letter from a woman poet to Dr. Paterson. In other words, a document, like Pound's frequent allusions to
historical documents but more personal, more local, and easier at first to
grasp, since in far more complete form. Then a shift back to verse, and to
the river, whose falls now seem to have something to do with the fall of
man. (Again as in *Finnegans Wake*, the basic myth of Paterson concerns
death and rebirth, the fall and redemption.) Longer lines of poetry introduce Paterson's giantess companion, the mountains cradling the city. These
are followed by an excerpt from the history of the city Paterson, the story of
a shoemaker, David Hower, who in 1857 found pearls in oysters, told in

prose, another of Williams' documents, this time public rather than private. The section ends (arbitrarily on my part) with a brief satirical view of Dr. Paterson, who twice a month "receives / communications from the Pope and Jacques / Barzun," and a return to the motif, "no ideas but in things."

The "thing" that dominates the lines described above is clearly the Passaic River, which weaves in and out of the various fragments of experience presented by Williams. He, far more than Pound, gives a clear, sensuous impression of his images; Pound's *Cantos* are filled with actions, Williams' *Paterson* is often closer to a collection of objects. But rather than describing the object, in this case the river, Williams identifies with it, experiences the world from the river's perspective; for the very identification of the city Paterson with Dr. Paterson implies that the relationship of the animate to the inanimate world is far more intimate than generally acknowledged. The waters move like thoughts; Williams has but to draw on his own inner world to understand the workings of the object:

> Jostled as are the waters approaching
> the brink, his thoughts
> interlace, repel and cut under,
> rise rock-thwarted and turn aside
> but forever strain forward—or strike
> an eddy and whirl, marked by a
> leaf or curdy spume, seeming
> to forget

Thus, while for Pound the poem is held together by the tension of small particles, in Williams the object creates its field of energy, a kind of gravitational center, that serves as the nucleus for other fragments. The two prose passages mentioned above begin motifs that cannot be fully understood in terms of the river. The theme of the poet in the modern world, and the theme of the prodigy of nature, the unexpectedly monstrous, have no obvious relation. But if we understand that for Williams, as for Pound, the river represents, among other things, the flux of experience, the importance of the poet encountering this flux becomes clear; and the monster becomes still another symbol of the artist alienated from his society, while the pearls are similar to Pound's "GREAT CRYSTAL," giving at least the illusion of fixity to the transient. As Williams wrote in book 5 of *Paterson,*

> Through this hole
> at the bottom of the cavern
> of death, the imagination
> escapes intact.

The last of the large-scale epics in the Objectivist tradition is Charles Olson's *Maximus* poems. Before examining Olson's means of creating a poetic field, it will be useful to look at his criticisms of the methods used by Pound and Williams:

> Ez's epic solves problem by his ego: his single emotion breaks all
> down to his equals or inferiors (so far as I can see only two, possi-

bly, are admitted, by him, to be his betters—Confucius & Dante. Which assumption, that there are intelligent men whom he can out-talk, is beautiful because it destroys historical time, and

thus creates the methodology of the Cantos, viz, a space-field where, by inversion, though the material is all time material, he has driven through it so sharply by the beak of his ego, that, he has turned time into what we must now have, space & its live air. . . .
the primary contrast, for our purposes is, BILL: his Pat is exact opposite of Ez's, that is, Bill HAS an emotional system which is capable of extensions & comprehensions the ego-system (the Old Deal, Ez as Cento Man, here dates) is not. Yet

by making his substance historical of one city (the Joyce deal), Bill completely licks himself, lets time roll him under as Ez does not, and thus, so far as what is the more important, methodology, contributes nothing, in fact, delays, deters, and hampers, by not having busted through the very problem which Ez has so brilliantly faced, & beat

(*Mayan Letters*)

By encountering history subjectively, Pound has turned time into space, into the arrangement of fragments that constitutes the *Cantos*. Williams, by identifying totally with the object (that is, the city Paterson, the Passaic River), has become as subservient to time as the object itself; it is, even from Williams' own point of view, the specifically human imagination that must triumph. Olson, then, devotes himself to the search for an "alternative to the ego-position." In theory, at least, he seems to have found it, in the identification of the human with the natural universe. If man turns inward, beyond his ego, he can project the objective world, in this way triumphing over both time and ego.

In the *Maximus* poems, Olson at least superficially resembles Williams more than Pound. As Dr. Paterson is to Paterson, New Jersey, so Maximus is to Gloucester, Massachusetts. Like Williams, Olson deals extensively with the history of the place, repeating whole documents and records at even greater length than Williams does, while mixing in the personal history of the artist, who is at the same time a part of his community and alienated from it. The first important difference is that Maximus, a kind of exile, writes *to* Gloucester. And as the poems go on, Olson establishes an increasingly universal context for both Maximus and Gloucester. The city becomes identified with the great maritime city-states, Maximus himself with legendary figures. In *Maximus IV, V, VI*, a mythological framework becomes almost dominant, as both city and hero become simply manifestations of the workings of the unconscious, and of the natural universe as interpreted by the unconscious.

Although there are poems in the sequence composed of fragments very much in the manner of Pound, or of Williams, Olson, while not always obvious, is generally more consecutive in his treatment of a subject; themes are carried through entire poems in reasonably recognizable form. The integrity of the line, however, supersedes even integrity of theme. Line is joined to line not as juxtaposition of image, but rather as energy-construct to energy-construct. Admittedly, this sounds like jargon; but the following selection from section 6 of "I, Maximus of Gloucester, to You," which is also about the creation of a poetic field, should illustrate:

> in! in! the bow-sprit, bird, the beak
> in, the bend is, in, goes in, the form
> that which you make, what holds, which is
> the law of object, strut after strut, what you are, what you must be, what
> the force can throw up, can, right now hereinafter erect,
> the mast, the mast, the tender
> mast!

In this particular instance, even the individual line is held together, not by syntax or grammar, but by the energy of staccato rhythms and serial organization. It is, in fact, the pulse beat, the breath, of these lines that allow the poet to give shape to his experience without relying on the distorting mechanisms of his own ego.

Pound, Williams, and Olson have all insisted at one time or another that the poem forms a reality of its own, a self-contained universe that does not imitate objective reality but rather impinges upon it, tests it. Art, said Olson, is life's "only twin." It was almost inevitable, then, that each of the epics came to a conclusion only with the death of its author. Pound never revised his *Cantos*, never attempted to give them final coherent form; new Cantos kept appearing until he no longer had the energy to write them. Williams made the only overt attempt to limit in advance the form of his poem. *Paterson* was to have consisted of four books. But after the four had been completed and published, Williams found that a fifth was necessary; a sixth was under way at the time of his death in 1963. Six books of the *Maximus* poems had been printed when Olson died in 1970; there is no suggestion they were approaching completion. The assault on traditional form in poetry has been in full force ever since the start of the romantic movement, but the notion that a poem not only would not, but very likely could not, take any given form (or any given lack of form), that it might endlessly grow and in growing alter whatever had preceded, is relatively new. Like the model of the universe they reflect, these poems, though finite, go on indefinitely, limited only by the accident of the author being unable to continue.

IV: Beat Poetry

Although one of the logical outcomes of the Projectivist aesthetic is a mystical approach to experience, and although Charles Olson was not afraid to face this implication and Robert Duncan embraced it, the Black Mountain poets are generally more involved with blood, breath, and muscle than with union with the One. The BEAT GENERATION poets—Beat as in "beatific," so named by Jack Kerouac—are aesthically a branch of the Projectivist group, separated by accident of geography and perhaps by their greater concern with cosmic consciousness. They did their earliest work in New York in the late forties and early fifties; ALLEN GINSBERG and Jack Kerouac were classmates at Columbia. The idea that they and GREGORY CORSO and the others, formed any sort of coherent movement was treated by them with irony; what they had in common, rather than philosophical or aesthetic principles, was largely a matter of personality, especially the personalities of Kerouac and Ginsberg.

Early in his career, Allen Ginsberg, who grew up in Paterson, N.J., was a disciple of William Carlos Williams; his first poems were in the Imagist-Objectivist tradition. But whatever debt Olson and Ginsberg independently owe Williams' Objectivist aesthetics, each moved in a direction completely opposed to Williams, though closely related to one another as far as metrics are concerned. For Williams, the notion of complete freedom in writing poetry was antithetical to the very essence of poetry. He continually searched for a means of giving formal control to the poetic line while at the same time maintaining enough flexibility to relate rhythm to the specific experience described. He finally hit upon what he called the "variable foot," which appeared for the first time late in *Paterson,* and the final triumph of which is probably "Asphodel, That Greeny Flower" (in *Pictures from Brueghel and Other Poems*). Each line is divided into three feet of varying length. For some critics, the fact that the foot is changeable leaves the line as free as before. Even if this is theoretically true, in practice the foot rarely contains more than three or four long beats and so represents a formal limitation. In contrast, both Olson and Ginsberg rejected the idea of preexisting metrical values independent of both poet and experience and based the length and rhythm of their lines on the poet's own biological and psychological characteristics.

In his notes for *Howl* (printed in Donald M. Allen's *The New American Poetry*), Ginsberg describes his abandoning of short-line patterns in favor of his "romantic inspiration—Hebraic-Melvillian bardic breath." It is Whitman in particular that Ginsberg has in mind. The unit is the breath. ("It probably bugs Williams now, but it's a natural consequence, my own heightened conversation, not cooler average-dailytalk short breath.") As for the difficulties of holding together the long line, Ginsberg says:

> Its natural inspiration of the moment that keeps it moving, disparate things put down together, shorthand notations of visual imagery, juxtapositions of hydrogen juke-box—abstract haikus sustain the mystery & put iron poetry back into the line: the last line of *Sunflower Sutra* is the extreme, one stream of single word associations, summing up. Mind is shapely, Art is shapely. Meaning Mind practiced

in spontaneity invents forms in its own image & gets to Last
Thoughts.

In other words, if you are a poet, what you write will be poetry. The specific dynamics of the line come directly from the aesthetics of Pound, Williams, and Olson, however, and "Sunflower Sutra," the example given by
Ginsberg, shows similarities to the passage from Olson quoted on p. 11:

—We're not our skin of grime, we're not our dread bleak dusty im-
   ageless locomotive, we're all beautiful golden sunflowers inside,
   we're blessed by our own seed & golden hairy naked accomplish-
   ment-bodies growing into mad black formal sunflowers in the sunset, spied on by our eyes under the shadow of the mad locomotive
   riverbank sunset Frisco hilly tincan evening sitdown vision.

                                              (from "Sunflower Sutra")

"Sunflower Sutra" is an appropriate title for a poem by Ginsberg, since it
was after reading Blake's "Ah! Sunflower" in a Harlem tenement that Ginsberg had his first mystical experience. It is inaccurate to suggest that any
poet associated with the Beats was automatically a mystic, though it is useful to note that Olson's definition of the unconscious as the universe flowing
in is perfectly consistent with a mystical approach to experience, that the
central principle of Projectivist verse is that by projecting what is deep
within the individual, beyond the conscious mind (that is, in body, or the
unconscious), one is able to order experience and dispense with the ego at
the same time. The suggestion is that the ego, something to be evaded or
pushed aside, is illusory, that reality cannot be experienced through it. In a
sense, the basic distinction between Olson and Ginsberg is that Olson offers
the poem as an alternative to the mystical experience, while Ginsberg sees
the poem as something that emerges from the mystical experience or its
equivalent, through drugs. (Ultimately, however, Ginsberg adopted a position far more compatible with Olson's.)

One characteristic usually associated with the Beat writers is the exploration of areas of experience—sexual and psychedelic—that had previously remained untouched. So quickly has our popular culture changed in the last
ten years that it is hard to recapture the shock that greeted the Beat poets,
the most refined example of which is Diana Trilling's essay "The Other
Night at Columbia" published in the *Partisan Review* in the spring of 1959.
The Beats now appear as a relatively gloomy forerunner of the hippie culture; and "Howl," the poem that made Ginsberg's reputation, seems mild
indeed in comparison with what is being published today.

The Beats' concern with varieties of sexual experience and with drugs is
clarified by Stanley Burnshaw's insistence in *The Seamless Web* that the
poem is an expression of the total organism rather than of the conscious
mind. By declaring sexual experience—and not simply conventional hetero-
sexual experience—as appropriate material for poetry, Ginsberg, Kerouac,
and the others were simply acknowledging their bodies; as Blake, Gins-

berg's spiritual mentor wrote in "The Marriage of Heaven and Hell," "that call'd Body is a portion of Soul discern'd by the five Senses, the chief inlets of Soul in this age." And by experimenting with consciousness-expanding drugs and mysticism, they proclaimed regions of the self beyond consciousness not only as suitable material for poetry, but as potential author of that poetry as well. As Burnshaw has suggested, the poem is more often done *to* the poet than *by* him.

Although in their origins, the Beat Generation writers were associated with New York City, particularly Greenwich Village, they made relatively little impact on the reading public until they moved, at least temporarily, to San Francisco. Here they became associated with the SAN FRANCISCO RENAISSANCE, which was already in progress, with LAWRENCE FERLINGHETTI and the already established poets Brother Antoninus (William Everson) and Kenneth Rexroth as its chief figures. Ferlinghetti, who ran the City Lights Bookshop and published City Lights Books, is of special importance. His publication of Ginsberg's *Howl* in 1956 led to a famous obscenity trial and opened the shutters on the Beat poets and the San Francisco Renaissance.

V: The New York Poets

In their preface to *An Anthology of New York Poets* (1970), Ron Padgett and David Shapiro disclaim the existence of a "school" of New York poetry. We can hardly blame anthologists such as Donald M. Allen or Padgett and Shapiro for wishing to avoid the categorization that denies the distinctness of individual poets, although we must at the same time recognize that the very existence of the anthologies suggests that the labels do describe something, albeit not as rigidly as the labelers might imagine. As far as general aesthetic principles are concerned, as far as their attitudes toward open poetry and tight forms, free verse and strict meter, the NEW YORK POETS, if we become convinced they really exist, are squarely in the Imagist-Objectivist-Projectivist tradition. There may, however, be a certain bias of sensibility that serves to make of these poets a distinguishable subdivision, to unite them even beyond accidents of geography.

JAMES SCHUYLER, who is generally included in any list of New York Poets, provided at least some evidence that they represented a separate sensibility:

> John Ashbery, Barbara Guest, Frank O'Hara, myself, have been or are among the poets regularly on the staff of *Art News*. In New York the art world is a painters' world; writers and musicians are in the boat, but they don't steer.
>
> Harold Rosenberg's Action Painting article is as much a statement for what is best about a lot of New York poetry as it is for New York painting.

Now there is a bit of naiveté in the suggestion that all New York poets inhabited a universe of Art, which at that time (the late fifties and early sixties) was dominated by painters. But it was a defining naiveté; apparently the New York Poets did, to a large extent, live in Schuyler's world. A further remark in the same piece, which appeared in Donald M. Allen's *The New American Poetry* (1960), may be even more illuminating:

> "Writing like painting" has nothing to do with it.
>
> For instance, a long poem like Frank O'Hara's *Second Avenue:* it's probably true to deduce that he'd read the *Cantos* and Whitman (he had); also Breton, and looked at de Koonings and Duchamp's great Dada installation at the Janis Gallery.

There are several points to be noted here. First, that Schuyler is not suggesting that the influences on these poets comes exclusively from painters; the poems rather exist in an aesthetic context that includes painting. Second, the influence of Pound and Whitman clearly links FRANK O'HARA to the poets we have been discussing. Finally, the mention of Breton and the Dadaists points to an influence not extensively shared by other Projectivist poets, and which, if it had its origins in the pictorial and plastic arts, nonetheless had a specific literary identity.

"The best American writing," Schuyler said, "is French rather than English oriented." This belief is certainly related to the Dadaist influence, clearly present, for example, in a poem like JOHN ASHBERY's "Leaving the Atocha Station." This poem is a kind of *collage* of perceptions, a few obviously related, a few related more in tone than in causal or perceptual sequence, but most not related in any discernible way. Now this is not far removed from the poetic "fields" that hold together the poems of Pound, Williams, and Olson. The main difference lies in what occurs in the mind of the reader. For in Pound, Williams, and Olson, tentative relationships between images and perceptions, possibly not the specific ones envisioned by the poets, are constructed by their audience. In other words, the reader's mind, working on the fragments the poet has presented it in given sequence, creates its own system explaining the universe. In Ashbery's poem, however, all attempts on the part of the reader to create a system fail; a good deal of unresolved tension remains after the reader has worked with the poem. (This is in itself a definite statement about the nature of experience, but it is nonetheless frustrating.) As Tristan Tzara put it fifty years ago, "The acts of life have no beginning or end. Everything happens in a completely idiotic way. That is why everything is alike. Simplicity is called Dada." This tendency may be at its most extreme in Ashbery, and much more extreme than usual in "Leaving the Atocha Station"; but it is still indicative of a turn from the generally traveled Projectivist path. The catalogs of experience that appear in O'Hara's *Second Avenue* and KENNETH KOCH's *When the Sun Tries to Go On,* for example, may be instances of the same vision of reality. As O'Hara said, writing of Jackson Pollock, the artist does not necessarily absorb or assimilate experience. For O'Hara, Ashbery, and

Koch, then, the poet may be in actuality what he pretends to be in Projectivist verse; in the poems of these New York Poets the cards are not stacked so that a "meaning" will be found by the reader.

There are French influences on the New York School more important still than Dada. O'Hara's remarks on Surrealism and Cubism (especially when we realize that a poem like "Leaving the Atocha Station" could as easily be called Cubist as Dadaist), from *Jackson Pollock* (1959), are instructive:

> The basic theory of Surrealism is a far greater liberation from the restrictions of preconceived form than any amount of idiosyncratic experimentation, and it finally destroyed the post-Renaissance vision of visual structure supported by the rationalizations and syllogisms of semi-popular science. That the principles of Surrealism were often expounded in painting by means perversely counter to the genuine accomplishment of Cubism does not negate the fact that Surrealism destroyed, where Cubism only undermined on the same rationalistic basis as before. Cubism was an innovation, Surrealism an evolution. The former dealt with technique, the latter with content.

If this distinction is valid, we can say that the work of writers like O'Hara, Ashbery, Koch, and Schuyler (and that of Ted Berrigan, Aram Saroyan, and others associated at one time or another with the New York School) is occasionally Cubist in technique, frequently Surrealist in orientation. Like Olson, Creeley, and Duncan, their chief concern is to release the mind from the conventions of archaic models of the universe and effect a more direct encounter with reality. In adopting the Surrealist perspective, they attack the primacy of the ego, the conscious mind, and assert the legitimacy of an alogical view of experience. André Breton has in fact pointed out "that the drift of surrealism has always and chiefly been toward a general and emphatic *crisis in consciousness.*" It is toward this crisis that the New York Poets and the Projectivist poets, and perhaps the greater proportion of all contemporary poets, address themselves.

Another French source for these poets—Symbolism—is one that has so thoroughly affected contemporary literature that it is pointless to suggest that any group of poets can be isolated by their indebtedness to it. It is important, therefore, to specify the sense in which this influence is felt in the case of the poets in question, for the sake both of accuracy and usefulness. The Symbolist doctrine of correspondences, in its attempt to unite spiritual and material worlds, can be taken to imply an order or harmony. Yeats, for example, greatly affected by the French Symbolists, constructed an entire system of significances with which to contain the violent disorder he perceived. The New York Poets, however, are symbolists in much the same way that Wallace Stevens was a symbolist: as creators of deliberate fictions. "What could be more natural," Stevens asked, "than a science of illusions?" But where Stevens insisted that "imagination is the power that enables us to perceive the normal in the abnormal, the opposite of chaos in chaos," Ashbery, for example, who in particular seems to have been influenced by Stevens, uses the symbolizing powers of the imagination to do away with notions of normal and abnormal, chaos and order. He, like the Projectivists in general, creates fictions as twins to life, realities that impinge upon our quotidian realities.

In 1959 Frank O'Hara wrote, partially tongue in cheek, partially in earnest, about founding a school in "Personism: A Manifesto":

> It does not have to do with personality or intimacy, far from it! But to give you a vague idea, one of its minimal aspects is to address itself to one person (other than the poet himself), thus evoking overtones of love without destroying love's life-giving vulgarity, and sustaining the poet's feelings towards the poem while preventing love from distracting him into feeling about the person.

(Quoted from *The Collected Poems*, 1971)

This, says O'Hara, leads to a poetry so removed from the abstract that we may have for the first time "true abstraction" in poetry. The paradox is probably related to Olson's conception of plunging into the subjective self much deeper than is generally done in order to achieve objectivity. It should also serve to remind us that no matter how far removed from order the poem may be, it is essentially a human creation; an absence of logical connections does not necessarily imply incoherence.

VI: The Confessional Poets

The Projectivist poets, if the term includes the Black Mountain poets, the San Francisco Renaissance, the Beat poets, the New York School, and any others who have followed directly in the Imagist-Objectivist tradition of Pound and Williams, form one of the largest and most important groups in contemporary American poetry. Granting a certain inevitable haziness in purpose and definition, they still represent the oldest continuing specific movement in American literature today, since such literary influences as symbolism can be said to have been so thoroughly assimilated as to no longer constitute a distinct movement. It is probably safe to say that more young poets begin in the Projectivist tradition than any other, if for no other reason than that the Projectivists come closest to offering a general method of writing. In spite of this, Williams, Olson, Ginsberg, and O'Hara have never been special favorites of the academic community, which, with the exception of the poets themselves, provides most of our critical evaluation of verse. If there is any single configuration of poets that receives more praise from academic critics than any other group, it is that group that for better or worse has been called the Confessional poets.

M. L. Rosenthal, who was one of the first to shape that phrase, has already questioned its usefulness. In his 1967 book on contemporary poetry, *The New Poets*, Rosenthal discusses ROBERT LOWELL, SYLVIA PLATH, ALLEN GINSBERG, THEODORE ROETHKE, JOHN BERRYMAN, and ANNE SEXTON in his chapters on CONFESSIONAL POETRY. His difficulties are clear at once.

He is not dealing with a common technical approach, nor with a common theme (unless the concern with inner anguish in all its varying manifestations is a common theme), nor even, precisely, with a common sensibility, though the last is no doubt closest to the mark. For the most part, with some important exceptions, there has not been the bond of close friendship, interchange of ideas and criticism, or even proximity to a single geographical center to provide coherence. The "movement" has the added disadvantage of being recognized retroactively. The classification occurred to Rosenthal when he saw Lowell's *Life Studies* (1959), but Roethke, Ginsberg, and even Berryman in his *Sonnets* had already employed the confessional mode. Rosenthal similarly attributes a short life span to the movement, considering it ineffective as an inspirational source after 1963, the year in which both Theodore Roethke and Sylvia Plath died. By this time it must be clear that the real question is not when the movement ended, but whether it existed.

It is probably best to start on the firmest ground available. In 1958–59, Sylvia Plath and Anne Sexton, who did not previously know one another, sat in on a class taught by Robert Lowell at Boston University. Both were greatly influenced by a man generally recognized as one of the two or three finest American poets to have come into prominence since the war. At precisely that time Lowell was effecting radical innovations in his own work. If there is historically a Confessional school, it must be traced from this conjunction of poets.

Anne Sexton, who had not so far read any of Lowell's poems when she studied under him, acknowledges an earlier debt to W. D. SNODGRASS' *Heart's Needle*, which, she says, "kind of gave me permission" to write the very personal poetry she had in mind. *Heart's Needle*, the title sequence of which deals with the poet's relationship to his daughter after he had separated from his wife, and which is still the finest achievement of Snodgrass' career, had been published in 1959; so Snodgrass must be considered one of the direct ancestors of the "movement." It is clear, though, that Lowell was ultimately influential in Sexton's work. Sylvia Plath certainly acknowledged his importance in her own writing:

> I've been very excited by what I feel is the new breakthrough that came with, say, Robert Lowell's *Life-Studies*. This intense breakthrough into very serious, very personal emotional experience, which I feel has been partly taboo. Robert Lowell's poems about his experiences in a mental hospital, for example, interest me very much. These peculiar private and taboo subjects I feel have been explored in recent American poetry—I think particularly of the poetess Anne Sexton, who writes about her experiences as a mother; as a mother who's had a nervous breakdown, as an extremely emotional and feeling young woman. And her poems are wonderfully craftsmanlike poems, and yet they have a kind of emotional and psychological depth which I think is something perhaps quite new and exciting.
>
> (Quoted in A. Alvarez, "Sylvia Plath,"
> *Tri-Quarterly*, No. 7 [Fall 1966])

The question is whether a breakthrough did actually take place. While it is simple to dismiss the label of critics as a new name for something old, it is another matter to quarrel with a fine poet who believed something new had occurred; the very fact that she thought this was so merits discussion.

There is nothing innovative about declaring one's emotional reactions to experience as appropriate material for poetry. Catullus is one of the early examples of a great poet who in dealing with personal feelings wove into the fabric of his verse the events of his own life as surely as Lowell, Sexton, or Sylvia Plath. Was Catullus, then, a Confessional poet? The answer is probably yes, if we use the term "Confessional" in its broadest sense; in that sense there is clearly nothing new about it. But this is not really the kind of experience Sylvia Plath had in mind when she spoke of the "private and taboo subjects" of Confessional verse. Certainly Catullus did not deal with the kind of taboos Plath had in mind. It is even questionable whether his poetry is "private" in the sense she intended, nor is it clear to me that that distinction between public and private can be made at all until a much later period in the history of Western culture. I suspect that the split between public and private worlds is intimately connected to the split between intellectual and emotional life, between spiritual and material realities, which T. S. Eliot described in his phrase "dissociation of sensibility" while discussing the seventeenth-century metaphysical poets.

In "The Canonization," however, John Donne establishes the notion of an inner, private reality that is fully as significant as the world of public accomplishment. The friend who has obviously suggested that Donne's career is being ruined by his love, Donne scornfully invites to better his own position; for himself, "As well a well wrought urne becomes/The greatest ashes, as halfe-acre tombes." It may be argued that this juxtaposition of public and private worlds does not differ qualitatively from the similar contrast in Catullus' "Vivamus, mea Lesbia, atque amemus," in which Lesbia is enjoined to ignore the household spies, those who will report their love to the world at large. It is nonetheless true that the world of Catullus and Lesbia and the world of the spies are essentially the same, not mutually exclusive. In Donne's poem, subjective and objective realities *are* mutually exclusive—and the subjective is clearly not the less valid experience.

With the romantic poets, however, the possibilities of subjectivity are carried to their logical conclusions. Wordsworth's *The Prelude*, to cite a major example, is the spiritual autobiography of the poet. If we except such works as Dante's *La Vita Nuova*, in which genuine sentiment is placed in the service of an abstraction tending toward allegory, *The Prelude* is one of the first attempts to focus attention on a truly private universe. Much of *The Prelude* would seem to deserve the label "Confessional" if any literature ever did. The incident of stealing a ride in the boat, for example, is confession in the same sense that Augustine's account of stealing pears is confession. But the incidents described are not "taboo"; there is not the sense of descent into the underworld that seems almost a defining characteristic of modern Confessional poetry. Two outgrowths of romanticism were, however, in many ways crucial to the development of Confessional poetry: French Symbolism and the poetry of madness.

In the Symbolists we find the attempt to reassociate the dissociated sensibility of the romantics. As a consequence, the inner world is given a new kind of legitimacy; it is linked with the outer world in a new way. In Baudelaire's "Correspondances" (1857), man passes through a forest of symbols; the natural world corresponds to the spiritual, the spiritual evokes the material. What occurs subjectively in the human mind is linked to what occurs objectively without. The Symbolists were not, of course, the only, or the first, group of writers to have embraced the doctrine of correspondences. A well-established tradition of theosophical literature, beginning in ancient times with Hermes Trismegistus, led to the mystics Jakob Boehme and Swedenborg and to British poets like Vaughan, Traherne, Blake, and Yeats. In America, the Transcendentalists, and Emerson in particular, found the natural world a book of spiritual truth; Hawthorne and Melville knew it as well as Hermes: as above, so below. But Baudelaire, Rimbaud, Mallarmé, and Verlaine have a special relevance to Confessional verse. The inner world of the Symbolists is, perhaps for the first time with any clarity, partially located in the unconscious, in the world of dream and illusion, fantasy and imagination. Rimbaud's "Le Bateau Ivre" plunges into a subjective landscape, and in turning inward for his vision, Rimbaud has already begun that displacement of the ego, the old notion of the self that so characterizes contemporary Confessional verse. The imagery of the poem has origins beyond the limits of conscious experience; in it, Surrealism already has tangible existence. Finally, the Symbolists admitted the ugly and the sordid into the world of form and beauty, as for example, in Baudelaire's "Une Charogne," to name just one of the many poems for which the Symbolists became notorious. In a dark time, nightmare overshadows dream.

Closely linked to Symbolism is Surrealism. By mingling unconscious and conscious perceptions, by refusing to recognize the boundaries between dream and objective reality, the Surrealists made possible a unity of inner and outer worlds that had not existed since before the Renaissance, and in their case the underlying assumptions favor inner experience.

Symbolist subjectivity and Surrealist breakdown of consciousness lead us finally to the "taboos" referred to by Sylvia Plath, with the addition of a further dimension, one that possibly distinguishes Confessional poetry from the traditions out of which it has evolved. The work of Lowell, Roethke, Plath, Sexton, and the others must be placed in the context of not only private, confessional poetry, but of the poetry of madness as well. As the demonic hero of the romantics led to the tortured heroes of the Symbolists, to Rimbaud crying for a *dérèglement de tous les sens* ("disordering of all the senses"), to the Surrealists, the distance between the poet's own voice and the voice of the madman decreased. Christopher Smart, Blake, and "that sweet man John Clare," the mad poets in whose company Theodore Roethke placed himself in "Heard in a Violent Ward," still had links with the divine; we are not sure whether they were mad or inspired. The artificial madness of drug-produced reveries became a legitimate source of po-

etry in the early nineteenth century; the agony in the lives of the Symbolists was more than a romantic myth. Yet through the first half of the
twentieth century, madness fell short of being both the means and the subject matter of poetry—that is, until Lowell and the Confessional poets. More
than that, with Confessional poets, madness not only became secularized
but at least partially deromanticized.

"What's madness but nobility of soul/at odds with circumstance?" asked
Theodore Roethke in "In a Dark Time"; but in his poetry, and in the poetry of Lowell, Plath, Sexton, Berryman, Ginsberg, and W. D. Snodgrass,
we find, maybe for the first time, madness stripped of nobility; we explore
extremes of emotion to discover not only prophecy but the mean, the petty,
the embarrassing. There is a nakedness about this verse that at the very
least differs quantitatively from what has come before.

The mad poet, or the poet under extreme emotional stress, has special insight into the human condition. Not because he is the transmitter of divine
insight into human affairs—his knowledge has painfully human origins—yet,
in spite of the distortions implicit in his situation, he is somehow able to see
more clearly. In our time, changes have taken place in our conception of
what there is to see. The idea of a solid, knowable universe, accessible to
reason and the orderly functioning of the five senses, has gradually dissolved. To perceive that world, a strong center of consciousness, a clearly
defined, finely balanced ego, seemed essential. But now the fictions of the
ego begin to appear as socially acceptable, even socially dictated, structures
that get in the way of unbiased perception of the real world. Sanity, then,
becomes suspiciously like a screen designed to separate the individual from
his self and its relation to the rest of being. Confessional poetry is less a revelation of intimate personal detail than it is an attempt to redefine human
identity.

It is, in fact, curious to note how few readers have noticed how impersonal Confessional poetry is. That is not to suggest that these poems do
not emerge from the particular emotional events of the poet's life. But a
reader is required to know less biographical material in reading Roethke,
Lowell, Plath, or Sexton, than in reading *The Pisan Cantos* by Pound or
many of Yeats's poems. What biography is needed is generally supplied by
the poet. Even this is often less biography than myth, a carefully selected,
distorted portrait of the artist. These poets inhabit a world that is beyond
personality; they have transformed what is particular, and very often pathological, in their own lives into something that is universal and existential in
their poetry.

This world beyond personality cannot, apparently, be visited without serious consequences. There is a price to be paid, and it is no accident that the
image of descent into the underworld is common in Confessional poetry.
Many critics, and some psychiatrists, have addressed themselves to the
question of whether this is a price willingly paid in the interest of one's art,
or an unavoidable consequence of illness and stress in the poet's personal
life.

Quite naturally, Sylvia Plath, whose life and art were cut short by suicide, has been the object of much speculation along these lines. A. Alvarez, the poet and critic instrumental in making the American Confessionals a potent influence in England, commented in his article "Sylvia Plath":

> The achievement of her final style is to make poetry and death inseparable. The one could not exist without the other. . . . Poetry of this order is a murderous art.

In a postscript to a reprinting of the essay (in Charles Newman's *The Art of Sylvia Plath*, 1970), Alvarez explains that he suggests that neither madness nor suicidal tendencies would produce good poetry, nor that they were the inevitable result of extremist poetry.

> But I did mean to imply that this kind of writing involves an element of risk. The Extremist artist sets out deliberately to explore the roots of his emotions, the obscurest springs of his personality, maybe even the sickness he feels himself to be prey to, "giving himself over to it," as I have written elsewhere, "for the sake of the range and intensity of his art."

M. L. Rosenthal, in *The New Poets*, although less absolute, is in substantial agreement:

> [Sylvia Plath] chose, if that is the word, what seems to me the one alternative position to Lowell's along the dangerous confessional way, that of literally committing her own predicaments in the interests of her art until the one was so involved with the other that no return was possible.

In his biography of Theodore Roethke, *The Glass House* (1968), Allan Seager arrives at a similar interpretation of creativity. He devotes an appendix to a discussion of the possibility that mental disorientation may be not only artistically productive but actually a movement toward health:

> In a recent book, *Positive Disintegration* (Little, Brown, 1964), the Polish psychiatrist, Casimierz Dabrowski, against the teaching of Freud and his followers argues that some neuroses, even psychoses, may be benign. Personality, Dabrowski says, develops primarily through dissatisfaction with and the fragmentation of one's existing psychic structure. . . . Finally reintegration occurs at a higher level and the personality evolves to a new plateau of psychic health.

Seager does not seriously attempt to establish the benignity of Roethke's illness in most areas of his experience, but he does make a case for the illness being crucial to his art. Roethke himself, citing Rimbaud's *"dérèglement de tous les sens,"* seems to have felt that he provoked his own breakdowns; Seager, while attracted by this possibility, points out that the belief itself may be a symptom of the illness.

These theories hint that a disintegration of the self is crucial to the Confessional vision of reality, that there is a horror at the core of the self that Medusa-like destroys whatever looks upon it. If so, the role of the poet becomes almost sacrificial. Risking self-destruction, he acknowledges, or even commends, aspects of existence that the ordinary man refuses to encounter. This is a difficult proposition to come to terms with. It requires acceptance of the romantic notion of self-destruction for the sake of one's art, or of an abstract human community. We can, however, avoid this difficulty if we suppose that although there is a paradoxically clear insight into the nature of reality to be derived through conditions of mental stress, or actual madness, the poet does not necessarily choose this condition. Rather than sacrificing for the sake of art, the artist may very well be using art as a protection against the chaos that threatens from within, an attempt to create form amid superficially senseless turbulence. The Confessional poets may be simply a group of writers whose own sense of self is so tenuous as to make it impossible for them to take it for granted; this affords them a more sophisticated awareness of identity at a time in which crises in identity, individual and communal, are commonplace, an awareness of pain and humiliation at a time in which the possibility of human dignity has been critically challenged.

The Confessional poets, then, are a product of World War II, very much in the way that the various seekers of order were the result of World War I. Just as the first war challenged the very conception of civilization, suggesting that it was a mere façade over unreasoning animality, the second challenged the very conception of human identity, suggesting that what is conventionally known as personality is no more than a collection of conditioned responses to organized pressures. World War II accelerated and made perfectly obvious tendencies that had previously been only imperfectly visible. The concentration camps, which carried the dehumanization of contemporary man to its furthest limits, were revealed as a microcosm of the totalitarian state, which itself was soon recognized as an exaggeration of the complex bureaucracies of the other great industrialized nations. The gas chambers of the Nazis and the American atom bombs dropped on Hiroshima and Nagasaki transformed even death into an impersonal experience. The real horror of what had taken place was not, in general, fully realized until the Eichmann trial of the early sixties. The revelation to the world at large that Eichmann was not especially monstrous, but was really a perfectly ordinary bureaucrat, removed any remaining doubt that what had happened during the war was any more than an exaggeration of the commonplace. When Sylvia Plath sees herself taken ". . . like a Jew./A Jew to Dachau, Auschwitz, Belsen" ("Daddy") or describes her lust "Greasing the bodies of adulterers/Like Hiroshima ash and eating in" ("Fever 103° "), when Robert Lowell identifies with "A Mad Negro Soldier Confined at Munich" or envisions ". . . Hiroshima boiling/over a Mosler Safe," then the Confessional spirit is most clearly linked to its public origins. In this updated application of the doctrine of correspondences, the holocaust without becomes a metaphor of the holocaust within. The private world of the poet is interesting to us precisely because of its relation to objective reality: not simply because this outer world has helped mold the

inner, but because in a certain sense the outer world is a possible consequence of deep-rooted urges.

Lowell, Plath, Sexton, Roethke, Berryman, and Ginsberg are certainly all
concerned with man as victim; but the quality that most solidly unites their
visions of reality is their pervasive sense of guilt. And it is a complex guilt,
born of the violation of both others and themselves. The deepest nightmare
of Confessional verse, rarely explicit but powerfully present nonetheless, is
the possibility that the poet himself is personally responsible for the holocaust, that he is ultimately his own victim. There are times when the sense
of guilt becomes maudlin, a thinly disguised form of self-pity. At best, however, the poems are courageous; when Berryman lies awake at night, counting up the people he knows to make sure he has not brutally murdered any
of them, when Plath rises from the ashes to "eat men like air," when
Roethke sees his several selves, "lewd, tiny, careless," scuttling under
stones, there is generated a self-irony that gives the poem a fine integrity.

In fact, although there is certainly no consistent philosophy or theology
to bind these poets together, the most appropriate possible metaphysical
gloss on their poems' psychological assumptions would probably be theolo-
gian Paul Tillich's *The Courage to Be* (1952). Although Freudian readings
provide insight, the anxiety that fills the poetry is basically existential; its
source is the confrontation of nonbeing—death, meaninglessness, condemnation. The only ways one can affirm one's being in the face of nonbeing, according to Tillich, is either neurotically to reduce the possibilities of that
being, or to eliminate the threat of nonbeing by absorbing it into one's being,
that is, by being willing to face the inevitability of death, the meaninglessness of human action, and the sense of guilt and condemnation. Or, as Tillich phrased it, "The courage to affirm oneself must include the courage to
affirm one's own demonic depth." For the poet, the poem remains a token
of the encounter with nonbeing and a record of the success or failure of this
encounter. The Confessional poets, after all, are not interested in confirming
Tillich's theories; it is their own sense of experience that they test.

Unlike the Projectivists, the Confessional poets do not practice anything
remotely resembling a common technique. Ginsberg, linked formally to the
Projectivists, substantially to the Confessionals (at least in "Kaddish"), is evidence that these labels measure different characteristics. The methodologi-
cal range of the group as a whole is huge; Theodore Roethke stands at both
ends. Capable of the formal lyric under the most rigid of limitations, he was
also a practicer of open verse in the mode of the Projectivists and actually
named William Carlos Williams as one of the spiritual fathers of "The Lost
Son." Although Roethke is frequently Confessional in both modes, it is interesting to notice that strictness of form in itself has the tendency to transform the private into the public. The prelogical world of the greenhouse
poems, the long, developmental poems of *Praise to the End!*, or the later
sequences exploring the adult psyche, "Meditation of an Old Woman" and
"North American Sequence," all seem to demand the freedom of open
verse; while the "Love Poems" of *Words to the Wind* and "Sequence,
Sometimes Metaphysical" in *The Far Field*, which depend upon the ulti-

mate unity of psychological and metaphysical perception, require a more formal organization. It is perhaps testimony to the fact that poetry which has its origins beyond consciousness can find its own rhythms, while poetry written in the service of a more abstract vision of reality invites a more abstract metric. Or so it seems in the case of Theodore Roethke.

Robert Lowell is similarly versatile in his ability to handle open as well as formal verse. But his changes of emphasis in technique seem less the choosing of options available at all times than the result of stages through which the poet has passed. *Lord Weary's Castle* (1946) and *The Mills of the Kavanaughs* (1951) are comprised almost exclusively of formal lyrics. Near the end of this period, during which time Lowell was at work on his translations of Racine, it is actually the rhymed couplet that is dominant. That *Life Studies*, whose publication in 1959 seemed to critics and poets alike an important breakthrough, should be not only "Confessional" but formally more flexible lends support to the theory that an intimate verse demands informal organization. This notion must be carefully qualified, however.

First, there is in the verse of Robert Lowell, even his "free verse," a tight control; the strain of energetic, strong lines against some shaping intelligence is more evident in his poetry than in that of most other practitioners of free verse. Lowell never entirely abandoned formal structure; its ghost, at least, is always present, in an occasional couplet, the hint of a rhyme. The attempt to isolate Lowell's Confessional verse from the rest of his work does not seem as reasonable in retrospect as it did in 1959. *Life Studies* is, to be sure, distinguished from Lowell's other volumes by the autobiographical prose section, "91 Revere Street." But from the very start, Lowell has been concerned with refracting the world of public experience through his own consciousness, in the effort to transform what is most personal into the universal. Certainly since *Life Studies* Lowell has been less "Confessional," that is, the events provoking the poetry have more frequently had an external origin. *For the Union Dead* (1964), *Near the Ocean* (1967), and *Notebook* (1970) increasingly reveal Lowell as a man vitally concerned with society as a whole, and with politics in particular, while determined to eschew abstraction and to deal with larger issues only in terms of his own sensibility.

At the same time, with the possible exception of the Yeatsian lyrics of *Near the Ocean*, the tendency of Lowell's verse has been to blur distinctions between formal and open poetry. Refusing to confine himself to strict stanzaic pattern and meter, he nonetheless persists in writing poems that tend to evoke in the reader's mind a vague formal expectation, as in the quatrains of "For the Union Dead," with their traces of rhyme, or as in the fourteen-line sonnets of *Notebook*, with occasional structural memories of conventional sonnets. It is an attempt to assert the formalness of a work of art, with the understanding that the word "formal" must be modified by the context of contemporary literature and culture.

John Berryman was still another poet trying to work out his intuitive feeling that art is related to pattern in opposition to his equally strong feeling that pattern is an inappropriate means of expressing the modern consciousness. *Homage to Mistress Bradstreet* (1956) is one of the remarkable examples in this period of a long poem written in intricate stanzaic form: $a^5b^5x^3b^4c^5c^5x^3a^6$ (with some variations). Berryman handled the pattern with skill and flexibility, the latter partially provided by the variable third and seventh lines, which are sometimes incorporated into the rhyme scheme and sometimes allowed to remain unrhymed. With all the admirable technique of *Homage*, and of the *Sonnets* (1967), Berryman was clearly most comfortable and productive in the pattern developed for *The Dream Songs* (1969): three stanzas of six lines apiece. The lines sometimes rhyme, sometimes not; the third and sixth lines of each stanza tend to be shorter than the rest, but sometimes they are not. The suitability of this pattern derives from its ability to shift from strict organization to relative chaos, depending on the condition of the psyche and the tone of the poet in each given song, while maintaining a distinct underlying unity. Berryman, then, seems another poet who moved to freer forms as his verse grew more Confessional.

Anne Sexton, in contrast, has never found pattern incompatible with feeling. *To Bedlam and Part Way Back* (1960), as Confessional as any volume she has published, is dominated by tight form. In fact, the tension between the control and organization of the poetry, and the wild surges of heart and mind that are the subjects of the poems, is the focus of the book. Succeeding volumes do, in fact, include a greater proportion of more flexible forms, but even Sexton's *The Book of Folly* (1972) has its share of stanzaic and metrical patterns.

The brief career of Sylvia Plath is, technically, a kind of recapitulation of Robert Lowell's. Her earliest work shows great concern for traditional form, at times a witty preoccupation with it. "Sow," for example, written in 1956, employs a variation of *terza rima*, itself a sufficiently difficult form: $a^5b^2a^5$, $b^2c^5b^2$, $c^5d^2c^5$, etc. The great poems of *Ariel* (1965) generally have some stanzaic organization, most often simply a fixed number of lines per stanza. Rhymes are frequent but unsystematic. It is especially instructive to compare "Sow," in the elaborate *terza rima* described above, with "Fever 103°," which, as a Dantesque parody, subtly suggests *terza rima*. In the case of Sylvia Plath, variations of technique are clearly an index of the poet's increasing mastery of her craft and not of degrees of confessionality.

Allen Ginsberg is among the Confessional poets discussed by M. L. Rosenthal in *The New Poets: American and British Poetry Since World War II*. In spite of "Kaddish," however, Ginsberg is not usually placed in this category but considered part of the Beat Generation or, in its broadest sense, the Projectivist movement. Nevertheless, Ginsberg cannot be excluded from the Confessional writers, who are defined largely in terms of subject matter. It is possible that Ginsberg's mysticism, presupposing a different view of the self from that of the Confessional poets, is a distinguishing characteristic. If both Ginsberg and the Confessional poets attempted to move beyond the conscious self, this is not to say that what is found there is identical in each case. For Ginsberg there is union with pure being;

for the other Confessional poets there is disintegration, possibly in the interest of reintegration on a higher plane as Dabrowski would suggest (see page 30), but always with the threat of ultimate annihilation. Sylvia Plath and, to some extent, Anne Sexton are not always certain that this annihilation is to be avoided; Plath, especially, seems to court it eagerly. But it is still annihilation and not mystical union she expects to find. "Blessed be He in Paranoia!" Ginsberg can cry near the end of "Kaddish." He ends in joy.

What emerges from this survey of six prominent Confessional poets is not the simplistic formula that open poetry is most appropriate to the materials with which these poets deal. There is, in fact, a link between free verse and poetry that springs from the other than rational centers of the body, poetry that attempts to describe experience beyond conscious perception. But unlike Projectivist verse on the one hand or mystically oriented verse on the other, Confessional poetry demands the presence of an ego, a consciousness, however disintegrated the form it may take. It is precisely out of the conflict between the movement toward psychic wholeness and the yearning for disintegration that the basic tensions of Confessional verse originate; and it is precisely in the conflict between the tendency toward form and the tendency toward complete freedom that this tension is poetically embodied.

VII: The New Black Poetry

Into one or the other of the two broad categories we have been discussing, Projectivism and Confessionalism, most of the more important American poets writing today would fall. Certainly these are the two largest, most commonly used classifications. A third group has only in the last two or three years begun to be thought of as a movement (and it is a different type of movement from the ones considered above). The Projectivists are defined in terms of technique; the Confessional poets in terms of subject matter; the poets of the NEW BLACK AESTHETIC must be defined in terms of moral purpose—the expressions of black consciousness.

In an age in which art is generally understood to be beyond moral categories, this sense of purpose has probably been an obsctacle to ending the exclusion of black writers from the white world of letters. This exclusion is not merely a thing of the less aware past. In 1970 the fifth edition of one of the most frequently used college anthologies, *Chief Modern Poets of Britain and America* (edited by Sanders, Nelson, and Rosenthal), was published without a single black poet represented. It is possible to argue that of the thirty best American poets since Dickinson, none happens to be black. Still there is, at the very least, room for skepticism. Although the exclusion of any black poets in earlier editions might have been simply a part of the automatic rather than conscious exclusion of blacks from all areas of significant experience, in 1970, among sophisticated academicians, this is unlikely. Far more probable is a confusion of criteria. For this reason we must be especially careful to turn to the new black poets and critics themselves for the movement's informing aesthetic.

Clarence Major's essay "A Black Criterion," which originally appeared in *The Journal of Black Poetry* Spring 1967), provides a basis for discussion. He begins:

> The black poet confronted with western culture and civilization must isolate and define himself in as bold a relief as he can. He must chop away at the white criterion and destroy its hold on his Black mind because seeing the world through white eyes from a black soul causes death. . . . The black poet must stretch his consciousness not only in the direction of other non-western people across the earth, but in terms of pure reason and expand the mind areas to the far reaches of creativity's endlessness to find new ways of seeing the world the black poet of the west is caught up in.

In the context of this survey of contemporary American poetry, an important distinction is immediately obvious. The writers we have considered to this point, whatever their differences, have been united by their wish to break through and, most frequently, to destroy the traditional ego. The black poets are here enjoined to do precisely the opposite: to strengthen the ego to a new clarity and definition. The white writers have sought to transcend the particular, and even the racial, self, to find the unity of all human experience, even, in some cases, the unity of all being. Major enjoins the black poets to concentrate on their separateness, to resist at all cost absorption into a common center. There is, however, one common enemy: the white, Western sense of self that binds and dominates both inner and outer worlds. To the destruction of this approach to experience, Projectivists, Confessional poets, and black poets alike seem committed. But if this commitment is epistemologically inspired in the first case, therapeutically in the second, it is chiefly a moral commitment in the last.

In fact, the real foundation of Major's criterion is not derived from the specifically black experience, but rather from a view of the poet that is almost as old as Western civilization. In "A Black Criterion" Major writes, "I believe the artist does owe something to the society in which he is involved; he should be involved fully. This is the measure of the poet, and the black poet in his—from a white point of view—invisibility must hammer away at his own world of creative criticism of this society." The writer's commitment to his society—be it positive or negative—is generally a controversial subject; it most emphatically is now. The notion that the shape and content of literature must be determined by the accidental nature of society is difficult to accept for one brought up under the NEW CRITICISM, which began in the thirties to teach that the poem must be understood in relation to itself, as a self-contained universe, and that poetry as an improver of manners and morals went out with the eighteenth century. So much emphasis has been placed on the form of a work of literature that content begins to seem incidental, hardly a legitimate basis of judgment. Even Major is very much aware of the dangers—literary dangers, that is—of what he exhorts: "We black poets can write poems of pure creative black energy right here in the white west and make them works of art without falling into the cheap marketplace of bullshit and propaganda. But it is a thin line to stand on."

As soon as literature begins to owe its main allegiance to an abstract principle rather than to the actual experiencing of reality, it endangers its value as art. But before we dismiss Major's aesthetic as valid social commentary but unacceptable criticism, we must take into account certain historical realities—or at least possibilities.

The New Criticism claimed its legitimacy by proposing a totally literary discipline. Any act, including the creative act, that takes place within the context of human society is, from a certain point of view, political. The New Criticism, however, saw literature as not being subservient to any other area of experience; consequently, it could be judged in terms of its own formal structure with no reference to external values. The political significance of a work of art might exist, but it was a secondary characteristic, not to be confused with the work's own significance. Similarly, the New Critics—John Crowe Ransom, Allen Tate, Cleanth Brooks, Robert Penn Warren—who happen to have been Southern Agrarians, are literarily of importance not for the Agrarian philosophy of the symposium *I'll Take My Stand* (1930) but for their formalist criticism. Alfred Kazin, defining the two untenable extremes of the thirties in *On Native Ground* (1956), describes the popular dichotomy of socially relevant and formally self-contained theories of literature: "The Marxist critic could study a work of art only in terms of its social relations; Tate would study literature—that is, only poetry of a certain intensity and difficulty—precisely because it had no social relations at all." Tate's assumption that a criticism divorced from political or social implications can exist is precisely what the new black critics challenge. In other words, they refuse to accept the possibility that the association of formalist criticism with conservative, even reactionary, politics may be coincidental.

The principle that the denial of political obligation is itself a positive political act is by now commonplace. Between the two world wars, formalist preoccupations in art were often linked to beliefs in law and order, continuing traditions, and a hierarchy of being. If fascism was not always the result, the advocation of an elitist, aristocratic culture frequently was. But this may be more than a simple symmetry of conviction, a vision of order in experience evoking a vision of order in art, or vice versa. The separation of art from social concerns is ultimately a denial of history; it is not so much counterrevolutionary as it is arevolutionary. Yet as such it exerts positive political force. Finally, the formalist approach may be an extension of the binding quality of the Western mind, whose assumptions are derived from conventional models of the self and the ego. It is probably no concidence that most of the post–World War II poets, not only the blacks, have found the New Criticism dangerous to their poetry. Claiming to be absolutely objective, it actually operates as the defender of a particular consciousness, one that is now being challenged.

The New Criticism itself, then, apart from the explicit political views of its proponents, can be understood to have political consequences in at least three senses: (1) as a formalist aesthetic lending support to a rigidly formal conception of society, (2) as an abandonment of radical political action in favor of "higher," individualistic values, and (3) as a perceptual bias, perpetuating a specifically Western, rather than universal, interpretation of experience. In this light, the New Black Aesthetic may appear not more biased but simply more honest than its purist counterparts. And in its deepest implications, this aesthetic is far more than a tool in the hands of black revolutionaries. The link between politics and vision is made clear by Major in his introduction to *The New Black Poetry* (1969):

> Our poetry is shaped by our experience in the world, both deeply personal and social. Unlike most contemporary white poets we are profoundly conscious of forces that ironically protect us from the empty patterns of intellectual gentility and individualism, and at the same time keep our approach fresh. We constantly mean our poems to reshape the world; in this sense, all excellent art is social; the proper movement of human art is to shatter illusion and make concrete the most explicit and useful reality.

White imperialism, for Major, is clearly the result of a white vision of reality; and by this vision black and white alike are enslaved. A writer like IMAMU AMIRI BARAKA (LeRoi Jones), for example, a "Projectivist" if defined by technique, a "new black poet" if defined by moral position, is doubly justified in his efforts to forge a new consciousness.

To suppose that all black writers subscribe to the view of literature presented by Clarence Major is, of course, an oversimplification. Poet Robert Hayden and critic J. Saunders Redding are only two of the many who believe in a more nearly universal, less nationalistic, conception of the artist's role. However, it seems reasonable to assert that the most energetic and successful black writers today see themselves in the tradition of Richard Wright rather than of Ralph Ellison. Although both men were primarily novelists, the choice between them—and the feeling that such a choice was necessary—is crucial to an understanding of contemporary Afro-American poetry.

Intellectually, both Wright and Ellison had roots in white, Western culture, albeit an aspect of it that has not flourished spectacularly in America. Both owed a good deal to Dostoevski; both created heroes best understood in terms of existential philosophy. But while Wright is stylistically an heir of the naturalists, Ellison is squarely in the camp of Eliot, a respecter of form in the face of chaos, tradition in the face of fragmentation. It is really to Ellison's aesthetics, and to his considerably less than militant posture in recent years, rather than to his *Invisible Man*, that black critics have most reacted against, although the generalization persists that Wright's heroes are truly black while Ellison's hero is a white man's black man. While I would not presume to comment on the relative blackness of these characters, it seems to me evident that Wright's Bigger Thomas and Cross Damon, almost classic existential heroes, have important dimensions to which the white consciousness can respond as powerfully as to the nameless Invisible Man.

In the end, what position will the new black poetry have in contemporary American letters? While it is certainly possible that some of the poetry will fall into "the cheap marketplace of bullshit and propaganda," just as so much white socially oriented poetry does, the best will express what is generally human in terms of what is specifically black. From a certain point of view, then, the new black poetry finds its place as still another manifestation of the dominant literary bias of our time: that the universal can be expressed or known only through the particular.

Although the new black poetry is moral rather than technical in orientation, it is not surprising to learn that the younger poets like IMAMU AMIRI BARAKA, DON LEE, and VICTOR HERNANDEZ CRUZ prefer freer forms and poets like ROBERT HAYDEN, respected by, but not generally associated with, the newer writers, are more concerned with traditional patterns. Seeing themselves as midwives to the birth of a new consciousness, the younger writers frequently regard literary convention as a vestige of the old consciousness. Their art is often oral rather than bound to the printed page; it operates in the interest of community rather than the one-to-one relationship between poet and reader. Still, the new black poetry is only incidentally innovative in technique; within its boundaries there is room for any method that will achieve its ends.

VIII: Deep Imagism

Although literary movements tend to exist primarily in the minds of critics, the writers associated with Robert Bly's journal, successively entitled *The Fifties, The Sixties, The Seventies,* can be viewed as a group. BLY, JAMES WRIGHT, LOUIS SIMPSON, and JAMES DICKEY, to name the most well-known members, may indeed share some significant common characteristics, though it is not always clear what that characteristic may be. They are thought of as relatively formal poets; but Bly has appealed for open verse from a perspective that sees even the Projectivists as preoccupied with technique and tradition rather than with the true roots of poetry. They have been described as translators; but this is chiefly true of Bly. They have been identified with the poetry of social protest; but again (except for Bly and Wright, who were much involved in the protest against the war in Vietnam) social protest is not conspicuously characteristic of their work in general.

The one quality that does in fact seem to link the work of the above poets, in turn connecting them with such New York-based poets as ROBERT KELLY and JEROME ROTHENBERG, is a strong interest in what has been described as the "subjective image" or "deep image." Both Bly and Kelly, the principal theorists of their groups, would agree that emphasis should be shifted from the syllable (as in Charles Olson's poetics) to the image as the poem's crucial component. "When the image, prima materia, is lacking," Kelly writes (in *Trobar 2*, 1961), "the verbal gesture is quickly emptied: the poem elapses instead of happening. The fundamental rhythm of the poem is the rhythm of the images; their textures, their contents, offer supplementary rhythms." Kelly appears, then, to be tracing modern poetry back to its origins in Pound and Hulme's IMAGISM. There may, however, be a confusion of terminology, and Bly lays special claim to the term *image*, contending that Pound and company were on false grounds. "Even the Imagists were misnamed: they did not write in images from the unconscious, as Lorca or Neruda, but in simple pictures, such as 'petals on a wet black bough . . .'" (*The Fifties* 3, 1959).

There is no point in entering the quarrel about who has a greater right to the term. The original Imagists, and those poets operating within their tradition, do tend to draw images for juxtaposition from the outer world, although that is not an absolute rule. And the poets of Bly's and Kelly's schools do tend to draw the images around which their poems are built from the inner world. The importance of the unconscious as a source of imagery to the "deep imagists" would suggest, however, that their true ancestors are the French Symbolists and the Surrealists.

The first stanza of Robert Bly's "Waking from Sleep" demonstrates this affinity:

> Inside the veins there are navies setting forth,
> Tiny explosions at the water lines,
> And seagulls weaving in the wind of the salty blood.

The image, which quite literally unites inner and outer realities, which breaks down barriers between conscious and unconscious perception, between imagination and "objective" reality, could justifiably be described as surreal.

Although the deep imagists and the NEW YORK POETS were both influenced by Surrealism, a distinction must be made. New York Poet Frank O'Hara pointed out that Surrealism represented a revolution in content, Cubism a revolution in technique. The New York Poets, affected by both revolutions, tend to present a fragmented version of reality, while the deep imagists struggle to achieve a unified, rather than multiple, perspective. The result is that for the New York Poets the unconscious becomes almost an alien presence, while for the deep imagists it is the key to a truly personal response to the world. It is no accident that the dominant theme of a poet like Robert Bly is the search for unity of being, the attempt to make coherent fragmentary experience, while a poet like Frank O'Hara celebrates that very fragmentariness of experience.

Another group of contemporary poets from whom the deep imagists must be distinguished is the Confessional poets. The Confessional poets, like the deep imagists, use imagery originating in the unconscious and a generally subjective approach to reality, but they tend to explore a private world, to encounter areas of experience more intrinsically painful than the deep imagists do. At times, however, the distinction becomes blurred. Robert Lowell, for example, usually classified as a Confessional poet, clearly makes use of the deep or subjective image in most of his later poetry. And Diane Wakoski, whose early work appeared in Kelly's *Trobar* and who is associated therefore with his group, is perhaps better identified as a Confessional poet. Clearly, the categorization of poets, always a dangerous process if taken too seriously, can be made neat only at the expense of reality, especially when the categories themselves approach poetry from different perspectives.

We would seem, then, to be dealing with two broad groupings of poets: the Projectivists (including the Black Mountain poets, the San Francisco poets, the Beats, the New York Poets) and the deep imagists (including the Confessional poets)—in other words, poets who are either objectively or subjectively oriented (with the new black poets somewhere in between, but closer to the Objectivists). But even here the lines cannot be too firmly drawn. Deep imagist Robert Kelly wrote: "Poetry, like dream reality, is the juncture of the experienced with the never-experienced. Like waking reality, it is the fulfillment of the imagined and the unimagined." This is not totally unrelated to Ezra Pound's remarks about the prototypical Imagist poem, "In a Station of the Metro": "In a poem of this sort one is trying to record the precise instant when a thing outward and objective transforms itself, or darts into a thing inward and subjective."

Neither school of poetry is interested exclusively in objective or subjective reality; both are concerned with the moment of contact between inner and outer worlds. And both schools implicitly demand a reevaluation of human consciousness, both question the legitimacy of the ego as providing the perspective from which reality must be viewed. In the long run, these common preoccupations may prove to be more significant than any superficial differences.

IX: The Formal Poets

Although the literary historian almost instinctively takes hold of "movements" as a convenient way of describing the period with which he is involved, the major writers of any age are not necessarily part of any specific school. When they are, that association is often of secondary importance in defining their own careers. In fact, this is almost inevitably the case. Writers known primarily for the movement of which they are part tend to be good illustrations of the movement's aesthetic; while writers of the first rank almost always transcend theory, even if the theory is their own. Yeats may be linked with The Rhymers' Club, or "the Celtic Twilight," but his stature as the major poet in English this century is more or less independent of these relationships. Theodore Roethke and Robert Lowell, the major poets of the period we have been considering, have been called Confessional, but insofar as the term is meaningful, it falls short of describing what is most powerful in Roethke's verse, and it is fully applicable to only a limited portion of Lowell's work. The obvious conclusion is that while a particular movement may well be of interest in and for itself, the most important writing may have contexts, both literary and nonliterary, of considerably more significance.

The post–World War II period has its share of nonaligned poets. ELIZABETH BISHOP, RANDALL JARRELL, W. S. MERWIN, HOWARD NEMEROV, KARL SHAPIRO, and RICHARD WILBUR are among the better known. A glance at any list of nonaligned poets provides the basis for still another generalized discussion, since the majority of them make use of conventional poetic form at a time when it has been rejected by most poets.

It is clear that at any moment of artistic upheaval there will still be practitioners of conventional form, and that some of the finest writers of the period are likely to be found among them. The first half of the century had at least three spectacular instances of this. While Ezra Pound and T. S. Eliot shook the poetic establishment of the English-speaking world at its foundations, Yeats, Robert Frost, and Edwin Arlington Robinson continued to use the most popular nineteenth-century forms, finding them perfectly adequate to their visions of reality, visions that were in other respects completely "modern."

Nonetheless, the use of strictly formal verse—and it should be noted that the nonaligned poets listed above, as well as other relatively formal poets like JAMES DICKEY and LOUIS SIMPSON, are neither totally nor consistently formal—in our age has implications it never had in the past. It is, for one thing, almost impossible now to use strict forms without a certain amount of irony, or at least without a tremendous tension between what is and what ought to be; the finest of the formal poets, Jarrell and Shapiro, for example, make good use of this built-in conflict, and few can successfully go against it. The utter seriousness and security of form of Frost and Robinson, which at its worst degenerated into moralizing, is no longer available to the contemporary poet. Strict form seems to imply a knowable universe, one that can be coherently organized. And this is an age that has abandoned the wish to dominate chaos, one that will gladly settle for some way of momentarily coming to terms with it.

There may well be a direct relationship between a poet's confidence in the conscious self, the ego, as the proper perspective from which reality should be viewed and his willingness to employ strict forms. Confronted with a meaningless universe, the poet's decision to write formally becomes absurd in the existentialist sense, as, for example, in the early poetry of Karl Shapiro. His early work is an assertion of the integrity of the self, of its dignity, at a time when the self seems to be totally at the mercy of inner and outer forces beyond its control; it is an assertion of the individual's capacity to give meaningful shape to his experience in spite of the fact that there can be no corroboration of the legitimacy of that shape.

Whatever their particular philosophies, however, the dominant bias of contemporary American poets has not been existentialist, if existentialism can be thought of as an attempt to reaffirm the power of the self to deal with experience. Contemporary American poetry, on the contrary, can be thought of as an attempt to escape from the tyranny of the self, to establish alternate modes of relating to reality.

AMMONS, A[RCHIE] R[ANDOLPH]   (*b. Whiteville, N.C. Feb. 18, 1926—*)

Of all contemporary American poets, there are few who have more thoroughly or more successfully appropriated the poetic stance of William Carlos Williams than A. R. Ammons. This is not to suggest that Ammons is simply an imitator; his voice and sensibility are peculiarly his own. But in his preference for the concrete, his responsiveness to the world of objects, his attempt to establish rhythmic patterns that are at once flexible and disciplined, he is recognizably within Williams' tradition.

Born in North Carolina, Ammons studied at Wake Forest College and the University of California at Berkeley. At the age of twenty-six, he was the principal of an elementary school in his home state. He later became executive vice president of a biologic glass company (to which experience one might be tempted to attribute his skillful attention to biological detail), and in 1964 he began teaching at Cornell University. His first collection of poems, *Ommateum*, was published in 1955. There was a nine-year interval and then what amounts to a sudden flood of books—no less than seven between 1964 and 1971. His poetic reputation, by now considerable, is therefore of recent vintage, reinforced by the publication in 1972 of his *Collected Poems*.

The respect possessed by Ammons for the world of objects originates in a realization, shared by many contemporary poets, that it is extremely difficult, maybe ultimately artificial, to draw distinctions between subjective and objective realities. And this major preoccupation is no more clearly expressed than in the title poem of *Corsons Inlet* (1965):

> in nature there are few sharp lines: . . .
>
> I have reached no conclusions, have erected no boundaries,
> shutting out and shutting in, separating inside
>> from outside: I have
>> drawn no lines:

Similarly, since particular forms of being are continually shifting into other forms, Ammons will "stake off no beginnings or ends, establish no walls."

The fact that Ammons is "willing to go along, to accept" this protean universe, that he will ". . . make/no form of/formlessness," seems to abdicate one of the artist's chief responsibilities, the creation of form out of flux. And if Stanley Burnshaw is correct in his observation in *The Seamless Web* (1970) that the business of art is to see underlying harmony in the face of apparent divisiveness, it is clear that without involvement in the world of divisiveness art must cease to exist. Of these considerations, Ammons is very much aware. Another poem in *Corsons Inlet*, "Guide," is an example:

> You cannot come to unity and remain material:
> in that perception is no perceiver:
>   when you arrive
> you have gone too far:
>   at the Source you are in the mouth of Death:
>
> you cannot
>   turn around in
> the Absolute: there are no entrances or exits
>   no precipitations of forms
> to use like tongs against the formless:
>   no freedom to choose:

Returning to "Corsons Inlet," we are now able to see that Ammons' purpose is not to assert his commitment to the "Absolute," but to balance precariously between the wish to impose rigid structures on reality and the impulse to immerse oneself in the oneness of being.

> . . . thousands of tree swallows
> gathering for flight:
> an order held
> in constant change: a congregation
> rich with entropy: nevertheless, separable, noticeable
> as one event,
>   not chaos: . . .

In change itself, there is order, an order that is constantly dissolving, but nonetheless perceptible. And Ammons concludes "Corsons Inlet":

> I will try
> to fasten into order enlarging grasps of disorder, widening
> scope, but enjoying the freedom that
> Scope eludes my grasp . . .

It is quite possible to go through Ammons' earlier work and cite texts to support first one then the other side of this quarrel between time and eternity. The tension, in itself fascinating, seems generally to have been resolved along the lines proposed in "Corsons Inlet." The temporal wins, as it must. *Uplands* (1970) and *Briefings* (1971) consist in great part of short, concrete perceptions, free verse frequently contained within two-, three-, and four-line stanzas, more than ever reminiscent of Williams. But it is important to recognize that these new poems emerge out of earlier tensions; they do not in the least repudiate them. In "Poetics" (in *Briefings*), Ammons makes it clear that he is interested in the *becoming* of things,

> from what black wells of possibility,
> how a thing will
> unfold:

He is concerned with form, in this poem a white birch tree "touched black at branches." (Like Williams, Ammons is fond of the sharp contrasts that make even a static scene dynamic.) But, he assures us, he is

> not so much looking for the shape
> as being available
> to any shape that may be
> summoning itself
> through me
> from the self not mine but ours.

It is tempting, perhaps even inevitable, in any brief discussion of a poet's work, to focus on those poems which most explicitly illuminate the basic principles that inform the poetry. However, in Ammons' case at any rate, most of the poems are applications rather than expressions of the poet's basic approach. "Storm," also from *Briefings*, is a good illustration of how the tensions of Ammons' early work manifest themselves in what would otherwise be a simple snapshot of a given landscape.

As a result of the storm, the branches of the trees are broken, "clean meat at the branch knot." The word "meat" helps dissolve the boundaries between the trees and the observer; the trees become more human, the man more a part of nature. The trees have sacrificed their weak parts in order to survive, and these losses are irreversible. The trees are not exactly given consciousness or will, but they are as dynamically involved in the confrontation with death as man, or as any individual, temporary form. The poem ends:

> . . . the trees, clarified,
> compress rootstrength
> into remaining flesh
> and the leaves that shake
> in the aftermath shake
> in a safe, tested place.

Again, "flesh" connects man with tree, and again the experience of the tree has obvious human application. But the poet's identification with the objective world is so strong that it would not be accurate simply to say that he has learned a lesson from the trees, a moral that he can bring to bear on his own experience; what he has seen is rather that the trees' experience *is* his experience.

Much of Ammons' poetry, then, is a study of the form of transformation, a search for permanence in the processes that produce change. In these explorations, Ammons is capable of a variety of responses: from detached observation, to terror, to self-mocking irony. If the terror is never far from the surface no matter what the tone, neither is the final joy in the simple fact of being. In *Briefings'* "The City Limits" (whose title may conceivably be an allusion to Robert Frost's terror-filled "Acquainted with the Night"), Ammons asks that the reader "consider the radiance" that pours uniformly into "every nook and cranny" of existence and consequently realize that

> . . . the dark
> work of the deepest cells is of a tune with May bushes
> and fear lit by the breadth of such calmly turns to praise.

Selected Bibliography:
By AMMONS:
Ommateum. Philadelphia: Dorrance & Co., 1955.
Expressions of Sea Level. Athens, Ohio: Ohio State University Press, 1964.
Tape for the Turn of the Year. Ithaca, N.Y.: Cornell University Press, 1965.
Corsons Inlet. Ithaca, N.Y.: Cornell University Press, 1965.
Northfield Poems. Ithaca, N.Y.: Cornell University Press, 1966.
Selected Poems. Ithaca, N.Y.: Cornell University Press, 1968.
Uplands. New York: W. W. Norton & Co., 1970.
Briefings. New York: W. W. Norton & Co., 1971.
Collected Poems: 1951–1971. New York: W. W. Norton & Co., 1972.

About Ammons:
Bloom, Harold. "Dark and Radiant Peripheries: Mark Strand and A. R. Ammons," *Southern Review*, 8 n.s. (January 1972), 133–49.
Howard, Richard. *Alone with America*. New York: Atheneum Publishers, 1969. Pp. 1–17.

ASHBERY, JOHN (*b. Rochester, N.Y., July 28, 1927—*   )

Of those writers associated with the NEW YORK POETS, only FRANK O'HARA has achieved a stature more impressive than that of John Ashbery. And yet the demands that Ashbery makes upon his readers—demands that they carefully reconsider what constitutes poetry—are probably even more extreme than O'Hara's. Working out of literary traditions that include the French Symbolists, Surrealists, and Dadaists on the one hand and Charles Olson on the other, but probably even more influenced by the theory and practice of American abstract expressionist painters, he writes poems that even his admirers find occasionally exasperating and that drive his more severe critics to despair or contempt. If we begin, however, with the proposition that poetry need not obey any sets of rules but rather must somehow communicate a particular vision of reality, then Ashbery's poetry must be taken seriously; for in this last respect, at least, it frequently succeeds.

Born in Rochester, Ashbery grew up on his father's farm in Sodus, New York. He received his B.A. from Harvard in 1949, his M.A. from Columbia in 1951. He did his thesis on British novelist Henry Green and studied

French literature, both of which interests make themselves felt in his poetry. After a few years in publishing, in 1955 Ashbery went to France on a Fulbright scholarship. He lived there for most of the next ten years, working for the Paris *Herald Tribune* and the New York-based *Art News*. In 1965 he returned to New York to become executive editor at *Art News*.

In one of the finest essays in *Alone with America*, Richard Howard makes the point that although the identification of Ashbery with *avant-garde* writing has a certain legitmacy, he is nonetheless firmly rooted in the traditional past. Howard can refer to the sestinas, sonnets, other intricate stanzaic forms, as well as the literary influences cited above to support his case. But most of the proofs of this, especially the concern with strict forms, occur early in Ashbery's work, and even in *Some Trees* (1956) he uses conventions in decidedly unconventional ways.

A good example in *Some Trees* is "Canzone," which seems to be modeled after a particularly intricate Provençal pattern, of the kind used by Arnaut Daniel in the twelfth century. The stanzaic pattern may be diagrammed as follows: *a b a a c a a d d a e e   e a e e b e e c c e d d   d e d d a d d b b d c c c b c c e c c a a c b b   b c b b d b b e e b a a   a e d c b.* The letters here represent not simply identical rhymes but identical words. The adoption of so demanding a pattern is generally seen as a demonstration of virtuosity, and, although this is unlikely in our time, could also be an expression of the intricate harmonies of the universe. Ashbery, however, seems to be using it for a different purpose. The surrealistic imagery plays tricks with the original conception. Stanza 4 will show the effects:

> The sprinkling can
> Slumbered on the dock. Clay
> Leaked from a can.
> Normal heads can
> Touch barbed-wire grass
> If they can
> Sing the old song of can
> Waiting for a chill
> In the chill
> That without a can
> Is painting less clay
> Therapeutic colors of clay.

It is clear that Ashbery's intention is not to show that he can write intelligible verse in spite of the obstacles of the pattern. His disjointed images and syntax have the effect of producing planes of reality that seem to impinge on one another but never coincide. Probably what attracted Ashbery to odder verse forms was not the challenge of making them work, but rather the perception that they did in spite of themselves communicate a sense of reality often analogous to that communicated by abstract or Cubist art.

Traditional forms give experience order. Ashbery, on the other hand, simply wants to show us what is there. But conventional realism—that is, the commonsense perception of reality—is itself an ordering of the universe that imposes on it a complicated series of unquestioned assumptions. Like de Kooning or Jackson Pollack, Ashbery is interested in showing us what is there not in terms of intellectual systems but in terms of textures, patterns, rhythms. He is an apostle of, to use the title of one of his poems, "The New Realism." He tells us this more clearly than he tells us most things in the poem "Some Trees." "You and I" suddenly become

> . . . what the trees try

> To tell us we are:
> That their merely being there
> Means something . . .

It is not the artist who orders the sensory world; it is rather the sensory world that gives shape to the artist, and it is that shape that Ashbery tries to record.

The most difficult of John Ashbery's books is *The Tennis Court Oath* (1962). "Leaving the Atocha Station," typical of many of the poems in the book, is the subject of a careful essay by Paul Carroll in *The Poem in Its Skin*. After pointing out some incomplete similarities with Dada, and even less satisfying similarities with Surrealism, Carroll never really succeeds in coming to terms with the poem. He does, however, remain convinced that it deserves further reading.

The poem simply refuses to make conventional sense. To the reader of contemporary poetry that in itself should not be totally damning. Nor should the absence of a consciousness that orders experience. What is really disconcerting is its absolute refusal to accept time as sequential or space as continuous. The first four lines will illustrate:

> The arctic honey blabbed over the report causing darkness
> And pulling us out of there experiencing it
> he meanwhile . . . And the fried bats they sell there
> dropping from sticks, so that the menace of your prayer folds . . .

Ezra Pound, of course, juxtaposed fragments in the *Cantos* but with an ordering consciousness. Besides, there is an integrity of line and syntax in Pound that is only rarely violated, and then only for a particular effect. In Ashbery's poem, it is not even always possible to tell whether words in a given line have been wrenched from ordinary syntax but are still internally related or whether they are simply listed in series.

The refusal to accept consecutive time and space, the insistence on experiencing the world from a perspective that has no center and is therefore a contradiction in terms, is itself a comment on the nature of reality. And somehow the accumulated fragments of the poem do amount to a vision that has a kind of unity if no coherence. One senses that "Time, progress and good sense" are being attacked; that the violence of machines and sexual experience are somehow linked; that our society is corrupt and decaying; that experience is essentially absurd.

The difficulty of evaluating this kind of performance still remains. Could not anyone put together a poem like this? Maybe. But some of the images taken in isolation are quite striking and would not be easily duplicated. Perhaps the appropriate analogy is with Jackson Pollack. Although Pollack poured the paint onto his canvas, apparently lacking—though he had previously proved his aesthetic credentials—the traditional artist's disciplines, he remains one of the most difficult of all artists to duplicate.

In John Ashbery's next two volumes of poems, *Rivers and Mountains* (1966) and *The Double Dream of Spring* (1970), the poet shifts to less frustrating techniques. Not that he has become an "easy" poet. He seems more and more attracted to quasi-meditative poems, similar to those written by Frank O'Hara at one stage in his career. There is more abstraction, more discursive statements that the reader can take hold of, but the imagery is still quite surreal, and there is nothing resembling an orderly development of thought. When Ashbery employs abstractions, he seems to do so not with any ultimate faith in their validity, but rather in an attempt to make them part of his world of patterns and textures. They are played off against alternate ways of perceiving reality, not offered as absolute interpretations of that reality.

"Clepsydra" in *Rivers and Mountains* is relatively typical of this genre, as well as being one of Ashbery's most successful poems. A clepsydra is a water clock, a measurer of time, a way of formulating man's relationship to his world. The business of poetry, of course, is also to attempt to define and understand that relationship. But for Ashbery this is a difficult, if not ultimately impossible, process.

The poem begins with a vaguely defined landscape: hills, sky, clouds, sun. The cyclical patterns of nature are alluded to and then rejected as a definitive statement about what has actually been experienced:

> This means never getting any closer to the basic
> Principle operating behind it than to the distracted
> Entity of a mirage. The half-meant, half-perceived
> Motions of fronds out of the idle depths that are
> Summer. . . .

More explicitly than before, Ashbery's poetry is epistemological; the poem's subject is itself. There is no final truth here. The mirage is what we have to deal with. If the search for the "true" nature of things is what focuses the poet's attention on a particular experience, however, the fact that he will never find it is not especially discouraging.

> . . . Each moment
> Of utterance is the true one; likewise none are true,
> Only is the bounding from air to air, a serpentine
> Gesture which hides the truth behind a congruent
> Message, the way the air hides the sky . . .

What is remarkable about this interplay of precise abstraction and relatively vague imagery (the imagery seems concrete, but try to visualize it) is the fact that the indefinite imagery has more reality than the definite statements. That, of course, is Ashbery's point. A poem like "Clepsydra" explains not only itself, but the frustrating poems of earlier vintage as well. The perception itself is the only truth, not the sense we try to make of it.

The most complete statement of Ashbery's aesthetics probably is in this passage from another poem in *Rivers and Mountains*, "The Skaters":

> This, thus is a portion of the subject of this poem
> Which is in the form of falling snow:
> That is, the individual flakes are not essential to the
>   importance of the whole's becoming so much of a truism
> That their importance is again called in question, to be
>   denied further out, and again and again like this.
> Hence, neither the importance of the individual flake,
> Nor the importance of the whole impression of the storm,
>   if it has any, is what it is,
> But the rhythm of the series of repeated jumps, from
>   abstract into positive and back to a slightly less
>   diluted abstract.

These lines are relatively self-explanatory. It may be worthwhile, too, to point out that Ashbery here repudiates the New Criticism, and all related techniques that would attempt to make sense of "the whole impression of the storm," and all criticism that would attempt to meet that challenge by focusing on particular images, "the individual flake." If Ashbery's analysis of his methods is correct, what is called for is a criticism that will be able to deal with process, with the energy made available through juxtaposition of discrete images. Here, perhaps more than at any other place in Ashbery's work, the influence of Charles Olson, and his Projectivist poetics, makes itself explicitly felt.

In line with the increased proportion of discursive language in Ashbery's work, *Three Poems* (1972) consists of meditative prose poems. In "The Recital," Ashbery continues to work his aesthetic position back to its origins. The systematizing intellect seems to emerge as the interpolation between man and his reality, as Ashbery develops a more sophisticated Wordsworthian analysis of the loss of the child's ability to perceive the world as it is:

> But as the days and years sped by it became apparent that the naming of all the new things we now possessed had become our chief occupation; that very little time for the mere tasting and having of them was left over, and that even these simple, tangible experiences were themselves subject to description and enumeration, or else they too became fleeting and transient as the song of a bird that is uttered only once and disappears into the backlog of vague memories where it becomes as a dried, pressed flower, a wistful parody of itself. . . .

We must sing our impression of the world, Ashbery goes on, but that song leads us farther and farther from reality.

Nonetheless, "The Recital," which at times threatens to become a denial of all artistic possibilities, does not abandon all hope of obtaining insight into the nature of reality. Out of the tension of conflicting opposites, of light and dark, of outer and inner worlds, "something real did seem to be left over."

There is another notable shift in emphasis in "The Recital." It had always been implicit in the poetry of John Ashbery that when a poet writes about aesthetics, he is not necessarily limiting himself to a specialized area of experience, of interest only to the poet and his audience. In "The Recital," aesthetic frustration and a feeling of loneliness come together, as well as the suspicion that the creation of a poem and the act of loving are the only ways available to man of transcending his isolation.

See also the Introduction, section V.

Selected Bibliography:
By ASHBERY:
Turandot and Other Poems. New York: Tibor de Nagy Gallery, 1953.
Some Trees. New Haven: Yale University Press, 1956.
The Tennis Court Oath. Middletown, Conn.: Wesleyan University Press, 1962.
Rivers and Mountains. New York: Holt, Rinehart & Winston, 1966.
Selected Poems. London: Jonathan Cape, 1967.
The Double Dream of Spring. New York: E. P. Dutton & Co., 1970.
Three Poems. New York: Viking Press, 1972.

About Ashbery:
Carroll, Paul. "Leaving the Atocha Station" in *The Poem in Its Skin.* Chicago: Follett Publishing Co., 1968. Pp. 3–26.
Howard, Richard. *Alone with America.* New York: Atheneum Publishers, 1969. Pp. 18–37.

BARAKA, IMAMU AMIRI (*b. Newark, N.J., Oct. 7, 1934—   )*

In his prefatory remarks for *Black Magic Poetry,* Imamu Baraka turns his back on the Western or European literary tradition and on the work he himself produced while operating on the borders of that tradition. As poet and prophet aware of the power of names, he also leaves behind the tag by which he was well known to his abandoned culture: LeRoi Jones. Not surprisingly, Baraka's reputation in the largely white critical community has steadily declined, but whether this is mainly due to changes in poetic methodology or because of an increasingly militant political posture is not clear.

Born and raised in Newark, New Jersey, Jones attended Rutgers University for one year, then transferred to Howard where he received his B.A. in English in 1954. He took advanced courses at Columbia and at the New School for Social Research, and also served more than two years in the

Strategic Air Command. In the late fifties, Jones taught poetry and writing at the New School. In the sixties several of his plays were produced off-Broadway, including the Obie-winning *Dutchman* (1964). Founder and director of the Black Arts Repertory Theatre in Harlem, he later became associated with the Spirit House Movers and Players in Newark. He has written fiction as well as poetry, plays, and criticism, most notably the semiautobiographical novel *The System of Dante's Hell*, and has been an editor of *Yugen* and *Kultur*. Jones is also well known for involvement in direct political action, especially in his native Newark, where he has frequently acted as spokesman for the black community.

Except in its final poem, Jones's first book, *Preface to a Twenty-Volume Suicide Note* (1961), is not the work of an obviously black writer. References to Jack Kerouac, John Wieners, Michael McClure, and Gary Snyder correctly identify Jones as being associated with the Projectivist poets, with the Beats, and in general with the poets represented in Donald Allen's *The New American Poetry* of 1960, in which Jones's work received its first wide exposure. Titles such as "In Memory of Radio," "Duke Mantee," and "The Death of Nick Charles" reveal an interest in Pop Culture, in what was soon to be proclaimed as "camp." The phrase "one of Kafka's hipsters" ("For Hettie in Her Fifth Month") serves to define his stance in relation to his world. It echoes Ginsberg, to whom a poem ("One Night Stand") is dedicated, and Jones is very often like a Ginsberg stripped of his beatific vision.

Although there is accumulation of detail, although there is some encyclopedic overview of a dying culture and the subcultures it has produced, Jones at his best in *Preface to a Twenty-Volume Suicide Note* is too in love with details to pass over them quickly, too in love with the moment to abandon it to the description of an age. "Ostriches & Grandmothers!" ends:

> It's these empty seconds
> I fill with myself. Each
> a recognition. A complete
> utterance.
>
> Here, it is color; motion;
> the feeling of dazzling beauty
> Flight.
>
> As
> the trapeeze rider
> leans
> with arms spread
>
> wondering at the bar's
> delay

In a sense, this poem fits in perfectly with Jones's predominantly existential position. But it is only secondarily the expression of a *weltanschauung;* it is a poem in praise of the perceptual process. There is something of the *tour de force* here, and elsewhere in this first small book, the feeling of a poet in love with his poetic powers. Also in this book, however, is an attempt to get beneath the surface of that which dazzles. In "Theory of Art," the poetic process is described in terms of sexual love. The poem, which begins by asserting that the "root is . . . an animal" and emphasizes the smells and tastes of love, becomes a probe into the dark core of experience rather than an exercise in romanticizing it. It is the promise to combine the love of surface perception with the refusal to be content with that surface that accounts for the enthusiastic reception Jones's work received.

Although the book's final poem, "Notes for a Speech," confronts the poet's blackness, it is still at a far remove from the poetry of Imamu Baraka. It is a sad poem rather than an angry poem, although the seeds of anger are there. Its sadness is that of a black man returning to Africa to find that he is no more at home there than in America:

> . . . Africa
> is a foreign place. You are
> as any other sad man here
> american.

His color is not theirs; he is lighter. Implicit throughout, though barely spoken, is the black man's alienation from America as well as Africa. But this alienation is still not distinguishable from the response of anyone living in what is felt to be a life-denying culture, the response of a Ginsberg or a Kerouac.

The Dead Lecturer (1964) is closer in tone and style to the book that preceded it than to those that were to follow. Titles such as "Green Lantern's Solo," "*Duncan spokes of a process.*" "A Poem For Speculative Hipsters" are in themselves enough to establish continuity. And the promise of *Preface to a Twenty-Volume Suicide Note* is largely fulfilled. In "The dance," which elaborates one of the book's principal metaphors, he asserts

> . . . That there
> was some bright elegance
> the sad meat of the body
> made. . . .

And then he pins down what seems to be the dominant energy of his verse:

> I want to be sung. I want
> all my bones and meat hummed
> against the thick floating
> winter sky. I want myself
> as dance. As what I am
> given love, or time, or space
> to feel myself.

The poem from *The Dead Lecturer* that ended by receiving most attention, and not necessarily from literary critics alone, was "BLACK DADA NIHILISMUS." Here Jones appears to be calling on a black god of destruction to annihilate the white oppressors. Nor is this very far from the truth; but it is far enough from it to require further examination. The lines most often quoted from the poem are:

> . . . Rape the white girls. Rape
> Their fathers. Cut the mothers' throats.

One could not ask anything clearer than that. The following lines, however, which are rarely quoted, are much more ambiguous, and much more interesting.

> Black dada nihilismus, choke my friends
>
> in their bedrooms with their drinks spilling
> and restless for tilting hips or dark liver
> lips sucking splinters from the master's thigh.

The point is, these friends *are* his friends. And it is the tension between the wish to destroy and the wish to preserve and remain part of at least one segment of white society, and not some unambiguously destructive energy, that makes the poem so powerful. The jews, who will increasingly become Jones's principal target, are already present. Here they are identified by their "ugly silent deaths"; like the blacks, they are victims. But they were passive victims. If this is what the blacks have been, they can be that no longer. The dark power of destruction unleashed in this century by the white man is an ironically appropriate instrument.

Still the poem has its roots in the West it would destroy. Even the title comes from a specifically Western movement in the arts, albeit a movement that had as its enemy the middle-class, industrial, commercial world the West had become. In this antagonism, Jones remains in the company of most white artists. But there is an absoluteness about Jones's negation that opens the door to something entirely different. He appeals to "Black scream and chant," and these are the weapons he will begin to substitute for the dead white rhetoric.

Another instance of the blending of black and white traditions in *The Dead Lecturer* is the Crow Jane sequence. Taking the name from a refrain by Mississippi Joe Williams, Jones inevitably reminds the reader of Yeats's Crazy Jane poems. The sequence is summarized in the sentence ". . . She is looking/for alternatives." She does not find them. And Jones concludes by calling on the god named toward the end of "BLACK DADA NIHILISMUS":

> . . . And Damballah, kind father,
>   sew up
>   her bleeding hole.

Of Jones's various talents, it is his ability to sum up his anger in sharp concrete images that he seems most spectacularly to be developing in his second book.

The next three books, *Sabotage, Target Study,* and *Black Art,* are col-

lected in *Black Magic* (1969). The author now signs his preface Baraka; the
Newark riots have occurred, and he has become increasingly involved in
the politics of that city in particular, in black militant movements in general. In the prefatory remarks to *Black Magic*, Baraka cites the preoccupation with death, his own, in his first two volumes, and describes his newer
work as studies in the destruction of white society. It is only a beginning,
for the center of attention is in a sense his own psyche; he is ridding himself of the final chains. In "leroy" (in *Black Art*), he writes:

> . . . May they pick me apart and take the
> useful parts, the sweet meat of my feelings. And leave
> the bitter bullshit rotten white parts
> alone.

Sabotage is stylistically still very close to the earlier work. Although the
theme of poet as black man has finally broken through and now dominates,
a poem like "Tight Rope" could easily have come from an earlier period:

> We live in fragments
> like speech. Like the fits
> of wind, shivering against
> the window.
>
> Pieces of meaning, pierced
> and strung together. The bright bead
> of the poem, the bright bead
> of your woman's laughter.

Target Study, the middle book, is in some ways the most interesting.
While the tight control, the disciplined technique, is still there, the poetry
is more straightforward, clearer. It is meant to be spoken, and when it is
spoken it will be understood. And it will help create a sense of community.
In "A Poem for Black Hearts," Baraka's tribute to Malcolm X, the poet is at
his best. Beginning with Malcolm's eyes, ". . . when they broke/the face of
some dumb white man," Baraka moves like an orator rousing a crowd, ex-
horting them never to "breathe a pure breath" if they fail, ". . . and white
men call us faggots till the end of /the earth." What distinguishes this
from most of the poetry of *Black Art* is its continuing commitment to concrete imagery and metaphor, its dependence on these things for much of its
effect.

In the poem "Black Art," Baraka turns his back on stylistic judgments. It
is no longer how a poem says something that matters; it is what it says:

> Poems are bullshit unless they are
> teeth or trees or lemons piled
> on a step. . . .
> . . . We want "poems that kill."
> Assassin poems. Poems that shoot
> guns. . . .

Strangely enough, this particular poem stands up quite well by the criteria Baraka is abandoning. But *Black Art* contains many examples of the kind of poetry Baraka means. The first poem, "SOS," begins "Calling black people," and is developed simply as a radioed distress signal. It depends on repetition and on the importance of what it says. This is not to imply that there is nothing beyond the repetition that is recognizable as poetry in traditional terms. In "Race," Baraka writes:

> . . . Our strength is in the drums,
> the sinuous horns, blow forever beautiful princes, touch
> the spellflash of everything, all life, and the swift go on
> go off and speed. . . .

What has happened is this: Baraka has not stopped being a poet, but he has stopped believing in the perceptual instant as the means of liberation; he has rejected the imagistic bias of our poetry, which has become so ingrained in our critical judgments that we have ceased to discuss it. And the reason for this change is that freedom and dignity are no longer questions of consciousness; they are questions of action.

It would be less than honest to insist that Baraka's new poetry does not have its ugly moments. There is, for example, a deeply anti-Semitic strain running through it, with which it is difficult to come to terms even if one takes it as a reaction to a particular set of circumstances rather than the generalized hatred it appears to be. But the same critic who complains that Baraka has abandoned form for content, the substantial for the superficial, has limited his right to attack the content. If the message is of the greatest importance, then a poet has perfect justification in concentrating on it.

For Baraka, the writing of poetry is a political act. And this adds to the complexities of literary judgment the complexities of political judgment. Probably the best we can do while we are attempting to unravel the tangle is to accept the poems on their own terms. If they are intended to express anger and hatred, how well do they do it? If they are intended to raise consciousness, to ready people for action, how well do they do that? In these terms, it is difficult to accept the proposition that Imamu Baraka has declined as a poet. He has turned from the personal to the communal experience, from problems of consciousness to problems of action, from the power of imagery to the power of rhetoric, from poetry bred of print to poetry that must be read aloud. The fact that he is as disturbing a poet as he is, is a mark of his achievement.

See also NEW BLACK AESTHETIC and the Introduction, section VII.

Selected Bibliography:
BY BARAKA:
Preface to a Twenty-Volume Suicide Note. New York: Totem/Corinth, 1961.
The Dead Lecturer. New York: Grove Press, 1964.
Dutchman and The Slave: Two Plays. New York: William Morrow & Co., 1964.
The System of Dante's Hell. [Novel.] New York: Grove Press, 1965.
Black Music. [Criticism.] New York: William Morrow & Co., 1967.

The Baptism & The Toilet. [Plays.] New York: Grove Press, 1967.
Tales. [Short stories.] New York: Grove Press, 1967.
Black Magic: Sabotage, Target Study, Black Art. Indianapolis: Bobbs-Merrill Co.,
    1969.
Four Black Revolutionary Plays. Indianapolis: Bobbs-Merrill Co., 1969.
Raise Race Rays Raze: Essays Since 1965. New York: Random House, 1972.
Home: Social Essays. New York: William Morrow & Co., 1972.

BEAT GENERATION

The Beat Generation grew out of an association of writers based loosely in
New York—although nearly continual movement around the country characterized the group—in the late forties and early fifties. When Jack Kerouac
half seriously proposed the term "Beat Generation" to ALLEN GINSBERG and
LAWRENCE FERLINGHETTI, he had "beatific" in mind; but unquestionably
the connotations of defeat were intended. These opposites are reconciled in
the group's rejection of a materialistic, spiritless society, identified with Moloch in Ginsberg's *Howl*, which oppressed them so that they felt beat, from
which they wished to escape in a quasi-mystical way.

Jack Kerouac and William Burroughs were the most important novelists
in the group, Ferlinghetti, GREGORY CORSO, and MICHAEL MCCLURE among
the more significant poets. It was Allen Ginsberg, however, with the publication of *Howl* in 1956, who brought the movement to the attention of literary and mass audiences. The poem itself had instant appeal, seeming to
speak for Ginsberg's generation in very much the same way that *The Waste
Land* spoke for T. S. Eliot's; and the obscenity trial that followed did not
hurt the poem's popularity.

Ironically, *Howl* marked the beginning of the end of the Beat Generation's influence on contemporary American poetry (although the fiction of
Kerouac and Burroughs, to which *Howl* called attention, had increasing impact). When Ferlinghetti's City Lights Press published Ginsberg's poem,
the SAN FRANCISCO RENAISSANCE, which brought together BLACK MOUNTAIN
POETS and Beat poets, took on a life of its own, muting specifically Beat
characteristics under the broader blanket of PROJECTIVE VERSE. The existential bias, the interest in Zen and other forms of mysticism, the experimentation with drugs, developed into the hippie movement of the sixties, while
Beat poetry became impossible to distinguish from the increasingly important body of antiacademic, open poetry that came into its own after *Howl*.

See also the INTRODUCTION, section IV.

BELL, MARVIN (*b. New York City, Aug. 3, 1937–*   )

In a poetic age dominated by the principles of IMAGISM, by insistence on
the concrete, Marvin Bell writes discursively, often abstractly. At a time

when more and more poets are choosing to confront reality through the jux-taposition of fragmented perceptions, when they are seriously questioning the capacity of human consciousness to organize experience in any mean-ingful way, he puts his confidence in the self's integrity. Yet Bell's poetry is anything but anachronistic. It could only have been written after World War II. And, although superficially quite distinct, it is not totally unrelated to dominant tendencies in contemporary poetry.

Born in New York City, brought up on Long Island, Bell attended Alfred University and the University of Syracuse. He received his M.A. from the University of Chicago in 1961, his M.F.A. from the University of Iowa in 1963. He began teaching in the writing program at the University of Iowa in 1965.

Only rarely is Bell's poetry at all descriptive. He is chiefly concerned not with landscapes or sensory perceptions, but with actions and human rela-tionships. On the basis of subject and theme alone, it would seem logical to classify him as a Confessional poet, for the poetry is often very private in-deed, very much concerned with the more painful areas of the poet's expe-rience. This suggestion, however, simply succeeds in making us realize that Confessional poetry cannot be exclusively defined in terms of subject or theme. The following passages from "Pieces" (in *Things We Dreamt We Died For*), one of Bell's most powerful poems, will serve to illustrate not only his distinct approach to the agonies of the human condition, but the techniques that are essential to that approach as well:

> My first wife feared
> gas and the night,
> and feared the two
> would suck her inside
> out, if she relaxed.
> Everyone needed
> the help she needed,
> she guessed, and she was wrong.
> . . . .
> I tried to afflict her
> with affection,
> I tried making her
> knuckle under.
> I tried to let her go
> crazy, and it worked.

Straightforward statement is used instead of surreal imagery, and no at-tempt is made to probe the depths of the unconscious. Reality is defined through actions. It is apprehended by the conscious mind. As a conse-quence, the individual is not absorbed into any larger reality—for example, the objective universe of the Projectivists, the unindividuated unconscious of the Confessional poets—but confirmed in his separateness. He is further confirmed in his sense of responsibility for the actions that define his reality.

If Bell's poetry can often be called abstract, this is true primarily in the sense that it is not centered on concrete imagery. But the actions and thoughts Bell presents (and even the thoughts are actions in the sense that they define the thinker's attitudes toward experience) are in their own way quite concrete. One could even argue that this non-Imagist poet obeys the three Imagist precepts formulated by Ezra Pound and F. S. Flint: direct treatment of the thing itself, no excess verbiage, rhythm appropriate to the experience of the poem. Experiences are presented starkly and directly; Bell tells us what has happened rather than talking about what has happened. A poetry of action is dominated by verbs; the quoted passages from "Pieces" clearly are. There are no adjectives, no ornaments. The short lines, the repetitions of words and sounds, set up a tension between rapid movement and futile repetition, which is clearly appropriate to the poem's meaning.

"Pieces" is a rather extreme example of what is generally characteristic of Bell's earlier work. His later poems are likely to contain not only adjectives, but even crucial images. Nonetheless, the emphases of his earlier methods of composition are reflected in later poems. The final stanza of "Service for Two" (in *The Escape into You*) is an illustration:

> We only wanted to fill up with pain
> on the crumbs of love, not these dumb
> animals which enter our blood daily.
> Hunger surmounts hunger; the spirit
> spits on the body; the heart chews
> on the heart, for the sake of the other.

The "crumbs of love," the "animals which enter our blood," the spirit spitting on the body, heart chewing heart, are images that grow successively more powerful. They are not simply present; they are carefully orchestrated. Nonetheless, adjectives are still kept to a minimum, verbs still dominate. And the poet's interest is still in describing objective correlatives for extreme emotional states.

Marvin Bell is as aware as any poet writing today of the difficulties involved in surviving as a whole human being. He is at least equally suspicious of any answers that can be codified, converted into a knowable, rational system. But it is precisely his knowledge of its probable impossibility that makes his faith in the mind's ability to master irrationality believable. He continually probes his history—both his ancestry, Jewish and Russian, and his personal experiences—never really expecting to dominate it, but achieving a kind of victory in the process itself. He is, in short, whether he would subscribe formally to that philosophy or not, one of the few existential poets writing today. The best epigraph to his work can probably be found in one of his own poems, "The Music of the Spheres" (in *The Escape into You*). Speaking of people he has loved, now dead, he says:

> They gave us guilt and the past,
> and we sing what we know best.

Selected Bibliography:
By BELL:
Things We Dreamt We Died For. Iowa City: Stone Wall Press, 1966.
A Probable Volume of Dreams. New York: Atheneum Publishers, 1969.
The Escape into You. New York: Atheneum Publishers, 1971.

BENEDIKT, MICHAEL (*b. New York City, May 26, 1935—*)

Although Surrealism has had a very definite impact on contemporary American poetry, Michael Benedikt is one of the few poets writing today in whose work it appears in its purest form. For while the chief appeal of Surrealism in recent years has been its implicit breaking down of barriers between conscious and unconscious worlds, and while this is clearly of great importance to Benedikt, he is also very interested in the sense of the sheer absurdity of human experience that Surrealism communicates.

Born in New York, where he has lived most of his life, Benedikt has been an editor of *Art News* since 1963. He has been involved in multimedia performances of poetry and has a special interest in the theater. He has also taught modern poetry at Bennington and Sarah Lawrence colleges.

Benedikt's interest in drama is reflected in *The Body* (1968) in "Some Litanies." The alogical nature of experience characteristic of Surrealism certainly plays a part in the poems. But connections with what has been rightly or wrongly labeled the "Theater of the Absurd" are even more conspicuous in passages such as the following:

> Will you ever marry?
>
> No.
>
> Have you ever been married?
>
> I don't remember.
>
> Do you love your husband?
>
> Yes.

It is easy enough to go through Benedikt's poetry picking out instances of the surreal, the absurd: "Carrying in the black bundle/the evening paused on the road" ("Motions"); "A lip which had one been stolid, now moving/Gradually around the side of the head" ("Divine Love"). Benedikt is generally witty, often simply funny. Nevertheless his verse has deadly serious underpinnings. In a way, his poetry presents another side of Robert Lowell's Lepke (in "Memories of West Street and Lepke"), waiting to be executed, "hanging like an oasis in his air/of lost connections. . . ." Connections, in Benedikt's world, are indeed lost. Common sense has no

place where surfaces are revealed as the flimsiest of illusions, where boundaries among forms of being are constantly shifting. In "Procession," Benedikt characteristically moves from the light to the serious, ending the poem
with:

> All will be water all will be pouring
> Descending from the skein of the firm and the packed
> There is no pleasanter exercise on earth than metamorphosis
> Time passes
> And all things that we love must be changed

That is one way of putting it. In "The Debris of the Body" is another,
which is probably more representative of Benedikt's approach to a world in
which the lines separating the self from the other cannot be clearly drawn:

> There, the sea is inundated with the flower of fallen hair, worn skin, finger-
> nail pairings, nose pickings, oozed blood, used sperm (love's leavings!),
> annoying old scabs, tears accidentally escaped in wind, tears meant to
> be wept, the nether wastes, the shit and piss of the skin, superan-
> nuated wart parts, etc.

Selected Bibliography:
BY BENEDIKT:
The Body. Middletown, Conn.: Wesleyan University Press, 1968.
Sky. Middletown, Conn.: Wesleyan University Press, 1970.
Mole Notes. Middletown, Conn.: Wesleyan University Press, 1971.

BERRYMAN, JOHN   (*b. McAlester, Okla., Oct. 25, 1914–
d. Jan. 7, 1972*)

Although his first collections of poetry appeared in the early forties, recognition of John Berryman's work was, until recently, generally limited to
other poets and academicians. Educated at Columbia (A.B., 1936) and at
Clare College, University of Cambridge (B.A., 1938), he was firmly connected with the academic world. He taught at Wayne State University,
Harvard, Princeton, and the Universities of Washington, Cincinnati, and
Minnesota (where he was professor of humanities), and wrote a highly
praised critical biography of Stephen Crane. *Homage to Mistress Bradstreet*
(1956), however, won him critical acclaim; *77 Dream Songs* (1964), which
received the Pulitzer Prize, and *His Toy, His Dream, His Rest* (1968)—
published in 1969 in one volume as *The Dream Songs*—established him as
one of the more important, certainly one of the most widely read, modern
poets.

In "Changes," an essay prepared for Howard Nemerov's *Poets on Poetry*
(1966), Berryman said that the influence of Yeats and Auden early in his
career had preserved him from "the then crushing influence of Pound and

Eliot." In the same essay, Berryman singled out two poems (both from *The Dispossessed*, published in 1948) that, for him, marked the beginnings of a style and voice of his own. The first, "Winter Landscape," is at least superficially about Brueghel's *Hunters in the Snow* (and so bears some kinship to Auden, in his Brueghel poem "Museé des Beaux Arts"). Berryman describes three men going down a snowy hill with their "poles" and their dogs, "the arrangement of trees," the life of the town in the background, three birds that watch and a fourth that flies. Berryman, however, denies that his poem is either a verbal equivalent of the painting, or, like Auden's, an interpretation of it, insisting that what is most significant in his own piece is the way it departs from its inspiration. Berryman's thoroughly somber tone is new; he, unlike the hunters, is aware of "the evil waste of history" but, ironically ignoring their destructive nature, calls the spears "poles." "Winter Landscape," written in 1938–39, a product of visits to France and especially Germany, is a vision, albeit an indirect one, of the coming war. Whether the reader, without Berryman's own commentary could, or even should, derive from the poem anything more specific than a vague sense of foreboding is not clear, but the technique at least is crucial to Berryman's later work. What is most important here is what is not said by the poet—and what he distorts. Silence, often dramatically more effective than sound, is from this point one of Berryman's central methods.

The second poem, "The Ball Poem," introduces problems of a different sort. The subject is "The epistemology of loss." A small boy loses his ball on the street, and, once this particular one is gone, it is "No use to say 'O there are other balls.'" Technically interesting is the ambiguity of pronouns, the movement back and forth from "he" to "I." "The poet himself is both left out and put in; the boy does and does not become him and we are confronted with a process which is at once a process of life and a process of art." Berryman's analysis sheds light on "The Ball Poem." It is even more interesting as manifesto for his more important work, as the key to the confusions of identity in *The Dream Songs*, and to the less confusing alternations of identity in *Homage to Mistress Bradstreet*.

Not published until 1967, *Berryman's Sonnets* were written during the early forties, and so offer still another glimpse of the poet forging his mature style. The sonnet sequence, 115 poems long, more or less tells the story—there is nothing here so clear-cut as a plot—of the protagonist's affair with Lise, the wife of a good friend. Of greater interest than the story are the methods used by Berryman to tell it; if "Winter Landscape" and "The Ball Poem" test tone and perspective, the greatest tensions here arise from language itself. "Crumpling a syntax at a sudden need" (Sonnet 47), says Berryman, and "I prod our English" (Sonnet 66). What appear at first to be simply archaic inversions turn out to be more reactionary still; Berryman pushes English as close to the forms of Latin and Greek as it has been in centuries: "Whom undone David into the dire van sent/I'd see as far" (Sonnet 21); "Demand me again what Kafka's riddles mean" (Sonnet 73); "What can to you this music wakes my years . . . Be . . . ?" (Sonnet 92). The device does not always work; when it does, the effects are remarkable.

In their new syntactical settings, old words are recharged with energy. Berryman's play with language owes much, it would seem, to Gerard Manley Hopkins, perhaps more to Joyce's *Finnegans Wake;* indeed, the dreamlike sense of a multitextured reality of the later poems is surprisingly present at this relatively early date.

The major breakthrough for Berryman, certainly in terms of critical reception, came with *Homage to Mistress Bradstreet,* which was called by so eminent a critic as Edmund Wilson "the most distinguished long poem by an American since *The Waste Land,*" and by so eminent a poet as Robert Lowell "the most resourceful historical poem in our literature." Asked why he decided to write about "this boring high-minded Puritan woman who may have been our first American poet but is not a good one," Berryman wrote in "Changes" that he found common ground in "the almost insuperable difficulty of writing high verse at all in a land that cared and cares so little for it." The poet's alienation from his society is certainly one of the poem's central themes, but it is only part of a larger complex of antagonisms and separations in Anne Bradstreet's life that give shape to Berryman's *Homage.* The first section centers on Anne's reactions to being uprooted from the country of her birth and placed in a rude, hostile environment, and to her childless early years in the new world; the second, on the limited fulfillment of her marriage; the third, on growing awareness of age and death. The preoccupations with spatial, personal, and temporal distance (from homeland, husband, and youth) are finally subordinate to the hopeless gap between poet and protagonist, which the poet nonetheless, and with a curious kind of success, attempts to span.

Homage begins with an exordium and concludes with a coda in the voice of the twentieth-century poet, which, according to Berryman's notes (which emulate, maybe parody, the notes to *The Waste Land*), modulates into and from the voice of Anne Bradstreet; there are also interruptions by the modern poet, as well as a dialogue between living and dead. This kind of ambiguity of identity we have encountered before, in "The Ball Poem." The tension between subjective and objective reality is what Berryman called "at once a process of life and a process of art." The temptation, of course, is to resolve the ambiguity, to decide whether Anne Bradstreet is a projection of the poet's psyche, a kind of *anima* through which the poet attempts to resolve his own psychological crises as in Roethke's "Meditations of an Old Woman," or whether she is an external object of the poet's love, as Catherine Tekakwitha is for the narrator of Leonard Cohen's novel *Beautiful Losers.* The two are not really incompatible; in either case, the poet's probing love for Anne Bradstreet leads to the exploration of his own inner self.

In *Homage to Mistress Bradstreet,* Berryman brought together for the first time on a large scale the techniques he had been developing for twenty years. In addition to the dramatic play of shifting identities, there is the terse, often indirect, exposition, which would be difficult to follow without the notes, and the wrenched syntax that, belonging neither to the world of Anne Bradstreet nor to that of the modern poet, manages to bridge both. Perhaps most impressive of all is Berryman's stanza (with variations,

$a^5b^5x^3b^4c^5c^5x^3a^6$), developed from Yeats's "In Memory of Major Robert Gregory." Berryman makes this into a flexible unit of meaning, tone, and rhythm, handling it, as M. L. Rosenthal has pointed out, even more effectively than the line, avoiding monotony but maintaining a very solid frame of reference.

In the introductory note to *His Toy, His Dream, His Rest* (1968), sequel to *77 Dream Songs*, Berryman attempts to set straight the critics who "went so desperately astray" in reading the first volume. Explaining that the songs should be treated as a single poem, he concludes:

> The poem then, whatever its wide cast of characters, is essentially about an imaginary character (not the poet, not me) named Henry, a white American in early middle age sometimes in blackface, who has suffered an irreversible loss and talks about himself sometimes in the first person, sometimes in the third, sometimes even in the second; he has a friend, never named, who addresses him as Mr Bones and variants thereof.

77 Dream Songs, which contains books 1–3 of the long poem, does in fact deal with this sense of loss, and perhaps even more with the accompanying sense of guilt of the protagonist, who is variously "Huffy Henry," "Sir Bones," "Henry Pussy-cat," "servant Henry," "gross Henry," "bitter Henry," "Ol' Marster," "subtle Henry," and "seedy Henry." With his epithets his moods vary, as does the tone of the poems, from the parody of the Eisenhower press conference in "*The Lay of Ike*" (Song 23) to the elegy "*A Strut for Roethke*" (Song 18). Prevalent, perhaps, are the tone and subject of "Henry's Confession" (Song 76), which begins: "Nothin very bad happen to me lately./How you explain that?" For Henry expects something to happen to him, as if he deserves it, although we never learn why. Maybe Henry himself does not know. He can only speculate, sometimes spectacularly, as in Song 29:

> But never did Henry, as he thought he did,
> end anyone and hacks her body up
> and hide the pieces, where they may be found.
> He knows: he went over everyone, & nobody's missing.
> Often he reckons, in the dawn, them up.
> Nobody is ever missing.

In his songs, Berryman mines the depths of the self, comic or terrible, usually both at once. Always aware of events around him, from Modern Language Association conventions to the cold war, he does not approach his experience from the historical perspective of, say, Robert Lowell's *Notebook* (1970) but almost escapes time in a kind of archetypal universality which, again, resembles Joyce's *Finnegans Wake*. The actions of the poems are in fact as likely to occur in the world of possibility or fantasy as in the world of objective, external reality, but they are none the less real, none the less disturbing, for that. The voice of the "blackface" friend sums up what Henry learns:"—Mr Bones, we all brutes & fools" (Song 62).

The poems of books 4–7, in *His Toy, His Dream, His Rest,* are not sharply differentiated from the first three books, in *77 Dream Songs.* Henry goes his way, affected by public affairs, but generally caught up in more personal matters, loving, laughing, but usually quite troubled. If there is any shift in emphasis, it is from the sense of loss in the vague past to the sense of coming loss in the indefinite but rapidly approaching future; to the epithets mentioned above are added "lonesome Henry" and "mortal Henry." Each of the poems of book 4 are labeled "*Op. posth.*" A significant proportion of the songs in the whole book are elegies: Robert Frost, Theodore Roethke, Wallace Stevens, William Carlos Williams, Ernest Hemingway, John F. Kennedy, Randall Jarrell, Delmore Schwartz, Sylvia Plath, Richard Blackmur, Yvor Winters, all dead, most of them within a few years before the publication of the book. Most of them, too, were near contemporaries of the poet. Jarrell and Schwartz in particular are singled out for sequences of their own, and Song 153 is a complaint against the "god who has wrecked this generation," taking Roethke, Blackmur, Jarrell, and Schwartz, while "In between he gorged on Sylvia Plath." Whether Henry himself has died and been reborn, whether he has in any sense come to terms with death, is far from clear; this is probably due to the very fluidity of personality, the difficulty in seizing the moment long enough to say what one *is,* while he is already becoming something else.

The Dream Songs are not, in fact, especially easy to understand. That did not disturb Berryman in the least: "These Songs are not meant to be understood, you understand./They are only meant to terrify & comfort" (Song 366). Still, the difficulties are not as overwhelming as some have supposed, and William Meredith's suggestion, that if one were to read the poems through, concentrating on the relatively easy ones and not getting bogged down in the more impenetrable ones, the entire sequence would gradually be illuminated, is probably correct. It is also useful to keep in mind the steps by which Berryman's verse evolved to this present point: the dependence on indirect methods to communicate crucial discoveries; the wrenching of syntax to revitalize language; the confusing of identities (here supported by a surreal combining of unrelated areas of experience). This last technique is of special importance to *The Dream Songs.*

Confusions of identity, which can be explained largely in terms of dramatic effects in earlier poems, raise the questions first asked in *Homage to Mistress Bradstreet* about what actually constitutes identity; "I am less impressed than I used to be," Berryman said, "by the universal notion of a continuity of individual personality." Most obvious of the multiple voices is the friend, speaking in minstrel-show blackface, who addresses Henry as "Mr Bones"; but someone who may be Henry himself uses the same diction. As white society has isolated aspects of its own collective identity and projected them upon the black community, so Henry seems to have done in creating his friend in these dialogs of self and soul. The friend is sometimes simply a straight man for Henry (as in "The glories of the world," Song 26); more often he takes the offensive: "Mr Bones . . . you strikes me as ornery" (Song 13). His name for Henry suggests both sexuality and mortality, and it is with these parts of the protagonist that he is most usually associated. Asking whether the friend is a distinct personality becomes almost irrelevant if we take seriously, as we are surely intended to do, the dream world of the sequence. But if this is a dream, are the other characters who appear throughout really totally separated from Henry? Any answer to this must be the one that would apply equally to *Finnegans Wake*. Humphrey Chimpden Earwicker, the dreamer of the *Wake,* contains within him all the book's characters, that is, Everybody. And we may say the same of dreaming Henry.

Although it is certainly *The Dream Songs* that made a literary star of John Berryman, his critics are not at all sure that it represents his best work; many favor *Homage to Mistress Bradstreet.* Most problems center on the question of whether *The Dream Songs* holds together as a single, unified poem (placing the sequence in the very respectable company of Pound's *Hugh Selwyn Mauberley* and Hart Crane's *The Bridge*). The disadvantages of *The Dream Songs* when compared to the earlier poem are obvious: while *Homage* has a clear narrative thread within which to connect the poem's varied movements, and a relatively classical organization, *The Dream Songs* is by necessity composed of fragments without any obvious rational sequence; and while *Homage* consists of fifty-seven beautifully handled eight-line stanzas, the poems of *The Dream Songs* (most of which take the form of three flexible six-line stanzas) form discrete units, which cannot be run together, and which can relate to other materials in the poem only by juxtaposition. In any case, few have denied the brilliance of a large number of the songs, which represent Berryman at the height of his poetic powers.

Love & Fame (1970), the last of Berryman's books to be published in his lifetime, received generally less enthusiastic critical response than had *The Dream Songs.* Although this can be understood as the usual response to an established poet altering the style that has dominated his work for several years, in this case there seems to be at least some justification for the reaction. The poems of *Love & Fame* lack some of the magic, and a good deal of the density of language, of *The Dream Songs.* These poems, like those that preceded them, are largely rooted in the poet's own experience; but while the earlier work enters the terrain between the conscious and unconscious mind, explores dreams and fantasies, and dramatizes the fragmentation of the self, the newer poetry stays near the surface of experience, records reactions without probing their sources. And there is a corresponding shift from passages of inspired madness to what is often simply aphoristic, as in these lines from the painfully prophetic poem, "Of Suicide":

> A basis rock-like of love & friendship
> for all this world-wide madness seems to be needed.

On January 7, 1972, John Berryman jumped to his death from a bridge over the Mississippi River. In 1972, *Delusions, Etc.,* Berryman's real *opus posthumus,* was published. Although the poems of this volume do not represent a retreat to older modes (in spite of two leftover Dream Songs), they are on the whole far more successful than those of *Love & Fame.* It is paradoxically by looking outside of himself, by examining his relation to God, that Berryman rediscovers the power of his inner voice. Although *Delusions, Etc.* contains a good proportion of secular verse, it is the book's religious themes that give it unity. Many of the poems record Berryman's arduous struggle back toward God. It is a painful, exciting, inconclusive struggle, which can best be summed up by the concluding line of "Certainty Before Lunch":

I know You are there. The sweat is, I am here.

See also CONFESSIONAL POETRY and the Introduction, section VI.

Selected Bibliography:

BY BERRYMAN:

Poems. New York: New Directions Publishing Corp., 1942.

The Dispossessed. New York: William Sloane Associates, 1948.

Stephen Crane. [Biography.] New York: William Sloane Associates, 1950.

Homage to Mistress Bradstreet. New York: Farrar, Straus & Giroux, 1956.

77 Dream Songs. New York: Farrar, Straus & Giroux, 1964.

Berryman's Sonnets. New York: Farrar, Straus & Giroux, 1967.

Short Poems. New York: Farrar, Straus & Giroux, 1967.

His Toy, His Dream, His Rest. New York: Farrar, Straus & Giroux, 1968.

The Dream Songs. New York: Farrar, Straus & Giroux, 1969.

Love & Fame. New York: Farrar, Straus & Giroux, 1970.

Delusions, Etc. New York: Farrar, Straus & Giroux, 1972.

See also Berryman's essay "Changes" in *Poets on Poetry.* Edited by Howard Nemerov. New York: Basic Books, 1966. Pp. 94–103.

About Berryman:

Evans, Arthur and Catherine. "Pieter Brueghel and John Berryman: Two Winter Landscapes," *Texas Studies in Language and Literature,* 5 (Autumn 1963), 310–18.

Johnson, Carol. "John Berryman and Mistress Bradstreet: A Relation of Reason," *Essays in Criticism,* 14 (October 1964), 388–96.

Meredith, William. "Henry Tasting All the Secret Bits of Life: Berryman's Dream Songs," *Wisconsin Studies in Contemporary Literature,* 6 (Winter–Spring, 1965), 27–33.

Rosenthal, M. L. *The New Poets: American and British Poetry Since World War II.* New York: Oxford University Press, 1967. Pp. 118–30.

BISHOP, ELIZABETH (b. Worcester, Mass., Feb. 8, 1911—   )

Superficially, Elizabeth Bishop has the characteristics of a minor poet; she is clearly a fine craftsman, yet the subjects of most of her work seem restricted, frequently nothing more than a study of surfaces. But there is an uneasiness among the critics about consigning her to minor status—even the suspicison that she may outlast most of the poets who now seem to be potentially major figures.

Elizabeth Bishop was born in Worcester, Massachusetts, in 1911, in the same city—within two months of the actual date—as fellow poet Charles Olson, who took an entirely different path, striking testimony to the diverse possibilities of contemporary American poetry. Her father died before she was a year old; frequent breakdowns left her mother permanently ill. She was raised by grandparents and an aunt in Nova Scotia and Boston. She graduated from Vassar in 1934, the same year she met Marianne Moore, and soon began the travels so important to her life and art—first Europe, then Mexico, finally Brazil, where she has lived more or less permanently since 1951. She has received numerous awards, most notably the Pulitzer Prize in 1956 and the National Book Award in 1970; she was appointed consultant to the Library of Congress; she has spent some time at Yaddo, the artists' colony in New York State. A good friend of Robert Lowell's, she has nonetheless avoided literary circles. She belongs to no school, unless it be a distant corner of that of Marianne Moore, herself an eccentric among American poets, or unless it be one that she has founded and occupied by herself.

The reader of Elizabeth Bishop's poetry, especially the early poetry, is generally first struck by the poet's exact eye, her meticulous descriptions, her devotion to the subtlest detail. This precision, strangely enough, is a characteristic Bishop shares with fellow-Worcesterman Olson; for each, the act of perception itself seems the poem's chief concern, the concrete world its chief subject. From that point on, the differences between the two poets become overwhelming. Where Olson scorns traditional forms and seeks the shape of his poems in the shape of experience, Bishop generally follows an exacting discipline of meter and stanzaic pattern; she frequently seeks out the most restrictive set of limits available, making within these limits her most effective poems, as in the sestina "A Miracle for Breakfast" and in "Roosters," which consists of rhyming triplets. While for Olson the act of perception is largely arational, an act shared by the senses, and has the quality of simultaneity, for Bishop it is refined by consciousness and wit, largely visual—there are exceptions, some excellent ones, for example, Bishop's "Varick Street," but the rule stands—and most often linear. Still, it is possible that all this is outweighed by the initial assumptions made by both Olson and Bishop, that the human universe is dependent upon the act of perception for its existence, that the writing of a poem is itself the creation of a world, a world that may bear important relation to what we generally name reality but one that has an integrity of its own.

"The Map," from Bishop's first volume, *North & South* (1946), is a good instance of the descriptive bias that dominates her poetry. A map, apparently of the northern Atlantic (Newfoundland, Labrador, and Norway are named), is described not as a representation of a portion of the earth or of human civilization, but as an object in itself. The colors assigned by the printer take precedence over natural colors; the water seems "more quiet than the land is." There is a temptation, after one has duly admired the poem's craftsmanship, to attack the perversity that would turn the poem into a lens that records but does not judge, that would exclude the specifi-

cally human. But this is only a first impression. A photographic lens is precisely what the poet avoids, and a sense of humanity is what the poem especially succeeds in communicating.

The map is above all things a human creation, which, like the poem
itself, takes its starting place in the real world, but which ultimately becomes important not for the geographical information it imparts, but rather
as bearing the imprint of creative energy. Bishop cites "—the printer here
experiencing the same excitement/as when emotion too far exceeds its
cause." The map—and we can be sure, by implication, the poem itself—is a
projection of its creator's consciousness, while at the same time it possesses
total existence and deserves to be considered apart from its creator. The
map has laws that may differ from the laws of objective reality, but which
are equally valid. The questions asked by the poet—whether the land tugs
"at the sea from under," whether the colors are assigned or chosen by the
countries (the *map* countries, that is) themselves—formally recognize this
validity. Always, however, even if only by indirection, the map retains its
identity as mediator between inner and outer worlds, between a judging
human intelligence and the material universe. "These peninsulas take the
water between thumb and finger/like women feeling for the smoothness of
yard-goods."

"The Man-Moth," another poem from this first volume, and one of the
most often anthologized of her works, is perhaps an even clearer illustration
of Bishop's creation of imaginative worlds that exist parallel to our own,
both frighteningly the same and frighteningly different. Seeing a misprint
for the word "mammoth" in the newspaper, she conjures up an image from
the lost nightmare regions of the mind, a queer Man-Moth, climbing the
façades of buildings at night, hoping to reach and investigate that small
hole at the top of the sky, the moon. Returning to the ground, and beneath,
the Man-Moth rides the subways, riding always backwards at a rate "he
cannot tell." Finally, the poem builds to its climax. If you can get hold of
him, the poet suggests, hold a flashlight to his eye.

> . . . Then from the lids
> one tear, his only possession, like the bee's sting, slips.
> Slyly he palms it, and if you're not paying attention
> he'll swallow it. However, if you watch, he'll hand it over,
> cool as from underground springs and pure enough to drink.

The influence of the surrealists is surely present in the poem, but modified
by Bishop's clarity of vision, giving many of her poems the feeling of a fantastic dream that, while it lasts, seems more real than the waking world.

The Man-Moth, who only rarely pays his visits to the surface, is in some
ways like Dostoevski's "underground" man, fearful and withdrawn from the
world of human relationships. He is also like a leprechaun, hard to find but,
if trapped, forced to hand over a valued possession. There is a fine ambiguity in these last lines of the poem. Does the shining of the light (representing perhaps insight into the nature of reality or human contact) lead to
communion and salvation by producing the tear that is "cool as from under-

ground springs and pure enough to drink"? Or does it lead to final destruction, as when the bee loses its sting. So fully, however, has the poet realized the world of the Man-Moth that interpretation is discouraged, and the last line of Beckett's *Watt* is brought to mind: "No symbols where none intended."

One of the hallmarks of Elizabeth Bishop's poetry has been the relative detachment of the poetic voice. The author seems content simply to point out, to select materials, always from the world outside, rarely from the inner life of Bishop herself. However, as we have seen, the process of selection and arrangement of material objects is itself an expression of that inner life. This is the point of "The Monument," which describes a wooden "monument" built like a box, or a pyramid of boxes, apparently without interest, without discernible significance.

> The monument's an object, yet those decorations,
> carelessly nailed, looking like nothing at all,
> give it away as having life, and wishing,
>
> . . . .
>
> It is the beginning of a painting,
> a piece of sculpture, or poem, or monument,
> and all of wood. Watch it closely.

Calling attention to the world of objects, the poet makes the reader aware of its having special significance without necessarily revealing, or perhaps even knowing, precisely what that significance is. Occasionally, the poet herself participates in the poem's action, but when she does there is a studious avoidance of motivation, of anything outside the observable world.

"The Fish" is such a poem. The action is simple. The poet announces that she has caught a fish; she describes it; she lets it go. There is no explanation—that is, no explicit explanation—of the final act, which was clearly not in the fisherman's mind at the poem's beginning. But the development of the wish to throw the fish back is there; it can be traced through the perceptual mechanism of the poem. The fish's skin is first compared to wallpaper; it is seen as a decorative object that in no way touches the core of the fisherman's being. Next, the fish is seen both as the victim and potential inflictor of violence: his gills, forced to breathe the "terrible oxygen," are also "frightening gills . . . that can cut so badly." The fisherman imagines the fish's entrails and then looks into the eyes of the fish, probably with the impulse to sympathize, but there is no contact: "—It was more like the tipping/of an object toward the light." After seeing the old fishhooks embedded in the jaw, however, the fisherman is able to enter the world of the fish, or rather to bring the fish into the world of men; the hooks are like medals, the bits of fish line like ribbons and also like a beard of wisdom. When the fisherman lets the fish go, it is perfectly clear why she has done so. But it has been explained by a psychology of seeing and doing rather than one of thinking and analyzing.

In *A Cold Spring* (1955), while the old themes and techniques are certainly present, there is a noticeable redefining of limits, which if it may be said to diminish the purity of some of the poems, increases range. A more dramatic kind of poetry is introduced in "Faustina, or Rock Roses," in which the white woman ". . . in a crazy house/upon a crazy bed" is tended by Faustina, who has a "sinister kind face." "Varick Street" has a re-frain, "*And I shall sell you sell you/sell you of course, my dear, and you'll sell me.*" In these poems, there is a sense of inner life, as well as a more fre-quent toughness of rhythm, that makes it difficult not to assume the influ-ence of Robert Lowell. There is also in this book a tentative approach to-ward abstraction, albeit abstraction firmly grounded in concrete reality. "At the Fishhouses" ends:

> If you should dip your hand in,
> your wrist would ache immediately,
> your bones would begin to ache and your hand would burn
> as if the water were a transmutation of fire
> that feeds on stones and burns with a dark gray flame.
> If you tasted it, it would first taste bitter,
> then briny, then surely burn your tongue.
> It is like what we imagine knowledge to be:
> dark, salt, clear, moving, utterly free,
> drawn from the cold hard mouth
> of the world, derived from the rocky breasts
> forever, flowing and drawn, and since
> our knowledge is historical, flowing, and flown.

In "The Map," Elizabeth Bishop concluded, "More delicate than the histo-rians' are the map-makers' colors." The movement in her poetry is, in fact, from the more delicate in the earlier poems to the less, from the emphasis on the perceptual present to the historical sense of consciousness. Even so, she remains more mapmaker than historian.

The title poem of *Question of Travel* (1965) draws a parallel between traveling and the exercise of imagination—or rather travel is suggested to be a symptom of a lack of imaginative power: " '*Is it lack of imagination that makes us/come to imagined places, not just stay at home?*' " As in a poem, the trees along the traveled road are "really exaggerated in their beauty." Travel forces upon the traveler an awareness of reality that is unreal. Why travel in order "to see the sun and the other way around?" That travel is in some sense an evasion extends to become a suggestion of the limitations of the human imagination, of poetry itself. "The Armadillo," one of the finest poems in the book, makes effective use of this awareness.

The detached perspective with which "The Armadillo" begins, and in-deed which continues until the final stanza, is a familiar one in the work of Elizabeth Bishop. It is the time of year, we are told, that the "illegal fire balloons" are loosed beneath the mountains in honor of a saint; the balloons become indistinguishable from the planets, a typical device of Bishop's, flat-tening three-dimensionality, reducing the scene to its visual aspects. The balloons, however, are potentially dangerous; and last night, the poet tells us, one ". . . splattered like an egg of fire/against the cliff behind the house."

A small fire breaks out, and a pair of owls, whose nest has probably been destroyed, an armadillo, and a baby rabbit, apparently on fire, flee the blaze. The contrast between the abstract visual imagery, the picture that the poet's imaginative eye has painted, and the experience itself, is painful, so painful that in the last stanza, for one of the first times in her verse, Bishop allows her emotional response direct expression:

> *Too pretty, dreamlike mimicry!*
> *O falling fire and piercing cry*
> *and panic, and a weak mailed fist*
> *clenched ignorant against the sky!*

It is significant that the outcry does not make for better poetry; but at the same time the inadequacy of the original detachment is fully revealed. The total poem is now a function of the tension between its conflicting parts, between detached observation and intense involvement.

"The Armadillo" is appropriately enough dedicated to Robert Lowell, whose own poetic kingdom lies more fully in the emotion-charged world that Bishop generally avoids directly confronting. The poem illustrates the thorough mastery of technique that seems to have been Miss Bishop's from the very start of her career, and which certainly has not declined with use. It is written in quatrains, with a line of roughly three hard beats forming the basic meter; variations on meter are frequent and effortless. The final, italicized stanza employs a four-beat line, emphasizing the poem's departure from its matter-of-fact tone. The rhyme scheme of the intial stanza is *a b a b;* but the first rhyme, after a near miss in the second stanza, disappears completely in the poem's movement from harmony to the threat of chaos.

The title calls special attention to the armadillo, which would otherwise be inconspicuous among the other fleeing animals. The armadillo is the poem's central symbol and will reappear, slightly altered, in the poem's last lines, as ". . . *a weak mailed fist/clenched ignorant against the sky!*" No service is done the poem by limiting the suggestiveness of this crucial image, but surely, among other things, the poet is revealing the insufficiency of all armor against experience. And it is difficult not to see the armadillo as symbol of the poet herself, stepping out from the protection of aesthetic detachment and helplessly confronting a contingent universe. *Questions of Travel*, with poems like "Squatter's Children," "Manuelzinho," "The Burglar of Babylon," and "First Death in Nova Scotia," seems to signal a new poetic direction, or at least the clarification of an old one. Bishop's specifically human concerns are more obvious than ever before.

This trend is continued in the new poems of *The Complete Poems* (1969) (which also contains, in addition to most of the three earlier volumes, a series of prose beast fables, some fine translations from the Portuguese of Carlos Drummond de Andrade and João Cabral de Melo Neto, and a few new and uncollected poems). "House Guest" is about the "small and thin and bitter" seamstress who stays in the poet's household for a month.

Everything she does is with hopelessness, even watching TV, whose distorted pictures she will not attempt to adjust; there is nothing, apparently, that will distract her. Even her sewing is "decidedly mediocre." A vague feeling of guilt creeps into the poet's attitude toward the woman; surely her presence must signify something. She tries to understand her, and finally discovers that the seamstress had wanted to be a nun but was discouraged by her family. This knowledge, however, seems of limited usefulness. And the almost comic—though it is never really comic—tone of the poem takes a turn toward the sinister at its conclusion:

> Perhaps we should let her go,
> or deliver her straight off
> to the nearest convent—and wasn't
> her month up last week, anyway?
> Can it be that we nourish
> one of the Fates in our bosoms?
> Clotho, sewing our lives
> with a bony little foot
> on a borrowed sewing machine,
> and our fates will be like hers,
> and our hems crooked forever?

At work here is the same imagination that created "The Man-Moth," but instead of a fantasy that impinges upon the "real" world, we find the real world itself vehicle of the fantastic. The poem never drops the witty tone, prevalent here and in so much of Bishop's earlier work, but that wit is more openly than ever in the service of a far more serious apprehension of the human condition.

Elizabeth Bishop's poems have come slowly. She is a careful poet and a careful critic of her own work. She has by now accumulated enough fine poems to found a substantial reputation, and she has revealed enough of her moral self to repudiate early critics who could see in her work nothing but meticulous description. From what appeared to be a collection of random particulars, she has created a moral universe.

Selected Bibliography:
By Bishop:
North & South. Boston: Houghton Mifflin Co., 1946.
Poems: North & South—A Cold Spring. Boston: Houghton Mifflin Co., 1955.
The Diary of Helena Morley. [Translation.] New York: Farrar, Straus & Giroux, 1957.
Brazil. [with editors of *Life.*] New York: Time-Life Books, 1962.
Questions of Travel. New York: Farrar, Straus & Giroux, 1965.
The Complete Poems. New York: Farrar, Straus & Giroux, 1969.
See also Elizabeth Bishop's statement in *Mid-Century American Poets.* Edited by John Ciardi. New York: Twayne Publishers, 1950.

About Bishop:
Fowlie, Wallace. "Poetry of Silence." *Commonweal* 65 (February 15, 1957): 514–16.
Jarrell, Randall. *Poetry and the Age.* New York: Alfred A. Knopf, 1953. Pp. 212–14.
McNally, Nancy L. "Elizabeth Bishop: The Discipline of Description." *Twentieth Century Literature* 11 (January 1966): 189–201.
Mills, Ralph J., Jr. *Contemporary American Poetry.* New York: Random House, 1965. Pp. 72–83.
Stevenson, Anne. *Elizabeth Bishop.* New York: Twayne Publishers, 1966.

BLACK AESTHETIC, NEW   See New Black Aesthetic.

BLACKBURN, PAUL (*b. St. Albans, Vt., Nov. 24, 1926—d. Sept. 13, 1971*)

Although never directly involved with Black Mountain College, Paul Blackburn was from early in his career associated with the movement that took its name from that school. While his methods by and large conform to Charles Olson's Projective verse—that is, emphasis on open rather than strictly formal verse and on composition by field, by tension between juxtaposed fragments, rather than by logical coherence—Blackburn's individuality, like that of most of the Projectivists, emerges quite clearly. His unique stamp can be at least partially attributed to a strong interest in the medieval poetry of France and Spain, particularly that of the Provençal troubadours.

Educated at New York University and the University of Wisconsin, Blackburn spent a good part of his adult life in France, where he was a Fulbright lecturer at the University of Toulouse, and in Spain. He also worked as an editor in New York and taught writing at the City College of New York. His career was cut short by cancer in 1971.

"Sirventes," in *The Cities,* is an early example of the poetry that emerged from the tensions between the impulse to create a new sense of form and the concern with highly articulated tradition. Like Ezra Pound, much of whose poetry contained similar tensions, Blackburn seems to assume a universality of experience that makes it possible to create modern equivalents to perceptions of reality originally recorded in distant times and places. Blackburn, however, never tries to obliterate temporal and spatial distinctions as systematically as Pound. Although the poem contains its allusions—the most inevitable one to Peire Guillem of Toulouse, to Peire Vidal, and to the classical pantheon that Provençal poets might well have invoked—they are assimilated into Blackburn's personal vision rather than remaining undigested fragments of imaginary reality.

The Provençal *sirventes* often took the form of an attack against a particular place, usually for political reasons; the poet would attack the enemies of his patron. Blackburn, however, writes a very private diatribe against Toulouse:

> . . . this ravel-streeted, louse-ridden, down-river,
> gutter-sniping, rent-gouging, hard-hearted,
>   complacent provincial town,
> where they have forgotten all that made this country the
> belly of courage, the body of beauty, the hands of heresy,
> the legs of the individual spirit, the heart of song!

The effect of substituting personal for political motivation is parody. The poem turns finally on the poet, whose own frustrations with language are projected on the now bourgeois, once passionate, city. Blackburn, a lecturer at the university ("Whole damn year teaching/trifles to these trout with trousers"), finds that his identity as a teacher of "bourgeois dolts" is smothering his passionate poetic core. This kind of self-irony—not present in all of Blackburn's work but there frequently enough, undercutting the poet's own perspective—helps to define Blackburn's reality.

"El Camino Verde" in *The Nets* makes far more explicit the connection between inner reality and that of the objective world that is fundamental to Blackburn's work. As with most of the Projectivist poets, the point is not that the outer world corresponds to the inner but that there is no absolute distinction between the two. The poem begins by asserting that there is a green road, on which the sun's rays filtered through leaves cast "obscene/beautiful patterns," and a hot, oppressive road of sand, which the poet has chosen to travel.

> In the green road,   pale
> gray-green of olives, olive-wood twisted
> under the burning wind, the wet
> heat of an armpit, but in the mouth
>
> this other road.

The poem is almost allegorical, yet it is not in the least abstract. It operates almost entirely in terms of sensuous perception. What have traditionally been thought of as opposing ideas are here transformed into contrasting bodily apprehensions of reality. Stanley Burnshaw's dictum that the poem is an expression not simply of the conscious mind but of the entire organism is here forcefully demonstrated.

The cities in the book of that name (1967) are principally those of America and Spain: New York, Málaga, Barcelona. The emotional states associated with these cities are not totally conventional. In earlier poems, such as "Meditation on the BMT," New York is indeed a place of emptiness. In *The Cities* as well, it has those connotations. In "Brooklyn Narcissus," for example, the city becomes one huge image of isolation. But in "Here They Go," the city, an artificial construct cutting man off from nature, has gone so deeply into itself that it seems to have come out the other side. Talking of the young, Blackburn says:

                    The generation,
                    or two if you like, ahead of them
                    uses deodorants.
                            They, tho,
                            like the smell of hot flesh
                            suffering relief of its passion.

At the poem's conclusion, a new world rises "from the dark waters/from dark grass," in contrast to "Brooklyn Narcissus," which concludes: "The dirty window gives me back my face." "Here They Go" is not without its ironies, it is far from a totally positive vision. The point is that the cities are complete imaginative realities, not just fixed symbols of some particular aspect of those realities.

In "MÁLAGA, port," conventions are similarly reversed. Here, ". . . the sheer/machinery of docking" is what saves the city, normally thought of as one of the more passionate centers of Andalusia, from being provincial. Provincialism is clearly an important concept for Blackburn; his distrust of it functions as a protection against sentimentality, against allowing some worn-out "romantic" ideal to interfere with the all-important process of confronting reality in its totality.

In the second half of the poem, Blackburn does in fact get to the wine, the gypsies, "the dull strain of guitars;" but even here, he makes important distinctions. What he seeks is

                    . . . not
            any dream of release but real
                                    cold
                                        and flowing
                release we cannot beg or steal . . .

The response to experience Blackburn is after is clearly expressed in "The Pastures of the Eye":

                    The eye, yes
                                    aging in its pool,
                    but open

            O P E N

This openness is the precise opposite of provincialism. It is the need of the poet, and particularly the Projectivist poet, to see the world freshly rather than through stock responses.

Selected Bibliography:
BY BLACKBURN:
Proensa. [Translations.] Palma de Mallorca: Divers Press, 1953.
The Dissolving Fabric. Palma de Mallorca: Divers Press, 1955.
Brooklyn–Manhattan Transit: A Bouquet for Flatbush. New York: Totem Press, 1960.

The Nets. New York: Trobar Books, 1961.
The Cities. New York: Grove Press, 1967.
The Reardon Poems. Madison, Wisc.: The Perishable Press, 1967.

BLACK MOUNTAIN POETS

Black Mountain College, an experimental community in the foothills of North Carolina, was in the forefront of innovation in art and education. Founded in 1933 by dissident faculty members from Rollins College, Florida, who felt that greater flexibility of curriculum was educationally necessary, the school was in continual financial and structural difficulties. It closed in 1956, possibly a victim of its own virtues. (See Martin Duberman's *Black Mountain: An Exploration in Community.* New York: Dutton, 1972.)

In the late forties, CHARLES OLSON replaced Edward Dahlberg as instructor at Black Mountain College; from the early fifties until the school's closing, Olson was rector. John Cage, ROBERT CREELEY, ROBERT DUNCAN, Merce Cunningham, and Franz Kline were at one time or another on the faculty. John Weiners, EDWARD DORN, Michael Rumaker, and JOEL OPPENHEIMER were among the students. Creeley's *Black Mountain Review,* its seven issues published at the college from 1954 to 1957, included the poetry of PAUL BLACKBURN, PAUL CARROLL, Larry Eigner, and DENISE LEVERTOV, as well as that of Olson, Duncan, Dorn, Oppenheimer. Another journal associated with these poets was Cid Corman's *Origin,* which appeared from 1951 to 1957.

Like Ezra Pound for another generation of poets, Olson, who was very much influenced by Pound, provided the aesthetic theory and much of the original energy for this group of poets. His essay "Projective Verse," originally published in *Poetry New York* in 1950, is still the most important statement on poetics to come out of the movement and in fact serves to define it. More recent theoretical contributions have been made by Robert Creeley and Robert Duncan.

See PROJECTIVE VERSE.

BLY, ROBERT (*b. Madison, Minn., Dec. 23, 1926—*   )

The central concern of the poetry of Robert Bly, whose first two volumes of poetry contain no less than five epigraphs taken from the writing of Jakob Boehme, is the relationship between inner and outer realities. For Bly, as for the Projectivists and for the line of Theosophists running from Boehme through Blake, it is human intellect that forms the barrier between these worlds of being. Consequently, poetry must be defined as the attempt to break through or by-pass that barrier, to establish the existence of underlying harmonies where the human consciousness perceives divisiveness. Bly is attempting to write a poetry "which disregards the conscious and the intellectual structure of the mind entirely and by the use of images tries to bring forward another reality from *inward* experience." It is these subjective, or "deep," images that form the basis of his art.

Robert Bly was born on a farm near Madison, Minnesota, growing up in a setting that would provide the essential landscape for much of his verse. After a time in the Navy during World War II, he attended St. Olaf College and then Harvard, from which he graduated in 1950. Living on a farm in Minnesota and earning his living through translations and poetry readings, he has been very much influenced by European and South American poets. Bly has published much of their work in his magazine, *The Seventies* (in earlier versions *The Fifties* and *The Sixties*), as well as his own poetry and that of James Wright, Louis Simpson, and William Duffy, among others associated with DEEP IMAGISM. In 1966 Bly founded the American Writers Against the Vietnam War and has edited anthologies of protest poetry with David Ray.

According to Jakob Boehme, man exists in two worlds: the inner and the outer. He is in a sense two men: an inner man and an outer man. The epigraph by Boehme in *Silence in the Snowy Fields* (1962) describes the general human condition: "We are all asleep in the outward man." It is the Theosophist's job, and, Bly suggests, the poet's job, to wake the inner man by perceiving connections between inner and outer realities. In a poem like "Solitude Late at Night in the Woods" the attempt is rather explicit. "The body is like a November birch facing the full moon," the poem begins. The harmony between man and nature, broken by human consciousness, is perceived by the body. The leafless trees become symbolic of the poet's own state, in which consciousness has been minimized; the trees lack "ambition," they are "Nothing but bare trunks climbing like cold fire!"

The landscape Bly creates is complex. The poet identifies with only part of it: the trees reaching for the sky, making the connection between the spiritual and the material. The sodden leaves, the "trapped fields" to which the poet must return after this transitory experience, are reminders that man does, after all, exist in two worlds. But the joy taken in the scene is a clear indication that the perception of unity, albeit brief, is one that illuminates the poet's life.

The poem, like so many of Bly's, has a tripartite organization, almost suggesting a thesis, antithesis, synthesis arrangement (the skyward-reaching trees, the links with earth, the final expression of joy). The lines are written in tightly controlled free verse, observing units of breath and meaning, with frequent end-stops. Although the reader forms the impression that the poem's imagery is predominantly visual, this is not in fact the case. Touch and smell are more important than sight; most important is the sense of entering the perceptual range of the natural world, very much in the manner of William Carlos Williams and Theodore Roethke.

In some poems, the process is reversed. "Summer, 1960, Minnesota," for example, begins with the description of a landscape. Instead of reaching out to the external scene, Bly here internalizes it: "Inside me there is a confusion of swallows, / Birds flying through the smoke." But here as in most of the poems in this volume, the call is for unity of being. As Bly concludes in "Poem in Three Parts":

> The strong leaves of the box-elder tree,
> Plunging in the wind, call us to disappear
> Into the wilds of the universe,
> Where we shall sit at the foot of a plant,
> And live forever, like the dust.

How Bly's poetic preoccupations led him to an overriding interest in politics, or rather in political poetry, is not immediately evident. But even in *Silence in the Snowy Fields*, Bly's social concerns make themselves felt. In "Poem Against the British," that same wind through "the box-elder trees" that called for the poet's merging with the natural world, reminds him of "rides at dusk" and the Revolutionary War. The very same conviction that man must know himself as part of a natural unity, which in a poem like "Depression" can be translated into a longing "to go back among the dark roots," into a passive death wish, can also lead Bly to struggle with all his might against a society that emphasizes man's separateness from nature, that replaces his intuitive responses with mechanization, and that answers his wish for peace with war.

The Light Around the Body (1967), while not losing its connections with Jakob Boehme, is a largely political book. The fact that it is a product of the sixties rather than the fifties, of Johnson's escalation of the Vietnam war rather than Eisenhower's vagueness, should be sufficient to explain the shift in emphasis. At times, the need for direct political statement leads Bly into a kind of poetry somewhat different from his earlier work. "Counting Small-Boned Bodies," for example, suggests that if we could only make bodies "The size of skulls, / We could make a whole plain white with skulls in the moonlight!" And if we could get them smaller yet, we could fit them on a desk; we could even fit a body into a ring. The intentionally grotesque image seems a product of bitter wit rather than a surreal or deep image; it seems to emanate from the conscious mind rather than the unconscious. The image is, however, complex. Bly is not only playing with the idea of the body count but is reaching back into Asian history for Tamerlane's pyramid of skulls. So if Bly is not here interested in exploring the relationship between man and nature, he still persists in constructing his poems out of the tension between the particular and the universal; the American performance in Vietnam becomes a special case in the vast waste of history.

More often than not, however, Bly responds to social reality within a natural context. "The Great Society," for example, is characterized chiefly by its uneasy relationship to what might be called domesticated nature. "Dentists continue to water their lawns even in the rain; / Hands developed with terrible labor by apes / Hang from the sleeves of evangelists." Bushes grow over outdoor grills, vines grow over yachts. In the center of the poem, "The President dreams of invading Cuba." It is difficult to tell whether the gloomy landscape has driven the President to thoughts of desperation or whether the landscape is itself a manifestation of irresponsible thought. The poem's other political images—"murdered kings," "the coffins of the poor," "a mayor sitting with his head in his hands"—are juxtaposed with movie theaters, junkyards, "the chilling beach," with no attempt made to fix causal relationships. Bly is presenting a state of being rather than assigning blame. The poem functions equally well as a description of a society that has betrayed its natural heritage (those "Hands developed with terrible labor by apes") or as a portrait of a man in despair.

If we had not otherwise been able to deduce it, a poem like "Romans Angry about the Inner World" would provide the key to the political implications of Bly's dualism. Two Romans, representing soldiers, statesmen, administrators, and rulers of the world, torture to death a woman representing the inner world. They are public men to whom inner reality is a threat; they do not seek unity of being, for it would render meaningless their power. They do not seek harmony with the natural world; they wish to conquer it. It is clear that for Bly, as for Robert Lowell in *Near the Ocean,* we are the Romans.

The final poems of *The Light Around the Body* return to the more personal search for unity of being. The fact that Bly has led us through the political overtones of this search is not easy to forget, however; it adds an extra dimension to the poetry. "In Danger from the Outer World" repeats the theme and much of the imagery of "Solitude Late at Night in the Woods." The heavy leaves are present, the flesh is "opaque"; this is body neither in harmony with nature nor united to spirit. At the poem's conclusion, there is reference to "Some shining thing, inside, that has served us well," and the warning that "It may be gone before we wake. . . ." The transitoriness of the experience produces not the joy of "Solitude Late at Night in the Woods" but an ominous threat to survival: "The black water swells up over the new hole. / The grave moves forward from its ambush."

Robert Bly's poetry perfectly fits the contention made by Stanley Burnshaw in *The Seamless Web* (1970) that "every . . . imaginative expression must be at least in part a denial of civilization, a self-assuring cry of the organism that freedom and wholeness and joy have not been lost." The poet's faith in the possibilities of such affirmation waivers, as indeed it must, for the absence of tension between public and private worlds would probably mean the end of art; there seems, however, little danger of that. Nonetheless, if Bly is a dark poet, he insists on his vision of light; if man seems bound by his body to the outer world, it is also through the body's potential harmony with the rest of creation that hope lies. This hope is clearly expressed in the conclusion to "Looking into a Face":

> I have wandered in a face, for hours,
> Passing through dark fires.
> I have risen to a body
> Not yet born,

Existing like a light around the body,
Through which the body moves like a sliding moon.
See also the Introduction, section VIII.

Selected Bibliography:
By Bly:
Silence in the Snowy Fields. Middletown, Conn.: Wesleyan University Press, 1962.
The Light Around the Body. New York: Harper & Row Publishers, 1967.
Sleepers Joining Hands. New York: Harper & Row Publishers, 1972.

About Bly:
Howard, Richard. *Alone with America*. New York: Atheneum Publishers, 1969. Pp. 38–48.
Stepanchev, Stephen. *American Poetry since 1945*. New York: Harper & Row Publishers, 1965. Pp. 185–87.

BROOKS, GWENDOLYN (*b. Topeka, Kans., June 7, 1917—   *)

Not least remarkable of Gwendolyn Brooks's achievements is that without compromising her identity as a black woman in America she has been able to earn the admiration of an overwhelmingly white critical establishment— in 1950 she won the Pulitzer Prize for *Annie Allen*—and then, in the late sixties, took her place among the new wave of younger black poets who seemed to repudiate the very critical criteria by which she was first acclaimed. Her keen sense of poetic discipline never diminished her commitment to expressing the specifically black experience; her shift from relatively closed to open forms constituted a change in style similar to the development of such poets as Theodore Roethke, Robert Lowell, and W. S. Merwin rather than a change of fundamental perspective.

Although born in Kansas, Gwendolyn Brooks was raised, and has spent most of her life, in Chicago. She graduated from Wilson Junior College in 1934. Through the years, she has given frequent readings of her poetry and has taught creative writing. In 1971 she was Distinguished Professor of the Arts at the City College of New York. Since the late sixties she has devoted much of her energy helping to launch the careers of young black writers, partly through her involvement with the Broadside Press in Detroit.

Much of Gwendolyn Brooks's versatility is already on display in her first volume of poems, *A Street in Bronzeville* (1945). She demonstrates her mastery of the formal sonnet, of a language that is totally "literary." "Gay chaps at the bar," for example, concludes:

. . . No stout
Lesson showed how to chat with death. We brought

> No brass fortissimo, among our talents,
> To holler down the lions in this air.

It is a Petrarchan sonnet; the technique is extremely sophisticated. The play with diction—the colloquial "holler down" against the formal "brass fortissimo"—is characteristic. So is her use of half-rhymes: "dash, lush," "taste, iced," "love, off," "islands, talents," "hour, air," "stout, brought."

Equally impressive is her use of the ballad form, her drawing on folk and spiritual traditions. The ballad has most frequently been a reporting of disaster, and there is all too great an abundance of material for Brooks in the world of black men and women in white America. The "Ballad of Pearl May Lee" is the story of a rape and lynching. "The murder" tells of a baby burned alive by his brother, who has committed the act intentionally but without any real sense of what he has done. These poems border on excessive pathos. Only simplicity and understatement, with the understanding that the materials speak forcefully for themselves, can save them, and generally they do.

There is still another form that Brooks handles with great success. It consists of iambic lines of varying length, often without a recurrent pattern, bound together by rhymes and half-rhymes. The following passage from "Matthew Cole" is typical:

> And the red fat roaches that stroll
> Unafraid up his wall,
> And the whiteless grin of the housekeeper
> On Saturday night when he pays his four
> Dollars . . .

And there are poems like "southeast corner," a memorial to the dead "Madam": three iambic tetrameter quatrains, with a foot dropped from the last line of each quatrain. There is something here reminiscent of Jonson and Herrick, nowhere more obviously than in the concluding lines: "While over her tan impassivity / Shot silk is shining."

A discussion of the formal methods of Brooks's first book, however, may mask its essential quality. It is dominated by ghetto portraits, in a way a black *Spoon River Anthology*, a vision of pain and suffering, of occasional joy, of dignity and defeat.

The prize-winning *Annie Allen* (1949) is generally acknowledged to be Gwendolyn Brooks's best book. It unquestionably contains some of her finest work. *A Street in Bronzeville* focused on a particular ghetto; this volume focuses on a single woman. In a way, however, the themes are identical; Annie, although possessing a distinct personality, is universal.

The book's structure is novelistic. It begins with an elegy to Ed Bland, killed in Germany in 1945. He will turn out to be the man, loved by Annie, who goes off to war (or an equivalent of that man; part of the poems' universality derives from the fact that the "story" might either be taken from one life or a composite of various lives that are at critical moments interchangeable). The next section is entitled "Notes from the Childhood and

the Girlhood." The first poem, "the birth in a narrow room," sets the tone
—a sense of paradox, of hope and despair never canceling each other out,
always in tension. Annie is "Wanted and unplanned." She has been born,
but born into a confined space that is the symbol of the space in which she
will always live. Still, she is not yet aware of her limits and plays happily,

> . . . where the bugs buzz by in private cars
> Across old peach cans and old jelly jars.

The imagery is wonderfully appropriate. Though it is a vision of garbage, it
is a kind of fairyland to the child. This reminds us of Ed Bland, who "grew
up being curious," but whose life channeled him inexorably to the place in
Germany where he was killed.

The next section is "The Anniad," a miniature epic in seven-line stanzas
of truncated trochaic tetrameter. Again, the technique is glittering:

> Think of thaumaturgic lass
> Looking in her looking-glass
> At the unembroidered brown;
> Printing bastard roses there;
> Then emotionally aware
> Of the black and boisterous hair,
> Taming all that anger down.

The trochees are especially effective when the man in the poem is drafted:
"Names him. Tames him. Takes him off. / Throws to columns row on row."

The final section is "The Womanhood," which begins with a five-sonnet
sequence, "The Children of the Poor." In the context of the book as a
whole, the sonnet form begins to take on special significance. It is tightly
controlled, something like the room in which Annie Allen's life began; it is
therefore both protective and confining, both an emblem of courage in the
face of destruction and a grim reminder of human—and especially black—
limitations. This double edge runs throughout the sequence, nowhere more
expertly than in the fourth sonnet, which begins "First fight. Then fiddle."
Here, Brooks conflates the imagery of playing the violin with the imagery of
war, the language of harmony and love with the language of hate. The
poem moves toward a terrible but inevitable resolution:

> Win war. Rise bloody, maybe not too late
> For having first to civilize a space
> Wherein to play your violin with grace.

After the sonnet sequence, the forms are somewhat freer, and a world of
possibility seems to open. The primary hope, of course, is in the children.
The poem beginning "Life for my child is simple" ends: "His lesions are
legion. / But reaching is his rule." There is more than a little irony here.
This is the way Ed Bland and Annie Allen began; the volume's final lines
are appropriately ambivalent: ". . . We are lost, must / Wizard a track
through our own screaming weed."

In *The Bean Eaters* (1960), Gwendolyn Brooks continues to exercise her already proven talents, as, for example, in the fine sonnet "The Egg Boiler." Nevertheless, the book is not at all a mere repetition of past accomplishments. First, there are stylistic experiments. "The Bean Eaters" begins by resembling a ballad and ends with flat prose: "As they lean over the beans in their rented back room that is full of beads and receipts and dolls and cloths, tobacco crumbs, vases and fringes." "A Bronzeville Mother Loiters in Mississippi. Meanwhile, a Mississippi Mother Burns Bacon" deals with material that is self-consciously appropriate to the ballad form, but it is written in the free verse that Brooks has begun more and more frequently to use. The often anthologized "We Real Cool," about seven pool players, strips language, and experience, down to its bare essentials:

> We real cool. We
> Left school. We
>
> Lurk late. We
> Strike straight. We
>
> Sing sin. We
> Thin gin. We
>
> Jazz June. We
> Die soon.

More striking, perhaps, is the presence of poems about the murder of Emmett Till, about Little Rock. What has been introduced to Brooks's work is neither more nor less than history. Her earlier almost anonymous ghetto portraits were based on individual lives, but on lives that followed the same fundamental patterns, boxed-in existences that offered only vague hope of escape from deadly cycles. In *The Bean Eaters* the experiences are painful, but something is happening—public events around which an entire people can rally. The anger present in Brooks's earlier books is now beginning to take definite focus.

In the Mecca (1968), Gwendolyn Brooks's last book published before her move to Broadside Press, was received with less favor by the white critical establishment than any of her previous volumes. Whether this reception was related to the book's themes or not, Brooks's path from this point on is unmistakable. In the long title poem, she writes of fellow poet Don L. Lee:

> Don Lee wants
> not a various America.
> Don Lee wants
> a new nation
> under nothing;
> . . . .
> wants
> new art and anthem; will
> want a new music screaming in the sun.

If Brooks's wishes are not identical with those of the younger black poet, they are not far from them. Many of the *In the Mecca* poems are occasional, again involved in history. The subjects are Medgar Evers, Malcolm X, the Blackstone Rangers (a street gang), the dedication of a Picasso sculpture in Chicago. Her new directions clear, much of the ambivalence of Brooks's earlier work is gone; not, however, the force with which she expresses her vision, as in the conclusion of "Medgar Evers":

> Roaring no rapt arise-ye to the dead, he
> leaned across tomorrow. People said that
> he was holding clean globes in his hands.

The epigraph to the title poem of *Riot* (1969) is Martin Luther King's definition: "A riot is the language of the unheard." In some ways, the voice of these poems is less personal than that of Brooks's previous work; she is speaking for the unheard as well as for herself. And yet, if the structure of her poems is less intricate than before—intentionally—the control of language is equally evident, even when the language is angry, as in "The Third Sermon on the Warpland":

> Fire.
> That is their way of lighting candles in the darkness.
> A White Philosopher said
> 'It is better to light one candle than curse the darkness.'
>   These candles curse—
> inverting the deeps of the darkness.

Having proven her credentials as a superb craftsman, she is not at all uncomfortable with the idea that the artist has obligations that extend beyond the practice of his craft. In *Family Pictures* (1970), she quotes one of three "Young Heroes" as saying

> *Art is life worked with:* is life
> wheedled, or whelmed:
> assessed:
> clandestine, but evoked.

In retrospect, this is what Gwendolyn Brooks's art has always been about.
    See also NEW BLACK AESTHETIC and the Introduction, section VII.

Selected Bibliography:
BY BROOKS:
A Street in Bronzeville. New York: Harper & Row Publishers, 1945.
Annie Allen. New York: Harper & Row Publishers, 1949.
Maud Martha. [Novel.] New York: Harper & Row Publishers, 1953.
The Bean Eaters. New York: Harper & Row Publishers, 1960.
Selected Poems. New York: Harper & Row Publishers, 1963.
In the Mecca. New York: Harper & Row Publishers, 1968.
Riot. Detroit: Broadside Press, 1969.
Family Pictures. Detroit: Broadside Press, 1970.

The World of Gwendolyn Brooks. [Collected poems and *Maud Martha.*] New
  York: Harper & Row Publishers, 1971.
Report from Part One: An autobiography. Detroit: Broadside Press, 1973.

CARROLL, PAUL (*b. Chicago, Ill., July 15, 1927—)*

Paul Carroll is probably best known as editor of the magazine *Big Table,*
which he published and edited from 1959 to 1961, printing the verse of
such poets as John Ashbery, Paul Blackburn, Robert Creeley, Allen Ginsberg, Robert Duncan, and Charles Olson. A millionaire's son, he received
his M.A. from the University of Chicago in 1952 and was poetry editor of
the *Chicago Review* before founding his own journal. He has taught English and creative writing at Iowa and the University of Illinois Chicago
Circle campus; recently he has been chairman of the English Department
at Columbia College in Chicago. In the late sixties, Carroll began publishing Big Table Books (in association with Follett Publishing Company). In
this series his own collection of poems (*Odes,* 1969) and critical essays (*The
Poem in Its Skin,* 1968) appeared, but the main function of the press has
been to introduce new writers.

  Like the poets he has published, Carroll prefers open to tight forms, free
accumulation of images to systematic symbolism. Much of his recent work,
including the "Ode to Severn Darden," printed on a five-foot fold-out, invites comparison with Ginsberg. But it was not always so: *Odes* is arranged
in reverse chronological order, becoming a kind of deepening probe into the
author's poetic past. The earlier the poem, the tighter the form; some intricate stanzas in syllabic meter in the earlier poems bring to mind Marianne
Moore in everything but diction. The most recent section displays more independence of method, often combining the control of earlier work with the
ribald and rich imagination of the later. It is probably no coincidence that
Carroll at this point in his career decided to bring out his first volume.

  The clearest statement of the aesthetic of Carroll's own verse can be
found in his analysis of contemporary trends, "Faire, Foul and Full of Variations: The Generation of 1962" (in *The Poem in Its Skin*). Examining
Ginsberg's "Message," Carroll calls it an "impure" poem.

> Its impurity exists in the lack of organic function or justification of
> the three images: the images are simply there. . . . In the midst of
> writing a conventionally organic love lyric, Ginsberg suddenly for-
> gets or ignores his natural tendency as poet to edit or refine material
> floating from his unconscious. . . . As far as I know, "Message" is
> the first example of the inorganically impure image in American
> verse. And the point of course is: the three impure images are not
> Dada or Surrealist poetry. On the contrary, skyscrapers, dirigible
> and dancing women exist within an otherwise perfectly traditional
> organic poem. That is the impure quality.

It is certainly possible to quarrel with Carroll about the uniqueness of Gins-berg's poem. Even granting the premise, one can argue that the uncon-scious itself provides a form of organic unity, although not an obvious one. But Carroll makes his point: he will not submit his work to the principles of the NEW CRITICISM; he will opt for poetry produced by the entire human psyche rather than limit art to areas of conscious control. And in addition to the inhabitants of the unconscious, "Concrete autobiographical facts from past and present can also be included." Clearly, serious evaluatory problems have been introduced. If the poet's own critical faculties are to be sus-pended, what criteria are available by which the reader can judge the poem? Serious as the difficulties may be, an art that would do away with the more rigid critical dicta is not completely unappealing. There is ulti-mately no way to judge a poem except to enter its universe, just as there is no way to know a man except to see the world from his perspective. Or, as Carroll puts it in "Ode to the Angels":

> Best of all,
> each poem wears its own skin
> the bones of style being
> (like any successful marriage)
> only ½ of what it's all about.

Selected Bibliography:
By CARROLL:
The Poem in Its Skin. [Criticism.] Chicago: Follett Publishing Co., 1968.
The Young American Poets. [Editor.] Chicago: Follett Publishing Co., 1968.
Odes. Chicago: Follett Publishing Co., 1969.

CONCRETE POETRY

The defining characteristic of Concrete poetry is that whether or not the poem has any referential significance, its emphasis is on the way in which the letters are presented on the page. Although message may very well be involved, medium is clearly central. Concrete poetry may range, therefore, from nearly conventional poetry in the modes of e. e. cummings or Charles Olson to photographic distortions that border on pure graphic art.

Concretism has not been a specifically American movement; its flavor is distinctly international. Such American writers as Aram Saroyan, Emmett Williams, and Mary Ellen Solt, however, are known for their Concrete po-etry. And poets like JEROME ROTHENBERG have gone far beyond ordinary typographical experiments to write occasional poems that are unmistakably Concrete.

In his afterword to *The Chicago Review Anthology of Concretism* (Chi-cago: Swallow Press, 1967), Eugene Wildman writes:

> Literature as it has developed so far, and this includes so-called non-realistic literature, is tied to verisimilitude in that it uses language symbolically. . . . Concrete poetry aims, in general, at the ideogrammic state. . . . Thus concretism begins where literacy begins. If we got used to literature being keyed to a movement of presentation, how much more intense an experience would be possible than anything poetry and prose now offer. Every turn of the page would be crucial. There would be, for the first time really, a non-oral tradition. For what we have had till now has been hardly more than the transferring onto paper, with not a great deal of essential difference, of what could just as easily have been the work of an oral poet.

This manifesto presents difficulties even for those who would not in the least wish to deny Concrete poetry's legitimacy as an art form. The question is whether poetry is not precisely an oral tradition, as opposed to the novel, whose rise to popularity seems unmistakably linked to the printing press. Poetry from Homer to the troubadours and beyond was principally oral, and while it has been significantly modified by print, the real test of its success has never really ceased to be its effectiveness when read aloud. The entire Projectivist school of poetry, with its emphasis on line units determined by breath, and the new black poetry, with its concern with the communal experience of the poetry reading, suggest that we are not in an age in which poetry's oral dimension is on the decline.

It would at first seem ironic that Concrete poetry would come into prominence just when Marshall McLuhan was announcing the end of the age of print. But it is probably a question of inevitable consequence rather than accidental irony: separating print from its symbolic function, and concentrating instead on its concrete reality, minimizes the significance of interchangeable type as a medium that affects our way of knowing the world—in this case the analytic and sequential sense of experience inherent in being able to break entities into component parts and to string them together again. From that point of view, Concrete poetry is a parody of the printed word rather than a reaffirmation of its importance.

In the end, however, whether it is poetry or graphic art, Concrete poetry exists. The fact that it cannot be dealt with in the manner of conventional poetry is not at all an argument against it.

CONFESSIONAL POETRY

One of the first to use the term *confessional poetry* was M. L. Rosenthal, in a review written in 1959 of Robert Lowell's *Life Studies*. In *The New Poets* (1967) Rosenthal more precisely explained what he had meant by the term, and included essays on LOWELL, SYLVIA PLATH, ALLEN GINSBERG, THEODORE ROETHKE, JOHN BERRYMAN, and ANNE SEXTON as examples of the Confessional school, all the while acknowledging the difficulties involved in asserting that such a school, as a meaningful focus of poetic activity, actually existed.

The best historical evidence for the existence of a school is the fact that Anne Sexton and Sylvia Plath were students of Robert Lowell's at Boston University in 1958–59. But it was probably *Life Studies* rather than anything said by Lowell that year that opened new possibilities to Sylvia Plath; Anne Sexton in fact credits W. D. SNODGRASS's *Heart's Needle* with introducing her to a poetry grounded in painful areas of experience; and Roethke, Berryman, and Ginsberg had already begun their explorations of the confessional mode before 1959. Thus this school, if it can be said to exist, has to be thought of as a series of nearly contemporary, independent discoveries, rather than as a group of poets inspired by a single writer's theories, as, for example, the Projectivists were by Charles Olson.

It is similarly difficult to spell out what breakthrough the Confessional poets are responsible for; yet one has the sense that Plath, Sexton, and Rosenthal were correct when they suggested that some sort of breakthrough was in fact made. The Confessional poets make poetry out of their own experience, but lyric poets have always done that, from Sappho and Catullus on. The Confessional poets invade their own privacy and suggest that their private worlds are as significant as any public universe, but so did Donne. The Confessional poets draw upon the unconscious for insight and imagery, and insist upon the capacity of inner life to illuminate what is outer, but so did the French Symbolists and the Surrealists. Finally, the Confessional poets have understood madness to be not necessarily a distortion but rather an intensification of the human condition, but so did many of the romantics.

Nonetheless, a sense of significant differences persists. The very bringing together of these characteristics and concentrating them in one poetic sensibility would itself justify that impression. There is more: madness in Confessional poetry is neither divine nor demonic. It is painful rather than ecstatic, embarrassing rather than noble. Its legitimacy lies not in the fact that it is an intenser assertion of the self's power in the world, but rather in the fact that the boundaries between the self and outer reality have themselves been brought into question. At the core of all Confessional poetry is a crisis of identity, a crisis which in our time has come to seem not pathological but rather a defining feature of the human condition.

See also the Introduction, section VI.

CORSO, GREGORY (*b. New York City, Mar. 26, 1930—   *)

For Gregory Corso, the poet is more important than the poetry, and the fact that one is a poet assures that what is produced will be poetry. Corso has remarked that he did not worry when he lost poems "because I felt myself to be inexhaustible." This feeling is undoubtedly related to the Zen notion that if one perfects one's being, the appropriate action will follow as a necessary consequence. And this in turn reveals a fundamental connection

between the BEAT GENERATION poets—of whom Corso is one of the more
more prominent—and the Projectivists, since in each aesthetic poetry is seen
as the expression of a total organism rather than simply of the conscious
mind.

Born in Greenwich Village, Corso spent much of his childhood in or-
phanages and foster homes. Back with his father after he remarried, Corso
ran away several times, ending up once in Bellevue, finally in prison. In the
early fifties, he met Allen Ginsberg and Jack Kerouac and became one of
the Beat poets.

Some of Corso's earlier work, although fully committed to open rather
than restricted poetic forms, is relatively conventional. "Uccello" in *Gasoline,* for example, opens:

> They will never die on that battlefield
> nor the shade of wolves recruit their hoard like brides of
> wheat on all horizons   waiting there to consume battle's end

The poem continues as a kind of set piece on art and life, eternity and time,
a reasonable performance in a familiar mode.

Far more characteristic of Corso's verse are the less disciplined poems, or
rather those poems ruled by a less obvious discipline, whose rhythms are
determined by breath rather than intellect, whose images wildly clash. "But
I Do Not Need Kindness" (also from *Gasoline*) is this kind of poem, echoing
both the theme and methods of Ginsberg's *Howl.*

> I have known the strange nurses of Kindness,
> I have seen them kiss the sick, attend the old,
> give candy to the mad!
> I have watched them, at night, dark and sad,
> rolling wheelchairs by the sea!

The poem works by accumulation of images, by taking an inventory of experiences organized by parallel structure and waves of rhythm. And the
tone, like Ginsberg's, is at once despairing and ecstatic.

Most characteristic of all in Gregory Corso's poetry is its combination of
humor and terror. In his best-known poem (in *The Happy Birthday of
Death*), "Marriage," a long monologue on whether or not he should get
married, he merges these conflicting tones as expertly as anywhere in his
work. A brief passage taken from the concluding lines will illustrate:

> Because what if I'm 60 years old and not married,
> all alone in a furnished room with pee stains on my underwear
> and everybody else is married! All the universe married but me!

If Ginsberg is the prophet of the Beats, mingling blissful mystical union
with a horror at the way the One manifests itself in individualized forms,
then Corso is his more mundane equivalent, mingling the terribly funny
with the simply terrible.

Selected Bibliography:
BY CORSO:
The Vestal Lady on Brattle and Other Poems. Cambridge, Mass.: Richard Bru-
   kenfeld, 1955.
Gasoline. San Francisco: City Lights Books, 1958.
The Happy Birthday of Death. New York: New Directions Publishing Corp.,
   1960.
American Express. [Prose fantasy.] Paris: Olympia Press, 1961.
Long Live Man. New York: New Directions Publishing Corp., 1962.
Selected Poems. London: Eyre and Spottiswoode, 1962.
The Mutation of the Spirit. New York: Death Press, 1964.
*There Is Time Yet to Run Back Through Life and Expiate All That's Been Sadly
   Done.* New York: New Directions Publishing Corp., 1965.
Elegiac Feelings American. New York: New Directions Publishing Corp., 1970.
See also Corso's essay "Some of My Beginning . . . and What I Feel Right Now"
   in *Poets on Poetry.* Edited by Howard Nemerov. New York: Basic Books,
   1966. Pp. 172–81.

About Corso:
Howard, Richard. *Alone with America.* New York: Atheneum Publishers, 1969.
   Pp. 57–64.

CREELEY, ROBERT *(b. Arlington, Mass., May 21, 1926—   )*

In light of his years at Black Mountain College and his frequently expressed
allegiance to the principles of Charles Olson, Robert Creeley is generally associated with the Projectivist poets. This attribution demonstrates as well as
any the limitations of labels. For Creeley's concern with the subtleties of his
feelings and with the qualifications and modifications of his reactions at any
given moment places him, in a curious way, with the Confessional poets.
But it is Creeley's commitment to analysis and definition, in an age in
which most have felt the analytic process inadequate to deal with the world
of emotional response, that is most telling; it makes him, in an even more
curious way, our clearest heir to the tradition of Henry James, albeit an heir
who, to rephrase E. M. Forster, would quite have incinerated the pages of
a James novel.

Creeley has been by necessity an avowed enemy of the academy, but his
career has been consistently linked with the academic world. He studied at
Harvard—before and after a year in the American Field Service in India
and Burma during World War II—but never received his degree there.
Leaving Harvard in 1947, he went to Europe with his first wife, spending
some time in southern France and Mallorca, where he founded the Divers
Press. His time abroad also included work on Rainer Gerhardt's magazine
Fragmente and Katue Kitasono's *Vou.* In 1954 he went to Black Mountain
College at the invitation of CHARLES OLSON; there he finally received his
B.A., taught creative writing, and edited the *Black Mountain Review,*

which, for its seven issues, was one of the most successful, if somewhat partisan, literary enterprises of its kind in recent years. He earned his M.A. at the University of New Mexico in 1959 and has taught at the State University of New York at Buffalo; he gives frequent lectures and readings at college campuses across the country, and is perhaps the one member of the Projectivist, or Black Mountain, school who has felt most keenly, both in print and on the rostrum, his responsibility to act as apologist for his poetic persuasion.

Although Creeley is more than willing to talk about poetics, the connections between theory and practice are not always especially obvious. He quotes Olson in particular, speaks of composition by field, open poetry, units of breath, but his poetry does not look or sound anything like Olson's, or, for that matter, like that of most other Projectivists. His poems are short and tightly knit—the ghost of some precise form seems always hovering, though is rarely explicit. But if we listen closely to Olson, or at any rate to what Creeley says about what Olson says, we come to understand how broad the Projectivist tradition is.

Creeley is probably very near the heart of things when he explains why the academy has remained hostile to Olson:

> Some, then, would not only not hear what Olson was saying, but would even deny, I think, the relevance of his concerns. The great preoccupation with symbology and levels of image in poetry insisted upon by contemporary criticism has also meant a further bias for this not-hearing, since Olson's emphasis is put upon prosody, not interpretation.

("Olson & Others: Some Orts for the Sports")

Generally of greatest interest in Creeley's verse, therefore, is not the analysis to which he has subjected his experience, but the rhythmic tensions that hold the poem together. A man fond of qualifications, Creeley's final irony in a host of ironic poems is the qualification of form itself, the undercutting by the choppy, usually unpredictable movement of lines. It does not look like Olson's work because the vision it attempts to communicate is fundamentally dissimilar; but the relation of form to vision and the emphasis on the problems of perception provide important common ground.

Creeley is also insistent on a principle that has been crucial historically to the tradition within which he operates. Pound, Williams, and Olson have all warned against the dangers of description, and to this literature Creeley adds:

> A poetry denies its end in any *descriptive* act, I mean any act which leaves the attention outside the poem. . . . *Description* does nothing, it includes the object,—it neither hates nor loves.

("To Define")

Creeley has taken this caveat more seriously than most practitioners of the Projective art. For a poet writing in what is still an essentially imagistic age, Creeley is remarkably sparse in imagery. For a poet vitally concerned with the specific contexts of the artist's performance, he is remarkably grudging about the contexts of the relationships that form the subjects of a good deal of his work, with the result that attention focuses on the relation itself rather than on the people involved in the relation, on the present moment as it stands out of time rather than on history (and here is the real reason that Creeley, appearances to the contrary, ultimately does not qualify as a Confessional poet—he lacks their preoccupation with time past). "The process of definition," Creeley has written, "is the intent of the poem." It is perhaps the central statement he has made about his verse, whose moving impulse seems always to be the wish to give shape or definition to discrete fragments of the flux of experience.

Although there has been continuing development in Creeley's art, it is not especially easy to pinpoint. The passion for definition, almost to the point of compulsiveness, has certainly predominated. There are, however, pervasive characteristics that seem to shift. *For Love* (1962), for example, which collects the most important work of the first decade of Creeley's career, is relatively stronger than later volumes in the kind of quasi allegory exemplified by "The Traveller":

> Into the forest again
> whence all roads depend
> this way and that
> to lead him back.
>
> Upon his shoulders
> he places boulders,
> upon his eye
> the high wide sky.

The temptation to identify Creeley's Traveller with Everyman is great. If this poem is allegory, however, it is allegory in the Kafkaesque mode, where static forms of reference are made ludicrous by the incomprehensibility, if not absurdity, of the universe. Where the Traveller is going, what his purpose might be, even his own response to his condition, are none of the business of the poem. All we know is that roads that lead him into the forest seem to conspire to lead him back, that he carries a burden represented by the "boulders" on his shoulders, that he has vision as signaled by the "high wide sky" on his eye. A wide range of possibilities suggest themselves, from Dante's dark woods to Camus's boulder-pushing Sisyphus; but the poem gives insufficient data for any such interpretation. The only secure ground for the reader—and this is hardly very secure—is the irony of the rhyme scheme, which develops from the slant rhymes of the first quatrain to the full rhymes of the second that are both naive and out of place in the context of the poem.

The use of rhymes for ironic emphasis, in the manner of Pound's *Hugh Selwyn Mauberley*, is prevalent in *For Love*, as, for example, in the opening stanzas of "The Friend":

What I saw in his head
was an inverted vision,
and the glass cracked
when I put my hand in.

My own head is round
with hair for adornment,
but the face
is an ornament.

The almost metaphysical conceit of the first stanza is appropriately representative of Creeley's dreamlike, surreal version of the analytic process.

For Love is also abundant in poems like "A Wicker Basket" (analyzed in detail by Paul Carroll in *The Poem in Its Skin*), richer by far in knowable context and sensible imagery than the more skeletal poetry to which Creeley has increasingly given himself.

Words (1967) collects the poems from that period of Creeley's career in which the poet's own perception of the complexities of human relationships amounts almost to obsession. I have already noted that Creeley, unlike the Confessional poets, has no preoccupation with the details of his own past, yet these poems are centered on the self to a degree that poets such as Lowell, Roethke, and Plath never really approach. Creeley's concentration on the act of perception as crucial to the existence of an objective universe leaves him uninterested in observing from without; in a very Jamesian way, Creeley provides the reader with a definite center of consciousness, a consciousness very much aware of its role as observer.

"Something" examines the ". . . finally foolish/question of how it is,/then, supposed to be felt,/and by whom." The poet remembers an occasion in a rented room, when, having made love to a woman, she, embarrassed, "sat spread-legged, turned on/one faucet and shyly pissed." Creeley's concluding remark is, ". . . What/love might learn from such a sight." The poem exploits the tension between the cerebral, the need to understand, to assign every experience its proper place, and the bodily, the need to piss and the act of making love itself. Unity of being is clearly something that eludes Creeley, assuming that he seeks it to begin with. The very asking of the question, how it is supposed to be felt, and by whom, implies a world out of joint, of self-conscious emotion that seems to lose its genuineness as it is experienced. To be fair, it is unlikely that Creeley himself is unaware of the irony with which his personae, who generally seem indistinguishable from the poet, are presented. Creeley's voice is cool, detached, superior; but the cumulative effect, at least in *Words*, is finally the impression of nearly desperate defensiveness.

Again, with all of Creeley's passion to understand, it is less the specific interpretation of an experience than the form within which this interpretation is cast that engages the reader. "The Mechanic," one of the most successful poems in the book, is a good example:

Were we now to fall
to our stubborn knees
and sink to rest, my-
self sunk in yours, then

what would hold us
together but uninteresting
weight. Do you believe
love, and how much.

The use of "uninteresting weight" counts for much; but with the last sentence the poem threatens to dissolve into banality, a threat not infrequently present in the conclusions of Creeley's poems. The ambiguities, even obscurities, of syntax and the unexpected rhythms enforced by line endings, however, succeed in rescuing the poem from what it seems to say. This configuration occurs time and again in the body of Creeley's work.

One poem in *Words* (given below in its entirety) was particularly irritating to critics, "A Piece":

One and
one, two,
three.

That reviewers found this poem exasperating is not surprising. It should be no more of a surprise to know that Creeley, who mentions the poem in "Contexts of Poetry," considered it "central to all possibilities of statement." "To count, or give account," he goes on, "tell or tally, continuingly seems to me the occasion." What has in fact occurred is an at least superficial abandonment of the specifically human dimensions of experience, in favor, on the one hand, of the value in words themselves ("Words/are/pleasure./All/words," he says in a recent poem), or, on the other, of abstractions as valid definitions of reality. Creeley's next book, *Pieces* (1969), picks up the cue from "A Piece."

The poems of this volume reach heights of abstraction only sketched out before, as in this section of "As real as thinking":

Inside
and out

impossible
locations—

reaching in
from out-

side, out
from in-

side—as
middle:

one
hand.

The individual identity of the poems themselves seems threatened. Frequently, poems are separated only by three dots, sections of the same poem
by one, so that the reader is confident—or at least relatively confident—of
which poem he is reading only after checking with the table of contents.
The discrete work of art is apparently relegated to the same limbo as the
discrete human personality as Creeley carries the principles by which he so
seriously works to something approximating their logical conclusions.

Probably the most important piece in *Pieces*—theoretically, if not
aesthetically—is "NUMBERS," in which the poet's movement toward the simple bones of experience is most successful. Most striking about the entire sequence, from "One" to "Nine" to "Zero," is that the universe that Creeley is
now dealing with is—if possible—more exclusively human than before.
There is no attempt here systematically to utilize traditional symbologies in
order to make the human connection (although it is neither possible nor de-
sirable to Creeley to keep traditional references from intruding occasionally). The poet works rather in terms of personal associations, with the curious result that the most abstract part of Creeley's opus is also very nearly
the most subjective as well. The way that he operates here is well illustrated by the beginning of "Four":

> This number for me
> is comfort, a secure
> fact of things. The
>
> table stands on
> all fours. . . .

Creeley's linking of extreme subjective and objective worlds of reference is
not unlike what Olson attempts in the final *Maximus* poems. As always,
however, the ways in which these two poets literally see the world are as
nearly distinct as two sensibilities could dictate.

Whatever the virtues of Creeley's *Pieces*, they are not without liability.
His tendency toward the meaningless and the banal is still present, and the
reader must judge whether it is always redeemed by subtleties of rhythm
and syntax:

> What
> by being not
> is—is not
> by being.

("Zero")

The critic must be wary: Creeley has a way of writing those things it seems anyone could have written, but actually no one else remotely could have. He has a unique voice, and *Pieces* has expanded the possibilities of that voice, not by ranging outward to new areas, but by mining still deeper in the preserve Creeley has already so successfully staked out.

See also BLACK MOUNTAIN POETS, PROJECTIVE VERSE, and the Introduction, section II.

Selected Bibliography:
BY CREELEY:
Le Fou. Columbus: Golden Goose, 1952.
The Immoral Proposition. Highlands, N.C.: Jargon Books, 1953.
The Kind of Act. Palma de Mallorca: Divers Press, 1953.
The Gold Diggers. [Short stories.] Palma de Mallorca: Divers Press, 1954. New York: Charles Scribner's Sons, 1965.
All That Is Lovely in Men. Highlands, N.C.: Jargon Books, 1955.
If You. San Francisco: Porpoise, 1956.
The Whip. Worcester, Eng.: Migrant, 1957.
A Form of Women. New York: Jargon/Corinth, 1959.
For Love: Poems 1950–1960. New York: Charles Scribner's Sons, 1962.
The Island. [Novel.] New York: Charles Scribner's Sons, 1963.
Words. New York: Charles Scribner's Sons, 1967.
Pieces. New York: Charles Scribner's Sons, 1969.
A Quick Graph: Collected Notes and Essays. New York: Taplinger Publishing Co., 1970.
The Charm: Early and Uncollected Poems. London: Calder & Boyars, 1971.
A Day Book. New York: Charles Scribner's Sons, 1972.
See also "Robert Creeley: In Conversation with Charles Tomlinson," Kulchur, 4 (Winter 1964–65), 4–16; "Contexts of Poetry," *Audit,* 5 (Spring 1968), 1–18.

About Creeley:
Cameron, Allen B. " 'Love Comes Quietly': The Poetry of Robert Creeley." *Chicago Review,* 19(1967), 92–103.
Carroll, Paul. "A Wicker Basket," *The Poem in Its Skin.* Chicago: Follett Publishing Co., 1968. Pp. 29–38.
Duberman, Martin. *Black Mountain: An Experiment in Community.* New York: E. P. Dutton & Co., 1972.
Howard, Richard. *Alone with America.* New York: Atheneum Publishers, 1969. Pp. 65–74.
Rosenthal, M. L. *The New Poets: American & British Poetry Since World War II.* New York: Oxford University Press, 1967. Pp. 148–59.
Stepanchev, Stephen. *American Poetry since 1945.* New York: Harper & Row Publishers, 1965. Pp. 151–57.

CRUZ, VICTOR HERNANDEZ (b. Aguas Buenas, Puerto Rico, 1949–)

Chiefly because the generation of Puerto Ricans for whom English is a first language has only recently attained significant numbers, Puerto Rican writers have lagged behind blacks in creating a new force in contemporary American literature. Victor Hernandez Cruz is then one of the first Puerto Rican poets to have reached a large audience.

Although born in Puerto Rico, at the age of five Cruz came to New York, where he later attended Benjamin Franklin High School. His poetry is very much the poetry of New York. Or rather it is the poetry of a Puerto Rican in New York.

There is probably no better way to give a sense of the content of Cruz's poetry, as well as its methods, than to quote the short poem that opens *Snaps* (1969), "HALF A Page from Square Business." °

> It is cold Tuesday.   gray sky.   hot tar.   your misery
> working.
>   imagine:
>   glass sticking out of tar.   wind
>   blowing.   your daughter dead.
>   all your horror dreams come true,
>   at the same time.
>   your wife felt up by brown wrinkled
>   hands.
> it is 12 midnight.   all this belongs to me & it is
> beautiful.
>   but my true nature is gentle
>   & the stare of a mad eye.

There is a great deal of pain in the poem, and if it were just that it would have legitimacy as an expression of pain. The last lines, however, reveal something beyond the pain, something beyond the anger, without in the least denying them. The ability to confront the horror of experience, to possess it, leads to a perception of beauty. An appropriate gloss on the poem might well be derived from Paul Tillich, who asserts that it is necessary to affirm one's being by encompassing the negations that threaten it. In fact, the title of Tillich's most famous work, *The Courage to Be,* could easily serve as the epigraph to *Snaps*.

In technique, Cruz is true to his perspective. The ordering of experience must be accomplished without distorting it; beauty must be found in the world as it is rather than in the world as it should be. The rhythms are the rhythms of speech and breath, often sharp and excited. The poems are filled with disjointed fragments of experience, not predigested elements of a coherent system. The poem quoted above is a quieter moment; often the

° From *Snaps,* by Victor Hernandez Cruz. Copyright © 1968, 1969 by Victor Hernandez Cruz. Reprinted by permission of Random House, Inc.

stream of experience flows unstoppably and is organized by repetition of words and rhythms rather than a contemplative consciousness:

> there was fire & the people yelling. running crazing.
> screaming & falling. moving up side down. there was fire.
> fires. & more fires. . . .

(from "Urban Dream")

The participles hold the lines together. The poetry of Victor Hernandez Cruz is indeed a poetry of verbs; it never loses contact with the world of human action from which it sprang.

Selected Bibliography:
By CRUZ
Snaps. New York: Random House, 1969.

DEEP IMAGISM

The term "deep image," coined by JEROME ROTHENBERG, is used by ROBERT KELLY, editor of *Trobar* magazine, to affirm the importance of the unconscious as a significant source of poetic imagery at a time when an increasing number of poets seem to be striving for "objectivity" in their verse. Although the term originates with Rothenberg and Kelly, critics such as Stephen Stepanchev have accurately noted its applicability to a significant range of American poetry. Kelly, Rothenberg, and Diane Wakosi (associated with *Trobar*) and Robert Bly, James Wright, Louis Simpson, and William Duffy (associated with *The Fifties*, a magazine that has changed its name with each decade) are especially linked to the movement, which appears to be a direct descendant of Surrealism.

The emphasis on subjectivity, however, has the paradoxical effect of undermining the ego, the conscious self, the traditional locus of subjective experience. This kind of subjectivity breaks down barriers between inner and outer worlds, between unconscious and conscious, and broadens the base of the poet's response to his experience.

Like most "movements," deep imagism is a reaction against a particular kind of poetry, the kind that is best represented by the work of Charles Olson and the Projectivist poets. The Projectivists see man as an object directly related to an objective universe, a view in complete opposition to the subjectivity of the deep imagists (although in each case the end result is the undermining of the ego). More to the point probably is the feeling, expressed by both Kelly and Bly, the group's principal theorists, that the Projectivists place too much emphasis on technique and not enough on the content of poetry.

See also the Introduction, section VIII.

DICKEY, JAMES (*b. Atlanta, Ga., Feb. 2, 1923—   *)

In the time between the publication of his first book of poems in 1960 and the collected volume put out in 1967, James Dickey established himself as one of the most widely read poets in America today. Not that his acceptance as a major figure—or even, in some instances, as a very good poet—is universal; a prolific and active critic of poetic methods alien to his own, he has himself been a frequent target. But indignation as well as praise have contributed to his present stature. Whatever evaluation will finally be placed on his career as a whole, he has written enough poems of overwhelming impact to define him as a very good poet indeed.

Dickey was born in Atlanta. In verse and prose the implications of his Southern heritage have been of primary importance: there is both guilt over having inherited and profited from a system that essentially demanded that another human being be deprived of his humanity and a sense of coming from a tradition basically opposed to the life-denying values of a materialistic, industrial society. He studied at Clemson, where he played football, and at Vanderbilt, from which he graduated magna cum laude. During both World War II and the Korean War he was a night-fighter pilot, decorated three times for bravery.

A fine guitar player, a hunter and woodsman, Dickey has interests that, at least superficially, do not seem particularly compatible with the vocation of poetry. After teaching at Rice Institute and the University of Florida, he worked five years for advertising agencies in New York and Atlanta, until his success in the business of poetry made possible, and even demanded, a more exclusive concentration of energies. He has been writer-in-residence at Reed College in Oregon, San Fernando Valley State College, and the universities of Wisconsin and South Carolina; he has served as poetry consultant to the Library of Congress and is a highly successful reader on the college circuit.

Dickey himself, in his essay "The Poet Turns on Himself," provides a fine description of his developing interest in poetry—he was a relatively late starter, about twenty-four—and of his discovery of the poetic methods most appropriate to his approach to experience. Although Dickey has a great deal to say about poetic form, it is significant that his first concerns are with content.

> I discovered that I had, as everyone has, a life and the memories engendered by it. When I examined these memories, I found that certain of them stood out in my mind and recurred to me at odd times, as if seeking something, perhaps some act of understanding, from me. Some recollections seemed more important than others, without my being able to tell why. Later, I saw that these incidents, the more important ones, were not only potential raw material for the kind of poetry I wanted to write, but were in fact the principal incidents in my life: those times when I felt most strongly and was most

aware of the intense reality of the objects and people I moved among.

Vaguely Proustian in tone, and to some degree in substance, the essay provides the basis of a poetry that is not simply autobiographical—in fact there is a free use of fantasy and dream and, especially in later work, frequent adoption of personae that belie autobiography in the narrowest sense—but essentially anecdotal. Dickey is not, however, the author chiefly of straightforward narrative verse; the most fruitful preoccupation of Dickey's poems is his concern with the powers of the human imagination to modify man's existential predicament and the consequent merging of the world of illusion with what is generally known as "reality."

Dickey is not at all unconcerned with formal values in poetry, nor does he passively accept existing conventions for their own sake. Rhyme, for example, he rejected from the very start since he found it not disciplining his expression of inner feelings, but rather leading him away from those feelings. Rhythm is the real key to form in Dickey's poems; the rhythms are often there even before the words. Dickey, through most of his career at any rate, does not vary the rhythm from line to line; and even if he does not often attempt a rhyme scheme, regular stanzaic pattern was for a long time the rarely broken rule of his verse. But his use of meter has always been flexible, and in his latest work he has begun to experiment with what, in "The Poet Turns on Himself," he calls

> the "open" poem: a poem which would have none of the neatness of most of those poems we call "works of art" but would have the capacity to involve the reader in it, in all its imperfections and impurities. . . . I was interested most of all in getting an optimum "presentational immediacy," a compulsiveness in the presentation of the matter of the poem that would cause the reader to forget literary judgments entirely and simply experience.

In a curious way, then, Dickey occupies a position much closer in theory and even in practice to the Projectivist exponents of "open verse" and "composition by field" than one might at first expect, although Dickey, a poet who must always feel in control of his materials, might not be flattered by the comparison.

Dickey's major obsessions are present from his first book, *Into the Stone* (1960). He begins his explorations of man's existential relation to that part of the universe that lacks consciousness, the part from which man emerged and to which he must inevitably return. One mode of examining this problem is exemplified by "The Vegetable King." Here the poet, a suburban home-owner, describes his yearly April ritual of sleeping out in a sleeping bag, escaping, at least temporarily, from a civilization that has severed him from even the vestiges of his natural roots. He begins to believe himself ". . . part of the acclaimed rebirth/Of the ruined, calm world, in spring"; he believes he becomes ". . . the chosen man,/Hacked apart in the growing cold" who now "by the whole of mindless nature is assembled." A nature god, he also intensifies that part of his self shared with mindless nature, that part of his being that is eternal and will survive the world of "human love," to which he must return at dawn. The direct appeal to myth, making conscious what is usually relegated to the darker portions of the mind, is characteristic of Dickey; he is really a teller of fairy tales for adults, tales that promise recovery not of a lost childhood world, but of a world of pre-consciousness, an almost mystical awareness of being. Here, his longing is similar, if not his means of execution, to that of a poet he much admired: Theodore Roethke.

Far more common a means of confronting the darkness of nonbeing in Dickey's verse can be located in the poems devoted to sudden and violent death, such as, for example, "The Performance." The fact with which the poet must come to terms is the death of his friend Donald Armstrong, beheaded by the Japanese in the Philippines during World War II. Armstrong, who was not naturally agile, had often amused members of the squadron with his vain efforts to perfect cartwheels and handstands. Dickey imagines him, in the moments before his execution, giving his captors a miraculously polished gymnastic performance, ". . . having done/All things in this life that he could." The terror is present in the poem; in fact, it never leaves it. All Dickey can do, all he can imagine Armstrong doing, is to contain it, to embrace it with beautiful form. Armstrong, as well as Dickey himself, are then paradigms of the artist; preoccupation with craft, with the perfection of one's art, is seen not as some extraneous, precious concern, but a matter of life and death.

Drowning With Others (1962), though an uneven volume of poetry, is nonetheless filled with virtuoso performances that are often selected for anthologies. "The Lifeguard" picks up the methods of "The Performance." It is told through the persona of a lifeguard unable to save a drowning child. Here the guilt implicit in the earlier poem—the inevitable guilt of the surviving comrade in arms—becomes explicit and dominant. The lifeguard returns to the lake at night—perhaps he has often returned—thinking of how he might save the boy "Who has already died in my care." In the end, he kneels in the moonlight, holding in his arms ". . . a child/Of water, water, water." It is a powerful poem, and gains from Dickey's refusal to define the boundaries between fantasy and objectivity. In some poems this results in the reader's inability to determine whether a particular incident occurs in the "real" world or only in the poet's mind. In "The Lifeguard," while it is clear that the lifeguard is in a world of fantasy, we do not know what his degree of awareness is. Is he consciously dramatizing his guilt, or has he been driven mad by his failure? It is necessary to point out that some critics have seen in Dickey's refusal to draw a clear line between the subjective and the objective an inability to resolve the tensions raised by his poems and a preference for the slick, easy ending. Although Dickey's avoidance of the rationally coherent resolution is by no means a proof of quality, it seems reasonably obvious that it is intentional and perfectly consistent with the way he sees the world. In effect, it is Dickey's moral vision with which the critics quarrel. To what extent does the imaginative world impinge upon the world of responsibility? is perhaps the question they really ask. And this is a problem of which Dickey himself is aware.

"A Dog Sleeping on my Feet" involves us in the same kind of interchange between conscious and unconscious nature as did "The Vegetable King." The poet experiences the "dream" of the sleeping dog; again, the poem is placed in the context of the poet "returning" to his wife and sons, to the specifically human universe—but not before the poet becomes aware of the extent to which the dog's perceptions of reality correspond to his own, albeit on a deeper level.

One of the truly fascinating poems in *Drowning With Others* is "The Heaven of Animals." Dickey envisions an eternal place very much like the one in which animals pass their temporal existence, but better, or at least richer, more extravagant. The first half of the poem contains nothing sinister, except, maybe, the fact that the landscape is ". . . desperately / Outdoing what is required"; but midway, the poem faces the fact that for some animals "It could not be the place / It is, without blood." The claws and teeth are "perfect," the animals more deadly than ever. And what of the hunted? This is "their reward," to be part of the cycle of natural existence: "They fall, they are torn, / They rise, they walk again." Since Dickey is himself a hunter, many critics have read the poem without seeing it in any irony at all; for them, it is a heaven of which the poet thoroughly approves, or one which he at least justifies. Paul Carroll, in his essay in *The Poem in Its Skin*, is one of the few not to take the poem at face value. After pointing out the nightmarish effect of some minor discordancies of diction and meter, Carroll observes that of all the things the animals might be doing, killing and being killed is the *"only* event" that occurs in Dickey's heaven. Actually, it is not essential to suppose that this is the only action: it is in fact the only action in this paradise of beasts that disturbs the poet, the only one with which he feels it is important to come to terms. Dickey himself, in his hunting, in his war experiences, is a man whose life has been touched by a continuing threat of violence, beyond the "ordinary" encounters with familial death. He is clearly not one to avoid violence—a nightfighter pilot of more than a hundred missions, a wielder of bow and arrow. But he is not comfortable about it either, as witness his introspection over bombing raids in "The Firebombing," in *Buckdancer's Choice* (1965), over an animal to be killed in "The Summons." Dickey's resolution to this conflict—if it is that—is to take the moment of violence out of time, to see it *sub specie aeternitatis* as a revelation of being. Thus the spring of the predator may last for years in its "glory" (and compare this to the expanded sense of time of the falling stewardess in a later poem, "Falling"). Again, it is the power of imagination that must accomplish this; the idealized landscape, the slow-motion focus on the hunting and the hunted, remind the reader that a human lens is being used. The paradox, of course, is that at the center of turbulence, at the heart of darkness, is calm, is light. As the blind child says in "The Owl King" (in *Drowning With Others*), one of Dickey's plunges into the deep worlds of myth and legend, "I see as the owl king sees,/By going in deeper than darkness."

The poems of *Helmets* (1964) are not markedly different in theme and method from those of *Drowning With Others*. Perhaps, as Dickey has suggested, there is the beginning of a movement away from the hallucinatory, an increasing commitment to objective reality as a source of insight into the still vitally important inner world. "Winter Trout," another hunting poem (the poet is armed with bow and arrow), is in this spirit. The poet, having missed the trout under the ice, reaches for his arrow:

> I froze my right hand to retrieve it
> As a blessing or warning,
> As a sign of the penalties
> For breaking into closed worlds

In the clarity of this image is a Frost-like element, a transcendental one perhaps, the suggestion that the concrete world contains within it emblems of the spiritual. Similarly, the invasion of the Kudzu vine in "Kudzu" seems unmistakably to invite connections with inner psychological states. "On the Coosawattee" does very much the same for its own body of water as Hemingway did for his Big Two-Hearted River.

Not all of Dickey's symbols are drawn from the natural world. In "Cherrylog Road," the persona keeps a rendezvous with his girl friend in the back seat of a junkyard wreck, "In the parking lot of the dead." If the poem's chief image is drawn from the world of men, its relation to nature is not forgotten either. The girl arrives "Through acres of wrecks . . . Through dust where the blacksnake dies/Of boredom." The sexual encounter brings back life not only to the back seat of the car, and to the lovers themselves, but also to ". . . the blacksnake, stiff/With inaction, curved back/Into life." The motorcycle on which the narrator leaves is similarly "the soul of the junkyard/Restored, a bicycle fleshed/With power." It is a wasteland myth in reverse, in which physical lovers resuscitate the dead land through animal energy; it is the Eden myth, again in reverse, in which the furtive sexual encounter (at all times under threat of reprisal by the girl's father) restores life to a landscape of bleak dullness.

Buckdancer's Choice, which received the National Book Award in 1966, is unusual in that it both refines existing techniques and initiates important breakthroughs. The volume begins and ends with two of the profoundest sources of Dickey's sense of guilt: his bombing missions ("The Firebombing") and the Southern heritage ("Slave Quarters"); significantly, both poems are in the new style, the "open" poem. Dickey had forged for himself in the course of his career a reasonably successful metrical technique, one that was extremely flexible at the same time that it provided a definite formal framework for the experience to be communicated. With many exceptions, the meter generally took the form of a three-beat line, with a varying number of unstressed syllables (this is especially prevalent in *Drowning With Others*, e.g., "The Heaven of Animals," "The Hospital Window"). Any poet must inevitably grow tired of a form at which he has, after repeated use, become exceptionally good, but Dickey had a special reason for trying to shed his former methods: to avoid the reader's consciousness of the poem as a mediator between himself and the experience, to "cause the reader to forget literary judgments entirely and simply experience."

The open poem has lines of irregular length, no repeated stanzaic pattern, sometimes the use of blank spaces instead of punctuation to draw the reader as much as possible into contact with the poem's auditory patterns. None of these devices are at all new; Dickey is rediscovering principles of composition with which many poets have begun their career. But here it is James Dickey using these methods, having arrived at them through his own particular development, as a modification of his own essential characteristics.

One can only speculate as to why, at a given stage of his career, a poet no longer wants to write what impresses his former audience as being poetry. There are hints that, in this case at least, Dickey is testing the adequacy of a poem to confront the world of experience at large; he is questioning the powers of the human imagination to cancel or redeem what has actually occurred. In "The Firebombing," the poet insistently tortures himself with the memory of a napalm raid over Japan:

> All families lie together, though some are burned alive.
> . . . .
> Twenty years in the suburbs have not shown me
> Which ones were hit and which not.
> . . . .
> . . . another
>
> Bomb finds a home
> And clings to it like a child. . . .
> . . . .
> . . . It is that I can imagine
> At the threshold nothing
> With its ears crackling off
> Like powdery leaves,
> Nothing with children of ashes . . .

As often as the poet recalls, or tries to recall, precisely what happened, he becomes aware of the separation between himself and the reality of the experience; in fact, the poem depends on an awareness of these dissociations of sensibility. The easy-living man in the suburbs, twenty years after the fact, is separated from the pilot who risked his life to kill others. That pilot himself is separated from his act of destruction—he does not see in detail what he has done, whom he has killed; he can directly perceive, ironically, only the beauty of the light patterns of the bombardment. And the poem itself may be an inadequate medium for dealing with what he has felt. It does not forgive:

Absolution? Sentence? No matter;
The thing itself is in that.

"The Firebombing" is Dickey's attempt to escape the poem to find the thing itself.

This poem is another illustration of the ambivalence toward violence to which any reader of Dickey's verse must grow accustomed. The poet does not see himself as a monster; he does not seem to be convinced of the unjustifiable evil of his actions. He is rather trying to grasp the inconceivable, the juxtaposition of his own suburban home with the destruction of the Japanese homes twenty years before. Dickey's unwillingness to accept time as real, his insistence on seeing the world from the point of view of eternity, brings into focus a man's life.

In "Slave Quarters," time is broken down on a still larger scale: ". . . two hundred years are turned back/On with the headlights of a car?" Dickey visits a deserted plantation; the experience at the other end of the pocket of time is in this case someone else's—the plantation owner's—but the connection, even at the most generalized level, weighs most heavily on the poet. Again, it is not the conventional and pious declaration of guilt that he wishes to impress upon us, but his attempt to comprehend the incomprehensible, to grasp the terrible logic of the human condition. Still drawn, sexually, to the ghostly slave quarters, he wonders

> . . . what
> It would be like   what it has been
> What it is to look once a day
> Into an only
> Son's brown, waiting, wholly possessed
> Amazing eyes, and not
> Acknowledge, but own?

The poems that recall Dickey's earlier verse are as successful as the new in this fine volume. "Pursuit from Under" describes the poet as a young boy, terrified in mid-August by a tale of the killer whale of the Arctic following under the thin ice the shadow of a victim and then breaking through the ice to reach his prey. The poem is a worthy successor to "Winter Trout," even more frightening, since the dark power underneath does not simply punish when disturbed, but actually stalks its victims. The vegetation myth appears again in "The Common Grave," the mixture of fantasy and objective reality in "The Celebration." *Buckdancer's Choice* is easily Dickey's most versatile, most consistent performance.

The section of new poems in *Poems 1957–1967* (1967) is entitled *Falling*. Perhaps more than any other single grouping of Dickey's poems, these poems serve to define those areas of experience Dickey has taken as his own. Not many other poets would care to dwell in detail on the fall of a twenty-nine-year-old stewardess from an airplane, examining her imagined reactions on the way down ("Falling"); not many would tackle the tale of "The Sheep Child," the legend of the woolly baby dead at birth used to frighten young farm boys, told from the perspectives both of the farm boy and the sheep child. One is reminded of Sylvia Plath's insistent facing of the unbearable, with the crucial difference that Dickey is somehow able to bear it, and sometimes, at least, can take his readers along with him.

He continues in this vein in his novel *Deliverance* (1970) and another volume of poetry, *The Eye-Beaters, Blood, Victory, Madness, Buckhead and Mercy* (1970). The arguments of some of the poems of *The Eye-Beaters* make the point: "Madness"—"A domestic dog wanders from the house, is bitten by a rabid female fox, runs mad himself, and has to be hunted down, killed, and beheaded"; "The Eye-Beaters"—The poet visits a home for children in which some have gone blind and walk about beating their eyes; "Blood"—the persona has slaughtered a woman (his wife?) and her children. And so it goes. The violent, the grotesque. At the beginning of Dickey's poetic career when he dealt with a beheading (in "The Performance"), the horror seemed contained within the framework of art; here, only the formal patterning of Dickey's open poetry stands as a hardly adequate shield between the reader and the full force of the nightmare. Not often a direct social or political commentator, Dickey is responding to the condition of the society in which he lives. He immerses himself in horror in order to be able to live with it. And he has, at least temporarily, returned to the approach to reality of "The Lifeguard." In a marginal note to "The Eye-Beaters," *"The Visitor begins to invent a fiction to save his mind."* Reason struggles with invention, but finally the persona accepts the fiction. The poetry of James Dickey is his own supreme fiction; but it does not exist primarily, as did Wallace Stevens', to give pleasure—it is a question of survival.

Selected Bibliography:
By Dickey:
Into the Stone and Other Poems in *Poets of Today, VIII.* New York: Charles Scribner's Sons, 1960.
Drowning With Others. Middletown, Conn.: Wesleyan University Press, 1962.
Helmets. Middletown, Conn.: Wesleyan University Press, 1964.
The Suspect in Poetry. [Criticism.] Madison, Minn.: The Sixties Press, 1964.
Buckdancer's Choice. Middletown, Conn.: Wesleyan University Press, 1965.
Poems 1957–1967. Middletown, Conn.: Wesleyan University Press, 1967.
Babel to Byzantium: Poets & Poetry Now. [Criticism.] New York: Farrar, Straus & Giroux, 1968.
The Eye-Beaters, Blood, Victory, Madness, Buckhead and Mercy. Garden City, N.Y.: Doubleday & Co., 1970.
Deliverance. [Novel.] Boston: Houghton Mifflin Co., 1970.
Self-Interviews. [Autobiography and criticism.] Garden City, N.Y.: Doubleday & Co., 1970.
Sorties [Journals and Essays.] Garden City, N.Y.: Doubleday & Co., 1971.
See also Dickey's essay "The Poet Turns on Himself" in *Poets on Poetry.* Edited by Howard Nemerov. New York: Basic Books, 1966. Pp. 225–238 (reprinted in *Babel to Byzantium: Poets & Poetry Now*).

About Dickey:

Boatwright, James and Carolyn Kizer. "A Conversation with James Dickey,"
  Shenandoah, 18 (Autumn 1966), 3–28.

Carroll, Paul. "The Heaven of Animals," in *The Poem in Its Skin.* Chicago: Follett
  Publishing Co., 1968. Pp. 41–49.

Friedman, Norman. "The Wesleyan Poets—II," *Chicago Review,* 19 (1966),
  55–72.

Howard, Richard. *Alone with America.* New York: Atheneum Publishers, 1969.
  Pp. 75–98.

Nemerov, Howard. "Poems of Darkness and a Specialized Light." *Sewanee Review,* 71 (Winter 1963), 99–104.

Rosenthal, M. L. *The New Poets: American & British Poetry Since World War
  II.* New York: Oxford University Press, 1967. Pp. 325–327.

Stepanchev, Stephen. *American Poetry since 1945.* New York: Harper & Row
  Publishers, 1965. Pp. 190–192.

Weatherby, H. L. "The Way of Exchange in James Dickey's Poetry." *Sewanee
  Review,* 74 (July–September 1966), 669–680.

DORN, EDWARD   (*b. Villa Grove, Ill., Apr. 2, 1929—*   )

A student at Black Mountain College, and by his preference for open verse
forms and breath-determined rhythms clearly within the Projectivist tradition born at that school, Edward Dorn's principal concerns are human relationships and, to a lesser degree, the social context within which the poet
operates.

Born in a prairie town in Illinois, Dorn was educated at the University of
Illinois and, in his words, "somewhat corrected at Black Mountain College."
He has taught at Idaho State University at Pocatello, and has been the edi-
tor of the magazine *Wild Dog.*

"The Song" (in *The Newly Fallen*) is a love poem, one that is especially
illustrative of the lyrical qualities that characterize Dorn's verse.

> Thus days go by
> and I stand knowing her hair
> in my mind as a dark cloud, its presence
> straying over the rim of a volcano
> of desire, and I take something
> so closed as a book
> into the world where she is.

The images have a rhythm of their own and a resonance that evokes much
more than is specifically said. It is this kind of imagery that transforms the
frequently specific detail of Dorn's poetry into archetypal experience.

If there is a tendency in Dorn's work to see things in terms of the universal, there is also a very powerful sense of the forces that compel us to deal
with our particular time, place, and condition. "We live," Dorn reminds us
in "The Biggest Killing" (also from *The Newly Fallen*), "in an earth of well-
dressed gangs." We are dominated by corrupt governments, which create

". . . that vileness falling in particles / of fine sifting daily poison sand," the radioactive fallout that serves as a symbol of the slow destruction of the natural world. In fact, the poem's major motif is that of man as dying leaves, doomed by a mechanized society:

> . . . we are the yellowing leaves, my friends and I
> heaped upon the slopes of the New World Trinity
> where grieves forth obsolescent landwrack
> to infinity.

See also BLACK MOUNTAIN POETS, PROJECTIVE VERSE.

Selected Bibliography:
By DORN:
The Newly Fallen. New York: Totem, 1961.
From Gloucester Out. London: Matrix Press, 1964.
Hands Up! New York: Corinth Books, 1964.
Idaho Out. New York: Matter Books, 1965.
The North Atlantic Turbine. New York: Horizon Press, 1968.
Geography. New York: Horizon Press, 1968.
Our Word: Guerrila Poems from Latin America. [Translations, with Gordon Brotherston.] New York: Grossman Publishers, 1969.
Gunslinger Part I. Los Angeles: Black Sparrow Press, 1968.
Gunslinger Part II. Los Angeles: Black Sparrow Press, 1969.

DUGAN, ALAN (*b. Brooklyn, N.Y., Feb. 12, 1923—*)

Containing his sense of the agonies of experience within his poetry's formal discipline, Alan Dugan is one of relatively few contemporary poets who attempts to confront the human condition with his isolated consciousness rather than to seek strength in the perception of underlying harmonies.

Born in Brooklyn, Dugan was educated at Queens College, Olivet College, and Mexico City College. His first book, *Poems* (1961), was published in the Yale Series of Younger Poets and won both the National Book Award and the Pulitzer Prize. Yale published his *Collected Poems* in 1969.

In "In the Forest," Dugan says,

> . . . Whoever it was
> who planned that place
> forgot the lighting
> although some claim to see.

This excerpt illustrates Dugan's basic approach to the human condition. The encounter with negation is obsessive in his work, in poems with titles like "On Zero," in his studies of solitude, defeat, despair, in his imagery of mutilation, especially castration. Against this Dugan sets the affirmation inherent in the very act of creating, a willingness to look at the darkness itself for renewed energy, an irony that can be turned on himself as well as directed toward his world, and the simple will to survive.

The act of creation is, for Dugan, complex, and it is complexly expressed in what Richard Howard has called his finest poem, "The Branches of Water or Desire." Read as a conceit, in which the stag's antlers—

> . . . poised
> against a branching need
> drumming in the red inside
> the arteries or antlers of the heart

—represent the poem, or the conscious poem-making faculties, it is as involved as anything produced by the seventeenth-century metaphysical poets. The notion of balance is crucial; it places the willful act of creation in relation to the body, the spiritual world in relation to what Yeats called the "complexities of mire or blood." The antlers, a potential "perch for . . . birdsong," become themselves a song. The act of creation is perhaps inseparable from the thing created. Then the antlers fall off, as they must if the process is to continue. Like Wallace Stevens, Dugan apparently believes that the products of imagination must be cleared away for a fresh start if the artist is to keep his essential connection with the outer world. A sense of strain and even violence is captured in the imagery, and Dugan skillfully embeds the abstract in the concrete, not as allegory but as radiant centers of meaning. Near the poem's conclusion, Dugan is Yeatsian in his use of straightforward language that, emerging inevitably from the preceding complexities, avoids the ring of epigram:

> the sounds and tines
> must be some excess of the flesh
> that wants beyond efficiency
> in time, but cannot find
> much permanence outside it . . .

Paul Tillich has defined "the courage to be" as the ability to confront nonbeing directly and to absorb it by the power of one's being. It is in terms of this kind of paradox rather than through any notion of clear-cut victory that Dugan's relation to the abyss must be understood. "From Heraclitus" begins: "Matter is palsy." The world is in flux, it is transient, it resists permanent shape. But even in the still of night, Dugan hears ". . . each thing wrestling with itself/to be a wrestler." It is the struggle of form to exist, the struggle of form to wish to exist. Life is possible only as strain or stress, and we are left with the poet "sentenced to a shape," but wrestling "through a gust of violence" to maintain that shape and yet feel some connection with the world of flux. It is clearly in the struggle itself, rather than in any vain hope of triumph, that the possibilities of human dignity reside. But possibilities are all we have, never certainties. In "Plague of Dead Sharks" where the ocean seems to be that destructive element in which Conrad insisted we must immerse, Dugan leaves us with only a question: "Who knows whether the sea heals or corrodes?"

What is remarkable about Alan Dugan's darkness is that it is not truly gloomy; it engenders its own dark light. This may be because of the obvious victories of his language—or his control of his poems' rhythms, which may be described either as tightly disciplined free verse or careful play with generally short iambic lines. It may be because of the wit with which he works out his imagery. It is certainly due, at least in part, to his ironic stance, which suggests a continual awareness on Dugan's part that he may be taking himself too seriously. "Noon's World" is a simple poem about a man who has slept late and finds himself eating "a lunch for breakfast." The last line is a rhetorical question offering cold comfort: "What have I missed except life?" When we are invited to take the day as a metaphor for an entire life, we are on the edge of self-pity. But the fact that in the final line the poem's persona himself makes the generalization, and that it is forced to compete with the triviality of what has actually happened on the poem's surface, banishes self-pity. The poem finally turns on itself, with the suggestion that even if one has missed "life," this is not much more important than having overslept.

Alan Dugan's virtues are considerable. He is essentially a poet of the passions—anger, fear, love are his dominant themes. He deals with them through his intellect, not by subjugation but by juxtaposition. He in fact questions, both in thought and method, the legitimacy of dissociating intellect from feeling. As Dugan writes in "On Being Unhappily in Love with Reason," "Rage" is "closest to reason in the mind."

Dugan's weaknesses are almost inevitable consequences of his virtues. He has a tight intensity that sometimes seems to limit what he can perform or even attempt. His language and his characteristic rhythms more than any quality of mind sharply circumscribe his range. Nonetheless, within his limits, he has been able to produce some unique and powerful poetry.

Selected Bibliography:
By Dugan:
Poems. New Haven: Yale University Press, 1961.
Poems 2. New Haven: Yale University Press, 1963.
Poems 3. New Haven: Yale University Press, 1967.
Collected Poems. New Haven: Yale University Press, 1969.

About Dugan:
Howard, Richard. Alone with America. New York: Atheneum Publishers, 1969,
    Pp. 99–106.

DUNCAN, ROBERT (b. Oakland, Calif., Jan. 7, 1919—   )

At a time when the criteria of what constitutes a good poem have never been less clear, Robert Duncan is an especially difficult poet to evaluate. He is singled out by some as the finest poet to emerge from the group of

BLACK MOUNTAIN POETS, more considerable even than Charles Olson or Robert Creeley, and is thoroughly condemned by others as a pretentious, pompous writer who betrayed his early promise. There is little doubt, however, that Duncan has written some first-rate poetry and has had something completely his own to contribute to the quasi-mystical tradition of poetry in English, to which much of his work belongs.

Duncan's mother died when he was born, whether in childbirth or from the flu is left ambiguous by the poet in an autobiographical fragment that appears in "A Sequence of Poems for H.D.'s Birthday" in *Roots and Branches*. His name at birth was Edward Howard Duncan. His father, presumably unable to support him, gave him up for adoption, and young Duncan became Robert Edward Symmes. He tells of falling and breaking his glasses while running toward his adopted mother—a possible explanation of how he became cross-eyed. Whatever the cause, cross-eyes appear in Duncan's work both as Christian pun and emblem of double vision and the conflict between illusion and reality. "Reach out and touch. Point to the one that is really there."

Duncan has kept careful track of the influences on his life and art. Of prominence are Sanders Russell, with whom he edited *The Experimental Review* (1940–41); Jack Spicer, whom Duncan knew in Berkeley between 1946 and 1950 as "mentor, censor and peer"; and since 1951, his companion, the painter Jess Collins. In the late forties and early fifties, Olson, Creeley, and the Black Mountain poets and artists were vitally important; Duncan himself taught at Black Mountain College in the mid-fifties and contributed to the group's periodicals, *Black Mountain Review* and *Origin*. He was also the most important link between Black Mountain and the SAN FRANCISCO RENAISSANCE.

Among the more prolific poets writing today (twenty-three separate books are listed opposite the title page of *Bending the Bow*), Duncan's reputation nonetheless rests on three books: *The Opening of the Field* (1960), *Roots and Branches* (1964), *Bending the Bow* (1968). "Often I Am Permitted To Return To A Meadow" is the opening poem of the first of the three; it is appropriate as an introduction to all of Duncan's work. The meadow seems to have its locus in the poet's past, in his childhood; a children's game, "ring a round of roses," is, in fact, under way. But it may transcend the poet's own personal past. It is, after all, "an eternal pasture folded in all thought," a part, maybe, of the collective memory of the race.

With a mixture of scholasticism and passion faintly suggestive of Dante's *Vita Nuova*, Duncan attempts to set in order the properties and characteristics of his elusive place. Insofar as it is a place made up by the mind, it is not his but "a made place"; it is, however, his insofar as it is so near to the heart. Like Pound before him, Duncan sees himself, not simply as molder of materials, but as a discoverer of forms as well. He writes in his essay "Towards an Open Universe" (in Howard Nemerov's *Poets on Poetry*):

> Central to and defining the poetics I am trying to suggest here is the conviction that the order man may contrive or impose upon the

things about him or upon his own language is trivial beside the divine order or natural order he may discover in them.

In the meadow is to be found "the First Beloved," or at least her image. Psychological or Platonic (Plato is certainly suggested in a place ". . . created by light/wherefrom the shadows that are forms fall"), she is the prototype of all beauty, the vivid reality of which all successors are no more than pale reflections. Finally, the meadow is described as ". . . a given property of the mind/that certain bounds hold against chaos." Like most of Duncan's poetry, "Often I Am Permitted To Return To A Meadow" is about poetry, about the creative process itself. However, like Wallace Stevens, Duncan understands poetry in its broadest sense, and the act of creation includes not simply the writing of a poem, or participation in a dance, but the very mechanics of coming to terms with reality. "Were it not for the orders of music hidden," says Duncan in "Four Pictures of the Real Universe," "we should be claimd by the preponderant void."

To a point, Duncan is simple enough to grasp. Art is the ordering of experience. The source of this order is an eternal perception, a glimpse of the world of forms. Or it is a glimpse of the child buried within the adult; the two are not in the least incompatible. Duncan's poetry does not derive its chief strength from the intricacy of its thought, however. There is a web of emotion woven almost invisibly. The "Queen Under The Hill" of "Often I Am Permitted To Return To A Meadow" is not necessarily threatening in herself, but in "Four Pictures of the Real Universe" she "dwells in the dark" rather than the light. And the light that is so essential to this scene in the meadow poem is itself fading, the sun is going down. The children play ring-a-round-a-rosy, and the circle they form keeps out the chaos. Yet the chaos is there, threatening; this "everlasting omen of what is" is sinister. The vision of eternity holds implicit the possibilities of time and death.

The poem that drew most attention in *The Opening of the Field*—and still is his most anthologized piece—is "A Poem Beginning With A Line by Pindar." It has all the hallmarks of Duncan's early poetry: the Cupid and Psyche myth provides still another opportunity to explore possible unions of mind and emotion; Goya and Pindar both make us conscious of the artist's part in this process; light-dark symbolism is conspicuous, and the image of the lamp shedding a circle of light in the darkness is an exact parallel to the children's ring keeping out chaos in the poem discussed above (in fact the image of children dancing in a ring reappears toward the end of "A Poem Beginning With A Line by Pindar"). The point of these preoccupations is underlined in Duncan's "Towards an Open Universe": "Our consciousness, and the poem as a supreme effort of consciousness, comes in a dancing organization between personal and cosmic identity." The poem becomes the point of balance between microcosm and macrocosm, between the mind's imagined order and the indifferent universe. Taking his cue from Olson, Duncan turns inward in order to turn out; the physical universe exists within man as surely as the human universe exists without. He writes in "Towards an Open Universe":

Charles Olson in his essays toward a physiology of consciousness has made us aware that not only heart and brain and the sensory skin but all the internal organs, the totality of the body is involved in the act of a poem, so that the organization of words, an invisible body, bears the imprint of the physical man.

Duncan adopts an aesthetic that celebrates the muscular rather than the visual:

In this aesthetic, conception cannot be abstracted from doing; beauty is related to the beauty of an archer hitting the mark. Referred to its source in the act, the intellect actually manifest as energy, as presence in doing, is the measure of our arêté (as vision, claritas, light, illumination, was the measure of Medieval arêté).

("Notes on Poetics Regarding Olson's 'Maximus' ")

Manifesto is generally far more extreme than practice, and, to return to the "Poem Beginning With A Line by Pindar," one must be struck by the extent to which "vision, claritas, light, illumination" are crucial both to form and content. There is an energy in the lines that suggests the concrete significance of Duncan's theories, which, incidentally, bear more than slight resemblance to the principles of action painting. The pace is quick even when action is slow or lacking; there is a sense of tension and energy even in simple description:

A bronze of yearning, a rose that burns
the tips of their bodies, lips,
ends of fingers, nipples. He is not wingd.
His thighs are flesh, are clouds
lit by the sun in its going down,
hot luminescence at the loins of the visible.

The shifting of units of breath and thought—as in "He is not wingd"—and similar linguistic alternations—as in "luminescence" in the midst of monosyllables—are typical of Duncan and help account for the sense of movement that cannot begin to be explained by a concentration of active verbs.

In *Roots and Branches* Duncan emphasizes roots. Not only are Pound, Williams, Creeley, Olson, and the others clear influences, Duncan here shows clear allegiance to a broader, certainly older, set of literary traditions that strongly modify his connections to the Projectivists. Dante is nearly ubiquitous, Blake of considerable importance; Hermetic lore forms a kind of unifying subtheme; Alpheus, Arethusa, Cyparissus—such names are as at home here as they would be in Milton. Duncan here more nearly resembles Pound, who forces upon the reader his own private sense of *the* literary tradition as prerequisite to his own work, than he does Williams, with whom many Black Mountain poets show greater affinity and who, though his range in time is great, remains essentially localized.

Dante seems especially important to an understanding of the book as a whole, not because he is alluded to far more than any other poet, but because his mode of seeing the world has affected Duncan's. In the fine sonnet "Now there is a Love of which Dante does not speak unkindly," Duncan picks up one of the *Commedia's* most striking images: "Sharpening their vision, Dante says, like a man/seeking to thread a needle." The strain of perception, perception on a cosmic scale, is Duncan's chief concern. The poem itself, still the most common of Duncan's specific subjects, becomes that place "where the disturbance is, where the words awaken/sensory chains between being and being . . ." ("Variations on Two Dicta of William Blake"). Vision is central, certainly; and there is a passion for order here that allies Duncan almost more closely with poets writing between the two world wars than with his own contemporaries.

If roots are obvious in this book, branches are evident as well; new directions are hinted at. In "Cover Images," Duncan joins the increasing number of poets who draw upon the Second World War for imagery. It is Duncan's way of leaving what Robert Lowell has called the "tranquillized Fifties," and entering a period in which the individual can no longer even pretend to ignore the realities of his society.

> . . . Strands
> of Belsen and Buchenwald
> issue from Eden where
> first were felt and return,
> if we are children of one Man,
> in us all, first-last
> intention,
>   transformations of rage
> and cruelty.

In *Bending the Bow*, Duncan's political concerns are far more explicit and contemporary. The war in Vietnam is his special concern and he is specific in attacking it. "Up Rising, *Passages* 25" begins:

> Now Johnson would go up to join the great simulacra of men,
>   Hitler and Stalin, to work his fame
>   with planes roaring out from Guam over Asia

and toward the end of "The Soldiers, *Passages* 26" he writes:

> the smoking fields, the B-52s flying so high   no sound   no sight
>   of them gives warning,   the fliers dropping their bombs
> having nor sight nor sound of what they are bombing.
>   This is Ahriman, the blind
>   destroyer of the farmer and his ox at their labor.

> The Industrial wiping out the Neolithic!   Improver of Life

> flying his high standards!

Ahriman, the Zoroastrian spirit of evil, performs the functions of Moloch in Ginsberg's *Howl*. Indeed, unmistakable similarities with Ginsberg emerge as Duncan enters the world of politics and social commentary, a world that Ginsberg had never really separated from the world of private emotion.

It is undoubtedly to this that poet-critics such as James Dickey refer when they announce Duncan's betrayal of early promise. The poetry of engagement often seems to favor the flat statement, to bury the necessity of agonizing labors of language under a mountain of facts. Certainly the poems of *Bending the Bow* are a long way from the part-mystical, somewhat nostalgic power of the poems of *The Opening of the Field*. Even the aesthetic of muscular poetry seems at least temporarily subordinated; some of the newer poems appear to have come full circle to the more sophisticated imagistic techniques of Pound and H. D. (Hilda Doolittle). "Envoy, *Passages* 7," for example:

> Good Night,   at last
>
> the light of the sun is gone
>
> under Earth's rim
>
> and we
>
> can see the dark   interstices
>
> Day's lord erases.

Critic Lawrence Lieberman, while recognizing an overhauling of poetic methods, finds at least the promise of purposeful direction: "Duncan's new esthetics of political engagement embodies his outrage in the most viable, grotesque emblems he has produced in any poetry. . . . It may well be that these agonizingly Dantesque, emblematic hymns point ahead to a full resurgence of Duncan's demonic genius."

It is, of course, possible that the shift in method had been overstated by friend as well as foe. Duncan himself provides a strong sense of continuity in the open-ended sequences that have appeared in his three major works: "Structures of Rime" (in all three books, so far twenty-six poems); "Passages" (begun in *Bending the Bow*, so far thirty poems); "Sonnets" (in the last two volumes, so far five poems). Probably misrepresented in the blurb to *Bending the Bow* as related to Pound's *Cantos*, Williams' *Paterson*, Louis Zukofsky's "A," and Olson's *Maximus* poems, these poems do tend to underwrite a consistency of direction in Duncan's work. If there is in fact a shift in emphasis to the public world, this concern was never wholly absent from his work. If poetry is no longer so nearly the exclusive subject of his verse, it is still a common theme. But the medium through which Duncan approaches experience is still recognizable, albeit qualified. The mythic structure is there, the theosophical preoccupation stronger than ever. Love as

well as war actually receives added attention in Duncan's newest work, and
we may be witnessing less a revision of method than an expansion of range.
  See also Projective verse and the Introduction, section II.

Selected Bibliography:
By Duncan:
Heavenly City, Earthly City. Berkeley: Bern Porter, 1947.
Poems 1948–49. Berkeley: Berkeley Miscellany Editions, 1949.
Medieval Scenes. San Francisco: Centaur Press, 1950.
Caesar's Gate. Palma de Mallorca: Divers Press, 1955.
Letters (Poems 1953–56). Highlands, N.C.: Jargon Books, 1958.
Selected Poems. San Francisco: City Lights Books, 1959.
The Opening of the Field. New York: Grove Press, 1960.
Roots and Branches. New York: Charles Scribner's Sons, 1964.
Bending the Bow. New York: New Directions Publishing Corp., 1968.
See also Duncan's "Page from a Notebook," in *The New American Poetry*. Ed-
  ited by Donald M. Allen (New York: Grove Press, 1960), 400–07; "Notes
  on Poetics Regarding Olson's 'Maximus,' " *Review*, #10 (January 1964), 36–
  42 (original version appeared in *Black Mountain Review*, 6 [1956]); "Towards an Open Universe," in *Poets on Poetry*. Edited by Howard Nemerov (New York: Basic Books, 1966), 133–46.

About Duncan:
Dickey, James. *Babel to Byzantium: Poets & Poetry Now*. New York: Farrar,
  Straus & Giroux, 1968. Pp. 173–77.
Duberman, Martin B. *Black Mountain: An Exploration in Community*. New York:
  E. P. Dutton & Co., 1972.
Lieberman, Lawrence. "A Confluence of Poets," *Poetry* 114 (April 1969): 43–
  44.
Rosenthal, M. L. *The New Poets: American and British Poetry Since World
  War II*. New York: Oxford University Press, 1967. Pp. 174–84.
Stepanchev, Stephen. *American Poetry since 1945*. New York: Harper & Row
  Publishers, 1965. Pp. 145–51.

EMANUEL, JAMES *(b. Alliance, Nebr., June 14, 1923–   )*

For James Emanuel, the wish to express his black identity is a necessary
consequence of being a black writer in today's America. He is, as a matter
of fact, notable for the fact that he continues to write nonracial as well as
racial poems, to use relatively strict as well as open forms, "literary" diction
as well as black dialect. But as he writes in the preface to *Panther Man*
(1970), he is more passionately involved in those poems "that attack the
cowardly authoritarianism which alone might make them seem overbold."
  Born in Nebraska, James Emanuel worked at a variety of jobs in the
West and Midwest before earning his B.A. from Howard in 1950, his M.A.
from Northwestern in 1953, and his Ph.D. from Columbia in 1962. He has

taught at the City College of New York since 1957 and in 1968 was visiting professor of American literature at the University of Grenoble in France.

The title poem of *The Treehouse and Other Poems* (1968) illustrates Emanuel's more "traditional" poetry. In a sense, the poem is allegorical. Each man, it asserts, has his treehouse, Spartan with regard to material comforts, but alive with natural energy, with delight. It is a childlike world, in the best sense of the word, that is, capable of illuminating the adult's twilight. And although it is an erotic world, in which ". . . every moving thing/was girlshaped," it is also prelapsarian, a state of wholeness from which a man inevitably descends. The poem ends:

> To every man
> His house below
> And his house above—
> With perilous stairs
> Between.

The ending renders more complex the poem's symbols, since taken by itself it would suggest an earth-heaven dichotomy, with possibly Purgatorial steps in between. Nevertheless, the poem succeeds primarily not because of its allegorical or symbolic qualities but because of its concern with detail and with precise, often unexpected, language. The memory of the treehouse is "A green splice in the humping years"; it recalls ". . . days of squirm and bite/that waved antennas through the grass."

"Panther Man," a poem characteristic of the volume it names, is James Emanuel's response to the pre-dawn killing by Chicago police of the sleeping Black Panthers Mark Clark and Fred Hampton. It is a poem bred of anger and frustration transformed into pride and a sense of power. One would not think to look at these men that they were so dangerous they had to be killed in that way. This is "Panther Man" 's main thrust, far less complex, less ambiguous, than "The Treehouse." The poem's form is freer, the language colloquial, the rhythms quicker and more exciting. There is a subtle control, however, that suggests that the same skill that went into composing the earlier poem is here as well. At the end the poet cries:

> Tell m, Panther!
> Get up out yr dead bed;
> if THAT'S the way he is
> even yr GHOST
> can take m.

Selected Bibliography:
BY EMANUEL:
Langston Hughes. [Criticism.] New York: Twayne Publishers, 1967.
The Treehouse and Other Poems. Detroit: Broadside Press, 1968.
Panther Man. Detroit: Broadside Press, 1970.

EVANS, MARI (*b. Toledo, Ohio, 1923–   *)

Although her poetry is consistent with the NEW BLACK AESTHETIC, with its
insistence upon the black poet's obligation to express the consciousness of
his people, its emphasis on the political implications of his art, Mari Evans'
poetic voice is rarely strident, frequently quite personal. The anger in her
work is anger that has been transmuted into a sense of dignity.

Born in Ohio, Mari Evans attended the University of Toledo. She has
worked as editor of an industrial magazine in Indianapolis, and more recently as writer-in-residence and assistant professor of black literature at Indiana University. She has also produced and directed a weekly television
program, *The Black Experience.*

What distinguishes Evans' work from that of such poets as IMAMU AMIRI
BARAKA and SONIA SANCHEZ is not subject matter, or the interpretation of
that subject matter, but tone. Her most political poems are informed by wit
and an irony that is almost gentle, but nonetheless powerful. In *I Am a
Black Woman,* in "The Emancipation of George-Hector (a colored turtle),"
for example, George-Hector is characterized as "spoiled"; accustomed to
staying in his shell, he now sprawls lazily, waiting to be admired. The
poem ends:

> he didn't use to
> talk . . .
> but
> he does now.

The lines balance delicately between self-mockery, pride, and unspoken
threat.

Even her most assertive poetry turns on a very serious sense of the ridic-
ulous:

> i'm
> gonna make it a
>   crime
>   to be anything BUT   black
>   pass the coppertone
>
> gonna make white
> a twentyfourhour
> lifetime
> J.O.B.
>   an' when all the coppertone's gone. . . ?

(from "Vive Noir!")

The key to Mari Evans' attitude can be found in a poem like "The Silver
Cell" (also from *I Am a Black Woman*), in which she asserts that she has
never been emprisoned except by herself, in which she sees herself as both

slave and master. She is not, here and elsewhere in her work, letting white America off the hook. She is rather placing emphasis on the black man's own power, the sense that his destiny is in his own hands rather than dependent on anything outside himself.

Technically, Evans' poetry is quite proficient and seems to fall squarely within the Projectivist tradition. Her lines are controlled by breath and emphasis; there is always a sense of tight discipline. Only rarely is her verse incantatory, for although she writes with a very definite sense of community, her perceptions are unmistakably individual. The core of her art is the transformation of these individual perceptions into an expression of universal black experience.

In "I Am a Black Woman," this metamorphosis is clearest.

> I lost Nat's swinging body in a rain of tears
> and heard my son scream all the way from Anzio
> for Peace he never knew. . . .

She is, of course, speaking as the *black* woman; but the experiences that define her are not generalized but expressed in the most concrete and personal terms imaginable. It is precisely this concreteness that makes believable her universality and thereby lends potency to the promise of the poem's final lines:

> Look
>   on me and be
>   renewed

Selected Bibliography:
By Evans:
Where Is All the Music? London: Paul Breman, 1968.
I Am a Black Woman. New York: William Morrow & Company, 1970.

FERLINGHETTI, LAWRENCE (*b. Yonkers, N.Y., ? Mar. 24, 1919—)*

Although he is in his own right a good poet, certainly one of the most popular poets of the post-World War II period of American literature, Lawrence Ferlinghetti's place in the literary history of his time has an importance his poetry alone could not earn him. In New York an original founder—along with Allen Ginsberg and Jack Kerouac—of the BEAT GENERATION, Ferlinghetti went to San Francisco in the early fifties and founded the City Lights Bookshop in 1953. It soon developed into the City Lights press, and with that the SAN FRANCISCO RENAISSANCE was born. Kenneth Rexroth was there, and Kenneth Patchen, and so was Robert Duncan. But it was Ferlinghetti's press, which was on solid ground after the publication of Ginsberg's *Howl* in 1956, that made the movement gel.

His most widely known book is still *A Coney Island of the Mind* (1958), which included selected poems from *Pictures of the Gone World* (1955). The characteristic method of that book, which Ferlinghetti handles with great skill, is the use of literary or cultural allusions to develop images of the modern world. The technique must be distinguished from the allusiveness of Ezra Pound or T. S. Eliot. One of the poems' popular appeals is undoubtedly the fact that the artists involved are generally well known, but when the specific allusions are not known to the reader, Ferlinghetti interprets his original in such a way that that knowledge is not essential. This is the method of W. H. Auden's "Musée des Beaux Arts," not that of *The Waste Land*.

A few examples from the beginnings of sections of poems will illustrate:

Sarolla's women in their picture hats
stretched upon his canvas beaches
                                beguiled the Spanish
                        Impressionists
                                (from "Pictures of the Gone World")

Dada would have liked a day like this
                                with its various very realistic
            unrealities
                                (from "Pictures of the Gone World")

In Goya's greatest scenes we seem to see
                                the people of the world
            exactly at the moment when
                they first attained the title of
                                'suffering humanity'
                                (from "A Coney Island of the Mind")

This is not, of course, a unique method. Many poets in addition to Auden have used it occasionally; for example, William Carlos Williams in "Pictures from Brueghel." It is in fact Williams' new metric, the triadic "variable foot" that seems to be echoed, if not imitated, by Ferlinghetti. But Williams stayed close to his originals while Ferlinghetti meditates and makes specific connections between the work of art and the modern world that Williams at best implies. The cumulative effect of Ferlinghetti's poems is different therefore, at least slightly, from that of his models.

The effect is, in fact, like visiting a gallery of pictures in which the pictures turn out to be mirrors, mirrors that reflect the poet, mirrors that reflect his world. The relation between illusion and reality is by necessity never far from the reader's mind, and the long title poem in particular becomes a series of essays on the nature of art. This is very unlike the aesthetic speculations of someone like Wallace Stevens, however, where the creative process becomes a paradigm for all human experience but where much of that human experience is excluded from the poetry. Ferlinghetti's eye is always on the human condition, its suffering, its absurdity; his point, in fact, is to make the connection for the reader between the realm of art and his ordinary existence. The section on Dada, for example, from "Pictures of the Gone World," is almost a reversal of Dadaist principles in their superficial sense. Instead of absent relationships, the poet gives us a world of definite metaphor, in which the accidental or unreal qualities of Dada are seen not as rejections of the commonplace but as its most precise artistic equivalent.

Ferlinghetti's clearest representation of the poet occurs in section 15 of "A Coney Island of the Mind." The poet, continually "risking absurdity and death," is "like an acrobat," who at any moment may destroy his delicate balance and, therefore, himself. He is a "super realist," a term whose full implications can be understood only if we take it as a translation of "surrealist." For he is in search of "Beauty," a reality beyond what is ordinarily considered the real.

> And he
> a little charleychaplin man
> who may or may not catch
> her fair eternal form
> spreadeagled in the empty air
> of existence

Even in Ferlinghetti's most explicit aesthetic statements, art is not defined in terms of itself but rather is grounded in the necessities of human experience. It is because we live in "the empty air of existence" that the poet must take his risks. And because he is aware of the enormity of human suffering and the absurdity of the human condition, the poet has a commitment to his world as well as to his art.

At times this commitment takes the form of a poem like "Autobiography," which, like Allen Ginsberg's "America," from *Howl and Other Poems*, is a confession not only of personal emptiness but also of the empty forms of the poet's society. As many of the other poems in *Coney Island* do, this piece depends largely on allusions to other literary works, often through parody. Ginsberg, Hart Crane, Walt Whitman, Ezra Pound, Thoreau, James Joyce, Yeats, and Melville are only a few of the figures that parade through the lines. It has the feeling of pastiche, almost of pop art. It also has justification within the context of the poem—because Ferlinghetti ends on an affirmative note, and it is evident that he has for himself replaced his meaningless surroundings with what is for him a living tradition, drawing from it the energy to create and possibly to revitalize his world:

> And I may cause the lips
> of those who are asleep
> to speak.

The lips may be those of the writers and artists referred to in the poem, or they may be the lips of those who possess merely the illusion of true existence. Ferlinghetti probably means both.

The form of "Autobiography" foreshadows the poet's methods in the years after *Coney Island of the Mind*. The poem is dominated by shorter lines, by repetitions, by series of parallel structures. The structure is largely rhetorical, although a poet so attracted to surrealism as Ferlinghetti obviously is will always depend upon striking imagery to make his point. And generally there *is* a point to be made, a quality that has undoubtedly contributed much to Ferlinghetti's popularity.

The title poem of *Starting from San Francisco* (1961) is very much in the same mode. As he travels cross-country, Ferlinghetti's response can probably best be summarized by his question, "Who stole America?" The poet himself supplies at least part of the answer in his more overtly political poetry, for example, "Tentative Description of a Dinner to Promote the Impeachment of President Eisenhower." Or in "One Thousand Fearful Words for Fidel Castro," which is much more a condemnation of the country trying to destroy Castro than it is praise of the Cuban leader. Again, Ferlinghetti employs relatively easy allusion to cement his perceptions.

> While lilacs last in the dooryard bloom, Fidel
> your futile trip is done
> yet is not done
> and is not futile
> I give you my sprig of laurel

By the allusion to Walt Whitman, Castro becomes identified with America's greatest political leaders; in trying to destroy Castro, this country is trying to destroy itself.

Because of Lawrence Ferlinghetti's early association with the Beat Generation, we often find ourselves searching his poetry for traces of the Beatific Vision, for some flirtation with Eastern mysticism, or perhaps some new doctrine of his own. And the traces are indeed there. But the title of one of his later books, *The Secret Meaning of Things* (1969), promises us more than a taste. As a matter of fact, the mystical vision is once again not there; what is there in its place provides a good explanation of why it probably never will be.

Most of the poems in the book were written in 1968; and in "Bickford's Buddha," Ferlinghetti quotes a book on Russian poets as saying " 'when guns are roaring/the Muses have no right/to be silent!' " The guns have been roaring, in Vietnam, in Washington, in Los Angeles, in Dallas. A poem like "Assassination Raga," with its repetition of a Sufi chant, "*La il-laha el lill Allah,*" is built around the tension between the poet's wish to participate in some greater unity, some wholeness that can survive the violent fragmentation he sees all around him, and his need to participate in the deadly events of his time, his need to confront the dark heart of experience rather than turn away from it.

From "Assassination Raga" and "Bickford's Buddha" Ferlinghetti moves to the world of possibility opened by LSD in "Through the Looking Glass," and in "After the Cries of the Birds" speaks of

> . . . a new visionary society
> now only dimly recognizable
> in folk-rock ballrooms

It is in some ways an optimistic poem; but Ferlinghetti has a way of intentionally undercutting his optimism. In that same poem, after invoking the "wish to pursue what lies beyond the mind," he then thinks of napalm, which he quotes as being described as " 'The eternal flame at Kennedy's grave.' "

There are limits to Lawrence Ferlinghetti's poetic powers. To what extent his poems are the direct communication of a reality rather than simply a commentary on that reality (a readily paraphrasable commentary at that) is a question often raised by critics. But at his best he possesses an unquestionable power. And he seems one of the finer examples of a man in whom the poet and the human being are not separated.

Selected Bibliography:
By FERLINGHETTI:
Pictures of the Gone World. San Francisco: City Lights Books, 1955.
A Coney Island of the Mind. New York: New Directions Publishing Corp., 1958.
Her. [Novel.] New York: New Directions Publishing Corp., 1960.
Starting from San Francisco. New York: New Directions Publishing Corp., 1961.
The Secret Meaning of Things. New York: New Directions Publishing Corp., 1969.
Tyrannus Nix? New York: New Directions Publishing Corp., 1969.
Back Roads to Far Places. New York: New Directions Publishing Corp., 1971.
The Mexican Night: Travel Journal. New York: New Directions Publishing Corp., 1970.
See also interviews in *The San Francisco Poets.* Edited by David Meltzer. New York: Ballantine Books, 1971.

FIELD, EDWARD   *(b. Brooklyn, N.Y., June 7, 1924—   )*

Originally associated with the NEW YORK POETS, Edward Field has gone his own way. Sharing with them a preference for open verse forms, possessing a sense of the grotesque that borders on the surreal, he does not seriously experiment with the perceptual universe but is content to record the absurdities of experience from the point of view of the coherent self.

Born in Brooklyn and raised on Long Island, Edward Field began writing poetry while serving in the Army Air Corps during World War II. After the war, he studied at New York University, and met Frank O'Hara, John Ashbery, and Kenneth Koch (although he names Robert Friend as the poet who helped him with his techniques). He wrote the narration for the prize-winning film *To Be Alive*, a prominent attraction at the 1964–65 New York World's Fair.

"The Dirty Floor" in *Stand Up, Friend, With Me,* illustrates some of the characteristics of Field's poetry. The poet finds the floor dirty not only with city soot but with fallen hair as well. This becomes a metaphor for the passage of time, and the world becomes a receptacle for "leavings." The poem's crucial phrase is brief: "Renewal is a lie." Somewhere behind all this is the law of entropy, the vision of a universe running down. What Field brings to this vision is a sense of the particular. It is happening to *him.* There is something truly unseemly about it:

> The floor having accumulated particles of myself
> I call it dirty; dirty, the streets thick with the dead;

One of Field's central themes is the bringing to life of the dead body of experience by eroticizing it. In "Graffiti," he blesses "all the kids who improve the signs in the subways," who bring often crude sexual reality to an unreal façade:

> They leave behind a wall scrawled all over with flowers
> That shoot great drops of gism through the sky.

Sometimes sexuality appears threatening, as in "The Bride of Frankenstein" in *Variety Photoplays,* where the monster, cheated of his bride by her terror, roams the earth, "his desire still ungratified," victimizing lovers and "children sleeping in their beds." But the destructiveness seems to lie in the repression, rather than in the energy, of the monster. Here as elsewhere, Field is insistent upon penetrating the veneer that dangerously covers our experience.

Selected Bibliography:
BY FIELD:
Stand Up, Friend, With Me. New York: Grove Press, 1963.
Variety Photoplays. New York: Grove Press, 1967.

About Field:
Howard, Richard. *Alone with America.* New York: Atheneum Publishers, 1969.
    Pp. 116–130.

GARDNER, ISABELLA (*b. Newton, Mass., Sept. 7, 1915—   *)

The poems of Isabella Gardner, the poet herself has remarked, "celebrate and affirm life, but they are also elegaic. My central theme is the interpersonal failure of love, the failure of the I-Thou relationship." She confronts her themes with a virtuosity of language and a variety of forms, which most often include rhyme and either iambic or syllabic metrical patterns.

Isabella Gardner attended the Foxcroft School and studied at the Embassy School of Acting in London. She was associate editor of *Poetry* under Karl Shapiro and has traveled widely, making New York City her home base.

The term "I-Thou relationship" suggests Martin Buber, and the epigraph to *Birthdays from the Ocean* (1955) is from Buber. Gardner's poetry is filled with expressions of affinity with the natural universe, but an affinity that does not lead to the merging of the self with the One. Through the conscious self the universe is perceived, and through that perception the identity of the self is affirmed. In "Of Flesh and Bone," the poet recalls her childhood refusal to acknowledge death's reality, her fear of ". . . the releasing/of the I." This fear has now been transmuted into a wish to choose "the hour of my negating" in order "to escape the meals and miles of waiting." It is the sensory apprehension of the natural world she prizes, all the more because of its inevitable negation.

> Now mornings are still miracles and my dear now-love is my true
> love and we fly we fly . . . O the sky was never once so bright and blue
> and I still wish to live with living's theft-
> ing and assault if even one sense will be left

The poem by Isabella Gardner that has probably received the most critical attention is "The Widow's Yard" (in *West of Childhood*), a good example of her handling of interpersonal relationships. The persona speaks to the "raw young widow" about the snails in her yard, about their frailty, their natural enemies, their shell-created isolation and consequent difficulty in mating. The widow replies that her husband knew the "snails' ways," that the garden was an Eden for them. She talks of how the snails go to earth in the fall, secreting lime at the openings in their shells. The poem ends:

> It is those little doors which sing,
> she said, when they are boiled.
> She smiled at me when I recoiled.

The poem has received various readings. Most convincing is that of Paul Carroll, who proposes that the poem be taken as an ironic comment on the persona (an interpretation supported by Gardner's own remark that her poems are often ironic). The persona chooses to speak of snails in order ". . . to spare/ the widow's vulnerable eyes/ the hurting pity in my gaze." The snails, as she describes them, however, become precise symbols of the vulnerability of the human condition. The widow is then a snail, and the persona has chosen, consciously or unconsciously, to bury her pity in metaphor. It is a condescending kind of pity, one behind which the speaker can comfortably shield herself from the touch of the widow's pain. In that sense, the persona herself is the snail; that the widow has perceived this, consciously or unconsciously, is revealed in the poem's concluding lines, which are both aggressive and evocative of just those feelings her neighbor wishes to evade. In the subtlety with which these portraits are drawn lies Isabella Gardner's art at its finest.

Selected Bibliography:
By Gardner:
Birthdays from the Ocean. Boston: Houghton Mifflin Co., 1955.
The Looking Glass. Chicago: University of Chicago Press, 1961.
West of Childhood: Poems 1950–1965. Boston: Houghton Mifflin Co., 1965.

About Gardner:
Carroll, Paul. "The Widow's Yard" in *The Poem in Its Skin*. Chicago: Follett
    Publishing Co., 1968. Pp. 51–62.
Mills, Ralph J., Jr., *Contemporary American Poetry*. New York: Random House,
    1965. Pp. 122–133.

GINSBERG, ALLEN (*b. Newark, N.J., June 3, 1926—*   )

In less than ten years, Allen Ginsberg moved from the position of a curiosity
on the borders of society to become the hero of a broad-based subculture;
in the late fifties, few except the more daring avant-garde publications
would touch his poetry, while in the mid-sixties a major work, "Wichita
Vortex Sutra," was printed by *Life* magazine. Ginsberg himself has been
reasonably consistent; his career is evidence in support of the predictive nature of art. That he was barely ten years ahead of his time may suggest
some of his limitations.

Born in Newark, New Jersey, Ginsberg grew up in Paterson. His father,
Louis, was a schoolteacher and a poet in his own right; his mother, Naomi,
the subject of "Kaddish," was severely paranoid, perhaps the most significant fact of Ginsberg's early life. In 1943, he entered Columbia College,
where he met Jack Kerouac and William Burroughs. He was suspended in
1945, for reasons by now shrouded in legend. Reinstated in 1946, he finally
received his degree in 1948; that year is important to Ginsberg, however,
not because of any academic achievement, but rather because of an experience more nearly central to his life and art. Living in an East Harlem tenement, Ginsberg heard the voice of William Blake intoning "Ah! Sunflower," and, staring out the window

> . . . I began noticing in every corner where I looked evidences of a
> living hand, even in the bricks, in the arrangement of each brick.
> Some hand placed them there—that some hand had placed the
> whole universe in front of me. . . . Or that God was in front of my
> eyes—existence itself was God. . . . what I was seeing was a vision-
> ary thing, it was a lightness in my body . . . my body suddenly felt
> *light,* and a sense of cosmic consciousness, vibrations, understanding,
> awe, and wonder and surprise. And it was a sudden awakening into
> a totally deeper real universe than I'd been existing in.

> (*Paris Review* interview in *Writers at Work*)

The search for a "totally deeper real universe" never stopped. On the road for the next few years—in fact, he has not for any length of time been off the road since—with and without Kerouac, Burroughs, Gregory Corso, his companion Peter Orlovsky, and the rest of the BEAT GENERATION writers, Ginsberg soon emerged as the group's major writer. From their origin in New York, the Beats soon shifted their base to San Francisco, joining Lawrence Ferlinghetti, Gary Snyder, Philip Whalen, Brother Antoninus, and others to form the SAN FRANCISCO RENAISSANCE. It was, as a matter of fact, Ginsberg's *Howl* (1956) that brought the group their most significant publicity when it was seized by the authorities and became the object of a now famous obscenity trial, ultimately won by Ginsberg.

Ginsberg's national, and international, stature has grown steadily in his readings given around the world. His attitudes toward love and drugs—he has recorded in his poetry responses to a remarkably complete assortment of hallucinogens—made him a natural idol for the hippie movements of Haight-Ashbury and the East Village. Involved in most of the major antiwar protests of the late sixties, a witness for the defense at the trial of the Chicago Eight, he has consistently impressed even political enemies with his sincerity, integrity, and dignity. He has not always fared as well at the hands of his literary "enemies."

The very openness of Ginsberg's verse, its apparent lack of craft—which Ginsberg's own accounts, if they are to be taken seriously, corroborate—has from the start insured opposition from the more formal poets, such as James Dickey and Louis Simpson. At first writing poems that looked like models of William Carlos Williams' "variable foot" experiments in both form and method, naturally enough since he was a kind of protégé of Williams', Ginsberg found his own mode through a "Hebraic-Melvillian bardic breath." Working independently of the Black Mountain poets, he arrived at a prosody similar in theory to that of the Projectivists in that it connected poetic rhythm with breath and other biological rhythms; in practice, however, he produced a far longer line.

> Actually, I keep reading, or earlier I kept reading, that I was influenced by Kenneth Fearing and Carl Sandburg, whereas actually I was more conscious of Christopher Smart, and Blake's Prophetic Books, and Whitman and some aspects of Biblical rhetoric.
>
> (*Paris Review* interview in *Writers at Work*)

It is in fact Whitman that the reader finds most relevant to Ginsberg's poetry, and to his life style as well. The long verse line reaches out to embrace all of experience, finding the spiritual in the sensual, wiping out distinctions between the temporal and the eternal. Ginsberg himself is a more cosmopolitan version of the wandering poet. The link between them is most explicitly stated in "A Supermarket in California," a poem in *Howl* that arrives at the core of Whitman's sensibility: "In my hungry fatigue, and shopping for images, I went into the neon fruit supermarket, dreaming of your enumerations!"

This "shopping for images" is not an entirely unfair description of Ginsberg's own poetic methods, and his work has frequently been criticized for its undisciplined accumulations. But Ginsberg is not without discipline, even if his poems proceed as spontaneously as he insists they do. The discipline involved is the discipline of *being* a poet, of being in touch with a "totally deeper real universe." From a state of heightened consciousness, according to Ginsberg, true poetry will of its own accord emerge, but only if the poet has taught himself to utilize that consciousness. A trip on LSD or peyote or mescaline or ayahuasco *can* lead to fine poetry, but not inevitably.

Approached coolly with the perspective of time, and with the battles with the censors well in the past, "Howl" seems both less spectacular and more impressive. That Ginsberg had been shopping in a particularly abundant supermarket for his images is evident from the no longer shocking first lines—

I saw the best minds of my generation destroyed by madness, starving hysterical naked,
dragging themselves through the negro streets at dawn looking for an angry fix,
angelheaded hipsters burning for the ancient heavenly connection to the starry dynamo in the machinery of night,

—through the "Nightmare of Moloch," in section 2, to the incantation to Carl Solomon in Rockland in section 3. The dislocation of adjectives, the telescoping of discrete images is hardly new in Ginsberg—the Symbolists had this, so did the Surrealists—but Ginsberg, claiming Cézanne rather than literary figures as inspiration, describes it this way in the *Paris Review* interview:

> . . . I had the idea, perhaps overrefined, that by the unexplainable, unexplained nonperspective line, that is, juxtaposition of one *word* against another, a *gap* between the two words—like the space gap in the canvas—there'd be a gap between the two words which the mind would fill in with the sensation of existence.

Nonetheless, it is probably not in the relation of word to word, the microcosm of the poem, that Ginsberg's innovations appear, but rather in the macrocosm, the relation of image to image. Following in the tradition of Ezra Pound and Williams, Ginsberg cites in the interview the example of the *haiku*, in which "you have two distinct images, set side by side without drawing a connection, without drawing a logical connection between them: the *mind* fills in this . . . this space." While both Pound and Williams make use of intellectually conceived frameworks in their longer works, Ginsberg moves in a different direction, toward what Paul Carroll has called in *The Poem in Its Skin* the "impure poem," in which the images pour out, emotionally rather than rationally linked; we are dependent upon the intensity of the poet's concentration for the poem's unity. Almost certainly there is a logic of association grounded in the poet's unconscious, but this logic is, of course, inaccessible to the reader, except perhaps in terms of his own un-conscious, if universal chords are struck. Ginsberg does rely, however, on syntax to provide a form strong enough to contain his howl. Of the first sec-tion's seventy-eight lines, fifty-eight begin with the word "who," two lines with "and who," forming, in effect, one huge sentence composed of a series of dependent clauses. The second section is held together by the insistent repetition of "Moloch," the final section by the repetition of "I'm with you in Rockland." The result is a kind of ceremonial chaos, a mixture of order and disintegration perfectly appropriate to the paradoxes of Ginsberg's mystical vision.

The catalog of Beat experiences that constitute "Howl" partakes of this paradox. Madness, anguish, suicide are dominant themes; the vision seems essentially nightmare. But the eternal is never far off, to be reached through drugs or power of will, and there is always a touch of joy in the most ex-treme surreal horror.

For many, the title poem of *Kaddish and Other Poems* (1961) represents the height of Ginsberg's achievement. In *The New Poets* M. L. Rosenthal compares it to Robert Lowell's *Life Studies*. As an exploration of the poet's family in intimate detail, as well as in its recognition of the impact of these details on the poet's own psyche, there certainly would seem to be good reason to classify at least this work of Ginsberg's with the school of CONFES-SIONAL POETRY. Some differences emerge from the very start, however. The irony that Lowell, Sylvia Plath, Anne Sexton, and John Berryman bring to their painful subjects is here barely present.

The opening lines of "Kaddish" serve effectively to place it:

Strange now to think of you, gone without corset & eyes, while I walk on
the sunny pavement of Greenwich Village.
downtown Manhattan, clear winter noon, and I've been up all night, talking, talking, reading the Kaddish aloud, listening to Ray Charles
blues shout blind on the phonograph
the rhythm the rhythm—and your memory in my head three years after—
And read Adonais' last triumphant stanzas aloud—wept, realizing
how we suffer—
And how Death is that remedy all singers dream of, sing, remember, pro-
phesy as in the Hebrew Anthem, or the Buddhist Book of Answers
—and my own imagination of a withered leaf—at dawn—

The strands that Ginsberg has chosen to interweave—the hip life of jazz-age New York; the kaddish, the Hebrew hymn to God and lament for the dead; the English literary tradition; the Buddhist Book of Answers—form a coherent whole. Ginsberg takes what is remote and makes it present. He translates the mystical sensibility, the romantic imagination, the entire weight of the past, into the language of his own private universe. In "Psalm III" (from *Reality Sandwiches*, 1963), he writes, "I feed on your Name like a cockroach on a crumb—this cockroach is holy." It is this combination of Blake and Kafka that most characterizes the mood of Ginsberg's verse. With the tone appropriate to this mood Ginsberg records the progress of Naomi's paranoia, threats of poison, Nazi plots, a world populated by conspirators, where no one can be trusted. It is not the sense of any delusion that Ginsberg strains to communicate; it is rather the validity of subjective vision.

"Kaddish" can be read with Ginsberg himself at its focus rather than Naomi, much in the way that Joseph Conrad's *Heart of Darkness* can be read with the narrator, Marlow, at its center, rather than Kurtz, the madman. It is perhaps not coincidental that our last view of Naomi has her denying Allen's identity, crying " 'The Horror' . . . 'The Horror' . . . 'The Horror!' . . . 'All the Horror!' " Naomi's madness, like that of Kurtz, whose dying words she echoes, opens doors on the universe.

Formally, in spite of its disjointed sentences and intermittent flow of fragments, "Kaddish" offers the reader relatively few difficulties. The poem is held together by its narrative—it has a story if not a plot—and its many concrete details fit easily into a larger picture. The rhythms, much more prosaic than usual for Ginsberg, also help to break down distinctions between poetry and fiction. There is a definite rhythmic structure, however, sensitively handled, in the alternation between long and staccato breaths, and, as always, the insistent rhythms of itemization.

Reality Sandwiches is Ginsberg's travelog. Most of the poems in it bear datelines from across the country, around the world, leading, cumulatively, to a sense of motion, of boundless energy. And there are fine moments in many of the pieces (as in "Psalm III," quoted above). But the volume lacks the sustained effort that shows Ginsberg at his best and is especially vulnerable to the criticism generally leveled against the poet. Often, his imagination seems without discipline, either conscious or unconscious; frequently irony—never Ginsberg's strong point—falls flat, as in "American Change." And the mystical vision, as Ginsberg himself feared, begins to turn into descriptions after the event rather than direct experiencings of it. In the *Paris Review* interview, given in 1965, Ginsberg said:

> On the train in Kyoto having renounced Blake, renounced visions—renounced *Blake!*—too. There was a cycle that began with the Blake vision which ended on the train in Kyoto when I realized that to attain the depth of consciousness that I was seeking when I was talking about the Blake vision, that in order to attain it I had to cut myself off from the Blake vision and renounce it. Otherwise I'd be hung up on a memory of an experience. Which is not the actual awareness of now, now.

In "The Change: Kyoto–Tokyo Express" (*Planet News,* 1968) Ginsberg begins to record his new direction: a commitment to the totally human—not that Ginsberg had in the past been alienated from the human universe. "Kaddish" in particular is distinguished by its deep involvement in the human condition. But in "The Change," inspired by Charles Olson's remark, "I am one with my skin," Ginsberg proclaims his commitment to the limits of the human condition:

I am not all now

but a universe of skin and breath
& changing thought and
burning hand & softened
heart in the old bed of
my skin

The shift is from the theological to the existential. "This form of Life needs Sex," one of the most successful poems in *Planet News*, is precisely the result of this new awareness of limits. "I will have to accept women / if I want to continue the race," Ginsberg begins by conceding, facing the darker side of the homosexuality for which he has never apologized.

You can joy man to man but the Sperm
comes back in a trickle at dawn
in a toilet on the 45th Floor—

There is a potentially tragic vision here, which Ginsberg flippantly rejects in the poem's last line—"and that's my situation, Folks"—but the poem at least suggests the possibility of a new dimension to Ginsberg's vision.

See also the Introduction, sections IV and VI.

Selected Bibliography:
By GINSBERG:
Howl and Other Poems. San Francisco: City Lights Books, 1956.
Kaddish and Other Poems, 1958–1960. San Francisco: City Lights Books, 1961.
Empty Mirror: Early Poems, 1946–1951. New York: Corinth Books, 1961.
Reality Sandwiches, 1953–60. San Francisco: City Lights Books, 1963.
The Yage Letters. (With William Burroughs.) San Francisco: City Lights Books, 1963.
Planet News, 1961–1967. San Francisco: City Lights Books, 1968.
The Fall of America: Poems of These States. San Francisco: City Lights Books, 1973.
See also Ginsberg's "Notes for *Howl* and Other Poems," in *The New American Poetry.* Edited by Donald M. Allen. New York: Grove Press, 1960. Pp. 414–18; and his *Paris Review* interview in *Writers at Work*, 3rd Series. New York: Viking Press, 1967.

About Ginsberg:
Carroll, Paul. "Wichita Vortex Sutra," in *The Poem in Its Skin.* Chicago: Follett Publishing Co., 1968. Pp. 65–109.
Ehrlich, J. W. *Howl of the Censor.* San Carlos, Cal.: Nourse Publishing Co., 1961.
Howard, Richard. *Alone with America.* New York: Atheneum Publishers, 1969. Pp. 145–52.
Hunsberger, Bruce. "Kit Smart's *Howl.*" *Wisconsin Studies in Contemporary Literature* 6 (Winter–Spring, 1965): 34–44.

Kramer, Jane. *Allen Ginsberg in America*. New York: Random House, 1969.

Menkin, Edward Z. "Allen Ginsberg: A Bibliography and Biographical Sketch." *Thoth* (Winter 1967): 35–44.

Ossman, David. "An Interview with Allen Ginsberg." *The Sullen Art*. New York: Corinth Books, 1962. Pp. 87–95.

Rosenthal, M. L. *The New Poets: American & British Poetry Since World War II*. New York: Oxford University Press, 1967. Pp. 89–112.

Rumaker, Michael. "Allen Ginsberg's 'Howl.'" *Black Mountain Review* 7 (Autumn 1957): 228–37.

Stepanchev, Stephen. *American Poetry since 1945*. New York: Harper & Row Publishers, 1965. Pp. 166–74.

Trilling, Diana. "The Other Night at Columbia." *Partisan Review* 26 (Spring 1959): 214–30.

GIOVANNI, NIKKI (*b. Knoxville, Tenn., June 7, 1943–   *)

True to the NEW BLACK AESTHETIC, Nikki Giovanni's poetry is almost always an exploration of black consciousness—of her own, of other individual blacks, of blacks collectively. But although she is in a sense moving toward a general definition of blackness, she is most successful when she focuses on the particular, as in her poems to Aretha Franklin, Angela Davis, a nameless woman whose voice she likes, a murdered black gangster, a lover. Here, in the tradition of novelists Richard Wright and Ralph Ellison, she reaches a core of common humanity without in the least diminishing the specifically black nature of her experience.

For a biographical entry in Clarence Major's anthology *The New Black Poetry* (1969), she wrote: "I'd like to have mentioned that I was kicked out of Fisk, plus I dropped out of a Masters Program at the University of Pennsylvania. And I was in love once." Even if her relationship to higher education has been uneasy, she has certainly learned whatever is essential to the craft of poetry. She is capable of using simple folk and blues rhythms and techniques and also the more sophisticated methods of Projective verse, sometimes combining both.

In fact, one senses in the work of Nikki Giovanni—more from its formal qualities than from its content—that there has been a conflict between the impulse to practice her art without restriction and her very strong sense of herself as a specifically black artist. But if this conflict did exist, it has been directly confronted. In "For Saundra" (in *Black Judgement*) she explains to the neighbor who feels her poetry contains too much hatred why she cannot write about conventionally beautiful subjects. She would like to write about trees, but Manhattan is covered with asphalt. She would like to write about blue sky, but clouds have been hovering low, especially since "no-Dick was elected." And it begins to occur to her that maybe she should not write poems at all, "but clean my gun / and check my kerosene supply." The poem ends:

             perhaps these are not poetic
             times
             at all.

Consequently, her poetry is frequently quite violent. In "The True Im-
port of Present Dialogue: Black vs. Negro" (in *Black Feeling, Black Talk*),
she asks, "Can a nigger kill a honkie/Can a nigger kill the Man." The
word "kill" holds the poem together. But the poem asks another significant question: "Can you kill the nigger/in you." While there seems little
doubt that Giovanni would not shrink from revolution if revolution would
accomplish her goals, killing a honkie and killing the nigger are two sides of
the same coin; they are assertions of blackness, assertions that must be
fought out in the black mind before they can have reality in any other
sense. And if the language is violent, we are reminded of Frantz Fanon's
conclusion that if a man has been deprived of his dignity through violence,
the psychology of the human mind dictates that it is only through violence
that that dignity can be recaptured.

Nikki Giovanni's more militant poetry is quite effective. But even more
effective, perhaps, are those poems which focus on particular black lives,
and whose call for revolution is implicit rather than explicit. Such a poem,
in *Re:Creation*, is "For Harold Logan (Murdered by 'persons unknown'
cause he wanted to own a Black club on Broadway)." Logan, a gangster, is
presented as an honest man, that is, one who may have operated outside
the law, but who dealt fairly with his customers. In bucking the white
order of things, he assures his destruction. It is significant that Giovanni
does not bother to inform us whether it is white gangsters or white politi-
cians who have Logan killed. The distinction would be pointless since in its
dealings with blacks the white establishment is seen as monolithic. The last
lines are:

                    a cleaning man came
                    and removed his life
                    said Broadway was getting
                    too dusty

It is impossible to discuss the poem without taking into account Harold Logan's blackness; it is his blackness rather than the fact that he is a gangster
that leads to his death. Yet the poet is unquestionably more disturbed that
this particular man's life has been extinguished than that the murder represents still another instance of white oppression of blacks. Giovanni describes
Logan as ". . . just a little/gangster with a high/voice/and a poetic
mind." She is responding to his humanity as well as to his blackness, to his
individuality as well as to his symbolic significance.

Nikki Giovanni's concern with black music becomes still another means of
defining black consciousness. This is nowhere more evident than in "Poem
for Aretha" (from *Re:Creation*), in which the power of Aretha's honesty and
directness, the fact that her singing is an expression of her full humanity, is
contrasted with the weaker performances of less dedicated artists. In other

poems black music provides not the subject but the method of Giovanni's poetry, as, for example, in "The Geni in the Jar" (in *Re:Creation*):

> take the air and weave the sky
> around the Black loom around the Black loom
> make the sky sing a Black song sing a blue song
> sing my song make the sky sing a Black song
> from the Black loom from the Black loom
> careful baby
> don't prick your finger

The last lines are especially characteristic of Nikki Giovanni's art. They break the rhythm, introduce a jarring, almost ominous note. They express the risk of being black, of being a poet.

Selected Bibliography:
By GIOVANNI:
Black Judgement. Detroit: Broadside Press, 1968.
Black Feeling, Black Talk. Detroit: Broadside Press, 1970.
Re:Creation. Detroit: Broadside Press, 1970.
My House. New York: William Morrow & Company, 1972.
Gemini: An Extended Autobiographical Statement on My First Twenty-five Years of Being a Black Poet. Indianapolis: Bobbs-Merrill Co., 1972.

GLÜCK, LOUISE (*b. New York City, Apr. 22, 1943–*   )

A language that is stripped of everything not essential, but which is brought into focus by sharp and powerful images, is at the heart of Louise Glück's poetry. Though her poems are filled with pain, or with a sensitivity to experience that borders on the painful, they are also capable of finding rebirth in death, the will to live in the face of bleakness. Her work often seems Confessional, but it is probably more accurate to think of her voices as personae exploring the possibilities of experience, testing the nature and limits of the self rather than asserting it.

Louise Glück attended Sarah Lawrence College and later studied with Stanley Kunitz at Columbia. A 1967–68 Fellow of the Rockefeller Foundation, she has more recently conducted poetry workshops at Goddard College.

In "Early December in Croton-on-Hudson," the sun is "spiked," the Hudson is "Whittled down by ice." The gravel sounds like "bone dice," the snow is "bonepale." Last year the tire had blown, the pines had been "pared down" and bare. The poem ends with a simple line: "I want you." In its literal sense, the scene has evoked a memory of a previous time, which sets off the persona's longing. That explanation, although accurate as far as it goes, does not account for the imagery of death preceding it. The sexual desire is at least partially elicited by the vision of death, death which is at once the absence of the lover and the absence of life. In the field of the poem, the short last line balances everything that has come before and because of that becomes all the more passionate.

At times, however, death is less cold and forbidding in Glück's poetry. In "Cottonmouth Country," one of her best poems, it is death itself that is seductive, representing a reunion with the oneness of nature, an escape from a painful world:

> Birth, not death, is the hard loss.
> I know. I also left a skin there.

The impulse toward life and the impulse toward death are inseparable in Louise Glück's poetry; the one can exist only in terms of the other. And it is this dichotomy that holds her poetry together.

Selected Bibliography:
By GLÜCK:
Firstborn. New York: New American Library, 1968.

HAYDEN, ROBERT   (*b. Detroit, Mich., Aug. 4, 1913—*   )

Along with GWENDOLYN BROOKS and MARGARET WALKER one of the most important black poets to come out of the forties, Robert Hayden has not been comfortable with the notion that he is a black poet rather than simply a poet. A good deal of his work is identifiable as having been written by a man with a fine eye for the concrete, with a good sense of the rhythms appropriate to the experience communicated, in short, by an excellent craftsman. Many of his most powerful poems, however, are deeply rooted in the specifically black experience, not only in the contemporary world but especially in its traditions, which he refuses to accept as nonexistent. Writing of Nat Turner, of anonymous runaway slaves, of the slave ship *Amistad*, he anticipated the resurrection of the black American history that had long been buried.

Robert Hayden received his B.A. from Wayne State University, his M.A. from the University of Michigan. The winner of many awards for his poetry, including the 1966 Grand Prize at the First World Festival of Negro Arts in Dakar, he has taught English, first at Michigan, for most of his career at Fisk University.

One does not have to read far in Hayden's work to find evidence of his technical skill. "The Diver," for example, describes a swimmer exploring the wreck of a ship who becomes so caught up in the experience that he is barely able to regain the surface. The detail is so fully realized, the short-lined rhythms so hypnotic, that the poem takes on the quality of an especially vivid dream, an archetypal night journey under the sea. And Hayden succeeds in this not by providing a pretentious context, but by limiting his perceptions to the immediate experience:

> With flashlight probing
> fogs of water
> saw the sad slow
> dance of gilded
> chairs, the ectoplasmic
> swirl of garments,
> drowned instruments
> of buoyancy,
> drunken shoes. . . .

So deep has the diver gone he is in danger of not being able to return. Whether the depths are understood as death—the poem echoes Keats's "Ode to a Nightingale"—or as the unconscious, or as any aspect of experience in which man is threatened by the loss of his individual self, the basic emotional structure of the poem remains valid.

Hayden's mastery is so complete that it sometimes gives the impression of a mere *tour de force*, as in this passage from "Veracruz":

> Here only the sea is real—
> the barbarous multifoliate sea
> with its rustling of leaves,
> fire, garments, wind;
> its clashing of phantasmal jewels,
> in lunar thunder,
> animal and human sighing.

Hayden's technical effects, however, usually prove to be appropriate to the poem's sense. In this case, the juxtaposition of more "refined" Latinate words with the blunter Anglo-Saxon reflects the tension between the ideal and the real, the dream and the actuality, which is at the core of this poem and of so much of Hayden's poetry.

His work as a whole is, in fact, bound together by those same tensions. The exploration of the possibilities of imagination is a frequent theme; so is the encounter with the ugliness of the objective world. "Night, Death, Mississippi" is a ballad-like poem—Hayden, here and elsewhere, is fond of using stanzaic patterns without their traditional rhyme schemes—telling of the castration and beating of blacks from the point of view of the whites. Interjections, like *"O Jesus burning on the lily cross,"* between the quatrains of the second section underline the poem's unifying imagery—the parallels with Christ's passion—as does the stanza:

> You kids fetch Paw
> some water now so's he
> can wash that blood
> off him, she said.

This is not an attempt to work within the folk tradition. The lack of rhyme, the irregular rhythms that strain against the lines, the intricacy of composition, are all indications of the sophisticated manner in which Hayden transforms the borrowed structural and narrative principles to his own uses. Similarly, "The Ballad of Nat Turner" proves to be not the expected recounting of Nat's doomed insurrection, but an interior monolog describing his visions in striking sensory detail.

The two concluding poems of *Selected Poems*, written about similar themes, display the full range of Hayden's art. "Runagate Runagate" is told from the perspective of a runaway slave, still in the process of gaining his freedom, threatened by the despair that will lead to apathy and capture. The poem is in free verse, the rhythms following the agitation of the slave's mind, interspersed with fragments of spirituals promising freedom.

> Runs falls rises stumbles on from darkness into darkness
> and the darkness thicketed with shapes of terror
> and the hunters pursuing and the hounds pursuing
> and the night cold and the night long . . .

"Frederick Douglass," whose fourteen lines and tight structure make it a sonnet in spite of its lack of rhyme or regular meter, is by contrast a conception if not of triumph at least of definite promise. With this poem, the tensions between dream and reality that have dominated the volume come into sharp focus. The gap between the world as it should be and the world as it is has not been the object of abstract, casual speculation, but a matter of great urgency, emerging from the experience of the black man in America. Douglass will be remembered, Hayden says,

> . . . not with statues' rhetoric,
> not with legends and poems and wreaths of bronze alone,
> but with the lives grown out of his life, the lives
> fleshing his dream of the beautiful, needful thing.

As the more recent *Words in the Mourning Time* (1970) suggests, Hayden's awareness is not restricted to past traditions. He is also responsive to the contemporary world, the world that made those traditions important to begin with. But although he is angry, he refuses to be caught up in the rhetoric of hate, he refuses to accept evil as deliverance from evil:

> Reclaim now, now renew the vision of
> a human world where godliness
> is possible and man
> is neither gook nigger honkey wop nor kike
>
> but man
>
> permitted to be man.
>
> (from "Words in the Mourning Time")

Selected Bibliography:
BY HAYDEN:
Heart-Shape in the Dust. Detroit: Falcon, 1940.
A Ballad of Remembrance. London: Paul Breman, 1962.
Selected Poems. New York: October House, 1966.
Words in the Mourning Time. New York: October House, 1970.

HECHT, ANTHONY *(b. New York City, Jan. 16, 1923—   )*

In spite of the fact that his recent poetry includes some fine free verse, Anthony Hecht is still very much committed to strict poetic forms. This, together with such dominant images as gardens secluded from the world and a certain elegance of style, may give the impression that he has staked out for his art a terrain somehow uninvolved in contemporary agonies. But that, of course, is not true. The garden is almost always an Eden from which man has been expelled. And if there is a central symbol in his Pulitzer Prize–winning *The Hard Hours,* it is the holocaust, making the entire volume a kind of descent into hell. The struggle of Hecht's art is to give reality some sort of coherent form that will not evade the destructive chaos that threatens on all sides, but will somehow come to terms with it.

Anthony Hecht studied at Kenyon College and Columbia University and was awarded a Writing Fellowship at the American Academy of Rome. He has taught at Smith, Bard College, and the University of Rochester. More significantly, perhaps, he served in the infantry in Europe during World War II, the marks of which are still evident in his poetry. He is an editor of *Hudson Review* and an executive of P.E.N. One of the remarkable facts about his career is that he has had published only two books of poetry, one in 1954, the next not until 1968. He is as disciplined in his attitude toward his work as a whole as he is toward individual poems.

Gardens are indeed important in *A Summoning of Stones* (1954). In "La Condition Botanique," the Brooklyn Botanical Gardens are a kind of Eden, but an Eden we can only temporarily visit:

> And we, like disinherited heirs,
>   Old Adams, can inspect the void estate
> At visiting hours: the unconditional garden spot,
> The effortless innocence preserved, for God knows what,
>   And think, as we depart by the toll gate:
>   No one has lived here these five thousand years.

Even this garden, however, this "throwback" to a less corrupt world, has implicit terrors. There is, for example, "The Mexican flytrap, that can knit/Its quilled jaws pitilessly." And Hecht compares the garden to a veteran of the Union army, who sees young men "march . . . for glory" past a reviewing stand on their way to death. Here, it is difficult to fix the tone. The language flows smoothly, with infinite grace, and meter and stanzaic pattern emerge effortlessly. The question is whether there is bitter irony in the contrasts or whether art succeeds in containing the terror.

"The Gardens of the Villa d'Este" makes one realize that Hecht's garden is a complex symbol, an Eden to be sure, a world of innocence that cannot be recaptured, but also a world intimately related to our own reality. These gardens, for example, are sexually charged. Of a fountain, Hecht writes: ". . . White/Ejaculations leap to teach/How fertile are these nozzles." It is a sexuality embedded in "lily-padded ease" but more exciting than one imagines could have existed in an Eden. This place, Hecht specifies, is not "Based on God's rational, wrist-watch universe." Here are wood lice, night crawlers, spiders. "Actually, it is real/The way the world is real." It begins to occur to us that the gardens represent not a prelapsarian paradise but the actual world ordered by the disciplines of art. And Hecht's aesthetics do in fact emerge from his description of the gardens:

> Controlled disorder at the heart
> Of everything, the paradox, the old
> Oxymoronic itch to set the formal strictures
> Within a natural context, where the tension lectures
> Us on our mortal state, and by controlled
> Disorder, labors to keep art
> From being too refined.

Hecht adopts the imagery as well as the central idea of Yeats's "Adam's Curse." Yeats wrote:

> . . . "A line will take us hours maybe;
> Yet if it does not seem a moment's thought,
> Our stitching and unstitching has been naught."
> . . . .
> . . . "It's certain there is no fine thing
> Since Adam's fall but needs much laboring."

The awareness of Adam's curse pervades A Summoning of Stones, not simply in the garden poems, but in pieces like "Japan" and "Discourse Concerning Temptation" as well. Nonetheless, it is not always certain that Hecht has succeeded in his labors to keep art from being too refined. The new poems of The Hard Hours (1968), however, both disclose the tremendous pressures that have made such tight control essential and show the poet capable of relaxing some of that control.

In a relatively subtle way, Anthony Hecht took notice of the darker side of experience in his earlier poetry. In fact, without that darker side, there could have been no poetry. In The Hard Hours, he faces it directly, so directly that the reader often flinches. One of the best poems, "More Light! More Light!" tells the story of a Pole ordered by the Nazis to bury two Jews alive. He refuses, and he is made to change places with the Jews. After he has been buried to his head, the positions are reversed again. This time he buries the Jews, then is shot in the stomach, taking three hours to die. The poem is written in orderly quatrains, but here there is no danger of artifice triumphing over feeling. The language is relatively bare, understated. Smooth rhythmic flow is broken by short sentences, end-stopped lines. The problem of what significance God can have to human life in the light of what man is capable of doing to man is clearly stated.

Nor is there any suggestion that the experiences of World War II are isolated phenomena in human history (even "More Light! More Light!" juxtaposes the contemporary atrocity with the death of an earlier martyr). "Behold the Lilies of the Field" tells in terrible detail of the humiliation and flaying alive of the Roman Emperor Valerian by barbarians, as recalled by one of his soldiers who has been shattered by what he witnessed. He is told repeatedly to relax, to "Look at the flowers." He concludes his monolog: "Yes. I am looking. I wish I could be like them." The fact that Valerian's soldiers are forced to witness everything that takes place is crucial. The implicit question is: how can man endure reality if he sees the horror at the center and not just the flowers? This poem is written in free verse, with Hecht making expert use of short sentences that break the narrative flow. The experience cannot be contained within the stricter forms.

If the principal biblical allusion in *A Summoning of Stones* was the expulsion from Eden, then in *The Hard Hours* it is the Book of Job. It appears near the conclusion of one of the volume's most interesting poems, "Rites and Ceremonies": ". . . Who/Fathered the fathering rain?" (The allusion is to "Hath the rain a father?" Job 38:28.) The poem, in four sections, again focuses on the holocaust, and again provides precedents in history. Hecht mixes free verse with stricter forms, chaotic experience with ritual.

> Neither shall the flame
> Kindle upon them, nor the fire burn
> A hair of them, for they
> Shall be thy care when it shall come to pass,
> And calling on thy name
> In the hot kilns and ovens, they shall turn
> To thee as it is prophesied, and say,
> *"He shall come down like rain upon mown grass."*

The difficulty of accepting this movement from Job to the Psalms when we have just seen the ovens, the two Jews and the Pole, Valerian, is at the very core of Hecht's art.

Selected Bibliography:
By HECHT:
A Summoning of Stones. New York: Macmillan Co., 1954.
The Hard Hours. New York: Atheneum Publishers, 1968.

About Hecht:
Howard, Richard. *Alone with America.* New York: Atheneum Publishers, 1969.
    Pp. 164–73.

HOWARD, RICHARD   (*b. Cleveland, Ohio, 1929–   *)

In addition to being a highly respected poet, Richard Howard is the author of one of the most impressive books interpreting post–World War II American poetry, *Alone with America* (1969). Although his criticism reveals a good deal of sympathy toward poets employing freer forms, as a poet Howard has elected to write within clearly defined restraints.

Born and raised in Cleveland, Howard later attended Columbia University and the Sorbonne. He gives frequent readings of his poetry, has worked as a lexicographer, and has been a prolific translator of modern French literature, having translated more than one hundred works.

Richard Howard's first book of poems, *Quantities*, was published in 1962. The poetry is formally structured, generally without rhyme but with definite meter. Howard prefers an iambic line, which he handles with great flexibility, often varying the number of feet per line in repeated stanzaic patterns. His concern with precise language gives the reader the sense that he had better pay careful attention to the particular word chosen because the poet surely has. This concern may even become explicit in the poetry, as in the conclusion to "Rumors of Real Estate":

> . . . How pat
> Our word *apartment* falls in here,
> For this is the life he divides
> From the others, a death apart.

The passage is rich in play with both the sound and sense of language. If Charles Olson drew attention to the importance of syllable and line, Howard defends the impact of the word.

Thematically, Howard foreshadows in *Quantities* the later achievements of *Untitled Subjects* (1969). He is interested, of course, in the problems inherent in the human condition—death, loneliness—and in the impulse to create in the face of emptiness. His focus is generally psychological. He emphasizes neither the perceptual universe nor man's interpretation of that universe—though he does not ignore them—but rather the process by which that interpretation is made. In his second book, *The Damages* (1967), in poems like "Bonnard: A Novel" and "The Author of 'Christine,'" Howard develops further the possibilities of narrative verse, and of monolog in particular, as a way of exploring more fully the areas of experience in which he is most interested.

In *Untitled Subjects*, which won the Pulitzer Prize, Howard's art reaches its full maturity. Except for an apostrophe to Wilkie Collins, the poems are dramatic monologs spoken by great Victorians, those closely associated with them, and some lesser-known figures. Robert Browning is very clearly in the author's mind throughout: Howard not only uses a favorite method of Browning's, the dramatic monolog, and sets the monologs in Browning's period, but he also handles the personae of the poems with an irony similar to Browning's. Howard's interest in the processes of the human mind, his learning, his wit, especially suited to the requisite ironies, even his particular concern with language, all fit in well with Victorian diction. The result is poetry that is at the same time anachronistic and totally modern. The book is a brilliant re-creation of the Victorian sensibility. Sharing with the late nineteenth century its passionate devotion to creating "characters," Howard has borrowed one of the most successful means of evoking them. His irony, however, is turned not only on individual speakers, but on the Victorian sensibility itself. And where he is not ironic, he is emphasizing those aspects of that sensibility that either are shared by our own age or have unmistakably developed into our own concerns.

It is difficult to convey through excerpts the sense of Howard's use of language in these poems; for the diction is appropriately chameleon-like, depending on mood or speaker. This passage from Mrs. William Morris's monolog ("1915") is one illustration of Howard's irony:

> You know what his rages were—
> I saw him drive his head against that wall,
> making a dent in the plaster. "With locks,"
> he said, "tinkering with locks, and too late . . ."
> With locks, did he say,
> or clocks? Clocks, I think.

And this passage from "1889," both parody of Browning and allusion to T. S. Eliot's *Waste Land*, typifies his mingling of sensibilities:

> It is a landscape
> out of "Childe Roland," more like Browning's barren
> than anything you have ever seen:
> bare, scored, broiled, scraped, blotched, scalped, flayed,
> flogged & ruined,
> a country calcined, grimy, powdered,
> parboiled, without trees, water, grass—*with* blank
> beastly orange-groves
> and senseless olive-clumps like mad cabbages
> gone indigestible. . . .

There are, of course, limits inherent in Richard Howard's triumph. Readers may suspect that a *tour de force* is less intrinsically valuable than work that requires less obvious virtuosity; they may wish to hear the poet's own voice. It is nonetheless a remarkable achievement.

Selected Bibliography:
By HOWARD:
Quantities. Middletown, Conn.: Wesleyan University Press, 1962.
The Damages. Middletown, Conn.: Wesleyan University Press, 1967.
Alone with America. [Criticism.] New York: Atheneum Publishers, 1969.
Untitled Subjects. New York: Atheneum Publishers, 1969.
Findings. New York: Atheneum Publishers, 1971.

IGNATOW, DAVID   *(b. Brooklyn, N.Y., Feb. 7, 1914—   )*

Beginning his poetic career in what he has called "the William Carlos Williams' school of hard core realism lyrically presented," David Ignatow has become increasingly surrealist in his writing. His essential view of life as tragedy has not materially altered, nor has his conception of poetic form as an extension of content, to be determined by the experience of the poem rather than drawn from preexisting conventions.

Born in Brooklyn, a friend and, for a time, disciple of Williams', David Ignatow became co-editor of the review *Chelsea* in 1968. He has taught or been poet-in-residence at the New School, Vassar, the University of Kentucky, York College of the City University of New York, and in the Master of Fine Arts program at Columbia University.

Frequently, Ignatow's use of surrealism is an attempt to explore the relations between subjective and objective realities. In "The Sky Is Blue" (from *Figures of the Human*), the poet's mother shouts that he should "Put things in their place." He is looking out the window, a toy at his feet.

> . . . The sky is blue
> and empty. In it floats
> the roof across the street.
> What place, I ask her.

The floating roof asserts the supremacy of the perceptual universe over the logically constructed universe. With that supremacy goes the relativity of experience, which is defined as a relation between observer and observed rather than something objectively knowable. Thus the reasonableness of the question "What place."

In other instances, Ignatow's surrealism is made more outrageous by being given objective reality. In "Simultaneously," two telephone poles, five thousand miles apart, simultaneously take off like missiles, exchange places, and begin "sprouting leaves." In part, the poem is governed by simple joy in considering the illogical. It is also, at least obliquely, social commentary, as the airplanes worried by the poles evoke deadly images of atomic war, and the return of the poles to their original identity of trees suggests that they are rebelling against an industrialized world. But the playful aspects of the poem are paradoxically more serious, questioning as they do our complacent certainty of a logical, predictable universe.

Ignatow's primary concern with the world of human relationships is demonstrated by a poem like "Marriage Song" in *Rescue the Dead*. Here again, he calls on surrealist techniques, this time to find a metaphor for a relationship that has become mechanized and painful in spite of itself.

> My role has been the face machine planed,
> slide slot of the lips, eyes sockets for ball bearings,
> and tongue the emery stick of the motor.

The poet sees himself as a cutting edge that inflicts pain. He also sees possibilities, albeit ambiguous ones, in the humanity that persists beneath the dehumanized surface.

. . . We meet here,
and I begin to soften, under a small tear
in your eye.

In the end, all of Ignatow's explorations beyond the limits of conscious, logically structured perceptions are brought to bear on a recognizably human universe.

Selected Bibliography:
BY IGNATOW:
Poems. Prairie City, Illinois: Decker Press, 1948.
The Gentle Weight Lifter. New York: Morris Gallery, 1955.
Say Pardon. Middletown, Conn.: Wesleyan University Press, 1961.
Figures of the Human. Middletown, Conn.: Wesleyan University Press, 1964.
Rescue the Dead. Middletown, Conn.: Wesleyan University Press, 1968.
David Ignatow: Poems 1934–1969. Middletown, Conn.: Wesleyan University Press, 1970.

IMAGISM

The first Imagist manifesto, written by Ezra Pound and F. S. Flint, appeared in Harriet Monroe's *Poetry* magazine in 1913. Flint contributed three basic rules:

1. Direct treatment of the "thing," whether subjective or objective.
2. To use absolutely no word that did not contribute to the presentation.
3. As regarding rhythm: to compose in sequence of the musical phrase, not in sequence of a metronome.

Pound elaborated the implications of these rules and added some famous definitions of his own, most notably:

An "Image" is that which presents an intellectual and emotional complex in an instant of time.

The first Imagist anthology, *Des Imagistes,* was edited by Pound and published in 1914. It included work by Pound, Flint, H. D. (Hilda Doolittle), Richard Aldington, Amy Lowell, and William Carlos Williams.

Although it is clear that Imagism began as a reaction against the excesses of discursive thought and of sentiment in late nineteenth-century British and American poetry, and that Ezra Pound provided the energy to turn theory into a vital poetic school, the precise historical origins of the movement are relatively clouded. T. E. Hulme, who called romanticism "spilt religion," and who insisted upon a return to spare, concrete verse, is generally credited with providing the theoretical background. And in 1909 a group of poets, including Pound, Flint, and Hulme, met in a Soho restaurant in London to discuss what later became Imagist principles. The Eastern *haiku* as well as the ideas of such Western philosophers as Henri Bergson influenced the discussions. However, the poetry of H. D., in addition to Pound's, seems to have been crucial to getting the movement launched, and, in his recent biography of Pound, Noel Stock credits Ford Madox Hueffer (later Ford Madox Ford) with major contributions to Pound's development as theorist.

The movement soon was out of Pound's control. Even before Amy Lowell put out three anthologies, all entitled *Some Imagist Poets* (1915, 1916, 1917), what Pound referred to as "Amygism" had begun. Wishing to dissociate himself from poetry he felt to be verbose and even sentimental, Pound shifted to VORTICISM, which was in one sense simply a broader term including all the arts, of which Imagism was a literary manifestation; but the shift also involved a sharpening of Pound's earlier principles.

The Vorticist journal, *Blast,* ran for two issues (1914 and 1915); but Pound's most important statement on Vorticism was an essay in *Fortnightly Review* in 1914. Here he said:

> The "one image poem" is a form of super-position, that is to say it is one idea set on top of another.

Pound had always insisted that Imagism was not merely descriptive. Here, for the first time, he isolates the notion of *montage,* the real dynamic force in Imagist poetry, the technique that was to be so important to Pound's *Cantos,* and to modern poetry in general.

Almost every important British and American poet of the time went through an Imagist phase—the list includes Pound, T. S. Eliot, William Carlos Williams, Wallace Stevens, D. H. Lawrence—before abandoning it. The form was too limited, effective in conveying momentary experience but incapable of bearing the weight of a comprehensive vision of reality. Imagism's impact on the subsequent course of modern poetry, however, can scarcely be overstated. It placed emphasis on the importance of concrete imagery, on the fragmentary nature of experience. By playing down the importance of abstraction, by pointing out the poetic possibilities inherent in man's relation to the objective universe, Imagism made possible the development of Objectivism and Projectivism, a progression that led to the insistence that poetry is the response to reality not of a disembodied consciousness but of a total organism.

See also OBJECTIVISM, PROJECTIVE VERSE, and the Introduction, section II.

JARRELL, RANDALL (*b. Nashville, Tenn., May 6, 1914— d. Oct. 14, 1965*)

Randall Jarrell grew up into the depression of the thirties and reached full manhood in World War II, but the recognition of loss that haunts so much of his poetry antecedes categories of time and space. The "lost world" that provides the title for Jarrell's last book of poetry is the world of childhood experience, that ambiguous paradise that is at once lost to us forever and continually accessible through the Proustian qualities of art. While in Proust the emphasis is finally on the past recaptured, on the participation in timeless moments that free the self from time, in Jarrell the emphasis is on the idea that all losses are final. That is the source of the pain so evident in his work; it is also, paradoxically, the basis of the vision of human dignity that Jarrell struggles to create in the face of all odds.

Randall Jarrell was educated at Vanderbilt University in the early thirties, when the Southern Agrarian writers were in full prominence. (Their magazine of poetry, *The Fugitive,* had been published in Nashville in the twenties; almost all of the authors of *I'll Take My Stand,* the Fugitive manifesto and collection of essays published in 1930, were at one time or another associated with Vanderbilt.) It is all the more remarkable, then, that in spite of his respect for that group of aristocratic intellectuals and his friendship with Southern regionalist John Crowe Ransom, whom he joined as a member of the Kenyon College faculty in the late thirties, Jarrell remained urban rather than agrarian, egalitarian rather than aristocratic, in his biases.

During the war, Jarrell was briefly a pilot, for the most part a trainer of pilots. Directly from these experiences come the great war poems of *Little Friend, Little Friend* (1945) and *Losses* (1948). These books established his reputation, and from the war until his death in 1965 he led the life of a distinguished poet and critic, lecturing and reading throughout the country, teaching chiefly in Greensboro, at the Woman's College of the University of North Carolina. As poetry critic of *The Nation, Partisan Review,* and *The Yale Review* at various times, he was respected, feared, and somehow loved in that role. Karl Shapiro probably says it best for the poets reviewed by Jarrell: "I felt as if I had been run over but not hurt." Even in the academic world, which is generally cool to criticism written by important poets, except insofar as it provides insight into the poets' own work, Jarrell earned a good deal of respect, most notably for his work on Robert Frost.

Blood for a Stranger (1942) was the first full book of poems published by Randall Jarrell. (*The Rage for the Lost Penny* had appeared in 1940 as part of a five-poet volume published by New Directions.) No poems from that book were reprinted in *Selected Poems* (1955), though one, "Eine kleine Nachtmusik," did find its way into *The Complete Poems* (1969). This early poem anticipated most of the major themes developed in Jarrell's poetry: loss, childhood, the merging of dream and reality, the strong sense of demonic presence in the world of innocence. *Blood for a Stranger* begins the elaboration of these preoccupations.

The significant fact about the vision of childhood in a poem from *Blood for a Stranger,* "Children Selecting Books in a Library," is that it is written with an adult's perspective, with sympathy, but from the outside; the poem does not function as a description of a child's reality but rather as the building of a bridge between man and boy. There is no idealized portrait of childhood: the children's ". . . tales are full of sorcerers and ogres/Because their lives are." The enemy is described as "the capricious infinite," embodied for children in parents, for adults in the nature of the universe. To deal with the terrors of experience, the children "hunt among the shelves" to find ". . . one cure for Everychild's diseases." It first seems as if the children are seeking to escape their realities, but they are, in fact, intensifying them; what they seek is themselves. The adult's escape is more complex, if essentially similar in kind. Jarrell suggests that

> . . . if we find Swann's
> Way better than our own . . .
> . . . .
> . . . it is because we live
>
> By trading another's sorrow for our own . . .

Again the suggestion is of a kind of escapism. If we look closely, however, it becomes clear that the other to whose world we escape is really the self, or rather the former self. "Swann's Way," while representing the world of literature, is more specifically, and more importantly, the door to one's own past. In any case, Jarrell concludes, this "disease" of men and children that causes them to turn to books is shortlived; for the disease is linked to the individual self, and may even be identified with the self. In that case, there is ". . . the great/CHANGE," leading us from one self to the next, obliterating the cares of previous worlds. The disease is, then, a cure, but only in the sense that death itself is a final cure. The poem in this way begins to turn in on itself: change, which leads to the dissolution of the self, also peoples the world with infinite selves, to whom the individual may ultimately return for solace. The circular movement is suggested by the imagery as well. The poem begins with a mural in which gray-eyed "Care" whispers to the baby hero "Words of a doom . . . blanched . . . with dew," and ends with "dewy-eyed" change. What begins as straightforward argument resolves itself only in paradox.

Formally, "Children Selecting Books in a Library" is typical of the craft Jarrell was to exercise throughout his career; it also illustrates the limitations of his methods that have qualified his acceptance as a major poet of his time. The poem is written in six-line stanzas of reasonably regular iambic pentameter, unrhymed, though with at least the ghost of rhyme in each of the six stanzas. The rhythm tends toward the prosaic, the conversational. While the poem is hardly without concrete imagery, there is a predominance of abstract statement not often found in contemporary poetry; even the imagery is for the most part descriptive, in the service of ideas, rather than being at the actual core of the poem. Here is where the problems arise. Can a relatively flat rhythm and diction that is sharp and precise rather than densely suggestive bear the weight of a vision as complex as Jarrell's? Without a voice as distinctive and yet flexible as, say, Frost's, the difficulties are great. The evidence is that Jarrell is most successful when his concrete vision is so extraordinarily powerful as to be able to recharge his abstractions with the energy of the source from which they are drawn.

The most famous poem of *Little Friend, Little Friend* (1945), probably the most widely anthologized of Jarrell's work, is a precise illustration of this point. "The Death of the Ball Turret Gunner" is only five lines in length, in itself remarkable when compared with the longish poems Jarrell generally wrote. Even so, it contains more concrete imagery than pieces many times its size, most spectacularly the vision of the gunner hunched in the plane's belly until his "wet fur froze," and the well-known last line: "When I died they washed me out of the turret with a hose." The situation itself is an affecting one; a simple statement of fact is enough to overwhelm the reader, in very much the way a good battle-field photograph does. The deeper emotional resources of the poem, however, are less dependent upon external event, more a function of Jarrell's familiar approach to experience. The turret becomes the womb; death, a release from that womb, becomes a type of birth. The sudden terrifying fall from womb to nightmare reality is also a telescoped vision of the fall from a childhood sense of eternity to an adult awareness of time and death. What is finally most significant about Jarrell's war poems is that they encounter war not as a perversion of the human condition, but, unfortunately, as a clarification.

In *Poet's Choice*, edited by Paul Engle and Joseph Langland, Jarrell wrote, " 'Eighth Air Force' expresses better than any of the other poems I wrote about the war what I felt about the war." However, it is no surprise to discover that the poem, which appeared in *Losses* (1948), expresses not a clear-cut judgment, but rather Jarrell's usual ambivalence and sense of paradox.

"Eighth Air Force" is set in the pilots' barracks; they are between missions. Three play Pitch, one lies there counting missions (Jarrell's note in *Selected Poems* tells us that this pilot has one more mission to fly). The identity of the speaker is not clear: he may be an outside observer, another pilot in the room, or the pilot lying awake counting missions—or there may be a shift of voice in the middle of the poem, in which case the shift is almost certainly to the pilot lying awake. Most likely of all, the speaker may be a former pilot who has already flown his last mission. In any case, the ambiguity does not obscure the poem's vision. The poet is fighting out within himself the conflict between the ideal of a just war and the inevitable logic of the proposition that a man who kills other men is a murderer. The poem's essential question is: ". . . shall I say that man / Is not as men have said: a wolf to man?" Searching for a justification, the poem's persona —and whoever he is, he shares the pilots' sense of guilt—compares the bombing of the cities of the Continent from British bases to the Passion of Christ. Again, the terms of the comparison are not explicitly worked out.

Jarrell's own note in *Selected Poems* seems to suggest that the pilots, modern "criminals and scapegoats," are being compared to Christ, "that earlier criminal and scapegoat about whom the Gospels were written." We do not need Jarrell's comment to see that this comparison is relevant. It is equally clear other roles from the Passion are being enacted by the pilots. Not only are they identified with Christ, and even with God (they are divided into three and one, and the one pilot with one mission left repeats

"One" three times, all of which suggests the Trinity), but they are obviously Christ's murderers as well. The three pilots play Pitch, a card game, but dice are suggested by the word, and these pilots seem analogous to the soldiers who pitched dice for Christ's robe. And, as Cleanth Brooks has pointed out in *Randall Jarrell: 1914–1965*, the persona speaks not only as Christ, but as Pilate (they are, after all, pilots), and even Pilate's wife, in the poem's last two stanzas.

Brooks has also seized upon the ambiguities of the concluding lines:

> Men wash their hands, in blood, as best they can:
> I find no fault in this just man.

Many readings are possible, but they all come to the same crux: are the murders justifiable, is man essentially good or an uncontrollable monster? It must be that both alternatives are true, although they seem to be mutually exclusive. The rhetoric itself, the confusions of role and perspective, embody meaning as surely as paraphrasable content. The poem's structure is elevated to symbol and provides an intensity that the central metaphor alone could not have created.

Another piece from *Losses* demonstrates that the child's world of innocence and terror has not become for Jarrell simply a vehicle for war poetry. In "The Märchen," the forests ubiquitous in Grimm's Tales become ". . . the Necessity/Men spring from, die under: the unbroken wood." What we learn from the tales is the need to escape from this necessity, that is, the need "to change, to change!" The magic of the fairy-tale world is thus identified with the human will to change. The suggestion is that the child lives with a sense of infinite possibility—in itself both terrifying and comforting—which is muted by adulthood. (Again it is a question of recapturing past sensibilities in order to survive in the present.) Jarrell himself, writing ostensibly about Robert Lowell's poetry in an essay in *Poetry and the Age* but like most poet-critics revealing even more about himself, provides the best gloss on the contrast between necessity and change:

> The poems understand the world as a sort of conflict of opposites. In this struggle one opposite is that cake of custom in which all of us lie embedded like lungfish—the stasis or inertia of the stubborn self, the obstinate persistence in evil that is damnation. Into this realm of necessity the poems push everything that is closed, turned inward, incestuous, that blinds or binds. . . . But struggling within this like leaven, falling to it like light, is everything that is free or open, that grows or is willing to change: here is the generosity or openness or willingness that is itself salvation; here is the "accessibility to experience"; this is the realm of freedom, of the Grace that has replaced the Law, of the perfect liberator whom the poet calls Christ.
>
> ("From the Kingdom of Necessity")

If we exchange Lowell's Christian framework for Jarrell's childhood world, we have a description of "The Märchen" and of much of Jarrell's other poetry.

The Seven-League Crutches (1951), as the title itself indicates, represents a fuller commitment to the worlds of dream and fantasy. To examine the kind and quality of Jarrell's verse at this stage of his career, we can do no better than to look at "A Girl in a Library," which Robert Lowell called the best poem in the book, and which Jarrell himself honored by placing it first in his *Selected Poems*. The poem takes the form of an internal monolog, that quasi-dramatic form that Jarrell used more and more as his art developed. The persona is in a school library, his thoughts drawn chiefly to a sleeping girl and, by way of contrast, to a more sophisticated woman. The girl is a major in physical education and home economics. She is apparently devoid of intelligence or any sense of culture, and the narrator's descriptions of her are generally condescending: ". . . One sees in your blurred eyes/The 'uneasy half-soul' Kipling saw in dogs'." The woman, Tatyana, seems to share his superiority to mindlessness and innocence; and yet, both Tatyana and the narrator are aware of a sense in which the sleeping girl is more fully alive than they are. The narrator is more firmly convinced of this, and certainly more explicit; the girl's "sturdy form" is sometimes ". . . modulated/Into a form of joy, a Lydian mode." With all her innocence of the possibilities of conscious human experience, she has maintained her contact with the child's intuitions about the nature of reality; as in a collective unconscious, mythic memory is embedded deep within her mind.

> . . . and I have seen
> Firm, fixed forever in your closing eyes,
> The Corn King beckoning to his Spring Queen.

Nonetheless, it would be a mistake to suggest that contempt is transformed into unreserved admiration or envy. To say that childhood or the unconscious holds perceptions of reality that ought to be unlocked to us is not to say that one should remain a child forever or that the conscious intelligence has no place in human experience. It is the tension between adulthood and childhood, between conscious and unconscious, that forms the basis of Jarrell's poetry, not the commitment to one world or another.

Randall Jarrell's first new book of poems after *The Seven-League Crutches* was *The Woman at the Washington Zoo* (1960). The title poem of that volume stands or falls with its central metaphor, which sometimes seems totally convincing, sometimes a heavy-handed contrivance. The poem is a kind of elaboration of Yeats's cry that he was "fastened to a dying animal." The woman, an employee in a government department, sees herself trapped by her own aging body; she is trapped the way animals in a zoo are trapped, except that she is her own cage and aware of the process of aging while animals are not. The poem ends with the woman's plea: "change me, change me!" It seems a clear echo of "The Märchen," in which the lesson of the tales was "to change, to change!" Change is again ambiguously understood, a principle of time, decay, and death, but also a principle of renewal, of rebirth.

An even more significant comparison can be made between "The Woman at the Washington Zoo" and "A Girl in a Library," which are ideal companion pieces. The girl is in the library, surrounded by dreams; the woman is in the zoo, surrounded by animal bodies. The girl is innocent of the terrors of reality; the more experienced, more aware, more intelligent woman has run the gamut of horrors from dullness and loneliness to aging and death. The girl cannot let spirit enter, while the woman cannot escape her flesh. Both poems are blank-verse monologs, but while the woman can reveal her own mind, the poet does not trust the girl's resources of language and insight and must speak for her. In this sense the poems represent respectively subjective and objective approaches to experience. At all times, however, with all the apparently absolute contrasts between the poems, it is perfectly evident that the reality being described by each poem is the same. The only change is of perspective. The woman at the zoo is for the most part more sympathetically drawn and seems a more admirable character. Yet her failure is as complete as the girl's; it is, after all, the vulture she calls upon to change her, emphasizing the negative side of that ambiguous verb. Jarrell is after what is almost impossible to obtain: that unity of being in which girl and woman, library and zoo, dream and reality, are brought together. Like Blake, like Yeats, like Rilke (whose poetry Jarrell has translated), Jarrell seeks that place where all contraries meet.

The last poem in Jarrell's last book of poetry, *The Lost World* (1965), is entitled "Thinking of the Lost World." It is a kind of summary of the poet's explorations of the relationship between past and present worlds. The poem's beginning is so Proustian that it is nothing short of parody. Jarrell takes a spoonful of chocolate tapioca instead of the madeleine dipped in tea in Proust's novel, but the result is the same, a journey through time to childhood. Jarrell, however, is struck by a perception that is only obliquely related to Proust's vision: he is puzzled to discover that age is so similar to childhood, to learn that life ultimately turns in on itself and ends where it started: ". . . our end copies/Its beginning." Memories and fairy tales are mixed in the attempt to recapture the past. But the success of this endeavor is expressed at last in decidedly equivocal terms; the past is difficult to grasp firmly:

> . . . my emptiness is traded for its emptiness,
> . . . .
> I hold in my own hands, in happiness,
> Nothing: the nothing for which there's no reward.

In one sense, this means that nothing has been found because nothing has been lost; the past is always present. But the exchange is described in largely negative terms. The self is transient; if we are seeking permanence then indeed we have nothing. It is only in the acceptance of the fluidity of the self, of the double-edged knife of change, of the nothingness itself that we can find "happiness."

See also the Introduction, section IX.

Selected Bibliography:
BY JARRELL:
The Rage for the Lost Penny (in *Five Young American Poets*). New York: New
    Directions Publishing Corp., 1940.
Blood for a Stranger. New York: Harcourt Brace Jovanovich, 1942.
Little Friend, Little Friend. New York: Dial Press, 1945.
Losses. New York: Harcourt Brace Jovanovich, 1948.
The Seven-League Crutches. New York: Harcourt Brace Jovanovich, 1951.
Poetry and the Age. [Criticism.] New York: Alfred A. Knopf, 1953.
Pictures from an Institution. [Novel.] New York: Alfred A. Knopf, 1954.
Selected Poems. New York: Alfred A. Knopf, 1955.
The Woman at the Washington Zoo: Poems and Translations. New York: Athe-
    neum Publishers, 1960.
A Sad Heart at the Supermarket. [Criticism.] New York: Atheneum Publishers,
    1962.
The Lost World. New York: Macmillan Co., 1965.
The Complete Poems. New York: Farrar, Straus & Giroux, 1969.
The Third Book of Criticism. New York: Farrar, Straus & Giroux, 1969.

About Jarrell:
Adams, Charles M. *Randall Jarrell: A Bibliography.* Chapel Hill: University of
    North Carolina Press, 1958.
Lowell, Robert; Peter Taylor; and Robert Penn Warren, eds. *Randall Jarrell:
    1914–1965.* New York: Farrar, Straus & Giroux, 1967. (Includes essays by
    Cleanth Brooks, Denis Donoghue, Sister M. Bernetta Quinn, and Karl Sha-
    piro.)
Rideout, Walter B. " 'To Change, to Change!': The Poetry of Randall Jarrell." In
    Poets in Progress. Edited by Edward Hungerford. Evanston, Ill.: Northwest-
    ern University Press, 1967. Pp. 156–78.
Stepanchev, Stephen. "Randall Jarrell." In *American Poetry since 1945.* New
    York: Harper & Row Publishers, 1965. Pp. 37–52.

JONES, LEROI   See *Baraka, Imamu Amiri.*

JONG, ERICA   (*b. New York City, Mar. 26, 1942—   *)

The poetry of Erica Jong's first book, *Fruits & Vegetables* (1971), is largely
erotic. But in addition to being erotic in the ordinary sense—which it most
emphatically is—its eroticism constitutes a theory of poetry. In one of the
book's epigraphs, Jong quotes Norman O. Brown: "Poetry, the creative act,
the archetypal sexual act. Sexuality is poetry." She carries this notion to its
conclusion in "Arse Poetica," section III of which is a marriage manual parody, in which the poet is the woman, the muse the man: "The poet sits up-
right & raises & lowers her body rhythmically until the last line is attained."
    Closely related to the sexual metaphors in the book—in fact part of them

—is eating. Eating pervades the book: the eating of fruits and vegetables, sexual eating; "The Teacher" actually concludes: "Eat this poem." Again, a Brown epigraph provides the key: "We must eat again of the tree of knowledge in order to fall into innocence." Eating is the ultimate act of union. Man, in his fall from harmony with nature, must consume it in order to be reunited. He must affirm his bodily as well as his cerebral existence. And the poet is in the vanguard of human consciousness: the writing of the poem is a sexual act, it is the act of eating.

> Far off, galaxies glitter like currants.
> The whole edible universe drops
> to his watering mouth . . .

> (from "Fruits & Vegetables")

The techniques of Erica Jong's poetry emerge quite logically from her vision of what poetry is. The surrealism that characterizes her verse is simply a denial of boundaries between subjectivity and objectivity, between the unconscious and the conscious. And it appears in poems with other than explicitly sexual themes, as in "His Silence":

> He still wears the glass skin of childhood.
> Under his hands, the stones turn mirrors.
> His eyes are knives.

Although *Fruits & Vegetables* contains some fine non-sexual poems, the sexual poetry dominates the book. Another aspect of the sexual theme is the reversal of the traditional sexes of poet and muse in section III of "Arse Poetica." At the same time an important dimension of Erica Jong's assertion of her sexuality is her affirmation of her identity as a woman. The strongest expression of this occurs in "Bitter Pills for the Dark Ladies," a serious parody of the new black poetry. The poem takes off from a remark made by Robert Lowell about Sylvia Plath: ". . . hardly a person at all, or a woman, certainly not another 'poetess,' but . . ." The poem concludes:

> . . . the ultimate praise is always a question of nots:
> > viz. not like a woman
> > viz. "certainly not another 'poetess' "

> meanin'

> > she's got a cunt but she don't talk funny
> > & he's a nigger but he don't smell funny

> & the only good poetess is a dead.

Ultimately, the entire book is directed against the arbitrary categories that separate us from nature, from other human beings, from ourselves.

Selected Bibliography:
BY JONG:
Fruits & Vegetables. New York: Holt, Rinehart & Winston, 1971.

KEES, WELDON   (*b. Beatrice, Neb., 1914—d. July 18, 1955?*)

Weldon Kees's poetry is truly naked poetry; it is a test of the power of art, unsupported by affirmative ideology, to confront the agonies of human existence. While all good contemporary poets confront the pain and loneliness of human experience, their visions are less bleak than Kees's; they balance anguish with joy, they purge their despair in ritual frenzy, or they shift to a perspective that reveals man's isolation to be an illusion based on the inability to perceive the essential oneness of being. Kees does none of these things, nor does he provide the humor that makes endurable the totally pointless world of a writer like Samuel Beckett. The only thing standing between Kees's vision of reality and absolute nihilism is the poetry itself, the fact that it exists.

Born in Nebraska, Weldon Kees spent most of his youth in New York City. He was not only a poet, but an Abstract Expressionist painter, a film maker, and a jazz pianist as well. He moved to San Francisco in 1951, and in 1955 he disappeared, leaving his car parked near the Golden Gate Bridge. It is assumed that he jumped from the bridge, but since he had talked both of committing suicide and of going to live in Europe under an assumed name, it is not absolutely certain.

Kees's initial perspective is clearly expressed in "Crime Club." A murder has been committed; there are only absurd clues. The entire situation is grotesque. The case remains unsolved. The detective has gone insane and is confined to a room where he sits,

> Screaming that all the world is mad, that clues
> Lead nowhere, or to walls so high their tops cannot be seen;
> Screaming all day of war, screaming that nothing can be solved.

Life is seen as a meaningless journey toward death. The possibilities of enduring it with dignity are severely limited. Kees's response to this view of reality is at times compassionate, at times bitterly cynical. An example of the latter tone is "For My Daughter" (possibly a mocking allusion to Yeats's "A Prayer for My Daughter"). He sees beneath his daughter's innocent flesh "hintings of death she does not heed." He sees "parched years," a "foul, lingering death." The poem ends:

> Or, fed on hate, she relishes the sting
> Of others' agony; perhaps the cruel
> Bride of a syphilitic or a fool.
> These speculations sour in the sun.
> I have no daughter. I desire none.

The poem succeeds because the trick ending does not reverse the mood but rather intensifies it by revealing the extravagance of the poem's pessimism.

Kees's poems about Robinson sound a more compassionate note, but this seems the result of a shift of point of view rather than a basic change in attitude. Robinson is a sad and lonely man:

> All day the phone rings. It could be Robinson
> Calling. It never rings when he is here.

> (from "Robinson")

In "Aspects of Robinson," he appears drunk and afraid, his heart "dry as a winter leaf." He goes through his meaningless routines; even in bars there is no relief. There are clear echoes of Edwin Arlington Robinson in these poems, recalling that poet's days in New York, struggling with loneliness and alcohol. But Kees's Robinson is a more universal figure. In "Robinson at Home," Robinson says in his sleep,

> "There is something in this madhouse that I symbolize—
> This city—nightmare—black—"

Equally important, Robinson is Kees's double. In "Relating to Robinson," the poet seems to encounter Robinson on the street.

> There was no chance. Just as I passed,
> Turning my head to search his face,
> His own head turned with mine
> And fixed me with dilated, terrifying eyes
> That stopped my blood. His voice
> Came at me like an echo in the dark.

The Robinson poems engender a curious struggle in the reader. He would like to isolate Robinson, to be convinced that Robinson is the totally other rather than a version of the self. The reader wishes to be certain that Robinson's case is pathological rather than existential. Robinson, however, with Kees's careful assistance, fights back by continually turning toward the reader, making him recognize an echo of himself.

Kees's poetic powers extend well beyond the direct statement of "For My Daughter" and the skillful characterization of the Robinson poems. Although his use of free verse, as well as iambic lines, is not spectacular, close examination reveals how carefully wrought his lines are. He is especially successful at breaking the flow of a breath-unit, introducing generally ominous pauses. Kees is similarly expert in his use of imagery, which is for the most part realistic, almost naturalistic, but handled in such a way as to make it nearly surreal, with all the power of what Robert Kelly later called the "deep image." "The Coming of the Plague," for example, concludes:

> And one day in a field I saw
> A swarm of frogs, swollen and hideous,
> Hundreds upon hundreds, sitting on each other,

Huddled together, silent, ominous,
And heard the sound of rushing wind.

In a first reading of Weldon Kees's poetry, the sense of horror and emptiness overshadows the poems' formal beauty. Gradually the formal beauty, a terrible beauty to be sure, begins to grow in importance. What results is not exactly hope, but it is not exactly despair either. The capacity to name one's terror, if it does not guarantee the ability to master it, is still an act implying dignity. The balance between beauty and terror is nowhere more evident than in the opening lines of "January":

Morning: blue, cold, and still.
Eyes that have stared too long
Stare at the wedge of light
At the end of the frozen room
Where snow on a windowsill,
Packed and cold as life,
Winters the sense of wrong
And emptiness and loss
That is my awakening.

The poet's pain is starkly present. The writing of a poem to communicate that pain, however, is a kind of victory, a victory over emptiness and loss, a victory over isolation. The probable outcome of Kees's own life indicates that his victories may have been temporary. But it is not at all obvious that any other kind of victory is possible.

It is inaccurate to say that Weldon Kees is an underrated poet, for though relatively few know his work, those that do value it highly. He is certainly the most underread poet of his generation.

Selected Bibliography:
By KEES:
The Last Man. San Francisco: Colt Press, 1943.
The Fall of the Magicians. New York: Reynal & Hitchcock (Harcourt Brace Jovanovich), 1947.
Poems 1947–1954. San Francisco: (privately printed), 1954.
The Collected Poems of Weldon Kees. Edited by Donald Justice. Lincoln, Neb.: University of Nebraska Press, 1962.

KELLY, ROBERT (b. Brooklyn, N.Y., Sept. 24, 1935—   )

Robert Kelly's original allegiance was to the Projectivist school of poets, to its experimentation with open form and its search for rhythms rooted in man's existence as a creature in nature. Fearing the possibility of becoming involved with technique for technique's sake, however, he has sought to "substitute the centrality of image for the centrality of syllable and line." With Jerome Rothenberg, with whom the phrase *deep image* originates, he has defined poetry as "the juncture of the experienced with the never experienced . . . the fulfillment of the imagined and the unimagined" ("Notes on the Poetry of the Deep Image," *Trobar 2*, 1961).

Kelly is a graduate of the City College of New York (1955). He studied medieval literature at Columbia and later founded no less than three literary magazines: *Trobar, Chelsea,* and *Matter.* He has taught at Wagner College, the State University of New York at Buffalo, and Bard College.

Kelly himself has suggested that his aesthetics have never been more clearly stated than in the "Prefix" to *Finding the Measure* (1968). Finding the measure, that is, the essential rhythm of the poem, "is finding the moon," "is finding/the natural articulation of ideas." The poem is a natural combination of the organisms of the macrocosm, of language, of the self. "Style is death. Finding the measure is finding/a freedom from that death." The rhythm of the poem, then, must emerge from a sense of man's affinity with the natural world, his sympathy with the objective universe. But it must also find its sources deep within the human psyche, in the world of dream and myth. Above all, it must not be a logically imposed system ("style"), legitimized by the conscious intellect. As Stanley Burnshaw points out in *The Seamless Web* (1970), poetry is the expression not simply of consciousness but of the entire human organism.

"Sun of the Center," from *Armed Descent* (1961), is less explicitly didactic, and therefore more characteristic of Kelly's methods. In a more imagistic way, it arrives at the same point.

> the shape of a man proceeds from all sides to center
> and he is the star whose body is called movement
> and in his hands the sun puts out branches
> leaves and petals break out of silver
> the corn is eaten, the animal howls, the sun flowers.

The surreal qualities link these lines to the unconscious as surely as they link man to the natural universe; the unconscious, alien to the ego, is part of that natural universe. These lines also clearly support Kelly's pronouncement in "Notes on the Poetry of the Deep Image": "The fundamental rhythm of the poem is the rhythm of the images; their textures, their contents, offer supplementary rhythms."

Of special interest in Kelly's more recent poetry is his attempt to ground his rhythms in myth and ritual, asserting again the connection between the archetypal unconscious and primal biological patterns. In "The Moon Closes," from *Twenty Poems* (1967), he writes:

> The moon closes
> down on us . she rises
> she enters her mansions & undoes our clothes
>
> (Ishtar at the gates
> relinquishing form).

The only need
is ritual. . . .
See also DEEP IMAGISM and the Introduction, section VIII.

Selected Bibliography:
BY KELLY:
Armed Descent. New York: Hawk's Well Press, 1961.
Her Body against Time. Mexico City: El Corno Emplumado, 1963.
Round Dances. New York: Trobar Books, 1964.
Lunes. New York: Hawk's Well Press, 1965.
Lectiones. Placitas, New Mexico: Duende, 1965.
Devotions. Annandale-on-Hudson, New York: Salitter, 1967.
Axon Dendron Tree. Annandale-on-Hudson, New York: Salitter, 1967.
Twenty Poems. New York: Matter Books, 1967.
H: D: A Joining. Los Angeles: Black Sparrow Press, 1967.
Finding the Measure. Los Angeles: Black Sparrow Press, 1968.
Sonnets 1967. Los Angeles: Black Sparrow Press, 1968.
Songs I-XXX. Cambridge, Massachusetts: Pym-Randall Press, 1969.
The Common Shore, Books I-V. Los Angeles: Black Sparrow Press, 1969.
Kali Yuga. London: Cape Goliard Press, 1970.

KINNELL, GALWAY (*b. Providence, R.I., Feb. 1, 1927—*   )

Galway Kinnell grew up during the Depression, reaching adulthood at the end of World War II, and, whether as a consequence or by coincidence, there is a grimness in his poetry appropriate to that historical background. There are visions of teeming city life informed by intermittent glimpses of the holocaust, visions of nature that do not provide refuge but are rather settings for man's brutalization. Even Kinnell's quieter moments tend to be meditations on time and death. But there is also a toughness in his work, which suggests that man can endure and conceivably, though not demonstrably, prevail.

Born in Providence, Galway Kinnell was raised in Pawtucket, Rhode Island. He received his bachelor's degree from Princeton in 1948, his master's degree from the University of Rochester in 1949. In the early fifties he taught at the Downtown Center of the University of Chicago. He traveled in France, taught in Teheran, and was involved in the civil rights movement in the sixties. He has been poet-in-residence at Reed College, at the universities of Washington, California at Irvine, Iowa, and at Queens College.

"The Avenue Bearing the Initial of Christ into the New World," which appeared in his first collection, *What a Kingdom It Was* (1960), is still one of Kinnell's most impressive poems. The long poem—it has fourteen sections —begins by establishing its setting, Avenue C in New York City. Kinnell, characteristically, works through concrete detail. There are descriptions of

people and places, Whitmanesque catalogs, like that of the store-window
signs in section 3. The street is inhabited chiefly by Jews, Puerto Ricans,
and Negroes. They are poor. The few brief, individualized portraits depict
sad lives. There is nonetheless a sense of life, a kind of abundance. But it is
a decayed abundance. Even the descriptions of the vegetables at the push-
cart market in section 6 are disturbing. There are dirty beets, "Cabbages
lying about like sea-green brains / The skulls have been shucked from." The
vegetables are pictured as ". . . uprooted, / Maimed, lopped, shucked, and
misaimed." As a crone comes to buy a pickle, we realize that these adjectives apply equally to the inhabitants of the street.

In section 7, the poem moves toward its literal and thematic center. An
"ancient Negro sits as usual / Outside the Happy Days Bar & Grill," singing
a spiritual. Suddenly Kinnell shifts to a new catalog, parallel in structure to
the ones that have preceded it, but terribly different in tone.

> Gross-Rosen, Maidanek, Flössenberg, Ravensbruck, Stutthof, Riga,
> Bergen-Belsen, Mauthausen, Birkenau, Treblinka, Natzweiler,
> Dachau, Buchenwald, Auschwitz—
>   Villages,
> Pasture-bordered hamlets on the far side of the river.

The annihilation of the Jews in these places becomes an indictment of God.
God has broken the promise. He has broken it too easily for the generation
of the victims or their children, many of them on Avenue C, to care.

Past and present are united in section 9. Children are setting fires in ash
cans. Then comes an image that the reader hopes—without a great deal of
confidence—is surreal: a child is burning in the flames. It is Isaac. "It was
not the plan." God washes his hands of the matter. Kinnell, however, does
not turn away, but broods on it. Considering the alternatives, perhaps death,
"Sane and Sacred Death," is not unacceptable. The next section concerns a
fire in Gold's junkhouse (God's junkhouse?). The avenue contains within itself the holocaust. And the avenue is not a sociological study of a particular
time and place but a general image of human life.

Some of the poem's most powerful imagery describes the fish market, in
section 11:

> Fishes do not die exactly, it is more
> That they go out of themselves, the visible part
> Remains the same, there is little pallor,
> Only the cataracted eyes which have not shut ever
> Must look through the mist which crazed Homer.

Because of the poem's title, the reader suspects the fish are a symbol of
Christ. This is soon confirmed, as the Jewish fishmonger, who "stands like
Christ," nails the fish to wood:

> . . . He lops off the heads,
> Shakes out the guts as if they did not belong in the first place,
> And they are flesh for the first time in their lives.

This is followed immediately by a form letter—with dashes for the names and dates—used to notify the wife of a concentration camp victim that her husband is dead. The effect of the juxtaposition is complex. Victim is also victimizer, Christ is a Jew and is killed by the Jews, death is both terrible and releasing. With all these undercurrents, these ambiguities, one dominant sensation, that of horror, emerges.

The poem moves to its conclusion as the imagery accumulates: in section 12 a baby crying in its crib "As if it could foresee everything"; the trucks collecting garbage. Finally, in section 14, the avenue is characterized as a place

> Where instants of transcendence
> Drift in oceans of loathing and fear, like lanternfishes,
> Or phosphorus flashings in the sea, or the feverish light
> Skin is said to give off when the swimmer drowns at night.

In darkness, there is light, in death birth, in fire and blood purification; the Jew Christ (here obliquely present as the lanternfish) is crucified and resurrected. On a symbolic level, the poem is beautifully resolved, though the poem's naturalistic detail threatens to overwhelm its symbolism. And the affirmation of human possibilities is qualified by the terrible mystery in which it is immersed.

In natural settings, when Kinnell is not caught up in the fierce struggles of man in nature (as in "The Wolves"), he is aware of their underlying harmony. In "Cells Breathe in the Emptiness," from *Flower Herding on Mount Monadnock* (1964), Kinnell contemplates the death of plants. He ends by questioning the distinction between plants and animals, between the animate and inanimate world:

> How many plants are really very quiet animals?
> How many inert molecules are ready to break into life?

From this perspective, death is illusory; it is merely metamorphosis from one state of being into another.

While this view may be perfectly satisfying to the detached observer—to one viewing all of creation as a whole—it is inadequate for man insofar as he is conscious of his separateness from the rest of creation, insofar as he tries to give shape and meaning to his own individual experience. Of this, Kinnell is very much aware. "Another Night in the Ruins," from *Body Rags* (1968), is a meditation on man's relation to eternity, which Kinnell perceives finally as nothingness. The last stanza alludes to the myth of the phoenix:

> How many nights must it take
> one such as me to learn
> that we aren't, after all, made
> from that bird which flies out of its ashes,
> that for a man
> as he goes up in flames, his one work

is
to open himself, to *be*
the flames?

Purification by fire has appeared often in Kinnell's work. In "Another Night in the Ruins" salvation is not a consequence of being consumed by fire; it is the process of being consumed. What Kinnell is suggesting is similar to Camus' interpretation of the Greek myth of Sisyphus: since Sisyphus' rock will always roll down the hill again, he can find his triumph not in any tangible accomplishment but in the struggle itself.

"The Bear" (also from *Body Rags*) welds together the themes of man's oneness with nature and the terrors of experience. The hunter, possibly a shaman, sets a trap that wounds the bear internally, hunts it down (in the process becoming as much a part of nature as the bear), kills it, and eats it. He has become one with his enemy during the hunt, and a dream in which he is the hunted bear confirms this identity. The hunt and union with the hunted is a rite of initiation, of metamorphosis, of rebirth. In order to perform the rite successfully, the man must penetrate to the very core of his existence. Yet he emerges from the experience not with certainty, but with inspired doubt. For Galway Kinnell the hunter's way of knowing the world is essentially the same as the poet's. The poem ends with its hero

. . . wondering
what, anyway,
was that sticky infusion, that rank flavor of blood, that poetry, by which I
    lived?

Selected Bibliography:
By KINNELL:
What a Kingdom It Was. Boston: Houghton Mifflin Co., 1960.
Flower Herding on Mount Monadnock. Boston: Houghton Mifflin Co., 1964.
The Poems of François Villon. [Translation.] New York: New American Library,
    1965.
Black Light. [Novel.] Boston: Houghton Mifflin Co., 1966.
Body Rags. Boston: Houghton Mifflin Co., 1968.
The Book of Nightmares. Boston: Houghton Mifflin Co., 1971.

About Kinnell:
Howard, Richard. *Alone with America.* New York: Atheneum Publishers, 1969.
    Pp. 258–71.

KIZER, CAROLYN (*b. Spokane, Wash., 1925—   *)

A responsiveness to concrete reality, a fine sense of irony when dealing with the social world, a mastery of both free and traditional rhythms: these characterize the poetic art of Carolyn Kizer. Born in the Pacific Northwest, the physical features of which are often recorded in her poetry, Kizer is a graduate of Sarah Lawrence College and a fellow of Columbia University. In Seattle she founded and edited *Poetry Northwest,* and she has been director of the literature program for the National Endowment for the Arts in Washington, D.C.

"The Great Blue Heron," from *The Ungrateful Garden* (1961), is one of Kizer's best-known poems. The poet, walking along the beach, sees a heron

> . . . standing
> Sunk in the tattered wings
> He wore as a hunchback's coat.
> Shadow without a shadow,
> Hung on invisible wires
> From the top of a canvas day,
> What scissors cut him out?

The sharpness of the imagery may bring to mind Eastern poetry, in which Kizer has been very interested, but this poem is not a *haiku*. The heron takes on a symbolic value that goes far beyond the immediate impact of the image. The "Shadow without a shadow" anticipates the "spectral bird" of the next stanza; the "hunchback's coat" anticipates a comparison of the heron's wings to "broken arms." Even the scissors take on almost sinister overtones of higher powers creating the scene, dictating events.

Seeing this bird takes the poet back fifteen summers, when, as a child, she had seen a blue heron and asked, "whose ghost are you?" She had called to her mother to see it and realized, "My mother knew what he was." Now as she sees the heron again, it is as if he had been there the whole time, waiting for the day

> When, like grey smoke, a vapor
> Floating into the sky,
> A handful of paper ashes,
> My mother would drift away.

Was the heron the mother's ghost? Was it death? In any case, it was her own death that the mother had seen. The poem implies connections and correspondences between material and spiritual realities. And its effectiveness depends upon its carefully orchestrated rhythm of images, for although the images are drawn from the objective world, they function very much in the subjective mode of DEEP IMAGISM. There are similar effects throughout Kizer's poetry, for example, in "A Widow in Wintertime," in which the sound of a cat making love becomes the sound of a baby gargling ". . . in the throes / Of a fatal spasm."

"From *Pro Femina,*" in *Knock upon Silence* (1965), illustrates Carolyn Kizer's ironic style. Appropriately composed in the hexameters of Roman satire, the poem attacks women as well as men who have conspired, through the establishment of arbitrary categories of behavior, to deprive both women and men of their full existence. In "Three" she writes:

But we'll always have traitors who swear that a woman surrenders
Her Supreme Function, by equating Art with aggression
And failure with Feminity. Still, it's just as unfair
To equate Art with Feminity, like a prettily-packaged commodity
When we are custodians of the world's best-kept secret:
Merely the private lives of one-half of humanity.

Selected Bibliography:
By Kizer:
The Ungrateful Garden. Bloomington: Indiana University Press, 1961.
Knock upon Silence. New York: Doubleday & Co., 1965.
Midnight Was My Cry: New and Selected Poems. New York: Doubleday & Co.,
     1971.

About Kizer:
Howard, Richard. *Alone with America.* New York: Atheneum Publishers, 1969.
     Pp. 272–80.

KNOTT, WILLIAM   (b. Gratiot County, Mich., Feb. 17, 1940—   )

Paul Carroll, in his foreword to William Knott's first book, *The Naomi
Poems, Book One: Corpse and Beans* (1968), tells of a letter

> allegedly written by a friend of the poet [that] stated that Bill Knott
> had committed suicide at 26 in his room in a tenement on North
> Clark Street in Chicago and that his body was on its way back to his
> native Michigan for burial. The letter went on to claim that Knott
> had killed himself because he was an orphan and virgin and that he
> couldn't endure any longer without being loved by somebody.

In one sense, the letter is Knott's announcement that with the death of his
relationship with Naomi, he ceased to live in any meaningful way and
found himself in a world that was not only now devoid of love, but always
had been. In another, however, it is a hint of the sensuous reality death assumes in Knott's verse. While his poetry is essentially a poetry of negation,
the negation is positively realized. Of two poems entitled "Death," for example, one goes like this:

> Going to sleep, I cross my hands on my chest.
> They will place my hands like this.
> It will look as though I am flying into myself.

Knott's need to experience death itself can be compared to the similar impulses of Sylvia Plath in such poems as "Lady Lazarus," where she has
come so near to being actually dead "They had to call and call / And pick
the worms off me like sticky pearls." If Plath is in some ways more spectac-

ular than Knott (hers is the poetry of one about to commit suicide as opposed to one simply fantasizing it), she is nevertheless willing to qualify the
possibilities of experiencing death in a way that Knott is not. There is no
reason that Saint Geraud, the pseudonym under which the Naomi poems
were written, cannot enter the abyss; he has been there all along.

Death is not the only subject of interest to Knott; Naomi is after all the
object of his love, a love that in its absoluteness conjures up an earthy
young Werther. But even the love poems share the preoccupation with
what is not more than with what is as in "Poem":

> The beach holds and sifts us through her dreaming fingers
> Summer fragrances green between your legs
> At night, naked auras cool the waves
> Vanished
> O Naomi
> I kiss every body of you, every face

"Vanished" is the fulcrum of the poem; the "Poem" sands announce the
transience of the relation between the poet and his beloved. The sense of
flux and impermanence, however, is offset by the intensity of the experience, the indelibility of what is written on the wind. Again, it is Knott's
willingness to encounter the negation of an experience that gives the poem
its sharpest definition.

Knott is at his best when he latches on to a particular sensuous detail
and expands its implications through his sharp, sometimes grotesque vision.
Naomi's hair, for example, is woven through the book like a thread in a tap-
estry. In "Hair Poem" it is defined as "heaven's water flowing eerily over
us"; in another "Poem" we are asked to envision the possibility—after her
death—of Naomi's hair escaping ". . . to become/a round animal, nameless." It is precisely in this realm of the neo-metaphysical bordering on the
surreal that Saint Geraud finds the chief sources of his strength; it is as if
Yeats's "hair tent poems" (as John Unterecker has called them) were subjected to a kind of psychedelic spectrum analysis. It is in this realm as well
that the poet's love for his beloved, barely managing to exist on the edge of
hyperbole throughout the book, becomes most believable.

Aside from love, death, and hair, Knott's major preoccupations are political; as he says in "To American Poets," "Pound's or Williams' theories on
prosody don't meet the cries of dying children." Here, however, the sen-
suousness of direct experience, or directly imagined experience, is replaced
by epigrammatic wit: "If bombing children is preserving peace, then/my
fucking you is a war-crime" ("Nuremburg, U.S.A."). The success of the political poems—within certain limits many of them are quite successful—must
be qualified. They are biting and to the mark, they are effective propaganda; lacking the complexity of experience, however, they tend to become
slogans. The poem "Secretary," for example, where Defense Secretary
McNamara is seen as a businessman at his desk stamping " 'PAID' on the
death-lists," avoids portraying the ambiguities of a man who was victim as

well as victimizer. This kind of oversimplification may be essential to political action but is dangerous to poetry.

At times, Knott is not just an oversimplifier; he is thoroughly outrageous:

> I don't know but I can't see much difference between John Ashbery or
>   Donald Hall or Barbara Guest or David Wagoner or William Mere-
>   dith or Anne Sexton or Sandra Hochman or Thomas Clark or Ken-
>   neth Koch or others writing
> a poem . . . and a U.S. aviator dropping a bomb on Vietnamese women
> and children: both acts in these hands are in defense of oppression and cap-
>   italism
>
> (from "I Don't Know")

It is hard to know how to handle a poem like this. Knott clearly means
what he is saying at the same time that he knows better. Perhaps it is another instance of oversimplification for the sake of making an emphatic
point, as in the poem about McNamara; or it could be that the irony cuts
both ways, with or without the consent of Saint Geraud.

Occasionally, the political and the personal are yoked together, as in
"(Poem) (Chicago) (The Were-Age)":

> History is made of bricks you can't go through it
> And bricks are made of bones and blood and
> Bones and blood are made of little tiny circles that nothing can go through
> Except a piano with rabies
> Blood gushes into, not from, our wounds
> Vietnamese Cuban African bloods
> Constellations of sperm upon our bodies
> Drunk as dogs before our sons

This poetic mode is, for Knott, a more effective way of dealing with the
public world; it allows again free play of the surreal and the sensuous, albeit in a more nightmarish way than before.

Formally, Knott is more difficult to place than one would first think. He
rarely rhymes; his brand of free verse could find its manifesto anywhere
from Pound's Imagists to the Projectivists. Many of the poems are quite
short (two or three lines) and focus on a single image, so that some sort of
identification with the Imagists seems indicated. But it is probably Sappho
and Catullus with whom comparisons are most fruitful, both in theme and
execution: love and death on the one hand, satire on the other. The hard,
evocative image, the sharp twist, but with a subjectivity that would strain
the bounds of the Imagist tradition, is possibly not as far removed from ancient Greece and Rome as one might think. At his best, Knott is a kind of
surreal classicist. The ultimate commitment to form is always at odds with
emotions that threaten to rip the poet apart. In this respect, he is not unlike
the Confessional poets, Sylvia Plath in particular.

William Knott's grotesque fertility of imagination sometimes threatens to
disintegrate into the gothic, into a love of the bizarre for its own sake.

Knott is a preposterous man, a quality that enables him to underscore what is preposterous in experience, which is to say, a good deal of it. But it also allows him on occasion to make his point too easily, in a way that impresses at first but diminishes with further reading. Liabilities not withstanding, he is already a formidable poet. His second book, *Auto-Necrophilia* (1971), contains both the strengths and weaknesses of his first (although what is intended to shock no longer shocks).

Selected Bibliography:
By KNOTT:
The Naomi Poems, Book One: Corpse and Beans. Chicago: Follett Publishing Co., 1968.
Auto-Necrophilia. Chicago: Follett Publishing Co., 1971.

KOCH, KENNETH (*b. Cincinnati, Ohio, Feb. 27, 1925—   *)

Along with Frank O'Hara and John Ashbery, Kenneth Koch is one of the most well-known of the NEW YORK POETS. Like most of the poets in the group, Koch displays some allegiance to Charles Olson's conception of PROJECTIVE VERSE. And like the others, he has been influenced by the painting of the New York School, although he was perhaps not as immersed in that world as O'Hara, Ashbery, or James Schuyler. The influence of Surrealism, discernible in many New York Poets, is especially evident in Koch's work, and it is Koch who often seems least reverent to the art he is practicing, who is most overtly satirical, who is fondest of parody.

Born in Ohio, Kenneth Koch received degrees from Harvard and Columbia, and has spent much of his adult life in New York. A professor of English at Columbia University, in 1968–69 he was involved in an experiment in teaching elementary-school children to write poetry.

In Kenneth Koch's earlier poetry, though the imagery is often grotesque and the events unexpected, there is a consistently coherent consciousness perceiving this bizarre reality. It resembles a painting by Dali, in which an identifiable world is presented in "unrealistic" combinations or distortions, as opposed to a Cubist painting, in which reality is fragmented, in which the components of objects, as well as the objects as a whole, are juxtaposed in unfamiliar ways.

"Fresh Air," an early poem reprinted in *Thank You and Other Poems* (1962), is set, more or less, at the meeting of the "Poem Society." The poem is an attack on institutionalized poetry, on any narrowing of possibilities. The chairman of the society, "bald with certain hideous black hairs," announces, ". . . The subject for this evening's discussion is poetry/On the subject of love between swans." It is the paradox of any poetry society that in the very process of identifying poetry as a significant part of their experience, the devotees may well end by limiting its scope, making the poem an end in and of itself rather than an expression of man's relation to his world. Koch's principal target, however, is not the Poem Society but its magnified reflection, the academy. Professors apparently constitute a good part of the society's membership. When they leave,

> . . . all that were left in the room were five or six poets
> And together they sang the new poem of the twentieth century
> Which, though influenced by Mallarmé, Shelley, Byron, and Whitman,
> Plus a million other poets, is still entirely original
> And is so exciting that it cannot be here repeated.

Irony is so heavy throughout the poem that it is difficult to know how to read these lines, to know whether these five or six poets do indeed represent the "new" poetry that will break through old boundaries, or whether they too, by their very presence at the meeting, must be considered pretentious. Probably, though, Koch is pointing at the handful of poets who are moving in the right direction, and his irony is directed at the critics who pretend to detect a myriad of influences, who can only understand poetry in relation to clearly established traditions.

Indeed, the next section of the poem takes on these traditions:

> Who are the great poets of our time, and what are their names?
> Yeats of the baleful influence, Auden of the baleful influence, Eliot of the
> baleful infulence

If the critics and their imposition of dubious categories earn a good part of Koch's wrath, another group angers him even more: the academic poets.

> Where are young poets in America, they are trembling in publishing
> houses and universities,
> Above all they are trembling in universities, they are bathing the library
> steps with their spit,
> They are gargling our innocuous (to whom?) poems about maple trees and
> their children,
> Sometimes they brave a subject like the Villa d'Este or a lighthouse in
> Rhose Island,
> Oh what worms they are! they wish to perfect their form.

This requires little explication; as is the case with a good deal of Koch's early work, the point is quite clear. In this instance, Koch is giving voice to the general sense of exclusion and resentment felt by the "non-academic" poets during the fifties. Although this dates that part of the poem devoted to attacking what has by now become a straw man, the remedy Koch proposes is still valid. It is contained in the title of the poem: "Fresh Air."

> Blue air, fresh air, come in, I welcome you, you are an art student,
> Take off your cap and gown and sit down on the chair.
> Together we shall paint the poets—but no, air! perhaps you should go to
> them, quickly,
> Give them a little inspiration, they need it, perhaps they are out of breath,

Give them a little inhuman company before they freeze the English language to death!

The fresh air clearly represents a sense of liberation as opposed to the restraint of the academies and conventional poetry. The fact that the air is an
"art student" may identify this freedom with creativity in general, and it
may also refer to what Koch saw as the healthy influence of painting and
sculpture on writing. The fact that the poets are out of breath, beyond the
obvious meaning, may allude to Charles Olson's dictum that the rhythm of
a line should be determined by the poet's breath.

Not all of Kenneth Koch's early poetry is as didactic as "Fresh Air." But
even when there is no clear-cut "message," even when it is impossible to
find prose equivalents for what Koch is saying in his poetry, the reader is
not likely to encounter much difficulty following the thread of the poet's
thought. "Taking a Walk with You" (also in *Thank You and Other Poems*),
for example, while it brings together a series of apparently disjointed images, is given unity as a catalog of things the poet does not understand, cul-
minating in his misunderstanding of the woman he is with. It soon becomes
evident that for Koch "misunderstanding" is a perfectly legitimate way of
knowing, possibly the way most appropriate to the artist. The lack of logical
sequence in the listing is not, then, an obstacle to the reader; it is instead
an obvious part of the poem's subject.

Two lines of "Taking a Walk with You" constitute a miniature aesthetic,
and in fact they prefigure the complications that later enter Koch's work:

It is Causation that is my greatest problem
And after that the really attentive study of millions of details.

Koch's "misunderstanding" of causation developed into a serious questioning of conventional interpretations of reality; the "attentive study of millions
of details" actually became the poet's chief business, his alternative to imposing man-made organizations upon experience.

"Sleeping with Women" in *The Pleasures of Peace* (1969) is one of
Koch's more recent poems. Again, the reader will have less difficulty sentence by sentence than with the work of O'Hara or Ashbery. It is no longer
a simple matter, however, to see precisely where Koch is going. The poem
has a kind of unity, provided by the insistently repeated refrain, "sleeping
with women." But since the names, places, and fragments of experience
linked with that refrain fall into no pattern, and since the refrain itself offers
no interpretation, the poem lacks conventional coherence. This lack of coherence does not necessarily constitute a weakness. Everything in an unor-
dered universe is juxtaposed with the stable reality of sleeping with women
—obviously, making love with them, but also, maybe more importantly, literally being asleep with them. That reality becomes a still point in a
turning world, a world that Koch examines in its infinite detail rather than
with any sense of meaningful connection.

See also the Introduction, section V.

Selected Bibliography:
By Koch:
Poems. New York: Tibor de Nagy Gallery, 1953.
Ko, or A Season on Earth. New York: Grove Press, 1959.
Permanently. New York: Tiber Press, 1961.
Thank You and Other Poems. New York: Grove Press, 1962.
Bertha and Other Plays. New York: Grove Press, 1966.
When the Sun Tries to Go On. Los Angeles: Black Sparrow Press, 1969.
The Pleasures of Peace and Other Poems. New York: Grove Press, 1969.

About Koch:
Howard, Richard. *Alone with America*. New York: Atheneum Publishers, 1969.
    Pp. 281–91.

LEE, DON L. (*b. Little Rock, Ark., Feb. 23, 1942—*)

"Blackpoetry in its purest form is diametrically opposed to white poetry," writes Don Lee in his preface to *Don't Cry, Scream* (1969). This statement follows logically from Lee's conviction—which he shares with Imamu Baraka and most of the newer black poets—that all poetry is political, that even the attempt to be apolitical is a political comment, and that politics for the black man in America is the expression of black consciousness. The nature of his audience also affects Lee's poetics. He is not interested in the praise of white critics nor concerned that his poetry meet their criteria. Therefore, although there is ample evidence that he understands the subtleties of his craft, Lee's voice is loud and direct. His message dictates the medium, and his message is essentially a call to blacks to cease being niggers and become black men and women.

Raised in Detroit, educated at Wilson Junior College and Roosevelt University, Lee has taught at Columbia College (Chicago), Cornell, Northeastern Illinois State College, Roosevelt University, and the University of Illinois. He has also been one of the most prolific of the newer black critics.

"Black Sketches," in *Don't Cry, Scream*, one of Don Lee's most effective poems, is an illustration of his attitudes and methods. Its eleven brief sections are partly autobiographical, partly the biography of blacks in America arriving at a consciousness of themselves. These threads are interwoven, each theme a commentary on the other. He writes of his parents marrying when he was five, and his lack of awareness that he was illegitimate until he started school; of having to use the men's room and not having a dime; of his mother dying at the age of thirty-five, "& nobody thought it unusual," not even Lee; and in section 10:

> in 1963
> i became black
> & everyone thought it unusual;
> even me.

White America receives its share of Lee's attack: the "mistake" someone made of sending the Peace Corps to Europe; the fantasy that Nat Turner returns to murder William Styron (and "his momma too"); General Westmoreland transferred to Chicago, where he is beaten again. But the bitterest lines are predictably reserved for blacks who have tried to become part of white America: Senator Edward Brooke sitting at his desk, crying and cutting his wrists, because someone called him black; and the poem's concluding section:

> the american dream:
>   nigger bible in
>   every hotel;
>   iceberg slim (pimp) getting
>   next to julia;
>   & roy wilkins on
>   the mod squad.

Each of the sections is simple and direct. The rhythms are prosaic; in fact, it is prose, prose fragments juxtaposed for poetic effect. It is the poetry of a man who wants to be understood rather than to mystify, who recognizes the complexities of experience but feels that certain very clear statements can be made—have to be made—before those complexities can be engaged.

It would be misleading to suggest that there are no ambiguities in Lee's poetry, or that it would be totally unacceptable if judged by the standards he refuses to recognize. His poetry is filled with juxtapositions far more striking than those of "Black Sketches," so that the texture of his work constitutes an attack on the belief in the mind's capacity rationally to organize experience. And if this attack is in part political—for the structures with which Lee has to contend are essentially white structures—it is also epistemological; and it is expressed precisely by the methods developed by the predominantly white poets of Projective verse, who share with Lee a profound mistrust of the Western ego's ability to interpret reality.

Probably the most interesting aspect of Don Lee's technique, however, is his use of rhythms. He demonstrates mastery of a wide range of possibilities, from the violent rage of "Don't Cry, Scream"—

> scream-eeeeeeeeeeeeeee-ing   sing
> SCREAM-EEEeeeeeeeeeee-ing   loud &
> SCREAM-EEEEEEEEEEEEEEE-ing   long with
>   feeling

—to the more delicate control of a poem in *We Walk the Way of the New World*, "A Loneliness":

> i stood there
> watching myself   feel
> feeling
> my own eyes   checking

my dark reflection against
the day's sounds.

Lee's more recent poetry has revealed a developing emotional range intimately related to rhythmic shifts. He is capable of gentleness as well as
anger, private as well as communal experience, without in the least sacrificing the goal of his art, the expression of black consciousness:

your beauty: un-noticed by regular eyes   is
like   a blackbird resting
on a telephone wire   that moves
quietly with the wind.

a southwind.

(from "Man Thinking About Woman" in *We Walk the Way of the New World*)

In view of Don Lee's aesthetics, it seems appropriate that he be evaluated by the audience for whom he is writing. He has been described by
Gwendolyn Brooks as "now the most significant, inventive, and influential
black poet in this country."
See also NEW BLACK AESTHETIC, and the Introduction, section VII.

Selected Bibliography:
BY LEE:
Think Black. Detroit: Broadside Press, 1967.
Black Pride. Detroit: Broadside Press, 1968.
Don't Cry, Scream. Detroit: Broadside Press, 1969.
We Walk the Way of the New World. Detroit: Broadside Press, 1970.
Directionscore: Selected and New Poems. Detroit: Broadside Press, 1971.
Dynamite Voices I: Black Poets of the 1960's. [Criticism.] Detroit: Broadside
     Press, 1971.

LEVERTOV, DENISE   (*b. Ilford, Essex, England, October 24,*
1923—   )

Although born in England, Denise Levertov has an unambiguous place
among contemporary American poets, not simply because she married an
American, Mitchell Goodman, and came to live in New York in 1948, but
because of her connection with the BLACK MOUNTAIN POETS. Though she
never visited Black Mountain College, she knew many of the poets associated with it, and her poetry appeared regularly in Projectivist-oriented
magazines, such as the *Black Mountain Review* and *Origin*. The best summary of the influences that transformed her from "a British Romantic with
almost Victorian background to an American poet" is probably her own biographical statement prepared for Donald M. Allen's anthology, *The New
American Poetry* (1960):

Marrying an American and coming to live here while still young was very stimulating to me as a writer for it necessitated the finding of new rhythms in which to write, in accordance with new rhythms of life and speech. My reading of William Carlos Williams and Wallace Stevens, which began in Paris in 1948; of Olson's essay, "Projective Verse"; conversations and correspondence with Robert Duncan; a renewed interest through Buber in the Hasidic ideas with which I was dimly acquainted as a child; the thoughts and shared experiences of my husband; an introduction to some of the concepts of Jung; the friendship of certain painters such as Albert Kresch—have all been influential and continue to be so.

"Beyond the End," which appeared in Levertov's first book published in this country, *Here and Now* (1957), embodies Projectivist aesthetics, not only in its breath-determined rhythms, but in its vision of reality. "In 'nature' there's no choice," the poem begins. Flowers, the wind, sun and moon, simply are. But human beings seem to fall short of totally experiencing their existence. We are reminded of Charles Olson's description of the ego, the soul, as "that peculiar presumption by which western man has interposed himself between what he is as a creature of nature . . . and those other creations of nature which we may, with no derogation, call objects." Man is cut off from his biological, his "natural" existence, from, in Levertov's words, "the humble rhythms, the/falling & rising of leaf and star."

The obvious problem is how to get back to the sources of one's energy. Levertov finds in art, in creativity, a means of reestablishing harmony with the universe. But it is important to distinguish between creativity as the imposition of man's intellectual perceptions upon reality, which Levertov, along with Olson, rejects, and creativity as a state of active receptiveness.

> . . . every damn
> craftsman has it while he's working
>   but it's not
> a question of work: some
> shine with it, in repose. Maybe it is
> response, the will to respond . . .

This is not Wordsworth's wise passivity, although it may in some ways be related to it. The word *will* is crucial; Levertov concludes by referring to the creative act as a kind of "gritting of the teeth," the wish to go ". . . beyond the end/beyond whatever ends: to begin, to be, to defy." The defiance is most likely of intellectual categories that cut man off from his full being, that produce an illusory sense of time, that leave him vulnerable to death.

The sense of harmony with nature to be found in a recognition of man's biological nature is not far from mysticism. Levertov's interest in Hasidic traditions suggests that she, like Robert Duncan, does not find these approaches contradictory. It is impossible to over-emphasize the activeness of Levertov's vision; she finds at the center of being, not eternal quiet, but eternal energy.

The theme is further developed in "The Way Through," which appeared in *Overland to the Islands* (1958). It has been raining, torrentially. The problem is to get an old car through a deep pool of water. The rain is characterized as ". . . real rain, sensuous,/swift . . ." Falling as it does from the "vague skies," it is both the physical world and eternity. It is frightening, the end beyond which man must penetrate to exist in the fullest sense of the word. To attempt to go around the edge of the pool will not work; the earth will simply crumble. The old car must charge directly through, and it does. The poem ends:

> Drown us, lose us,
> rain, let us loose, so,
> to lose ourselves, to career
> up the plunge of the hill

A good portion of Denise Levertov's poetry is didactic in that it advocates the position behind the aesthetic rather than simply demonstrating it. A poem like "The Goddess," from *With Eyes at the Back of Our Heads* (1959), is openly allegorical. The goddess—to whom the poet has paid "lip-service," but whose face she has not seen—finds the poet in Lie Castle. This in itself constitutes an explanation of the didacticism. The poet, who finds attractive the notion of man's essential unity with the rest of being, does not find it easy to accept totally the stance she has intellectually adopted. This may account for the great strain involved in coming to full awareness that produces the most interesting tensions in Levertov's poetry.

The lies of Lie Castle seem to be the abstractions that cut man off from reality. The castle encloses; and so the goddess violently flings the persona about until she lies beyond the outer walls. There she is brought in contact with the natural world:

> I bit on a seed and it spoke on my tongue
> of that day that shone already among stars

The poem concludes by defining the goddess as she

> without whom nothing
> speaks in its own tongue, but returns
> lie for lie!

Significantly, the quality of being fully alive is embodied in speech, linking it intimately with the art of poetry.

In spite of the often explicit attitudes toward experience of Denise Levertov's poems, their success depends ultimately upon her sense of the concrete, her responsiveness to detail. "Night on Hatchet Cove," for example, begins:

> The screendoor whines, clacks
> shut.   My thoughts crackle
> with seaweed-seething diminishing
> flickers of phosphorus.   Gulp

> of a frog, plash
> of herring leaping;
>   interval:

Nonetheless, the book in which this poem appears, *The Jacob's Ladder* (1961), is fully committed to the vision of reality developed in earlier works. The ladder of the title, taken from Martin Buber's *Tales of the Hassidim: Later Masters,* connects death-bound man with eternity; the angels of God ascend and descend, and their ascent and descent depend on man's deeds. Buber asserts that man cannot truly experience his own being until he has fully experienced the being of other men, of the natural world, and finally, of God. In Buber, and in Levertov, these are not separate processes; they form the single means by which man transcends the ego that prevents him from seeing the true nature of things.

Again, for Levertov, the natural world is the ground of eternity. "No man is so guileless as/the serpent," she writes in "Come into Animal Presence." Questioning the quality of joy she observes in animals: "What is this joy? That no animal/falters, but knows what it must do?" Only man, conscious of his existence as though apart from the rest of creation, is involved in the world of choice and doubt. Denying the fall from Eden except as a psychological phenomenon affecting man alone, she insists that the world is holy, ". . . only the sight that saw it/faltered and turned from it."

The same theme is continued in ". . . Else a great Prince in prison lies." All of the joy, the grace, and the peace that characterize animal existence, "dwell secretly behind man's misery." Even man's fall is not irrevocable; it is, in fact, illusory, a result of what Blake would have called "single vision."

In spite of her obvious sympathy with the mystic's way of knowing the world, however, Denise Levertov is in no sense shut off from the world of ordinary experience. On the contrary, it is the tension between ways of knowing that gives energy to her poetry, her love of the material world that makes believable her vision of the spiritual. Nor is she oblivious to man's involvement in history. In fact, one of the most powerful poems in *The Jacob's Ladder* is "During the Eichmann Trial." The poem is divided into three sections. The first places the poet's reaction to Eichmann within the context of her general vision of reality:

> He stands
>
> isolate in a bulletproof
> witness-stand of glass,
>
> a cage, where we may view
> ourselves, an apparition
>
> telling us something he
> does not know: we are members
>
> one of another.

Levertov is responding to perhaps the most terrifying aspect of the Eichmann trial: the man linked to the death of millions was revealed to be not an unnatural monster but the most ordinary of men. It would have been far more comforting to have been able totally to dissociate ourselves from him; but we cannot. It is, of course, precisely Eichmann's inability to see the common bond of humanity that makes him a murderer. The isolation of the glass booth is largely self-created.

Probably most significant is that Levertov's perception of the impossibility of separating ourselves from Eichmann does not lead to a passive acceptance of his actions, nor to any diminishing of horror in the fact that under the surface the multiplicity of experience is one and changeless.

The second section of the poem is an imagined reenactment of Eichmann's shooting of the boy who stole fruit from the tree (the one instance during the trial in which Eichmann was proved to have himself been the instrument of murder). It is characteristically the concrete rather than the abstract that excites Levertov's horror.

The most remarkable part of the poem is its final section, "Crystal Night." Here the universality and the particularity of the experience are merged in a kind of Jungian dream. Screams of fear shatter the poem:

> smashing the windows of sleep and dream
> smashing the windows of history
> a whiteness scattering
> in hailstones
> each a mirror
> for man's eyes.

As its title suggests, O Taste and See (1964) concentrates even more than Denise Levertov's earlier work on the perceptual universe. In "September 1961" the poet suggests that "the old great ones"—Ezra Pound, William Carlos Williams, and H. D. (Hilda Doolittle)—"leave us alone on the road." These are perhaps the best of the Imagist poets, and their legacy is an involvement in the concrete that has formed the core of modern American poetry. The message of their work is probably best summarized in the title poem of Levertov's collection, "O Taste and See." She begins by rephrasing Wordsworth: "The world/is not with us enough." In one sense, she is simply playing with the word "world," which Wordsworth used to designate worldly things and which she uses to mean the physical universe. However, the distinction may be more than casual. What Wordsworth and Levertov have in common is a sense of the importance of man's relationship to nature. But while Wordsworth is concerned primarily with a reality unmarred by civilization, Levertov's interest extends to the entire sensory world. More important, where Wordsworth seeks in nature permanent forms that relate significantly to human experience, Levertov is committed to the act of perceiving in and of itself. She is involved with ". . . all that lives/to the imagination's tongue," she wishes to "breathe them, bite,/savor, chew, swallow, transform/into our flesh our/deaths."

"The Garden Wall" provides an insight into Levertov's notion of what constitutes accurate seeing. The wall, built with bricks older than the house, attracts relatively little attention until a hose being used to water flowers is turned on the wall, revealing a world of color, rivaling the flowers, springing from the wall's "quiet dry brown":

> archetype
> of the world always a step
> beyond the world, that can't
> be looked for, only
> as the eye wanders,
> found.

It cannot be looked for. That is, there is no plan, no system, no preconceived discipline, no intellectual construct, that will provide insight into the nature of reality. But the act of perception is not therefore totally accidental. The fact that the eye is willing to wander, that it is curious, that it is responsive, is obviously essential.

"To Speak," from *The Sorrow Dance* (1967), begins:

> To speak of sorrow
> works upon it
>   moves it from its
> crouched place barring
> the way to and from the soul's hall—

In many ways the book as a whole is devoted to the speaking of sorrow. To be sure, there are expressions of joy in the sensuous world, there are love poems. But in "The Closed World," Levertov writes: ". . . the blinds are down over my windows, / my doors are shut." The difficulties involved in moving from the particular to the universal, never taken lightly in her work, are here overwhelming. This is the consequence partly of personal sorrow —the book's longest poem is a moving elegy to her sister, Olga Levertoff— partly of a world whose horrors cannot be avoided.

The principal public horror is, of course, the war in Vietnam. In "Life at War," one of several poems in *The Sorrow Dance* on that subject, the obvious, but nonetheless crushing, paradox is stated: that Man,

> . . . whose flesh
> responds to a caress, whose eyes
> are flowers that perceive the stars,

can feel nothing more than "mere regret" about

> . . . the scheduled breaking open of breasts whose milk
> runs out over the entrails of still-alive babies,
> transformation of witnessing eyes to pulp-fragments,
> implosion of skinned penises into carcass-gulleys.

The Sorrow Dance is a doubly tragic book. It is tragic because its dominant themes are death and suffering. It is also a tragedy of poetic consciousness. It is the work of a poet who sees just barely out of reach a world that will transcend human pain; but the pain is so great that it cannot be deserted.

Selected Bibliography:
By LEVERTOV:
The Double Image. London: Cresset Press, 1946.
Here and Now. San Francisco: City Lights Books, 1957.
Overland to the Islands. Highlands, North Carolina: Jargon Books, 1958.
With Eyes at the Back of Our Heads. New York: New Directions Publishing Corp., 1959.
The Jacob's Ladder. New York: New Directions Publishing Corp., 1961.
O Taste and See. New York: New Directions Publishing Corp., 1964.
The Sorrow Dance. New York: New Directions Publishing Corp., 1967.
A Tree Telling of Orpheus. Los Angeles: Black Sparrow Press, 1968.
Selected Poems of Guillevic. [Translations.] New York: New Directions Publishing Corp., 1969.
To Stay Alive. New York: New Directions Publishing Corp., 1971.
Footprints. New York: New Directions Publishing Corp., 1972.

About Levertov:
Howard, Richard. *Alone with America.* New York: Atheneum Publishers, 1969. Pp. 292–305.
Mills, Ralph J., Jr. *Contemporary American Poetry.* New York: Random House, 1965. Pp. 176–96.
Stepanchev, Stephen. *American Poetry since 1945.* New York: Harper & Row Publishers, 1965. Pp. 157–65.
Wagner, Linda. *Denise Levertov.* New York: Twayne Publishers, 1967.

LEVINE, PHILIP (b. Detroit, Mich., Jan. 10, 1928—   )

Hiroshima, the torture of Algerian prisoners, soldiers in eye-to-eye combat, generalized and brutal bigotry, a sick child watched by a father powerless to help him: this is a reasonably representative cross section of the subjects of Philip Levine's poetry. Usually focused on man's cruelty to man rather than the pain and suffering inherent in the human condition, Levine's poetry has evil as its dominant theme.

Born in Detroit, Philip Levine studied under John Berryman at Wayne State University. He attended Iowa and Stanford and later taught at Fresno State College.

Levine rejects coming to terms with human suffering rationally, that is, he rejects the containment of suffering within some justifying system. In "Night Thoughts over a Sick Child" (from *On the Edge*), seeing his son struggle "toward consciousness and the known pain," he says,

> If it were mine by one word
> I would not save any man,

> Myself or the universe
> at such cost: reality.

Levine is either alluding to or independently reformulating the question
Ivan asks of Alyosha in *The Brothers Karamazov:* would he be willing to
obtain happiness for mankind at the price of torturing a baby to death?
Levine's answer, like Alyosha's, is no, rejecting not only the specific proposition but, by implication, all attempts to reduce the impact of individual suffering by placing it in a larger context. All that Levine has to protect himself against possible disaster is the ". . . frail dignity / of surrender."

In most of his poetry, Levine's stance cannot be characterized as passive,
however. Again and again, he forces us to confront the unendurable, the
horror that man has created. "The Horse" begins with an impossible, surrealistic image:

> They spoke of the horse alive
> without skin, naked, hairless,
> without eyes and ears, searching
> for the stableboy's caress.

> (from *On the Edge*)

But the poem is dedicated to a survivor of Hiroshima; it is simple natural-
ism. We must be able to look at what we have done, to recognize that we
have broken down the boundaries between nightmare and literal truth.

Although it is difficult to pay attention to the techniques of Levine's
poems so powerful are his images, when the techniques are examined they
turn out to be perfectly appropriate to his material. He frequently uses
some formal framework, evidence of the strain to master the horror confronted. But his use of these forms is necessarily flexible (so much so that
his work was included in Berg and Mezey's *Naked Poetry,* an anthology of
poetry in "open forms"). While the quotation from "The Horse" shows a
reasonably full rhyme for lines two and four—there is a slight dissonance—
half-rhymes are far more typical. And that passage illustrates Levine's handling of meter, here a three-beat line, capable of great variety. (Notice especially how he manages to bring the three long feet together to reinforce
the horror of line two.)

There is a tendency on the reader's part to flinch, to turn aside from
what this poet wants him to experience. Levine makes that as difficult as
possible, implicating his audience when they would like to think he is talking of somebody else. In "Gangrene," from *On the Edge,* he describes in
detail the torture of three prisoners: one beaten and forced to swallow his
own vomit; another with his penis wired for electric shocks; a third beaten
on his genitals with a short ruler. The poem ends:

> . . . We must live
> with what we are,
> you say, it is enough. I
> taste death. I am among you
> and I accuse

you where, secretly thrilled by
the circus of excitement,

you study my strophes or
yawn into the evening air,
        tired, not amused.
Remember what you have said
when from your pacific dream
        you awaken
at last, deafened by the scream
of your own stench. You are dead.

Selected Bibliography:
By LEVINE:
On the Edge. Iowa City: Stone Wall Press, 1963.
Not This Pig. Middletown, Conn.: Wesleyan University Press, 1968.
They Feed They Lion. New York: Atheneum Publishers, 1972.

LOGAN, JOHN   (*b. Red Oak, Iowa, Jan. 23, 1923—*   )

For years pigeonholed as a religious poet, and one who was orthodox in his doctrine as well, it is only recently that John Logan's poetry has been recognized as transcending these limits. Consequently, his earlier work has been seen in retrospect as not having been quite so dogmatic after all. His early apparent dependence upon religious and literary epigraphs and materials masked the fact that he has spoken clearly, if not spectacularly, in his own voice all along.

John Logan attended Coe College in his home state of Iowa and received his B.A. in zoology in 1943. He earned an M.A. in English from the University of Iowa in 1949, and has subsequently taught at Notre Dame and at the State University of New York at Buffalo. He was poetry editor for *The Nation*.

In "Lines to His Son on Reaching Adolescence" (from *Ghosts of the Heart*), Logan writes:

> But for both our sakes I ask you, wrestle
> Manfully against the ancient curse of snakes,
> The bitter mystery of love, and learn to bear
> The burden of the tenderness
> That is hid in us. . . .

These lines announce the theme that dominates his work. It is easy to see how this could be read as a conventional piety—Logan himself is aware of this, since he compares his advice to that of Polonius. He is not arguing against love, or even counseling prudence. He is rather pointing out that it is necessary to love in order to live, and that the problems inherent in the human condition make love as complicated and difficult as it is necessary.

Another poem in *Ghosts of the Heart*, "A Trip to Four or Five Towns," makes the nature of Logan's preoccupations even more evident. The poem's verse form makes it more obviously "modern." (In general Logan has moved from conventional stressed meter in his first volume, to syllabic verse in his second and third, and finally to free verse, making frequent use of slant-rhymes, in his fourth.) The poem is an exploration of the possibilities of love. The first section gives a brief glimpse of a good marriage. The key word is "balance," and in the rest of the poem this balance is what is so difficult to achieve. The second section focuses on a marble *pietà* in a seminary. The poet leaves the seminary without confessing; he "never saved himself." His reasons, both for his need to confess and his failure to do so, are unclear—they are not the subject of the poem—but an uneasy note is struck that will continue to dominate the poem. In the third section, on a plane, he hears executives, ". . . manicured and/fat, fucking this and fucking that." He ends up at "the National Stripshow" and with a dream of "the negro girl's room."

The fourth section is a brief, green interval, leading to a portrait of a family, healthy and competent, in the fifth. In the sixth, the persona is with a Beat poet friend who pisses in a phone booth and gets knocked out for "horning in with the girl in the room over him." He thinks of Orpheus. "Do poets have to have such trouble with the female race?" Then they go to visit an older poet in New Jersey, clearly William Carlos Williams.

> That old father was so mellow and generous—
> easy to pain,
> white, open and at peace, and of good taste,
> like his Rutherford house.

The balance swings back. The "father" gives the love the child has been unable to find. What are we to make of all this? The poem seems to have no message, except perhaps that it is better to be happy than not to be happy; it is rather a vision of the full complexity, the vast variety, of human experience. The conclusion is characteristically ambiguous. He is on his way home,

> high, pure and clear,
> seemed like the right time
> to disappear.

Selected Bibliography:
By LOGAN:
Cycle for Mother Cabrini. New York: Grove Press, 1955.
Ghosts of the Heart. Chicago: University of Chicago Press, 1960.
Spring of the Thief: Poems 1960–1962. New York: Alfred A. Knopf, 1963.
The Zigzag Walk: Poems 1963–1968. New York: E. P. Dutton & Co., 1969.

About Logan:
Carroll, Paul. "A Century Piece For Poor Heine" in *The Poem in Its Skin.* Chicago: Follett Publishing Co., 1968. Pp. 111–136.
Howard, Richard. *Alone with America.* New York: Atheneum Publishers, 1969. Pp. 306–317.

LOWELL, ROBERT   (*b. Boston, Mass., Mar. 1, 1917—*)

Since the publication of *Lord Weary's Castle* in 1946, Robert Lowell has enjoyed the reputation of a master craftsman, one of the important poets of his generation. *Life Studies* (1959), which seemed to explore areas of experience previously unavailable to poetry, became what is probably the single most influential book of poems in English since World War II.

In both form and theme, Lowell's work has developed greatly in the course of his career, but the major preoccupations of his poetry were present from the start: defining the self through its historical context, its psychological integrity, its relation to God and nature. Although these are the great themes of Western literature, held in common by all significant writers, Lowell's particular genius contributes, first, a way of bridging private and public worlds that enlarges the dimensions of everything he writes about, and, second, a relentless scrutiny that allows neither reader nor poet an easy resolution to the complexities of human experience.

History, for Lowell, means both the public events that shape the destinies of men and nations and the private familial circumstances that mold individual personalities. Descended from one of the most prominent of Boston families, Lowell has probably found the conflation of public and private worlds easier than most. His ancestor Percival Lowle came to Massachusetts in 1639. Among his descendants, in addition to Robert, were poets James Russell Lowell and Amy Lowell, Harvard President A. Lawrence Lowell, and astronomer Percival Lowell. The maternal side of the family, Winslow, has even older credentials: Edward Winslow arrived on the *Mayflower* in 1620.

Robert Lowell was educated at St. Mark's School, Harvard, and Kenyon College. In 1940, he graduated from Kenyon and married writer Jean Stafford. During World War II he was, as he later recalls in *Life Studies,* "a fire-breathing Catholic C. O." ("Memories of West Street and Lepke"). He was a conscientious objector in protest against allied bombings of civilian populations. His reasons for conversion to Catholicism in 1940—the Lowells were, of course, good Protestant stock—are naturally less public and less clear, but rebellion against his own heritage and a search for some formal structure within which to contain his responses to experience, the experience of war in particular, must certainly have been involved. Whatever the reasons, Catholicism did not live up to Lowell's expectations or his expectations changed; he has for some time described himself as a "lapsed Catholic." In 1948 he divorced Jean Stafford and in 1949 married Elizabeth Hardwick.

Lowell has taught poetry at Kenyon College, Iowa State, Boston University, and Harvard. After a period of relative inactivity, which Lowell calls "the tranquillized *Fifties*" in "Memories of West Street and Lepke," he renewed his political commitments. His involvement centered on the war in Vietnam and its domestic implications. His widespread acceptance as America's preeminent living poet often made his protests newsworthy, as when he declined a dinner invitation from President Lyndon Johnson, or when he took part in the 1967 Pentagon March and became one of the leading figures in Norman Mailer's novel-history *Armies of the Night*. Although the world of public events has been so much a part of his life and has played an increasingly large role in Lowell's poetry, Lowell almost never writes poems of propaganda, nor does he even write conventional political poetry. Like Mailer, he writes with a phenomenological bias; events are important to him not as objective fact but rather as they are humanly perceived.

Another aspect of Lowell's biography is important in his poetry. As his poems reveal, he has often encountered "the kingdom of the mad." The fact that Lowell in his poetry deals with materials so personal seems to elevate what would ordinarily be gossip to the level of literary criticism; and perhaps it does. But we must carefully examine one of the assumptions generally made about what critic M. L. Rosenthal and others have called "CONFESSIONAL POETRY." It has been taken for granted that the persona of the poems and the author are totally identical, that the poet by literally confessing the most intimate details of his personal life captures his soul in the poem. Certainly, there is a close relationship between the poet and his voice. There is also a close relationship between James Joyce and Stephen Dedalus, between Ezra Pound and Hugh Selwyn Mauberley, but the differences between writer and the character created by him are as significant as similarities. Lowell has surely shared many of the experiences of his protagonist, but he may not necessarily *be* that protagonist. It is as logical, and much more likely, to say that Lowell creates a myth of the self, based on his own experience but selected, distorted, and arranged, until its final fidelity must be not to its creator but to itself. Except for the elucidation of certain details, biography cannot provide an explication of the work; the only Lowell we are interested in is the one who is revealed in his poetry.

Lowell himself attempted, in his *Paris Review* interview (in *Writers at Work*, 2nd series, 1963), to define the complex reality of the Confessional poems:

> They're not always factually true. There's a good deal of tinkering with fact. You leave out a lot, and emphasize this and not that. Your actual experience is a complete flux. I've invented facts and changed things, and the whole balance of the poem was something invented. So there's a lot of artistry, I hope, in the poems. Yet there's this thing: if a poem is autobiographical . . . you want the reader to say, this is true . . . . And so there was always that standard of truth which you wouldn't ordinarily have in poetry—the reader was to believe he was getting the *real* Robert Lowell.

There are several points to be noted here. First, the poems are *not* totally factual. Second, there is in these poems a link with the poet's own life that one would not necessarily expect in poetry. Third, the *reality* of these poems must impress itself upon the reader; the fictive Robert Lowell must sustain the illusion of essential humanity. It is not the particularity of reality but rather the quality of reality that Lowell's poetry must convey. Therefore, to return again to Lowell's "madness," whatever the poet's personal problems actually may be, their interest lies in the extent to which they reflect a sensitivity to the contradictions of the human condition and not as the manifestation of some private pathology.

Although *The Land of Unlikeness* (1944) is Robert Lowell's first book of poetry, most studies of his art begin with *Lord Weary's Castle* (1946), which won the Pulitzer Prize in 1947. The best poems of the earlier volume were reprinted in it, generally with substantial revisions. "Children of Light" offers a convenient starting point because it is in theme and method characteristic of Lowell's art at that stage of his career, and because it is short enough to quote in its entirety:

> Our fathers wrung their bread from stocks and stones
> And fenced their gardens with the Redman's bones;
> Embarking from the Nether Land of Holland,
> Pilgrims unhoused by Geneva's night,
> They planted here the Serpent's seeds of light;
> And here the pivoting searchlights probe to shock
> The riotous glass houses built on rock,
> And candles gutter by an empty altar,
> And light is where the landless blood of Cain
> Is burning, burning the unburied grain.

In 1935, Lowell left Harvard to study with New Critic John Crowe Ransom at Kenyon. "Children of Light" and most of the poems in *Lord Weary's Castle* bear testimony to Ransom's influence in that they lend themselves so totally to the approaches of the NEW CRITICISM. The poem's first two words place it in both a national and a familial context. The fathers are the early New England settlers in general, but, for Lowell, "Our fathers" is an explicit reference to his own family as well. There is also a slight hint of an allusion to the Lord's Prayer, an allusion that is not inappropriate to the poem's bitter irony. The "stocks and stones" from which the settlers "wrung their bread" refer literally to the stumps of trees and the rocky terrain that made early New England farming so laborious. The line could also allude to the stocks used for imprisonment in public squares and the stones used against the lawbreakers. The "Redman's bones" is a clear allusion to the genocide that began as soon as Europe began to settle the New World; the violence of the "fathers" was directed both outward and inward.

The "Nether Land" of Holland is both a pun on Netherlands and an epithet for Hades. The Pilgrims, Calvinists who went from England first to Holland and then to America, become children of Satan. They have been "unhoused" (that is, deprived of the Eucharist) by "Geneva's night" (Calvin), and now have come to the new land to plant "the Serpent's seeds": themselves—"seeds of light," children of light. The poem's effectiveness depends largely on Lowell's use of light where the reader expects to see darkness. The main source of irony is possibly the contrast between the ideals of this country, hope and freedom, and the reality, destruction and bondage. But it is also a comment on civilization in general, and on the individual in particular, masking a dark reality in the name of light.

The second half of the poem is built around three forms of light: the "pivoting searchlights," the candles guttering, the burning grain. The searchlights, be they God's or the devil's, appear to be searching out guilt. They probe the "riotous glass houses" (an ambiguous reference to expensive houses on the New England coast, the lighthouses themselves, or some specific, private allusion) while candles burn down in empty churches. Just as Puritanism represented an abandonment of the Catholic Church, the present time and place seems to represent an abandonment of all faith. The last two lines bear the moral weight of the poem. During the depression, in order to support the price of produce, the United States government burned grain, among other farm products. The light of the burning corn suggested to Lowell the interchangeability of light and darkness. In his indignation over the act of burning food while thousands upon thousands went hungry, Lowell combines a closely linked series of acts of violence against man and God: the Protestant revolt against the Catholic Church, the murder of the Indians, the murder of Abel by Cain, the burning of grain.

In a sense, the events of "Children of Light" are a reenactment of man's expulsion from Eden, a drama Lowell sees repeated throughout history. The poem abounds in possible allusions to Genesis: there are "gardens," "the Serpent's seeds" ("I will put enmity . . . between thy seed and her seed"), pivoting searchlights (suggesting the "flaming sword which turned every way,"), and "the landless blood of Cain." The "empty altar" and the burning of the grain may refer to Cain's unaccepted offerings. Although God's reasons for rejecting Cain may be obscure, the culpability of the "children of light" is clear.

It is also possible that the poem's second half concerns the violence of World War II, in which case the searchlights would serve a military purpose. Although many critics have read the poem that way, however, there is no confirming internal evidence. Whether this interpretation is true or not, the basic themes of man's destructiveness and the irony of light imagery remain.

Formally, "Children of Light" conforms to rigid patterns. The meter is iambic pentameter, energetic but reasonably regular. The rhyme scheme looks like this: $a\,a\,x\,b\,b\,c\,c\,x\,d\,d$. It divides the poem neatly into two five-line segments (the fifth line is end-stopped), and the poem does in fact pivot structurally around its midpoint, just as the searchlights pivot at that same spot: the past tradition is handled in the first part, the present in the second; the shift is prepared rhetorically by "They planted here . . ." in line five and by "And here the pivoting searchlights . . ." in line six. The poem is supported by a host of technical devices, appropriate if not in-

spired. Alliteration is especially noticeable, and also employed are assonance, consonance, dissonance, and remarkable networks of sonal relations,
such as the poem's concluding phrase: ". . . the landless blood of Cain / Is
burning, burning the unburied grain." In addition, the poem is held together by repetition of images, sometimes metamorphosed. In the first line,
for example, "bread" anticipates the "grain" of the last line. "Stones" looks
forward to "rock" and, perhaps, to "bones." "Houses" is at least an auditory
echo of "unhoused," but the relationship between being cast out of the
true Church and the "riotous glass houses" may be more than incidental.
And, of course, there is the continuous stream of light and darkness imagery, of allusions to God and the devil.

Generally singled out as the most impressive poem in *Lord Weary's Castle* is "The Quaker Graveyard in Nantucket," written in memory of Warren
Winslow, Lowell's cousin, lost at sea in World War II. Hugh Staples, author of the first full-length study of Lowell's poetry, has placed the poem in
the same elegiac tradition as "Lycidas" and "Adonais" since Lowell's elegy,
like Milton's and like Shelley's, places the individual's death within the context of a more comprehensive vision of reality. The usual conclusion of this
kind of elegy is that while the individual perishes, the One persists, that
death is an illusion. In the case of Lowell's poem, there is more ambiguity
of resolution than Milton, Shelley, or any of their predecessors permit; and
there is a violence and energy that threaten to break the tight formal structure of the poem and that are simply not characteristic of the genre.

The epigraph sets the tone: "*Let man have dominion over the fishes of
the sea and the fowls of the air and the beasts and the whole earth, and
every creeping creature that moveth upon the earth.*" Since section 1 of the
poem begins with the description of a shipwreck and a drowned sailor, the
irony of this quotation from Genesis is immediately evident. The emphasis
is on the grotesqueness of the corpse; it is a horror story in miniature,
dwelling on details that most elegies would eschew. The body is weighted
and returned to the sea from which it came. Then Lowell introduces two of
the three frames of reference that operate beneath the poem's surface: We
encounter "Ahab's void" (the first of many allusions in the poem to *Moby
Dick* and to the Nantucket whalers in general), and the section ends with
classical allusions—an image of destructive Poseidon ("earth-shaker") and
the advice, or command, to ". . . ask for no Orphean lute / To pluck life
back." The reference to "Orphean lute" may well be a version of the conventional complaint that the Muses were impotent to save their devotee. In
Lowell's poem, however, as opposed to "Lycidas" and "Adonais," the
drowned man is not a poet. Lowell alone plays the Orphean lute, and he
questions its power far more explicitly than Milton or Shelley. The terrible
reality of death seems expressible not in poetry but in "The hoarse salute"
of the warships' guns.

In section 2, the sea threatens even the land with a violent storm; and at
this violence the dead sailors long to return to the scene of destruction that
possibly cost them their lives. As in the first section, the language is grotesque and filled with horror:

> . . . The wind's wings beat upon the stones,
> Cousin, and scream for you and the claws rush
> At the sea's throat and wring it in the slush
> Of this old Quaker graveyard where the bones
> Cry out in the long night for the hurt beast
> Bobbing by Ahab's whaleboats in the East.

Section 3 reaffirms the connection between Warren Winslow, whose boat disappeared in the North Atlantic, and the sailors who hunted ". . . IS, the whited monster. What it cost/Them is their secret." Both Winslow and the whalemen are mysteriously swallowed up by the ocean, the news of their confrontation with death lost forever. "IS, the whited monster," is a clear allusion to Moby Dick. This clarity, however, is deceptive, since the symbolic figure to which Lowell refers is itself highly ambiguous. In the poem, the monster becomes equivalent to the German boat that presumably was responsible for the death of Warren Winslow. On the other hand, the name "IS" seems to suggest the ground of being itself, that is, God. This contradiction is not necessarily absolute. The Germans were not inhuman devils (certainly not in the view of a man who protested the indiscriminate bombing of their cities); the Quakers are ironically destructive. Nor is God necessarily moral in specifically human terms. The confrontation with God (the third frame of reference), that "fabled news," is in itself awful. Set in the context of man's own destructiveness (the war, the whalers), the face-to-face encounter may be beyond endurance.

Section 4 sees the *Pequod* "packing off to hell"; but the waters swirling over the New England ship become apocalyptic in their implications.

> Waves wallow in their wash, go out and out,
> Leave only the death-rattle of the crabs,
> The beach increasing, its enormous snout
> Sucking the ocean's side.
> This is the end of running on the waves;
> We are poured out like water . . . .

Is this a vision of the end of the world? Being poured out like water seems to suggest the flow of time, in both its particular and universal manifestations, and with this the notion that "IS, the whited monster," may be time itself. Subject to time, man is destined to tragedy. Only the intercession of an unreachable God can restore significance to human life. The section appropriately ends with a question rather than with a statement.

> . . . Who will dance
> The mast-lashed master of Leviathans
> Up from this field of Quakers in their unstoned graves?

The "mast-lashed master of Leviathans" is Ahab, trapped by his own harpoon-rope; it is also a possible allusion to Christ, mast-lashed in his crucifixion, master of Leviathans. Although it refers to the Judgment, the last question is ambiguous, referring either to Ahab's self-involved pride, which may place him beyond the possibility of redemption, or to Christ, whose symbolic resurrection within the individual human soul may no longer be a significant dimension of spiritual life.

Section 5 attempts to locate the beginning of that saving dance: in the heart of destructiveness itself. Images of the butchery of the whale—the sword sinking into fat, the ripping of the whale's "midriff into rags," "gobbets of blubber" spilling "to wind and weather"—becomes transformed into the crucifixion. "Hide," the section ends, "Our steel, Jonas Messias, in Thy side." Jonah, whose three days in the belly of the great fish, adumbrates the death and resurrection of Christ, becomes the promise of hope; the destructive instruments, lodged in his side, may yet become the means of salvation. Nonetheless, this promise is apparently buried in a flood of blood and blubber, "In the great ash-pit of Jehosaphat," as the ships' ovens become the scene of the Judgment, with the bones still crying for the white whale's blood. And it is the memory of the "death-lance" hacking out "the coiling life," not the final prayer, that dominates this section of the poem.

Section 6, "Our Lady of Walsingham," promises to be a plea for the intercession so desperately needed. The Virgin of Walsingham was a famous medieval shrine, destroyed during the Reformation, later restored. When England shall again go to Walsingham, it is said, England will return to the Roman Catholic Church. Lowell enlarges the scope, looking forward in the poem's last line to the time when "the world shall come to Walsingham." But the description of the statue, taken, Lowell's note tells us, from E. I. Watkin's *Catholic Art and Culture*, belies all hope, very much as the butchery of the preceding section limited the possibilities of the cross. (The original passage in Watkins is clear praise of the statue's inner beauty. A comparison of the two pieces shows that Lowell has intentionally or unintentionally blurred this clarity.) The Virgin's face, "Expressionless, expresses God." The poem does not seriously question God's existence; what it does question is the possibility of bridging the gap between man and God. The blank face "knows what God knows"; and what God knows may have nothing to do with the human condition.

In the poem's final section, the sea is again rough and filled with memories of drowned sailors. The enduring powers of wind and ocean so impress Lowell that he is moved to think of that time

> When the Lord God formed man from the sea's slime
> And breathed into his face the breath of life,
> And blue-lung'd combers lumbered to the kill.

It is an image of creation closely linked with an image of destruction. More important, together they establish the limitations of man's time. Even while man was being created, the huge waves "lumbered to the kill." From water man came, to it he will return; the brief interval is filled with pain and violence. There are signs of hope and salvation all about, but their powers are uncertain, caught in the world's welter.

It is impossible to come to terms with "The Quaker Graveyard in Nantucket" without dealing with the line that concludes its final couplet:

The Lord survives the rainbow of His will.

The line has generally been read as an affirmation of human possibilities; and there is no doubt that the rainbow, God's covenant with man after the Flood and, maybe, after the war, is a symbol of renewal after destruction. After each catastrophe, God endures, and, therefore, man's hope. All the same, the line remains troubling. The allusion earlier in the poem to Jehosaphat's "ash-pit" underlines the equivocation of the covenant: no more water, fire next time. And the word "will" reminds us that God is the ultimate mover of destructive forces; we are returned to the ambiguities of "IS, the whited monster." Finally, it is the *Lord* who will survive; in the context of the previous three lines, quoted above, the implication that man will not is hard to avoid.

It is impossible, and probably undesirable, to resolve finally and convincingly the attitudes of the elegy. Possibly, it is the poem of a traditional mystic; possibly, the poem of a man who has lost, or who is about to lose, his faith. Most likely, the poem works by means of the tension between these perspectives. And it is certainly the energy produced by this tension, and not any philosophical or theological position it might hood, that makes the poem work. Similarly, there is a parallel tension between the poem's superficial form and the attempt of language to shatter all constraint. The sections have involved rhyme schemes, which do not vary greatly from one section to another; the lines are iambic, generally pentameter, but with significant variations. Although half-rhymes are occasionally employed, this means of qualifying form perfected by Yeats is not important in the poem. Lowell does, however, rely on run-on lines, and combinations of assonance and alliteration in conjunction with powerful clusters of spondees to make an emotional impact analogous to that made by an angry ocean attacking a sea wall. These forceful passages are almost always associated with violence and chaos, the smoother ones with God and hope. Whatever his intentions, given this configuration, the relative weakness of Lowell's affirmations, the strength of his denials, is practically assured. If there is any elegy that Lowell's poem should be compared to, it is Gerard Manley Hopkins' "The Wreck of the Deutschland," with its similar vision of God's terror, its similar, though more pronounced, rhythmic breakthroughs. But unlike Hopkins, Lowell's powers diminish when he accosts salvation.

The religious sensibility of *Lord Weary's Castle* is, in fact, generally tinged either in gloom, as in the Puritanical darkness of "Mr. Edwards and the Spider" and "After the Surprising Conversions," or in the painful intensity so often found in Hopkins, as in "Colloquy in Black Rock": ". . . heart,/The blue kingfisher dives on you in fire." Again and again, possibilities are qualified, undercut, in the allusion to Dante's gate of Hell in "The Exile's Return," or in the ambiguity of the last line of "The Holy Innocents": "Lamb of the shepherds, Child, how. still you lie." There is a toughness in Lowell that can save him from the excesses of his passionate involvement in experience, a toughness that is present from the very start of his career.

The Mills of the Kavanaughs (1951) was a mild setback for Lowell. Although some critics praised it, and most found at least some good things to say about it, a sense of disappointment was prevalent. It is probably significant, however, that the standards being set for Lowell were already exceedingly high. The poems themselves can be seen both as finished products and as bridges to new techniques and new areas of experience. Most of the poems are narratives: "The Mills of the Kavanaughs," "Falling Asleep over the Aeneid," "Her Dead Brother," "Mother Marie Therese," "Thanksgiving's Over." More important, they are largely monologs, developments of the methods of "Between the Porch and the Altar" in *Lord Weary's Castle*. The focus is psychological rather than theological, although man's relation to his universe is still a dominant concern. In that sense, these explorations of consciousness begin to point the way toward more Confessional techniques, in which the mask Lowell assumes is his own.

Formally, the poems do not appear to connect the poet of *Lord Weary's Castle* with the one who wrote *Life Studies*. Couplets and quatrains and meters as regular as any Lowell ever wrote predominate. Lowell is, however, working out the difficulties of stream of consciousness and related techniques. He is also expanding the range of his tone, developing a sense of decorum that will contrast effectively with chaotic energy and not simply fall flat.

"Falling Asleep over the Aeneid" is a good example of what is happening in this volume. The poem is largely based on book 11 of the *Aeneid*. The structure is as tight, the allusions as important, as in an early poem by Eliot. The advice given by "the bird-priest" to the old man dreaming he is Aeneas—

> . . . "Brother, try,
> O Child of Aphrodite, try to die:
> To die is life." . . .

—can be seen as a Christian rejection of this world, or as a seventeenth-century pun on orgasm, an incitement to the son of Aphrodite to counter death with life. All this in skillful heroic couplets—a competent, if not spectacular, performance. But what makes the poem come to life is the plunge not into the present but into the past that takes place as the old man wakes up:

> . . . My Uncle Charles appears.
> Blue-capped and bird-like. Phillips Brooks and Grant
> Are frowning at his coffin . . . .

As interpretation of dreams, this is heavy-handed. Still, the Proustian shock of discovering that the past continues to have real presence works. The door to the life studies that no one could have anticipated on the basis of this volume is open.

The organization of *Life Studies* (1959) is obviously important. The book is divided into four parts. The first is dominated by images of war and exile. The second is an autobiographical sketch, superficially about the Lowells and Winslows, much more about Robert Lowell himself. The third deals with four figures significant to Lowell's life and art: Ford Madox Ford,

George Santayana, Delmore Schwartz, Hart Crane. The fourth part is itself divided into two sections: one dealing with the past, from his relatives to his own madness; the other encountering the present. If the poems along the way were not so good, one would be tempted to say that the book is devoted to providing a significant context for its powerful conclusion.

In different ways, each of the first poems develops historical context and prepares the way for the perception that public and private worlds of history are far from irreconcilable. "But who believed this? Who could understand?" so Lowell speaks in "Beyond the Alps" of the dogma of Mary's assumption, pronounced by Pius XII in 1950. Against a backdrop that moves from Caesar to Mussolini, the poem could be taken as a testament to the endurance of the Church as empires rise and fall, but Lowell makes this difficult to do. The movement from Caesar to Mussolini was not hindered by the Church: "God herded his people to the *coup de grâce.*"

There is a similar gloom to "The Banker's Daughter." History is seen cyclically, in terms of a succession of images introduced by Henry IV's pirouette in the first stanza. Marie de Medici, the prom's persona, has "brutal girlish mood-swings." The poem is in danger of being summarized when she notes that "Now seasons cycle to the laughing ring/of scything children." Marie ends by rocking her "nightmare son," who has, in fact, exiled her. Grotesque, subject to time, she is the embodiment of her civilization. Like it, she is at the border of madness.

The cold irony of "Inauguration Day: January 1953" points to a frightening possibility, implied in the previous poems, explicit here. The wheel of history is in trouble: "Ice, ice. Our wheels no longer move." The universe is seen coming to a stop at the "Cyclonic zero of the word." Anticipation of Eisenhower's years in office suggests to Lowell that history could turn so far in on itself that there would be no way back, or, as the next poem, "A Mad Negro Soldier Confined at Munich," will all but assert, there are extremes of madness that can bring time to its knees. Madness as apocalypse is a major intuition of the book.

"A Mad Negro Soldier" takes us fully into the world of *Life Studies*. The first three poems of part 1 carry the mark of *The Mills of the Kavanaughs*. The fourth poem has broken loose. It is composed of quatrains, the rhyme schemes shifting, probably in emulation of the soldier's wandering mind, but the rhythms are new. Lowell searches out the voice of his protagonist, not the seventeenth-century voice of *Lord Weary* nor the eighteenth-century voice of *The Mills*. It is the voice of the experience itself, exaggerated here, yet closely related to the flat, powerful diction of the later poems. Alienated in terms of color, nationality, language, and occupation, not to mention mental condition, the soldier is a mask for Lowell himself experiencing the escape from history through sequence-shattering madness. There is a violence here that is missing in the three preceding poems, a violence that becomes increasingly important toward the book's conclusion.

Part 2, "91 Revere Street," provides *Life Studies* with its familial orientation. In order to know Lowell, you have got to know his antecedents, it would seem. Much attention has been drawn to Lowell's chipping away at his father's manhood; not sufficient attention has been drawn to the fact that these memoirs do not focus on any of Lowell's relatives—they are not *about* them—but on the young boy. The real issue is not his father's manhood, but his own. ("To be a boy at Brimmer [the school Lowell attended, where the students in the upper grades were all girls] was to be small, denied, and weak.") And Lowell avoids cheapening "manhood." He is speaking not chiefly about sexuality, or even about psychology; manhood is a question not so much of masculinity as of humanity.

The four poems of part 3 help to establish a sense of literary and intellectual tradition for Lowell. While New England's religious and political histories, and his own family's history, connect him with the receding past, Ford, Santayana, Schwartz, and Hart Crane are contemporaries or near contemporaries; they are very much a part of his world. Each is pictured at the heart of a conflict, a split denying to them unity of being. Ford's estrangement, as he plays golf with Lloyd George, is political; Santayana's religious; Crane's, sexual; Delmore Schwartz is estranged from sanity itself. In addition to setting out the boundaries of the four corners of Lowell's own mind, these poems are highly individualized tributes to their subjects.

"Words for Hart Crane" is possibly still Lowell's finest sonnet, in spite of the prodigious output of *Notebook* (1970). The poem is characteristic of the methods of the second half of *Life Studies:* tough, prosaic rhythms, laced with spondees; a precision of diction generally associated with Yeats; a sense of irreducibility about the poems. It is this last quality that is probably most significant. It is not that the poems totally resist new critical approaches the way those of Williams do, or those of Olson, or most of Pound; it is rather that the sense of the whole is so powerful there is no danger of getting lost in fragments. Like the good symbol that is itself before it is anything else, all the while radiating infinite possibilities of meaning, the poem means precisely what it says, all the while being limitlessly resonant.

"Words for Hart Crane," beginning with a couplet, ending with a powerful unrhymed epigram—

> Who asks for me, the Shelley of my age,
> Must lay his heart out for my bed and board.

—successfully wrestles traditional forms to the ground, paving the way for the even freer *Notebook.* The sonnet rhymes: *a a b c x b x d e c f e d f.* It is appropriate that the poem both is and is not a sonnet, since it is about a man who both is and is not the prototypical American poet, who both is and is not a foreign outcast.

Part 4, section 1 (a series of eleven poems), operates as an emotional countdown. It moves from grandparents, aunt and uncle, father and mother, to his own stay in a "house for the 'mentally ill,' " and then focuses, more hopefully, on his child. At all times, however, Lowell himself is at the center of these poems. Reality exists as he perceives it. It is a subjectivity that begins to break down barriers between subject and object. Lowell is operating here like a painter who has discovered that the reality of his landscape depends upon himself, that perspective, for example, is not an inevitable visual perception, but a trained response that the artist can reinforce or repudiate. In fact, it is precisely a trick of perspective that makes a poem like "Commander Lowell" work. Cataloging in sequence his father's failures, Lowell concludes with a rapid, dizzying lunge into the past, to the pinnacle of his father's success in 1928, to the even more impressive promise of the beginning of his career:

> And once
> nineteen, the youngest ensign in his class,
> he was "the old man" of a gunboat on the Yangtze.

The technique is flashy. Still, the possibilities for irony may in themselves justify it. And what we respond to may not be excess but enthusiasm. Lowell is on the verge of plunging so deeply into the self that he will succeed in escaping it.

It is Lowell's father, and, more precisely, his father's death, that presides over the middle poems of the series—all events lead up to it, all that follows is in its shadow. In "Terminal Days at Beverly Farms," Lowell confronts the death itself in language that succeeds in being universal without being allegorical, or even, for that matter, symbolic:

> Father's death was abrupt and unprotesting.
> His vision was still twenty-twenty.
> After a morning of anxious, repetitive smiling,
> his last words to Mother were:
> "I feel awful."

There is a passivity here that seems to have been present throughout his father's life; and there is the attempt to transform even the encounter with death into a social occasion. The scene borders on the comic. But it is not comic; it is more nearly heroic. The father of "91 Revere Street" and the father of "Terminal Days" are easily identifiable as the same man. The poetic version has added a complexity of vision that allows for compassion, contempt, possibly admiration, to charge its crucial perception.

By the time the reader reaches section 2 of part 4, he has been through Lowell's stay in an institution ("Waking in the Blue") and his return home ("Home After Three Months Away"). The reader is ready for "Memories of West Street and Lepke," a powerful poem in its own right, even more painfully intense in the context of the entire volume. The guilt that Lowell may seem to have been earning throughout, but which he has probably simply been trying to come to terms with, finally breaks through, although not consciously in relation to his boyhood. A forty-year-old teacher living on a " 'hardly passionate' " street in Boston, where even a garbage scavenger is a " 'young Republican,' " Lowell subjects himself to the pitiless scrutiny that was to characterize Confessional verse.

"These are the tranquillized *Fifties,*/and I am forty." Here the themes of *Life Studies* are brought together. Public and private history are merged; the distinction, which is made, is revealed as barely worth making. The agonies of the depression and war years have given way to a dangerous peace, those of his madness to a suspicious calm. "Tranquillized" is a loaded word here. It insists that the tranquillity is artificial, that it is not an expression of reality but an evasion of it. "Ought I to regret my seedtime?" he asks. This is a crucial moment in the poem. The setting is ripe for self-pity, but the self-pity never materializes. Instead, he launches on a search for things past that in reality bring him directly back to the present. He recalls his days as "a fire-breathing Catholic C. O.," when he served a prison term with fellow "jailbirds" Abramowitz the pacifist ("so vegetarian,/he wore rope shoes and preferred fallen fruit"), Hollywood pimps, a Jehovah's Witness, and Murder Incorporated's Czar Lepke. The ironies are obvious, but effective. Lowell in jail while his country commits murder in civilian bombings. Lowell in jail with a professional murderer. Murder Incorporated and America move into conjunction, both contrasted with the pacifist poet. He in turn is less pacifistic than Abramowitz, who is therefore punished more severely than Lowell by being beaten by the pimps.

The prison is then an instrument of irony. Lowell seems to claim the right to paraphrase Thoreau's question: "what are you doing outside?" The prison is also like Lowell's "school soccer court," and the entire poem is opened by that perception. Is the poet a prisoner of his childhood? Is his being in prison an evasion of responsibility, the acting out of the role of a child when dealing with matters too complex? Does the prison represent the boundaries of the mind, of human reason, when confronted with moral dilemma? Ultimately, the prison is the prison; but the reader is not sure whether he is inside looking out, or outside looking in.

Working like a cameraman who has panned his scene, Lowell prepares for a final close-up of Lepke. Lepke is off by himself, enjoying benefits that other prisoners could not possibly afford—the prison is here clearly a microcosm of American society. He has ". . . two toy American/flags tied together with a ribbon of Easter palm," associating him specifically with the patriotic war effort and, for the first time, with religious experience, already in the reader's mind because Lowell is "a fire-breathing Catholic C. O." and because he makes a point of his ignorance of the Jehovah's Witnesses. It is almost more incongruous that Lepke is in prison than that Lowell is, he is so much a product of American capitalism and democracy. Since *Life Studies* is a book of spectacular endings, we must turn to this poem's conclusion to place it in the proper perspective.

> Flabby, bald, lobotomized,
> he drifted in a sheepish calm,
> where no agonizing reappraisal
> jarred his concentration on the electric chair—
> hanging like an oasis in his air
> of lost connections. . . .

The reader is jolted to recognition of Lepke's lobotomized, sheepish calm as an echo of Lowell's own tranquilization, although this equation was implicit in the relationships mentioned above. The identity, however, is not complete. No agonizing reappraisals disturb Lepke, while the entire poem has been for its author precisely that. And the "lost connections," a terrifying pun evoked by the electric chair, connections forever beyond Lepke's control, are exactly what Lowell is trying to reestablish in the course of the poem. Even after we have made these qualifications, Lowell and Lepke remain uncomfortably close. Although there is no confusion at all between the fire-breathing C. O. and the czar of Murder Incorporated, the years have blurred some of those distinctions. "Ought I to regret my seedtime?" was the question. Lowell has answered it.

"Tamed by *Miltown*, we lie on Mother's bed," begins the next poem, "Man and Wife," picking up the theme of tranquilization. The sun rises, red, like the poet's daughter in her "flame-flamingo infants' wear" in the beginning of the previous poem. The adjective Lowell uses to describe the scene is "Dionysian." The God who is ripped apart and brought to life again is an appropriate association for a man who has been brought back from "the kingdom of the mad." It is the descent into, and return from the underworld, the story of Eurydice and Orpheus—except that here roles are reversed: it is the poet, the man, who must be rescued by his wife. This is a possible reminder that it is on Mother's bed that most of the drama of the previous night has taken place, a place that is both protective and destructive.

The reader is unprepared for the sudden shift to the past in line 12. The recapturing of things past in Proust is most often a slow process, a difficult one, rarely fully realized; in Lowell it is something like suddenly stepping into a hole. And the poet is particularly skillful at exploiting the reader's sensations as he falls. From the agonies of the present, the reader is taken to Lowell's first meeting, or at any rate one of his early meetings, with his present wife. The passage can easily be related to what has preceded it and to what follows. The awe in which he holds his wife, this woman who has "dragged him home alive," is already present in his earlier "fainting" at her feet. Her scorching invective of that time anticipates the "old-fashioned tirade" with which the poem concludes. Yet there is a mystery about the episode that defies traditional analysis. The flashback fits perfectly, but why it does so is not perfectly evident. The tension between past and present is, of course, at the heart of it. But why this particular manifestation of that tension? The reader is convinced, at any rate, that the association is real, that the event from the past has in fact been conjured by the present. Whether it is artifice or the most undisciplined sincerity, the poet is making sure that the reader believes he is "getting the *real* Robert Lowell."

As usual, the poem's conclusion holds its power. The wife turns her back. In exhaustion? In rejection? She turns her back and holds her "pillow to your hollows like a child." To risk ambiguity at this point in a poem that has been anything but ambiguous does not seem reasonable strategy; yet that is precisely what Lowell does. Either his wife, motherly, holds the pillow to her as if it were a child, or she holds it to her as if she herself were a child. On Mother's bed—and that is Lowell's capital letter—this is a vital piece of information; it may define his relationship with his wife, whose tirade, "loving, rapid, merciless—/breaks like the Atlantic Ocean on my head." Does his wife comfort him like a mother, or is she herself a child? Does the Atlantic breaking over his head represent an assault on him, or is it an image of the sea engulfing him? Both loving and merciless, we must remember. Probably both sets of opposites are true. In his recognition of the importance of the subjective perceiver in knowing (perhaps even in creating) the objective world, in his total descent into the ego, Lowell seems to have eliminated, or at least challenged, the fixed point of view. For what is missing in Lowell's use of opposites is the sense of contradiction. In the world of "Man and Wife," life and death, sanity and madness, youth and age, love and hate, protectiveness and destructiveness, are mutually *inclusive.*

The poem " 'To Speak of Woe That Is in Marriage' " is placed between "Man and Wife" and "Skunk Hour" and cannot fail to derive some of its meaning from these poems. A quotation from the Wife of Bath's Tale, the title warns us that we are about to hear the woman's side of it, not necessarily the woman from the previous poem, but a woman involved in a similar relationship. A magnolia first connects the poems, then the violent, mad husband cements that connection. It is a savage piece, concluding with the pitiless couplet,

> Gored by the climacteric of his want,
> he stalls above me like an elephant.

The image of a razor blade is present—as it was in "Waking in the Blue" and "Home After Three Months Away"—suggesting the sharpness of the man's pain, its suicidal or homicidal undercurrents. In a sense, the poem is an act of sympathetic imagination, identifying as it appears to do with the victim of one's own violence. But if this is a poem about the poet as torturer, as seen by the victim, it is also a poem about the poet as victim, for his identification with the wife is complete, in spite of the quotation marks around the poem. Even in a poem whose structure is as relatively simple as this one, the problems of perspective are complex; whether the poem's voice is located totally outside the poet, or whether it is a persona that reveals some aspect of himself, is ultimately not resolvable. As before, both may be true.

The vision of "Skunk Hour" is equally bleak. Signs of sickness and decay are all about. The island's "hermit heiress" is "in her dotage"; she buys up all the "eyesores" and lets them crumble. The end of the summer season itself is described as "ill." Even the fairy decorator is filled with discontent. And this is all prelude to the poet himself, who, climbing the skull-like hill in his car looking for necking couples, decides: "My mind's not right."

The isolation of the next stanza is absolute. The "lost connections" of the Lepke poem, the lonely violence of the marriage poems, finally resolve themselves into what Lowell himself, commenting on the poem, has called a dark night of the soul. In this stanza, he says: "I myself am hell," echoing Marlowe's Faustus and Milton's Satan. He hears his "ill-spirit sob in each blood cell." One of the implications of his emptiness is a center that no longer holds, a unity of being dissolved into its characterless component parts. The poet has become indistinguishable from what he perceives. He is the hermit heiress, the summer millionaire, and the fairy decorator—in each case an outcast, fallen from grace. Searching the hill (with its suggestion of Golgotha or of the human mind) for evidence of love, which he can no more find outside himself than within, the specifically human is exhausted.

Enter the skunks. They march through the town, themselves outcasts. Only the animal is now adequate symbol for the human condition: the mother skunk "swills the garbage pail." There is a toughness in the final line: the mother skunk "will not scare." Whether this is true courage, or the false bravado of the ostrich, to whose tail her tail is compared in the preceding line, is far from clear. The orderliness of the skunks' march is played off against its distastefulness. The poem leaves room for the assertion of value in the valueless, but it does not complete that assertion.

Originally, *Life Studies* concluded with "Skunk Hour." When reprinted in paperback, however, Lowell added "Colonel Shaw and the Massachusetts' 54th," the poem that was later retitled "For the Union Dead." In effect this takes the reader back to the beginning of the volume, especially to the historical and public contexts within which the private experiences must be understood to have taken place. This adds to the book's sense of wholeness. On the other hand, the book loses the impact of ending at the dark zero of "Skunk Hour."

A word should be added about the presumably increased formal freedom of *Life Studies*. It is true that obvious poetic patterns are less evident here than in *Lord Weary's Castle* or *The Mills of the Kavanaughs*, and it is certainly true there is, especially toward the end of the volume, more "free verse" than before. On the other hand, it can easily be argued that there is as much of a rhyme scheme generally in use in part 4 of *Life Studies* as in "The Quaker Graveyard in Nantucket." (The first stanza of "Man and Wife," for example, rhymes: *a a b c d e e c f f g d h g i j d d g i h j;* this kind of pattern, since it is not repeated, may not be as difficult as others less intricate, but it clearly is not an abandonment of structured verse.) And the free verse in these poems is never terribly far from the iambic lines of varying feet used by Lowell in the earlier elegy. Nonetheless, the reader has the impression that Lowell is freer. It may simply be that the units of thought in Lowell's verse cut directly across units of line and pattern and that his ability to shape and control these larger units is by now consummate. In "Skunk Hour," for example, while working in stanzas of six more or less rhymed lines, he conveys the impression of prose, or at least free verse. So careful is the control, so fine the balance, that the only run-on from one stanza to the next, from the sixth to the seventh, coincides with the difficult shift from the human to animal:

nobody's here—

only skunks . . .

There is a new freedom in Lowell because there is a new power.

The poems of Lowell's next book, *Imitations* (1961), are translations that recognize the impossibility of translation. Imitating poets such as Villon, Baudelaire, Heine, Rilke, Pasternak, he remains firmly in the tradition made so important by Pound, characterized by a fidelity to the poem's impact rather than to its exact words. Technically, Lowell's verse in this book seems tougher, more energetic, more compressed, than comparable translations.

For the Union Dead (1964) seemed to signal a return to more public themes and to more controlled use of forms. But although in many ways what emerges from the book is a portrait of America in the late fifties and early sixties, Lowell only deals with generalities in terms of intense and localized perceptions; some of these poems, such as "Night Sweat," would have been perfectly at home in *Life Studies*. Themes more familiar at the beginnings of Lowell's career are picked up again. However, as is the case in "Jonathan Edwards in Western Massachusetts," there is a new sophistication and self-irony:

> Ah paradise! Edwards,
> I would be afraid
> to meet you there as a shade.
> We move in different circles.

That this wit can be perfectly serious is evident not only in the Edwards poem, but in poems such as "Caligula," in which the Emperor, who suffers more than the animals fattened for his arena, wishes "the Romans had a single neck!" Amid the puns and grotesque images emerges, in more spectacular form now, that remarkable tone, revealing a kind of colloquial ease when confronted with intense passion. It is as if Lowell must follow each emotional bath with a book devoted to modulation of tone; *Lord Weary* gives way to the *Kavanaughs*, *Life Studies* to *For the Union Dead*.

There is an important distinction. Where *The Mills of the Kavanaughs* returned Lowell to stricter forms, *For the Union Dead* does not. Whether working with loose stanzas or more obvious free verse, Lowell can be extremely flexible because he is in total control. There may even be the impression that with this book Lowell has reached that dangerous stage in his career where great poetry becomes too accessible.

One of the most interesting poems, probably the best, is a poem that bridges *Life Studies* and *For the Union Dead*, appearing in both: the title poem. Here Lowell is moving toward his new detachment that is, paradoxically, personal. The poet sees the wreck of the old South Boston Aquarium, recalls another scene in which an underground garage is being built, and turns to a Civil War relief in bronze of Colonel Shaw and his black regiment. Developing comparisons of old and new horrors, exploring the ironies of bigotry and war, Lowell moves logically to an advertisement showing ". . . Hiroshima boiling/over a Mosler Safe," and the defeated Negro schoolchildren he saw on television. He returns to the aquarium for his conclusion: "giant finned cars nose forward like fish." We are back in the age of dinosaurs suggested by steamshovels at the poem's beginning. It is a skillful job, it makes its point well through the manipulation of echoing images and ironies.

But that is probably not what the poem is about. The shifts in perspective are dazzling. Or it might be more accurate to say that Lowell, very much like Pound in his *Cantos*, eliminates perspective in the sense of a fixed point of view. Time is wiped out—a fixed point of view in time implies a fixed point in space, and here both are blurred. Although Lowell has described the poem as more "public" than the poems of *Life Studies*, it is possible that by plunging deep beneath the singleness of ego he has reached a public world that is nonetheless completely defined in terms of the self.

Near the Ocean (1967) received the coolest reception of any of Lowell's books since *The Mills of the Kavanaughs*. When a poet reaches a certain level of achievement and reputation, it becomes difficult to assess the true significance of critical response, provoked in this case partially by the poems, partially by the book's format, a more expensive edition with impressive illustrations by Sydney Nolan.

The book is organized around parallels drawn between ancient Rome and contemporary America, a comparison underlined from the start by Lowell's ironic bewilderment, in his introductory note, as to how one could make this connection, except, perhaps, by means of Nolan's drawings. In fact, the comparisons could hardly be clearer. Where Lowell's translation of Juvenal's tenth satire in the poem "The Vanity of Human Wishes" warns the reader to ". . . be prepared/to think each shadow hides a knife or spear," in "Central Park" "We beg delinquents for our life./Behind each bush, perhaps a knife." Lowell gives the edge to New York here, since ". . . each flowering shrub,/hides a policeman with a club." Yet, if the poet wishes to place man's contemporary insanities—Vietnam and the abuse of power, police brutality and civil injustice—within the broader context of continuing human folly, he does not in the least take the heat off the present.

The landscapes of *Near the Ocean* are bleak. A crumbling society dominates, the secular manifestation of a vanishing God: "When will we see Him face to face?/Each day he shines through darker glass" ("Waking Early Sunday Morning"). Human love fares no better: in "Near the Ocean," when Lowell's lovers meet in the park, they find themselves in a water-starved wasteland, with "all access barred with broken glass."

"Pity the planet," he writes in "Waking Early Sunday Morning," "all joy gone." And indeed, in the "modern" poems, there is little relief, except perhaps in the form of the poems themselves. Couplets are everywhere, often set within quatrains. There is the real sense that a vision of this sort needs an effective container to prevent it from indulging in despair. The use of off-rhymes and dissonance, however, has greatly increased, undercutting any illusion of stability.

The Roman poems are not much more hopeful. Although the wit of Juvenal's satire, with all its bitterness, lightens the load somewhat, it is rather on a poem that links the Roman world with the modern, Dante's *Comme-*

dia, that *Near the Ocean* focuses. Lowell's vision is gloomy, a perception of the futility of human existence, of life filled with needless cruelty, terminated by death. We are already in hell, Lowell intimates, and there is no real escape. And yet, the very fact that the cry of pain can be mastered is itself a kind of triumph. Most important is the figure created by Dante, re-created by Lowell in his translation from the *Inferno*—Brunetto Latini. Lowell had already alluded to Latini in the Santayana poem of *Life Studies;* in the context of *Near the Ocean,* his significance is even clearer. If there is indeed no escape from hell, here at least is proof that hell can be borne with dignity.

Notebook 1967–68 (1969; reprinted with revisions and additional poems as *Notebook* in 1970) appears at times a deepening of Lowell's commitment to public realities, at times a further withdrawal to private, subjective worlds. Actually, the distinction between inner and outer becomes meaningless. At the end of the book a list of dates of important events in the news allows the reader to place some of the individual experiences of the poems in order, reminding him that history is somewhere out there. "I am learning to live in history," Lowell writes in "Mexico," describing, possibly, his entire poetic career.

As crucial as the march of events may be, it is Robert Lowell's history that holds our interest—the world as it was lived by the poet, as it was interpreted by him. Lowell, in fact, de-creates history as fast as he creates it. He is after no system, no organization of facts. Nor is he bound by time, since he is as likely in this collection of sonnets to write about Clytemnestra, Sir Thomas More, Roland, Richard II, or Attila as about Che Guevara, Robert Kennedy, Eugene McCarthy, De Gaulle, or the Chicago police. This kind of history has nothing to do with sequence, it has nothing to do with analysis. It does have, however, a great deal to do with the phenomenological nature of a historical event. When Lowell's reactions to the murder and funeral of Martin Luther King become indistinguishable from completely personal experience (as in "April 8, 1968," the despair in which is related to King only by the date), the poet is not simply saying that the inner world is equivalent to the outer; he is arguing for the grounding of history in the concreteness of his own emotions as opposed to the abstractions of historians and journalists. Or, as Lowell says, less directly but more effectively, in section 1 of "Charles River,"

> if we leaned forward, and should dip a finger
> into this river's momentary black flow,
> the infinite small stars would break like fish.

The stars depend on the poet for their being. The very ambiguity of the metaphor indicates the phenomenological bias: it appears that stars are being compared to fish, while the probable daytime setting of the poem makes it more likely that the fish are being compared to stars. In any case, the event cannot be said to exist independent of the perceiver.

Most of the poems do not refer to the events in Lowell's list of events, not even obliquely. The *Notebook* is, after all, a record of the totality of the poet's experience. The poems are about friendship, love, marriage, children, poetry, fame, death. But there is always the backdrop of the historical chronology. Perhaps the book's power derives chiefly from the strain of the poet to live his life and somehow to preserve it from the chaos without, the chaos within. Futilely longing to touch history, not even certain it exists, Lowell simultaneously seeks to escape from its nightmare. The sheer details of day-to-day experience, carefully placed within a seasonal cycle (which Lowell preserved even when he expanded the book beyond the first year), do in fact supply *Notebook* with an oddly affirmative tone; but the affirmation does not cancel the horror. The tension stands, leaving the volume poised between birth and death, between its historical framework (from Vietnam to Vietnam) and its natural framework (from summer to summer).

The tension between form and formlessness within the poet's mind is firmly rooted in poetic technique. The series of sonnets seems at times the unified whole for which Lowell aimed, held together by theme, but mainly by the force of the poet's personality; at other times it seems a series of fragments. The very label "sonnet" is here problematical. Fourteen lines of blank verse is Lowell's description in his "Afterthought" (although he concedes that in places the lines take on "the freedom of prose"). The full and half-rhymes often provide at least the ghost of a set pattern toward which the reader feels drawn, but which he will never quite find. In other ways as well, the words struggle against their framework: run-on lines, often with pauses just before the line's end; private allusions, barely on the threshold of public accessibility; surreal images, juxtaposed without transition, fragmenting the poems and locating unity in the reader. Possibly order triumphs, but not by denying chaos.

In many respects, *Notebook* is Lowell's equivalent to Pound's *Cantos.* They are both visions of history's relation to the self; both mix historical event, literary or mythical incident, and personal recollection and experience without differentiating levels of reality; both are spatial rather than temporal constructs; both are encyclopedic; and both stubbornly refuse to be finished. The differences may be even more telling. Lowell's book is composed of uniform blocks of verse (which he does, however, break into uneven subdivisions) while Pound works with organically shaped materials. Pound sought to discover order where there appeared to be chaos, Lowell seems rather to seek to maintain the balance between freedom and necessity.

Still, Lowell is here closer to Pound than he has ever been before; he may have taken significant steps toward reconciling apparently disparate poetic traditions. A change made by Lowell in the Afterthought of the 1970 edition may shed some light on what is taking place. "I lean heavily to the rational," he writes in *Notebook 1967–68*, "but am devoted to surrealism." In the later edition, he replaces "surrealism" with "unrealism" throughout the essay. Precisely what Lowell had in mind is not yet clear. He is at least severing the connections between his own practice and that of earlier Surrealist poets, and suggesting that the term *surreal* is no longer an exact term. Lowell may mean that in spite of a certain superficial technical similarity, his own verse no longer can be thought of as having its roots in the unleashing of the unconscious mind, but rather as a process of defining what constitutes the real world.

If critical attention is a reliable indicator, Robert Lowell is the preeminent American poet who established his reputation since World War II. His range—in theme, method, and tone—is awesome; his skill is almost too great, his excellence is continually in danger of being overshadowed by his virtuosity. Yet although it is a difficult judgment to make in a man's lifetime, he has the equipment, and perhaps already the accomplishment, of a major poet.

See also the Introduction, section VI.

Selected Bibliography:
BY LOWELL:
Land of Unlikeness. Cummington, Mass.: Cummington Press, 1944.
Lord Weary's Castle. New York: Harcourt Brace Jovanovich, 1946.
Poems, 1938–1949. London: Faber & Faber, 1950.
The Mills of the Kavanaughs. New York: Harcourt Brace Jovanovich, 1951.
Life Studies. New York: Farrar, Straus & Giroux, 1959.
Imitations. [Translations.] New York: Farrar, Straus & Giroux, 1961.
Phaedra and Figaro [Translations.] New York: Farrar Straus & Giroux, 1961.
For the Union Dead. New York: Farrar, Straus & Giroux, 1964.
The Old Glory. [Play.] New York: Farrar, Straus & Giroux, 1965.
Near the Ocean. New York: Farrar, Straus & Giroux, 1967.
Prometheus Bound. [Play.] New York: Farrar, Straus & Giroux, 1969.
Notebook 1967–68. New York: Farrar, Straus & Giroux, 1969.
The Voyage. [Translation.] New York: Farrar, Straus & Giroux, 1969.
Notebook. New York: Farrar, Straus & Giroux, 1970.
History. New York: Farrar, Straus & Giroux, 1973.
The Dolphin. New York: Farrar, Straus & Giroux, 1973.
For Lizzie and Harriet. New York: Farrar, Straus & Giroux, 1973.
See also Lowell's *Paris Review* interviews in *Writers at Work,* 2nd Series. New
     York: Viking Press, 1963.

About Lowell:
Cambon, Glauco. "Robert Lowell: History as Eschatology." In *The Inclusive
     Flame.* Bloomington: Indiana University Press, 1963. Pp. 219–28.
Fein, Richard J. *Robert Lowell.* New York: Twayne Publishers, 1970.
Hardison, O. B. "The Poet and the World's Body." *Shenandoah* 14 (Winter
     1963): 24–32.
Jones, A. R. "Necessity and Freedom." *Critical Quarterly* 7 (Spring 1965): 11–30.
London, Michael, and Robert Boyers, eds. *Robert Lowell: A Portrait of the Artist
     in His Time.* With a checklist of materials on Robert Lowell 1939–1968 by
     Jerome Mazzaro. New York: David Lewis, 1970.
Mazzaro, Jerome. *The Achievement of Robert Lowell: 1939–1959.* Bibliography.
     Detroit: University of Detroit Press, 1960.
———. *The Poetic Themes of Robert Lowell.* Ann Arbor: University of Michigan
     Press, 1965.
Mills, Ralph J., Jr. *Contemporary American Poetry.* New York: Random House,
     1965. Pp. 134–59.

Ostroff, Anthony. "On Robert Lowell's 'Skunk Hour.'" In *The Contemporary Poet as Artist and Critic*. Boston: Little, Brown & Co., 1964. Pp. 84–113.

Parkinson, Thomas, ed. *Robert Lowell: A Collection of Critical Essays*. Englewood Cliffs, N.J.: Prentice-Hall International, 1968.

Perloff, Marjorie. "Death by Water: The Winslow Elegies of Robert Lowell." *Journal of English Literary History* 34 (March, 1967): 116–40.

Rosenthal, M. L. "Robert Lowell and 'Confessional' Poetry." In *The New Poets: American & British Poetry Since World War II*. New York: Oxford University Press, 1967. Pp. 25–78.

Staples, Hugh. *Robert Lowell: The First Twenty Years*. New York: Farrar, Straus & Giroux, 1962.

Stepanchev, Stephen. "Robert Lowell." In *American Poetry since 1945*. New York: Harper & Row Publishers, 1965. Pp. 17–36.

McCLURE, MICHAEL (*b. Marysville, Kans., Oct. 20, 1932—*   )

Michael McClure is generally identified as a poet of the BEAT GENERATION and a member of the SAN FRANCISCO RENAISSANCE. He came to San Francisco in 1953 to study painting with Mark Rothko and Clyfford Still, who had both left the city before he arrived. Instead he studied poetry with Robert Duncan. Evidence of that apprenticeship is deeply embedded in McClure's aesthetic philosophy. In an interview that appears in *The San Francisco Poets*, he says: "What I am most concerned with now is the river within ourselves. The biological energy of our selves is extrusions or tentacles of the universe of meat." The language is McClure's own (he did, after all, write a book entitled *Meat Science Essays*), but the theory is clearly an offshoot of Duncan's brand of PROJECTIVE VERSE theory.

Both Duncan and McClure believe that man's oneness with the universe can be expressed in biological terms, that there are certain essential rhythms and connections in the universe in which man participates. It is the poet's job to write not out of his consciousness alone, but out of his entire body—or, to use McClure's phrase, man "is able to feel with his meat."

This is what McClure, borrowing a term from Charles Olson, would call his "stance" from the beginning of his career as a published poet. At the start, under the influence of Donne and Blake, he did explore the possibilities of metrical and stanzaic verse. But by the time he published *Hymns to St. Geryon* (1959) he had found a technique more compatible with his philosophical outlook, a technique based on obeying the rhythms of the body, principally the rhythms of breath, rather than adopting prefabricated forms. In "Hymn to St. Geryon, I," he writes:

> To fill out the thing as we see it!
> To clothe ourselves in the action,
> to remove from the precious to the full swing.
> To hit the object over the head. . . .

This filling out of the thing is the Projective act, the projecting outward of the river within. "I am the body, the animal," he says toward the end of the hymn, "the poem/is a gesture of mine." The poem is a "field," to use again the language of Duncan and Olson, which the poet creates as a kind of equivalent to his own perceptual field. And it is the entire body, rather than the center of consciousness, that creates that field.

Or so the theory goes. Yet there is a paradox in McClure: the content of his poetry *is* largely the product of conscious intellect. He is often very philosophical in his insistence on the limitations of philosophy. For this reason, his poetry is much easier to paraphrase than the poetry of Olson, Duncan, or Robert Creeley, who subscribe to similar theories of composition. His work remains, perhaps, more in the tradition of Blake than does that of his contemporaries, although McClure is straightforward and direct in a way that Blake never is in his prophetic poems.

It is finally as prophet that McClure seems to see his role. Prophets, however, must make us feel their truths; simply to state them is not sufficient. The question in McClure's case is whether his formal qualities, his sense of free form, are enough to provide the tension that his imagery only occasionally produces. McClure is aware of his dilemma: his need for a philosophy and his certainty that that philosophy is beyond language. His statement of the problem below is characteristic of his methods, of his weaknesses and his strengths. In section 4 of "The Surge," a poem from *Star*, he writes:

> But desire to know and feel are not eased!
> To feel the caves of body and the separate
> physical tug of each desire is insanity. The key
> is love
> and yearning. The cold sea beasts
> and mindless creatures are the holders of vastest
> Philosophy.
> We can never touch it.

Selected Bibliography
By McClure:
Passage. Big Sur, Calif.: Jargon Press, 1956.
Hymns to St. Geryon and Other Poems. San Francisco: Auerhahn Press, 1959.
The New Book/A Book of Torture. New York: Grove Press, 1961.
Dark Brown. San Francisco: Auerhahn Press, 1961.
Meat Science Essays. [Essays.] San Francisco: City Lights Books, 1963.
The Beard. [Play.] New York: Grove Press, 1967.
Little Odes & the Raptors. Los Angeles: Black Sparrow Press, 1969.
The Mad Cub. [Novel.] New York: Bantam Books, 1970.
Star. New York: Grove Press, 1970.
The Adept [Novel.] New York: Delacorte Press, 1971.
See also interview in *The San Francisco Poets*. Edited by David Meltzer. New York: Ballantine Books, 1971.

MERRILL, JAMES (b. New York City, Mar. 3, 1926—   )

For James Merrill, the art of poetry is very much an art of seeing. He focuses now on the outer world, now on his inner self, but most often on the interlocking of the two. For the perception of underlying harmonies, the wit and elegance of Merrill's language is well suited.

Merrill was graduated from Amherst College in 1947. He has been in the army and taught school and is the author of novels and plays as well as poetry. He has traveled widely, living in Connecticut, New York City, and Athens.

"Foliage of Vision," from *First Poems* (1951), tells us a good deal about James Merrill's early poetic perspective. After rain, Merrill observes the ripe, fallen fruit, assaulted by wasps. ". . . What/A marvel is the machinery of decay!" he remarks. The imagery is almost allegorical: the fallen fruit, of course, suggests the fall of man; the wasp is identified as the agent of time and therefore of death. Although the scene is filled with potential terror, the terror is never given an opportunity to develop. In the very process of disintegration is both beauty and order:

> The eye attunes, pastoral warbler, always.
> Joy in the cradle of calamity
> Wakes though dim voices work at lullaby.
> Triumph of vision: the act by which we see
> Is both the landscape-gardening of our dreams
> And the root's long revel under the clipped lawn.

The mutuality of vision is a function both of the mind's shaping powers and of the intrinsic order of things; thus, it is not an imposition upon reality but rather a sympathetic response. Merrill clarifies this further when he talks of saints, "Sensational beyond the art of sense," and of Darwin, who perceives the natural world

> Dancing an order rooted not only in him
> But in themselves, bird, fruit, wasp, limber vine,
> Time and disaster and the limping blood.

The poem is formally an extension of its content, arranged in orderly, rhyming stanzas, with just enough dissonance in the rhymes to suggest the tension between order and harmony on the one hand, and chaos and decay on the other.

Although Merrill's early work appears to consist of the systematic denial or at least the mitigation of harsh realities, it is precisely to these harsh realities that he obsessively returns. In "Laboratory Poem," from *The Country of a Thousand Years of Peace* (1959), Charles, a favorite persona of Merrill's, watches Naomi cutting open live turtles. She does it with perfectly cold, scientific detachment, albeit with an undercurrent of hostility toward her lover, while he gags at the blood,

> . . . at the blind twitching, even after
> The murky dawn of entrails cleared, revealing
> Contours he knew, egg-yellows like lamps paling.

The language tends to overpower the experience, to contain it, but there is less complacency here than in "Foliage of Vision"; it is probably fair to say that this indicates the direction Merrill's development as a poet takes.

"Mirror," one of Merrill's finest poems, exemplifies the growing complexity of his conception of vision. The persona of this poem is the mirror itself. The children playing in front of it serve to define its essential qualities, for they are everything it is not. They ". . . embrace a whole world without once caring/To set it in order." The mirror is then a principle of order, symbolic, perhaps, of the fact that for Merrill vision is a question of sympathy between inner and outer worlds. But here, the principle of order itself is not permanent but subject to what Keats called "slow time." A generation or two has passed, and the mirror's reflective powers are now imperfect. ". . . As days,/As decades lengthen, this vision/Spreads and blackens." In the end, the mirror will be an image of the void. There seems less confidence in the inherent harmony of things; it may be that the perceiver is essential, and he himself part of the mutable world. If the mirror can be thought of as representing the poem, the work of art, then the capacity of art to brave time is severely qualified.

"An Urban Convalescence," from *Water Street* (1962), further explores the poet's growing doubts but also reaffirms his commitment to the powers of imagination. He walks through the city, where ". . . everything is torn down/Before you have had time to care for it." As in "Foliage of Vision," there is an identification of the poet with the scene he perceives. The urban equivalent to that pastoral experience, however, does not reveal joy in calamity. In "The massive volume of the world" he encounters

> Gospels of ugliness and waste,
> Of towering voids, of soiled gusts,
> Of a shrieking to be faced
> Full into, eyes astream with cold—
>
> With cold?
> All right then. With self-knowledge.

The natural, orderly process of decay has been replaced by pointless destruction, revealing emptiness behind façades. The poet returns to his office, takes a pill earlier than he should, allowing his imagination to operate, but not freely. Its concerns have become quite serious:

> . . . not that honey-slow descent
> Of the Champs-Elysées, her hand in his,
> But the dull need to make some kind of house
> Out of the life lived, out of the love spent.

The imagination, on the defensive to be sure, is at least going about its business of filling the void. And for the conclusion of this poem Merrill has returned to more orderly rhymed quatrains, as if to counter the less restrained, relatively free verse of the opening.

Nights and Days (1966), which won a National Book Award in 1967, takes Merrill more or less as far as he can go without actually repudiating the perspective of "Foliage of Vision." There is increasing concern with inner landscapes, for example in the dream poem "The Mad Scene." And in "Days of 1964," whose title echoes Cavafy's "Days of 1909" and "Days of 1911," it is love that must give meaning to experience, and love is understood to be very possibly an illusion. If it is an illusion, the poet, accepting its transience, simply wants it to last as long as it can. Any complacency there might have been in his earlier work is certainly gone by now, as the poem concludes:

> But you who were everywhere beside me, masked,
> As who was not, in laughter, pain, and love.

In *The Fire Screen* (1969) and *Braving the Elements* (1972), Merrill maintains his position on the edge of chaos, with imagination as his chief shield. His language is tighter than ever before, his imagery even more vivid. In "Log," from *Braving the Elements,* he provides lines that could stand as the epigraph to his work:

> Dear light along the way to nothingness,
> What could be made of you but light, and this?

We have but experience consuming itself, and the poem, the imagination, braving time.

Selected Bibliography:
By MERRILL:
First Poems. New York: Alfred A. Knopf, 1951.
The Seraglio. [Novel.] New York: Alfred A. Knopf, 1957.
The Country of a Thousand Years of Peace. New York: Alfred A. Knopf. 1959.
    Revised edition, New York: Atheneum Publishers, 1970.
Water Street. New York: Atheneum Publishers, 1962.
The (Diblos) Notebook. [Novel.] New York: Atheneum Publishers, 1965.
Nights and Days. New York: Atheneum Publishers, 1966.
The Fire Screen. New York: Atheneum Publishers, 1969.
Braving the Elements. New York: Atheneum Publishers, 1972.

About Merrill:
Howard, Richard. *Alone with America.* New York: Atheneum Publishers, 1969.
    Pp. 327–48.

MERWIN, W[ILLIAM] S[TANLEY]   (*b. New York City, Sept. 30, 1927—*   )

In one of those rare instances in which the literary critic has sufficiently understood the methods and purposes of a poet to engage in intelligent prophecy, James Dickey wrote of the author of *The Drunk in the Furnace:* "With tools like these and with the discoveries about himself that this book shows him intent on making, Merwin should soar like a phoenix out of the neat ashes of his early work" (*Babel to Byzantium*). W. S. Merwin, who has moved from the formal to the free, from the traditional to the innovative, has at the least forged a voice that is peculiarly his own. Never closely associated with any of the numerous schools of poetry currently functioning, Merwin is nonetheless very much in the mainstream of contemporary American verse; he is in many ways the representative poet of his time, having gone through a process that is not only common to many of his contemporaries, but a microcosm of the history of modern verse as well.

Born in New York City, Merwin grew up in Union City, New Jersey, and in Scranton, Pennsylvania. After graduating from Princeton, he was a tutor in various European countries and has lived much of his life abroad. Translations from French, Spanish, Portuguese, Latin, Yiddish, among other languages, have apparently brought Merwin more financial success than his "original" poetry. But these translations, many of them of works of medieval literature, have also brought an added richness to that original work, and, it might be argued, did much to support Merwin poetically as well as economically in the early years of his career.

W. H. Auden wrote the foreword to Merwin's first book of poetry, *A Mask for Janus*, which was the 1952 selection of the Yale Series of Younger Poets. Although one must view with suspicion anything that seems to pass as a key to a body of creative work, Auden is undoubtedly accurate in drawing attention to the importance of myth in Merwin's writing. Alice Benson increases our understanding by pointing out "Merwin's insistence on myth-making as a creative process by which existence is reduced from chaos to order through the ordering principle of language itself" ("Myth in the Poetry of W. S. Merwin"). The predilection for mythic materials is not the only, perhaps not even the most important, evidence of Merwin's search for order. The turn toward myth may well indicate not what Benson calls "the impulse to escape the miasma of personal statement and to find a sense of personality, a self, in reference to universal experience," but rather the desire to elude the self, to immerse it in a primal order that is in fact as close to chaos as human consciousness can tolerate.

The poems of *A Mask for Janus* are, for the most part, monuments to orderly vision. The book contains two sestinas, that most unmodern of forms that continually appears in modern verse, and a wealth of less demanding but still clearly defined forms. Descriptive words in the titles themselves reveal a pervasive awareness of tradition and genre: "rime," "ballad," "roundel," "danse," "epitaph," "ode," "song," "carol," "canción y glosa." Such attention to set forms may have several implications: it is almost certainly the mark of a poet learning his craft (the book is in some senses a collection of virtuoso pieces); it could possibly serve to define a sensibility, to announce a certain affinity with the medieval and renaissance worlds from which most of the poems derive their particular shape; or it might conceivably reveal a desperate clinging to solidity in a welter of change and disintegration. Does form completely confident of itself require constant naming, as if it were convincing itself of its existence? Included among the numerous myths alluded to by Merwin is, after all, Sisyphus, whom he describes in "Suspicor Speculum" as "A vain myth in the winter of his sense,/Capable neither of song nor silence." Like Wallace Stevens, Merwin understands the importance of the "mind of winter"; he knows that the final myth is the negation of all mythic possibilities.

"Ballad of John Cable and Three Gentlemen" is in many ways characteristic of the poems in A Mask for Janus, linking Merwin to old traditions, which it then proceeds to undercut. The "three dark gentlemen" have antecedents, from the anonymous "Ballad of Thomas Rhymer" to Keats's "La Belle Dame Sans Merci." Yet there are special problems here. The gentlemen, who have come to carry John Cable over the gray river, seem pretty clearly to represent death or some agency of death. But why three? Charon is singular; so is the king of the underworld. The Fates are three; but they are generally female. And the Devil generally avoids trinity. Though the difficulties are hardly insuperable, the reader is left with a vague uneasiness; at the least, he has not a clear-cut archetypal pattern, already neatly labeled, to fall back upon, he must grope for himself. Just as dissonance is achieved by sounds that almost merge rather than by those completely distinct from one another, so a kind of archetypal dissonance hovers above this story with which we are almost, but not quite, completely familiar.

This sense of uneasiness does, in fact, extend to formal matters as well. As the poem is printed on the page, the expectation is for the traditional ballad quatrain. But to begin with the rhymes are shaky, ranging from very rare full rhyme (years-tears), to conventional ballad off-rhymes (say-lie), to dissonance (said-side), to no rhyme at all (me-afternoon). Attempts to scan the poem metrically are doomed to similar frustration. Individual stanzas seem to offer clear patterns, which are then repudiated by adjoining stanzas, until the reader is no longer certain whether iambs or anapests form the dominant foot, or how many feet consistently appear in which lines. And, odd for a ballad, prosaic rhythms dominate, as in this stanza, which would certainly read like a sentence of prose were the line-endings eliminated:

> And this word, now I remember,
> Makes me sorry: have you
> Thought of my own body
> I was always good to?

All this illustrates the chief characteristic of Merwin's first volume of poems —that the poet shows fidelity to medieval materials and forms while endowing them with a peculiarly modern sensibility. One is left with the impression that Merwin has not falsified, but rather put his finger precisely on those discordant notes in medieval literature that have made the period so attractive to so many specialists in modern literature. In "Dictum: For a Masque of Deluge," Merwin writes: "A falling frond may seem all trees. If so/We know the tone of falling." It is perhaps this "tone of falling" that he employs to link past and present.

Merwin's second book, *The Dancing Bears* (1954), is in tone and substance not unlike *A Mask for Janus*. (Richard Howard is reasonably accurate in referring to Merwin's first six volumes as "braces" of books.) But the new work has a focus much sharper than that of the first. Filled with masks and mirrors, the poems are vitally concerned with the tension between inner and outer realities, between illusion and reality, between art and experience. The title is taken from a remark by Flaubert that language is "a cracked kettle" on which we pound tunes, hoping to win the stars, in reality making music by which bears may dance. Doubtless Merwin is saying that art falls short of its object, that, in Eliot's phrase, "Words strain,/Crack and sometimes break, under the burden,/Under the tension . . ." (*Burnt Norton*). But there is the suspicion that Merwin may think that it is not such a bad thing to have bears dance, that art receives not only its boundaries but its possibilities from the limits of the human condition.

In *The Dancing Bears*, death emerges more and more clearly as the defining characteristic of the human condition; it seriously threatens to deprive human experience of all significance. Paradoxically, however, it is precisely the awareness of ultimate extinction that leads to all that is finest in man's fate: the fact that there are a finite number of moments available to the individual makes it of crucial importance how those moments are disposed of; the fact that man is mortal and changeable makes him long for permanence. As Stevens said: "Death is the mother of beauty." In a Yeatsian mode, Merwin enters the tradition that might well be described as poetry's most nearly essential theme: the strain to transcend the temporal world, which leads to the work of art, the issue of both time and eternity:

> . . . "I imagine
> A song not temporal wherein may walk
> The animals of time; I conceive a moment
> In which time and that timelessness begin."
>
> Creation is not raw, is not refined.
>
> (from "Canso")

In "On the Subject of Poetry," the man in the garden, surely the poet, listens ". . . to the turning/Wheel that is not there, but it is the world." The ambiguity involved in what the man is listening to, whether it can only be the "world" or whether it is nonexistent but still of central importance, is yet another version of the paradox at the heart of Merwin's aesthetics. The imagination is both all and nothing, both infinitely powerful and totally impotent. Indeed, the mythic materials of Merwin's second book tend to be cast in the image of these poetics. In "East of the Sun and West of the Moon," a retelling of the Cupid-Psyche archetype, the imagination is both exalted and revealed as insignificant: the birds sing, "All magic is but metaphor." Again, the characteristic ambiguity. Is magic discredited or is metaphor recognized as having some relation to the real world? "O what am I . . . but a trick of light," says the heroine, while the lucid moon, the imagination, "Creates the image in which the world is." In "Proteus," the poet's concerns have been returned to sources, that is, to the perception of nothingness:

> . . . I am he, by grace of no wisdom,
> Who to no end battles the foolish shapes
> Of his own death by the insatiate sea.

In *Green with Beasts* (1956) vacant eyes become dominant images: what they "look" upon is darkness and emptiness. The influences and materials introduced in this volume seem chiefly designed as vehicles for these themes: the Anglo-Saxon influence of section one, the Kafka-esque quality of section two, the obsession with the sea of section three. (Since one of these is an influence, another a sensibility, the third a subject, there is the obvious possibility, maybe even the necessity, of overlapping.)

The rugged accentual Anglo-Saxon meter, whether as a direct result of the rhythm itself or simply by association with the actual content of much of Old English poetry, conveys the sense of a bleak, if not hopeless, existence, in which man is frequently called upon to confront the dark forces of the world, whatever forms they might take, whatever realities they might represent. One of the finest poems in this mode is "Leviathan": "This is the black sea-brute bulling through wave-wrack,/Ancient as ocean's shifting hills." As was the case in Merwin's use of continental medieval themes and techniques, however, there is an added dimension of complexity in his re-creation of an ancient experience. The great beast is himself a force of darkness, of tremendous potential destructiveness; and yet he is the conqueror of the dark, "Overmastering the dark sea-marches." Ancient as ocean, a "sea-fright," he is nonetheless "Like land's self." He is, in short, beyond categories. He was first; before consciousness, before instinct. The implication, unstated, is that he may also be last; the eye looking out on the empty waste, waiting for the world to begin, may, like Yeats's "rough beast" in "The Second Coming," find himself at both the beginning and end of a cycle.

To compare section two to the work of Kafka is perhaps an overgeneralization. Only a few, like "The Mountain" and "The Station," really qualify as parables of the absurd. But there are elsewhere frequent touches of surrealism and a pervading suspicion of the senselessness of existence. In "The Bathers," ". . . the mirror turns serpent/And their only sun is swallowed up like a voice." In "The Annunciation," there is "A great burning under the darkness," in a poem dominated by the words "darkness," "light," "emptiness," "falling." "The Station," however, is probably most typical, with its

ambiguous vision of the absurd relation between actor and action becoming
an equally undefined expression of courage and despair:

> Why some who perhaps sat there saying least,
> And not, to appearances, the bravest
> Or best suited for such a journey
> At first light would get up and go on.

Or we may turn to "The Master," who is both phony and genuine, for still
another indeterminate symbol of the shifting configurations of illusion and
reality, of the uncertain limits of the imagination. The master has exhausted
his vision, perfected it; he has defined a sensibility, shaped a way of seeing
the world, fashioned what Frost called "a momentary stay against confusion." In accomplishing this he has greatly restricted ways of seeing the
world; he has made it nearly impossible for his disciples to respond honestly
and directly to their own experience.

The sea poems close *Green with Beasts;* they begin *The Drunk in the
Furnace* (1960), uniting the two books into one of Merwin's "braces" of
books, as Richard Howard called them. Connections are in some cases extremely specific. In *Green with Beasts* appears "Fog," in *The Drunk in the
Furnace* "Fog-Horn." ("We cannot be saved here," from "Fog," could well
serve as an epigraph for all the sea poems.) The fog poems keep Merwin in
the bleak archetypal past; in both cases, a heavy Northern gloom prevails,
implying terrors that are almost beyond naming. "That throat does·not call
to anything human," he writes of the "Fog-Horn," "But to something men
had forgotten,/That stirs under fog." It is like the sound of a beast whose
"tethered" tongue can never "speak out in the light of clear day." The menacing voice of the foghorn is dark and inarticulate, like the caves of Forster's *A Passage to India*, in which all sounds are reduced to "Boum"; it suggests a formless undifferentiated being that surrounds and threatens to
engulf consciousness.

"The Bones" brings the series of sea poems to a conclusion. The poet, at
the seashore, remarks that he had never particularly "Considered shells as
being bones," until the "bones" of an old wreck are cast upon the shore by a
storm; then he becomes aware that he is surrounded by bones, of fish, of
men, and "of man's endeavors." The configuration is significant. It takes the
appearance of the man-made wreck to reveal the nature of reality, to lend a
name to diffuse experience. The sense of an infinity of sand, sea, and bones,
and of an awesome, relentless power driving all that lives to its destruction
is certainly felt. But Merwin is here almost optimistic. Although the prospect is nearly overwhelming, the emphasis is upon "nearly":

> . . . These things are not
> Limitless: we know there is somewhere
> An end to them, though every way you look
> They extend farther than a man can see.

In the final poems of *The Drunk in the Furnace*, Merwin engages—more
than he ever has before—the particularity of his own experience. Titles such

as "Uncle Hess," "Grandfather in the Old Men's Home," "Grandmother and Grandson" invite comparison with Robert Lowell's *Life Studies*. While Lowell draws his readers into the very center of his moral universe, however, Merwin creates a series of ambiguous parables, clearly defined though surreally grotesque, which seem closer to public myth than private nightmare.

It may be simply a coincidence that the family poems immediately precede the emergence of Merwin as a practitioner of open form; but it is tempting to the theorist to imagine that some sort of liberating process took place in *The Drunk in the Furnace*. Once a poet of intricate pattern, Merwin now uses free verse almost exclusively; the syntax is frequently fragmented, the language is less precious, less archaic, and much tougher. Most important, perhaps the cause of many of the more obvious distinctions, is the shift in perspective, in the essential voice. In "Grandfather in the Old Men's Home" (from *The Drunk in the Furnace*), Merwin writes of his grandfather's wife:

> . . . raising the family
> Through her needle's eye while he got away
> Down the green river, finding directions
> For boats. . . .

In "Sire," which appears in *The Moving Target* (1963), Merwin uses precisely the same figure:

> Sir, I would like to say,
> It is hard to think of the good woman
> Presenting you with children, like cakes,
> Granting you the eye of her needle,
> Standing in doorways, flinging after you
> Little endearments, like rocks, or her silence
> Like a whole Sunday of bells. . . .

In the earlier poem, the conceit is placed in the mind of the grandfather, in the later in the voice of the poet. "Sire" is dramatic rather than lyric, more objective than personal; Merwin has moved from an art that depended heavily on a continuous, logical texture to one that perceives reality as fragmentary. In place of the blank verse of "Grandfather in the Old Men's Home," Merwin has substituted lines in which participles govern breath, breaking the sentence into discrete units, suggesting a monotony that supplies some of the poem's irony. It is interesting to note that participles are grammatically of equal importance in the first poem, but do not contribute to the poem's structure. The creation of a language that operates as a universe in itself, and not merely as a medium by which thought is expressed, is probably the chief accomplishment of Merwin's new style. It is extreme to say that Merwin has moved from a use of words as ornamentation to a use of words as the essential components of reality, but that idea does indicate the direction of his development.

Because "Sire" shares with the earlier poetry a richness of metaphor, this poem somewhat obscures another distinction of his new voice in *The Mov-*

ing Target: the frequent use of spare language repeated with variations, as in the conclusion to "She Who Was Gone":

> We say good-bye distance we are here
> We can say it quietly who else is there
> We can say it with silence our native tongue

The sense of constriction here may at first be an irritant, but there is also a kind of freedom in the acceptance of limitations. The possibilities of varying a given line, and therefore of the nuances it may be able to carry, are nearly infinite. Merwin is one of the few poets since Eliot (in his *Quartets*) to have exploited this particular technique.

In "Now and Again" Merwin demonstrates that his new spareness is versatile:

> When you consider how learning happens
> You would think that once might be enough.
> You would suppose such pain would become knowledge
> And such knowledge would be wisdom
> And such wisdom would stay with us.
>
> Each time
> The leaves hesitate but finally they fall.

In this combination of abstraction with concrete image, the image is not simply an illustration of the abstraction. The process of development from pain to enduring wisdom is hypothetically described; the image of the leaves hesitating but finally falling may be the painful act of learning, or it may be the object of that act, the essential wisdom itself. What we are left with is a kind of finality without content, a language of silence. And that emptiness, that silence, is not an avoidance of reality; it is *the* reality.

The title of *The Lice* (1967) is explained by the book's epigraph from Heraclitus, who tells how Homer, wisest of men, was deceived by a boy's riddle: "What we have caught and what we have killed we have left behind, but what has escaped we bring with us." The answer, of course, is lice. The riddle is designed to illustrate how "all men are deceived by the appearances of things": the lice can be understood to be the assumptions about experience we carry with us, unquestioned. The main thrust of Merwin's poetry has been increasingly to penetrate the appearances of things, to be able to see—in the words of Wallace Stevens—"nothing that is not there and the nothing that is" ("The Snow Man"). To avoid the traps of subjectivity and yet to retain contact with the human universe—these are the artist's imposing tasks.

"For the Anniversary of My Death" is one of the most striking poems in the collection. The central idea of the poem is simple: each year contains the date on which the poet will finally die, each year he unknowingly passes the anniversary of his death. But the implications of this premise are complex. They involve nothing less than the total breakdown of conventional modes of apprehending time. Viewing time *sub specie aeternitatis,* granting equal reality to time future as is granted to time present and time past, Merwin labels the linear sense of time—that is, time as inexorable, un-folding, continual movement—as illusory. The "beam of a lightless star" is in one sense a metaphor of Merwin's own language of silence, the silence of death, the silence of meaninglessness. A beam emanating from a lightless star also suggests that from a sufficiently detached perspective, a dead star can appear still alive. It takes years—thousands, millions—for light to travel through the universe; in a sense the light exists eternally, although the source of that light may be long dead. This is a fine symbol of the poet's eternal longings. And it is a fine symbol of time as relative in a world of ab-solute being.

Merwin perceives that his death has already taken place in precisely the same sense that the present exists eternally. The temporal distinction is false. In the second stanza, however, he sets up new distinctions to replace the old. He will no longer "Find myself in life as in a strange garment." He will lose his divisive perceptions that isolate him from the rest of being. Merwin's response is characteristically ambivalent. He will no longer be "surprised at the earth/And the love of one woman." The uncomfortable world of time and change is also the realm of specifically human satisfac-tions. It is finally to this human universe that Merwin must return,

> As today writing after three days of rain
> Hearing the wren sing and the falling cease
> And bowing not knowing to what

Though the language is simple, it is capable of bearing much weight. The three days of rain, the singing bird, the image of falling which has, signifi-cantly, stopped, the mysterious bow—all suggest that language does not have to be sensuously rich in order to be archetypally profound. It is, as a matter of fact, the hallmark of Merwin's "new style" that his images consist not of detailed description, but rather of actions and essential types. In fact, in these poems the types become almost allegorical (as in "Crows on the North Slope")—a vestige, perhaps, of Merwin's early interest in medieval forms and sensibilities. But like all modern allegory it is not supported by an ordered universe; it is grounded in nothingness.

For Merwin, the shape of the universe is a function of human conscious-ness. At the beginning of "In the Winter of My Thirty-Eighth Year," the poet is found "Waking in fog and rain and seeing nothing," bringing to mind Robert Frost's "Acquainted with the Night." The poem ends with a rejection of the notion that the universe is in any way obligated to provide meaning for the individual:

> Of course there is nothing the matter with the stars
> It is my emptiness among them
> While they drift farther away in the invisible morning

Or, as he puts it in "The Widow": "There is no season/That requires us."

In many respects, the language of *The Carrier of Ladders* (1970) resem-bles the language of Merwin's preceding two volumes. Certainly, there is no sign of a retreat from the stripped diction and tough rhythms of these works. It is also clear that Merwin's style is still undergoing change. Most noticeable is his attempt to break down distinctions between the abstract and the concrete, to fragment language so that language becomes an object in itself rather than merely a describer of objects.

> on the right is fear I am I fear and
> the rain falling fear red fear yellow fear
> blue and green for their depth etcetera
> fear etcetera water fire earth air

> (from "Fear")

Repetition of phrase as well as word is central to much of his newer work, particularly in the four "psalms" in *The Carrier of Ladders*. The parallelism sometimes recalls the structure of Ginsberg's *Howl*, although Merwin's rhythms are rougher, his syntax less continuous. Most often Merwin weaves repetition of word and phrase, by now the chief characteristic of his poetry.

Curiously enough, Merwin now seems closer than ever to the beginnings of his career. It is as if he had not developed his style by metamorphosis, but rather by a stripping down, so that what we have now in the later poems are the bare elements of his earliest verse reduced to their essential forms. Almost entirely lacking is the occasional use of precious diction that made some of his early work seem bookish. But the sense of an allegorical universe—albeit Kafka's kind of allegory rather than Dante's—the appeal to central symbols and mythic patterns, are even more firmly at the heart of Merwin's poetic sensibility. The later poems are, it is true, closer to archetypal sources. Primitive American societies have replaced European myths as a starting point in such poems as "Words from a Totem Animal" and "The Gardens of Zuñi."

Merwin also seems involved in creating his own myths, myths rooted not in the historical experience of a nation (they may indeed contain oblique contemporary reference), but in landscape, or in action bereft of specific context, as, for example, in "Woman from the River":

> I thought it was an empty doorway
> standing there by me
> and it was you
> I can see that you stood that way
> cold as a pillar
> while they made the stories about you

The doorway, the pillar of stone, the river, are all suggestive of existing myths. Here, however, Merwin is reaching for the stuff that myths are made of rather than alluding to an existing body of legend. And the myth-making faculty is again revealed as a shield against emptiness, against the nothingness that at all times threatens. This is, after all, what his poetry has always been about.

Selected Bibliography:
By MERWIN:
A Mask for Janus. New Haven: Yale University Press, 1952.
The Dancing Bears. New Haven: Yale University Press, 1954.
Green With Beasts. New York: Alfred A. Knopf, 1956.
Favor Island. [Play.] in *New World Writing.* New York: New American Library,
     1957.
The Poem of the Cid. [Translation.] New York: New American Library, 1959.
The Drunk in the Furnace. New York: Macmillan Co., 1960.
Spanish Ballads. [Translation.] New York: Anchor Books, 1960.
The Moving Target. New York: Atheneum Publishers, 1963.
The Song of Roland. [Translation.] New York: Random House, 1963.
The Lice. New York: Atheneum Publishers, 1967.
Selected Translations 1948–1968. New York: Atheneum Publishers, 1968.
Products of the Perfected Civilization. [Translations of Chamfort.] New York:
     Macmillan Co., 1969.
Voices. [Translations of poems by Antonio Porchia.] New York: Atheneum Pub-
     lishers, 1969.
Transparence of the World. [Translations of poems by Jean Follain.] New York:
     Atheneum Publishers, 1969.
The Carrier of Ladders. New York: Atheneum Publishers, 1970.
The Miner's Pale Children. [Prose.] New York: Atheneum Publishers, 1970.
Asian Figures. [Translations.] New York: Atheneum Publishers, 1973.
Writings to an Unfinished Accompaniment. New York: Atheneum Publishers,
     1973.

About Merwin:
Benston, Alice N. "Myth in the Poetry of W. S. Merwin" in *Poets in Progress.*
     Edited by Edward B. Hungerford. Evanston, Ill.: Northwestern University
     Press, 1967. Pp. 179–204.
Carroll, Paul. "Lemuel's Blessing" in *The Poem in Its Skin.* Chicago: Follett Pub-
     lishing Co., 1968. Pp. 139–50.
Dickey, James. *Babel to Byzantium: Poets & Poetry Now.* New York: Farrar,
     Straus & Giroux, 1968. Pp. 142–43.
Howard, Richard. *Alone with America.* New York: Atheneum Publishers, 1969.
     Pp. 349–81.
Stepanchev, Stephen. *American Poetry since 1945.* New York: Harper & Row
     Publishers, 1965. Pp. 107–23.

MEZEY, ROBERT   *(b. Philadelphia, Pa., Feb. 28, 1935—   )*

Early in his career under the influence of critic and poet Yvor Winters—
with strictly formal poetry the result—Robert Mezey soon moved to the relatively open forms so much more congenial to his vision of reality. He is
interested in exploring his feelings, his relationships with other human
beings, not through analysis but rather through the use of suggestive imagery, more often than not drawn from the natural world. It often seems

that it is only by retreating, at least temporarily, to some isolated natural setting that he can understand his place in the world of men.

Born in Philadelphia, Mezey was educated at Kenyon College and at the University of Iowa, where he received his B.A. in 1959. He has taught at Fresno State College, Western Reserve, the State University of New York at Buffalo, and has lived in the Sierra Nevada with his wife and children.

"You Could Say" is characteristic of his poetic methods. It is the end of summer, and the poet is alone. His aloneness is placed in a natural context; it has a relation to the season. In fact, his aloneness seems to be part of the weather. The poem concludes:

> My love,
> it was my nature to want you,
> lascivious, aloof, a body
> fresh as new-fallen snow, and as
> cold. Like other men in my
> desire, I asked for it and now
> I have it—the wind, the black trees,
> scum of ice on the roadside pools—
> all that the rain promised, and more.

Mezey is always a careful craftsman, and there is as much discipline here as in his formal verse. Particularly evident is the way he uses line length to emphasize the first word of each new line.

It is finally his connection with the natural world that dominates Mezey's work. Since for Mezey man is defined not simply by his own consciousness but as part of the universe in which his entire organism participates, his verse does not grow out of an intellectual orientation. The rhythms of his poems are drawn from the rhythms of experience and not from preconceived cerebral constructs. Probably the clearest expression of Mezey's sense of harmony with the objective universe occurs at the end of "There":

> . . . I am sullen, dumb,
> ungovernable. I taste myself
> and I taste those winds, uprisings
> of salt and ice, of great trees
> brought down, of houses and cries
> lost in the storm; and what breaks
> on that black shore breaks in me.

Selected Bibliography:
By MEZEY:
The Wandering Jew. Mount Vernon, Iowa: Hillside Press, 1960.
The Lovemaker. West Branch, Iowa: Cummington Press, 1961.
White Blossoms. West Branch, Iowa: Cummington Press, 1965.
The Mercy of Sorrow. Philadelphia: Three People Press, 1966.
The Door Standing Open: New and Selected Poems 1954–1969. Boston: Houghton Mifflin Co., 1970.

MOSS, HOWARD (*b. New York City, Jan. 22, 1922—*   )

Although he has recently made use of freer forms, Howard Moss is generally most comfortable with tightly controlled stanzaic patterns and meters. Like the Projectivists, he sees connections between the human universe and the cosmos as a whole; very unlike them, he depends upon wit and intellect rather than spontaneous rhythms to perceive underlying harmonies.

Born in New York City, Howard Moss received his B.A. from the University of Wisconsin in 1943. He is the poetry editor of *The New Yorker*.

"Elegy for My Father" in *The Toy Fair* is one of Moss's best-known poems. It begins:

> Father, whom I murdered every night but one,
> That one, when your death murdered me,
> Your body waits within the wasting sod.

The meter is iambic pentameter, the stanzaic pattern: *a b c c a a b b*. Moss analyzes his emotions, couching them in intellectual terms. A chiasmus organizes the beginning of the poem ("murdered" appears in the first half of one line, the second half of the next, while the reverse is true of "one") and becomes almost an emblem of the balance between father and son. Alliteration and a variety of internal sound effects also knit the lines together. For most of his career, Moss has written the kind of poetry best approached through the methods of the NEW CRITICISM.

In a later poem like "Arsenic" (in *Second Nature*, there is more flexibility, as in the following lines:

> I have never killed.
> I have loved three times—
> Possibly four.
> I have two suits
> I will never wear.

The ghosts of stricter forms still hover throughout, producing an interesting tension in the poetry.

Selected Bibliography:
BY Moss:
The Wound and the Weather. New York: Reynal and Hitchcock (Harcourt Brace Jovanovich), 1946.
The Toy Fair. New York: Charles Scribner's Sons, 1954.
A Swimmer in the Air. New York: Charles Scribner's Sons, 1957.
A Winter Come, A Summer Gone: Poems, 1946–1960. New York: Charles Scribner's Sons, 1960.
The Magic Lantern of Marcel Proust. [Criticism.] New York: Charles Scribner's Sons, 1962.
Finding Them Lost. New York: Charles Scribner's Sons, 1965.
Second Nature. New York: Atheneum Publishers, 1968.
Selected Poems. New York: Atheneum Publishers, 1971.

About Moss:
Howard, Richard. *Alone with America.* New York: Atheneum Publishers, 1969. Pp. 382–95.

NEMEROV, HOWARD   (*b. New York City, Mar. 1, 1920—   *)

Howard Nemerov has been a significant figure in American poetry for almost the entire post–World War II period. One of the relatively few poets writing today within the limits set by traditional verse forms, he is also one of the few poets who has not radically challenged the integrity of the self as a point of view from which reality may be perceived.

Born in New York City, Nemerov received his bachelor's degree from Harvard in 1941, before entering the Royal Canadian Air Force. In American uniform, he then served with the RAF over the North sea. He subsequently taught at Hamilton, Bennington, and Brandeis.

Although Nemerov generally preserves the boundaries between the subjective self and the objective world, the relationship between the two is often at the heart of his poetry. The sense in which this is true can be illustrated by one of Nemerov's most successful poems, "The Goose Fish," from *The Salt Garden* (1955).

Two lovers embrace on the shore; their shadows become one. It is a prelapsarian scene, in which the lovers are in perfect harmony with each other and with their natural surroundings. Nemerov, in fact, describes them as "emparadised." The second stanza concerns their fall from grace, the effects of which they experience before they even begin to comprehend the cause. They are now "Embarrassed in each other's sight"; they feel "As though the world had found them out" when they see the embodiment of their uneasiness on the sand at their feet: a goose fish, dead, his head grinning. It is not immediately evident whether the fish is somehow the cause of their predicament, or whether their actions have actually invoked his appearance. He lies there in "the china light," "most ancient and corrupt and grey." He is certainly a symbol of the world of time and decay into which the lovers have fallen from their timeless Eden. But named as both bird and fish, and as the one before whom the lovers' shame is manifest, he is a god. He does in fact become their "patriarch," after they take the fish with his grin as

> . . . an emblem of
> Their sudden, new and guilty love
> To be observed by, when they kissed,
>   That rigid optimist.

The poem moves, then, from a sense of harmony with nature to a vision of nature as something grotesque and alien, out of which man is cast in disgrace. "The Goose Fish" is an example of Nemerov's perspective, which generally demands that the specifically human be placed in sharp juxtaposition to an unsympathetic natural world.

"The Pond" is another illustration in *The Salt Garden* of the kind of poetry Nemerov can write best. A narrative in blank verse, it reminds us that Nemerov's position is analogous to that of a representational painter in a world of abstract expressionists, cubists, and surrealists. Gradually, a result of exceptionally heavy rains, a pond appears in the meadow. That winter, it freezes over, and the children skate on it. The ice breaks, and the pond, still nameless, has its victim, a boy named Christopher.

From this tragedy, the water receives its name: Christopher Pond. As in "The Goose Fish," the encounter between man and nature leads to an awareness of time and death; that is, it leads to a sense of history. But also as in "The Goose Fish," nature's role is not passive, it is not simply sitting there waiting to be noticed. It materializes unexpectedly like a dead fish, or like water in a dry meadow. As Nemerov points out in the poem, nature has its own history. The pond appears, takes its toll, and begins to dry up the following summer. And during that summer, this place of death becomes a place of teeming life, a lush and thick swamp choking with birth,

> As though, in spite of all the feeding there,
> Death could not keep the pace and had to let
> Life curb itself . . .

In this image, life and death become almost interchangeable, or, at the very least, aspects of the same process. Nature's "history" is in part a question of catastrophe and subsequent renewal. It is also seen in the poem as the continuing cycle of birth, death, and rebirth, of continual metamorphosis, as in the image of the dragonfly near the poem's conclusion. The dragonfly is first "In a small way a dragon of the deep, / A killer and meat-eater." It then rises from beneath the surface of the pond and takes "a lighter part." Together with the name Christopher, and the Easter setting of the melting ice, this makes links between natural cycles and Christianity clear. No affirmation emerges, however, as a result of placing man within his natural context; at best the antagonism between man and nature quiets to an uneasy truce: "Not consolation, but our acquiescence."

It would be incorrect to suppose that Nemerov sees nature as a force actively hostile to man. Echoing Robert Frost's assertion that the time is neither wrong nor right, Nemerov says in "Deep Woods":

> Line, leaf, and light; darkness invades our day;
> No meaning in it, but indifference
> Which does not flatter with profundity.

Caught up by the indifferent universe, man is not capable of real tragedy. Nemerov's firm insistence on the self's integrity seems to come out of his awareness of how difficult it is to assert its existence.

In the title poem of *The Blue Swallows* (1967), the poet attempts to come to terms with the painful limitations of the human intellect. He remarks how long it has taken the mind

> . . . to see
> With opened eyes emptied of speech
> The real world where the spelling mind
> Imposes with its grammar book
> Unreal relations on the blue
> Swallows. . . .

Nemerov's reactions to this perception are not unmixed. The poem is, in a sense, a comment on his own poetry, which is so frequently involved in analyzing the complexities of experience. He refers to "That villainous William of Occam," a fourteenth-century English philosopher who undercut the possibilities of abstraction. But in this poem, more than anywhere else in his work, Nemerov reacts to the limitations of the mind not with pain or frustration or self-mockery, but rather with the anticipation of a new awakening. At the poem's conclusion he seems to assert, although ambiguously, the central importance of the mind in this new apprehension of reality:

> O swallows, swallows, poems are not
> The point. Finding again the world,
> That is the point, where loveliness
> Adorns intelligible things
> Because the mind's eye lit the sun.

Selected Bibliography:
By Nemerov:
The Image and the Law. New York: Holt Rinehart & Winston, 1947.
The Melodramatists. [Novel.] New York: Random House, 1949.
Guide to the Ruins. New York: Random House, 1950.
Federigo, or The Power of Love. [Novel.] Boston: Little, Brown & Co., 1954.
The Salt Garden. Boston: Little, Brown & Co., 1955.
The Homecoming Game. [Novel.] New York: Simon & Schuster, 1957.
Mirrors and Windows. Chicago: University of Chicago Press, 1958.
New and Selected Poems. Chicago: University of Chicago Press, 1960.
The Next Room of the Dream: Poems and Two Plays. Chicago: University of Chicago Press, 1962.
Poetry and Fiction: Essays. New Brunswick, N.J.: Rutgers University Press, 1963.
Poets on Poetry. [Editor.] New York: Basic Books, 1966. (Includes "Attentiveness and Obedience," an essay on his own poetry.)
The Blue Swallows. Chicago: University of Chicago Press, 1967.

About Nemerov:
Dickey, James. "Howard Nemerov" in *Babel to Byzantium: Poets & Poetry Now.* New York: Farrar, Straus & Giroux, 1968. Pp. 35–41.
Harvey, Robert D. "A Prophet Armed: An Introduction to the Poetry of Howard Nemerov." In *Poets in Progress.* Edited by Edward Hungerford, Evanston, Illinois: Northwestern University Press, 1967. Pp. 116–33.

NEW BLACK AESTHETIC

In his essay "A Black Criterion," originally printed in *The Journal of Black Poetry* in 1967, Clarence Major insisted that "seeing the world through white eyes from a black soul causes death." This probably expresses the very heart of the New Black Aesthetic. The traditional Western view of man's relation to the world in which he lives is not inevitable. Its history suggests that it is destructive and oppressive, based on ideas of separation rather than community, domination rather than harmony. "The artist," says Major, "does owe something to the society in which he is involved." The society in which black writers are involved is the society of black men bound by a white vision of reality; it is the obligation of the black writer to express the blackness of his people and thereby to liberate them.

Developed in the late fifties by such writers as IMAMU AMIRI BARAKA (formerly LeRoi Jones) and Major, the New Black Aesthetic has come under heavy attack by more traditional critics. The lines of battle are not new. To what extent should a writer take into account social reality? If art is the record of an *individual* man's response to his reality, as some critics maintain, how can the content of art be dictated by any general formulation of the human condition? Do not the complexities of experience go beyond the boundaries of any fixed system, and is not the precise task of the artist, as opposed to a philosopher, for example, to be faithful to these complexities rather than to any attempt to contain them?

There are, however, answers to these objections. To the notion that art is the expression of the individual consciousness, one can reply that this is not only a Western idea, but one that McLuhan would describe as print-begotten. Are not the *Iliad* and most of medieval literature expressions of a communal consciousness? To the charge that the New Black Aesthetic is political, one can reply that formalist criticism is in its own way political, a denial of history, an implicit acceptance of the status quo, an imposition of Western ideas of structure.

In any case, the New Black Aesthetic is a potent force among young black writers like DON L. LEE, SONIA SANCHEZ, NIKKI GIOVANNI, MARI EVANS. And some older writers, like GWENDOLYN BROOKS, have forsaken their allegiance to traditional standards of criticism in order to embrace it. It is important to remember that even as stated by such partisans of black consciousness as Baraka and Major, the new Black Aesthetic serves not only an important political function, but also constitutes a questioning of basic aesthetic assumptions at a time when they clearly need to be questioned.

See also the Introduction, section VII.

NEW CRITICISM

The New Criticism (1941) by John Crowe Ransom was a discussion of contemporary literary criticism focusing on the critical work of I. A. Richards,

William Empson, T. S. Eliot, and Yvor Winters. The term has generally been expanded, first to include other specific critics (principally those connected with Ransom at Vanderbilt—Robert Penn Warren, Cleanth Brooks, Allen Tate, for example) and finally to embrace all criticism emphasizing close reading of texts. The New Criticism was a reaction against the historically oriented criticism that had until the thirties dominated the academies and in its turn became the new orthodoxy. In recent years, the New Criticism has come under heavy attack by socially minded critics, particularly exponents of the NEW BLACK AESTHETIC.

The New Criticism seemed to be as apolitical as a critical method could be: it warned against the intentional fallacy—the idea that a poem could be explained by what its author thought he was doing—and the affective fallacy—the idea that a poem could be understood in terms of one's emotional response to it; in short, the emphasis was on art as a formal structure, with its own unity and integrity, which had to be approached through its own laws rather than through any imposed from without. The new black critics, however, are among those raising the question of whether the removal of art from the political and social world was not in itself tacit approval of the status quo, an implicitly conservative position. The fact that so many of the New Critics were politically conservative Southern agrarians reinforced this suspicion.

An equally serious problem arises from the heavily intellectual approach of the New Criticism. It is at its best dealing with ironies, ambiguities, cleverly developed structures of theme and motif. This approach is perfectly appropriate to certain poetic styles, the metaphysical poets, for example, and contemporary poetry influenced by the metaphysical poets. It can also be applied to most poetry studied in the academies, from Chaucer on. But from the very start it had difficulty with Pound's *Cantos* and most of the poetry of William Carlos Williams, with the result that these poets never received anything approaching the attention accorded T. S. Eliot and Wallace Stevens. And there is now an increasing body of work, particularly in the Objectivist-Projectivist tradition, to which the principles of the New Criticism seem barely relevant.

Nonetheless, the New Criticism has made available to the contemporary critic a valuable methodology. It taught the reader and scholar to look closely at the text, more closely than ever before, and that is not a lesson that will be quickly forgotten. Like Newtonian physics, proved inaccurate in the age of relativity, it remains more or less sound in many instances. Although contemporary poetry continues to experiment with the many ways the self can relate to the outer world, the methods of the New Criticism can still be applied successfully to poetry expressing a particular mode of that relationship.

See also the Introduction, section VII.

NEW YORK POETS

Although they lack a uniformly agreed-upon manifesto, and therefore may not constitute a "poetic school" in the conventional sense, the New York Poets have since the fifties been one of the most important groups of poets in America. FRANK O'HARA, JOHN ASHBERY, and KENNETH KOCH, the most prominent of the group, originally met at Harvard. They came to New York City in the early fifties; there they met such poets as JAMES SCHUYLER and EDWARD FIELD, and were associated with The Living Theater and the Artists' Theater. Even more significant was their connection with the contemporary art scene. O'Hara, Ashbery, and Schuyler, for example, were all editors for the Museum of Modern Art's *Art News* at one time or another.

The poetic school with which the New York Poets have been most closely associated is probably Charles Olson's PROJECTIVE VERSE. At any rate, they generally have preferred open to closed poetic forms and have agreed with Olson's assertion that an "alternative to the ego position" as a perspective from which reality can be viewed must be sought. Ashbery in particular has, like many of the Projectivists, looked to natural, biological rhythms for the sources of poetic energy.

But the New York Poets have their own defining characteristics, which set them off from the Projectivists as a whole. Most important is the influence of the painters working in New York at the time of their origins, especially Willem de Kooning and Action Painting. The notion that the process of creation is at least as important as the product and the sense of a fragmented reality are obvious manifestations of this influence. It is clear, however, that the *milieu* of the art world was as important as its aesthetics. In addition, the literary and artistic traditions of symbolism, Surrealism, and Dada have left their imprint on the works of the New York Poets.

With the death of Frank O'Hara in 1966, the group lost its most significant member. It has persisted, however, with remarkable vitality, considering the changes that have taken place in the world that gave it life and the lack of any clear-cut definition.

See also the Introduction, section V.

OBJECTIVISM

In 1931 William Carlos Williams, Charles Reznikoff, and George Oppen, who supplied financial backing, founded the Objectivist Press. Ezra Pound and Louis Zukofsky joined Williams on the press's advisory board. The press lasted about three years, published three or four books, including *An "Objectivists" Anthology* (1932) and Williams' *Collected Poems* (1934), and then folded. The Objectivist aesthetic, while it did not in itself rouse a great or enduring following, provided a crucial link between IMAGISM and the theories of PROJECTIVE VERSE propounded by Charles Olson in 1950.

Objectivism began as a reaction to, or rather a clarification of Imagism, which, "though it had been useful in ridding the field of verbiage," wrote Williams in his *Autobiography*, "had no formal necessity implicit in it." Seeing Objectivism as "an antidote" to free verse, Williams and the others argued that "the poem, like every other form of art, is an object, an object that in itself formally presents its case and its meaning by the very form it assumes." As Williams emphasized in his entry on Objectivism for the *Princeton Encyclopedia of Poetry and Poetics,* it was a question of structure.

By insisting that the poem derived its structure out of its objectness, by insisting on the poem's existence as a reality in itself, Williams helped open a door that was only potentially opened by Imagism: the escape from the ego. Pound had contended that Imagism was concerned with the moment the subjective became objective. He shifted the emphasis of the poem from subjectivity to its objective expression. Williams began where Pound left off. The poet, for Williams, has already entered the objective world: the world of external objects, the world of the poem itself. He has expanded the bounds of the human universe by seeing no significant distinction between the structures of objective reality and the structures of the human mind. Where Pound's Imagism juxtaposed objects, Williams' Objectivism could enter them. It was only one short step from this to Olson's perception that it is possible, maybe even necessary, to probe within, beneath consciousness, in order to find man's links with the objective universe.

See also the Introduction, section II.

O'HARA, FRANK   (*b. Baltimore, Md., June 27, 1926— d. July 25, 1966*)

Donald M. Allen's edition of *The Collected Poems of Frank O'Hara* (1971) is a surprising book. It is surprising first of all because of its size, nearly five hundred large, well-filled pages of the poetry of a man who published in his lifetime only a handful of slender volumes. The number of poems O'Hara never attempted to publish, or apparently even to preserve, is overwhelming. A second surprising fact is the overall quality of the work. This is not to say that no poems stand out or that none are particularly weak, but by and large the previously uncollected and unpublished work compares well to the poems already published. The poems, which are arranged chronologically, reveal a consistency of poetic powers that is evident even when a specific poem does not quite work. In a way, then, *The Collected Poems* is in its very nature the clearest statement we have of Frank O'Hara's conception of the poet: he is not someone trying to make sense out of his experience, concentrating it in a limited number of intense visions that illuminate the human condition; he is rather a man continually seeing the world freshly, who records rather than organizes his perceptual universe. Although obviously lacking even an attempt at thematic or structural unity, O'Hara's *Collected Poems* stands with Ezra Pound's *Cantos* as an encyclopedic record of how a man gives form to his reality.

Born in Baltimore in 1926, Frank O'Hara grew up and was educated in Massachusetts. Having served in the Navy during the Second World War, he obtained a B.A. from Harvard in 1950, majoring first in music and then in English. In 1951 he received an M.A. in creative writing at the University of Michigan, won an Avery Hopwood award, and then moved to New York and began working for the Museum of Modern Art. He was associated with the museum for most of the remainder of his life.

By this time his circle of friends included JOHN ASHBERY, KENNETH KOCH, Larry Rivers, and JAMES SCHUYLER. In the early fifties, he met New York painters Willem de Kooning, Franz Kline, Michael Goldberg, and Jackson Pollock. The resulting friendships may have had at least as much to do with his development as a poet as more literary influences. His first book, *A City Winter*, was published by the Tibor de Nagy Gallery in 1952, and subsequent publications included not only books of poetry but critical studies of painters as well, most notably his long essay *Jackson Pollock* (1959). On July 24, 1966, having been virtually ignored by the academic critics, and yet an almost legendary figure within his own circles, he was run down by a beach-buggy on Fire Island and died in the hospital the next day. He was forty years old.

The development of Frank O'Hara's poetic techniques is much more easily followed in *The Collected Poems* than in the earlier volumes of poetry. Even there, the development is generally a subtle one, especially when compared with that of O'Hara's contemporaries, for example, Robert Lowell, or Theodore Roethke. Some general observations are possible, however. Although O'Hara was using freer forms from the very start of his career, the early poetry contains a good deal of experimentation with strict patterns—there are, for example, a remarkable number of sonnets—that gradually disappears. Stanzas remain long after rhyme has become a rarity, but even these are finally abandoned. Similarly, the surrealist touch seems more pronounced in much of the early work. O'Hara is never a "realistic" poet, but while the shock of dislocation in early poems usually resides in the images themselves, in later work it is a result of fragmented syntax, and often of vision itself. Taken together, these tendencies suggest the increasing influence of Charles Olson and PROJECTIVE VERSE, in which rhythm and juxtaposition of perceptions are crucial. But it is a question of shift in emphasis rather than dramatic change; there is, in the end, a remarkable sense of unity in the poetry.

"The Young Christ," probably written in 1950 or 1951 and first published in *A City Winter*, is perhaps an extreme example of O'Hara's early methods. The poem's narrator is a Christ whose pain and triumph are surrealistically projected on the outer world, which in turn becomes an inner landscape:

> The hill my bones fornicate and thatch
> screams at the pure azure to get
> bloody, at the immaculate ocean to be
>
> purer than the royal motive . . .

The pain of crucifixion and the pain of sexual entry, in a specifically homo-sexual context, are brought together; the "skull which like a sow burns fat/was ovoid rectum to a frightened girl" and then that skull, the poem's central image, is thrust "between king's purple thighs/a burning child." It is a strange poem, taking place on that fringe of consciousness where events are felt but hard to follow. But the feelings are clear, communicated by the ubiquitous skull, verbs like "strains," "crash," "screams," the recurrent image of burning, the references to "a homosexual Pharisee" and Christ's fear that ". . . I must be a pansy/myself." What it all means, if that is a le-gitimate term to use in connection with O'Hara's work, is almost impossible to say, until one recognizes that the poem's dominant conceit must be re-versed. That is, this is not a poem about a Christ who sees himself as a ho-mosexual; it is a poem about a homosexual who sees himself as a Christ. With that perception, the poem falls into place.

While the surreal imagery is its most striking characteristic, equally inter-esting are its shifts in tone. For example, O'Hara can move in a few lines from the colloquial tone of "Nobody'll be playing on that striped beach" to the anachronistic inversion of "What think you?" Either the poem is flawed or we have been placing too much emphasis on unity of tone as a necessary poetic element. O'Hara's work in general stands as eloquent support of the latter possibility.

"The Young Christ" is written in unrhymed triplets, a form favored by Wallace Stevens as well as by O'Hara. A City Winter also contains far more formal poetry. The title poem, for example, is actually a short sequence of five sonnets, both Italian and English, conventionally unified in terms of theme and imagery. The meter is iambic pentameter, notable for its regular-ity, as in these lines: "I plunge me deep within this frozen lake/whose mir-rored fastnesses fill up my heart." The themes are familiar enough in O'Hara's work—loneliness, the night of the soul, fear and pain, homosexuality—and the surreal imagery gives the sequence its measure of success, but there is nothing here of the open verse that finally dominated O'Hara's work. This is persuasive evidence that O'Hara's methods emerged out of his own emotional and poetic needs rather than out of any blind de-votion to someone else's poetic theory.

"Chez Jane," first published in 1954 and reprinted in *Meditations in an Emergency* (1957), emphasizes another aspect of O'Hara's sensibilities. It begins:

> The white chocolate jar full of petals
> swills odds and ends around in a dizzying eye
> of four o'clocks now and to come. . . .

The lines seem at first almost a shameless echo of Wallace Stevens; but they are immediately followed by lines Stevens never could have written: ". . . The tiger . . . pisses/into the pot, right down its delicate spout." This shift in tone is analogous to the one that takes place in "The Young Christ," but this time the reader has unquestionably been set up to be cata-pulted suddenly into a universe that is uniquely O'Hara's. When "A whisper of steam goes up from that porcelain/eurythra," the poet seems to hear it whispering "Saint-Saëns!" making an association between the actions of the beast—is it a real cat, an imaginary tiger?—and music, music that later "scratches" the animal's "scrofulous stomach." Perhaps it is a complex metaphor. Is it the element of surprise that defines art, its deliberate irreverence; or the "truly menacing" quality with which the poem ends; or the conversion of piss into steam, the earthy transformed into the spiritual? It is possible to work with the poem in this way. And yet one feels a fool doing it. The vision is first and foremost a sensuous rather than intellectual one, it is playful rather than metaphysical, and something in the poem itself suggests that we leave it just at that. The NEW CRITICISM is all well and good when applied to the sequence "A City Winter," but the further one reads in *The Collected Poems* the less applicable the New Criticism becomes. If we are going to read O'Hara, we are going to have to learn to respond to precisely what is there. This is not to say that he is working without method. And the delight in deflation, in breaking down all imaginable rules of decorum, becomes increasingly prominent in the verse.

Although it is impossible to deal with it comprehensively in an essay of this size and purpose, O'Hara's long poem *Second Avenue* (1960), actually written in 1953, requires at least passing mention. The poem begins:

> Quips and players, seeming to vend astringency off-hours,
> celebrate diced excesses and sardonics, mixing pleasures,
> as if proximity were staring at the margin of a plea . . .

It begins with the dominance of intellect, reminding us, perhaps, of a Stevens gone wild. Hart Crane comes to mind when O'Hara writes, "your distinction is merely a quill at the bottom of the sea," and not simply because the bottom of the sea is mentioned. But soon we are again plunged into a world that is O'Hara's alone; in lines like these, the second-hand feeling totally disappears:

> . . . I am a nun trembling before the microphone
> at a movie première while a tidal wave has seized the theatre
> and borne it to Siam, decorated it and wrecked its projector.

If O'Hara's work, taken as a whole, is encyclopedic, then *Second Avenue* is a microcosm of the whole and affords us the opportunity to determine precisely what the adjective "encyclopedic" means when applied to O'Hara. It is first of all a personal poem. O'Hara introduces the word "proximity" at the start, and there is reason to assume that the poem's subject is in fact the poet's proximity to other human beings, to certain human beings in particular. If that is so, all distinctions between the poet's inner world and the world in its largest sense are broken down. The geographical range, for example, is immense. Among the localities that figure in the poem are: Siam, the Bronx, the Amazon, America, Lesbos, the Bering Sea, Tierra del Fuego, Japan, Victoria Falls, Pasadena, the High Sierras, China, Hollywood, Massachusetts, Venice, New Guinea, Vienna, and Mexico. And, of course, Second Avenue. This is not at all a travel poem, however; the places are not explored, but rather become the sources of imagery and metaphor. A catalog of the animals mentioned would be as varied. More instructive is this example of how O'Hara includes them: "And must I express the science of legendary elegies/consummate on the Clarissas of puma and gnu and wildebeest?" He says at one point, "I can only enumerate the somber instances of wetness." Enumeration is indeed the dominant method of the poem. Visual perceptions, recollections of the past, records of the present.

The cumulative result is an insistence on the individual detail or fragment, a discouraging of searches for overall patterns. Somewhat in the tradition of Pound, William Carlos Williams, and Olson, it lacks the broad mythic structures to which the reader can always retreat in their works when the concrete has exhausted him. It is either formless or demands a new definition of form. And yet, although the poem at times seems to be simply a listing of experiences, it is obvious that the experiences have been transformed by the poet's sensibility. This sensibility is, in fact, what the poem is "about." (In his notes on the poem, O'Hara concludes, "I hope the poem to *be* the subject, not just about it.") He does not make sense out of reality; he *does* invite us to perceive it with heightened awareness.

The long poem ends: ". . . 'You've reached the enormous summit of passion/which is immobility forging an entrail from the pure obstruction of the air.'" We end where we began: in obscure abstraction. It is helpful to know that O'Hara wrote the poem in the studio where Larry Rivers was sculpting. Even without knowing that, we can sense that this image alludes to the artist at work, identifying passion as the source of creative activity. More interesting, however, is the fact that the movement is not from experience to immobility, but rather from immobility to the guts of experience, or to the heights of prophecy, depending on how we read "entrail."

The title poem of *Meditations in an Emergency* (1957) will serve as an example of the many prose poems written by O'Hara. Superficially, it seems easier to read than the poems written about the same time. ("Meditations" was written in June 1954.) Each of the paragraphs, which function here like stanzas, is discursive and intelligible. However, there is no obvious movement from stanza to stanza; the various parts of the poem stand in juxtaposition rather than in logical sequence. This form is perfectly appropriate to the content of the poem; in some ways it is the content because like so much of O'Hara's work, the poem is a search for lost connections, and, paradoxically, a wish to avoid them.

"I am the least difficult of men," O'Hara says. "All I want is boundless love." He goes on to qualify this. He is attracted by the natural world, which seems to need *him*, but he prefers the city, a symbol of separation and loneliness. In another stanza, he feels the inexorable approach of heterosexuality, which he seeks to avoid. O'Hara turns his homosexuality into an expression of the paradox. It is his wish to be loved, and to love; but it is a particularly narcissistic form of love, and in some ways a reinforcement of his isolation. The poem reminds us of something that is always implicit in O'Hara's poetry, though rarely quite as explicit as in "Meditations": his poems, which often seem abstract in spite of, or perhaps because of, their accumulation of detail, are very personal assertions of the poet's being-in-the-world. In his statement for *The New American Poetry* (edited by Donald M. Allen, 1960), O'Hara denied that his "experiences are clarified or made beautiful." Instead, he suggests, "It may be that poetry makes life's nebulous events tangible to me and restores their detail."

"To the Harbormaster" (first published in *Meditations in an Emergency*) is one of Frank O'Hara's most well-known, most often anthologized, poems. Like many poems in that category, it is relatively atypical of its author. In this case, it is unified in imagery, syntactically correct, and easy to follow. It would, in fact, be very similar to a metaphysical conceit were it not for the fact that, while the elaborate image is there, the area of experience it represents is not specified. The poet begins to insist that he wants to reach the harbormaster; but his ship is continually caught in moorings, and, after tying up, he decides time and again to leave. Fighting against outer storms and inner enemies, like "the forms of my vanity," he still struggles toward the harbormaster. The poem ends:

> I trust the sanity of my vessel; and
> if it sinks, it may well be in answer
> to the reasoning of the eternal voices,
> the waves which have kept me from reaching you.

The poem is most intriguing in its ambiguity. A note informs us that the poem is about Larry Rivers. And clearly it works on that level, or as a more general statement about the relationship of the lover to the beloved. Neither interpretation, however, is incompatible with the notion that the harbormaster may represent Beauty, the goal of art. In any case, Richard Howard seems right in suggesting that ". . . the eternal voices,/the waves," should be identified with O'Hara's conception of personality, a constant that is ever in flux, a radiance without sharp boundaries. In this poem, however, O'Hara talks about his sense of self; in most of the other poems, he demonstrates it through his techniques.

"In Memory of My Feelings" (the title poem of a book published in 1967), more recognizably an O'Hara poem in its surreal imagery and sharp juxtapositions, isolates the idea of self even more explicitly:

> My transparent selves
> flail about like vipers in a pail, writhing and hissing
> without panic, with a certain justice of response
> and presently the aquiline serpent comes to resemble the Medusa.

The idea of transparent selves suggests the onion metaphor in Ibsen's *Peer Gynt;* but where Peer Gynt unpeels the layers of his selves and finds nothing at its core, O'Hara finds a serpent. But to the serpent, he says, "I am not quite you, but almost." The serpent is "coiled around" the poet's heart, and the combined image suggests Yeats's perception that all dreams begin in "the foul rag and bone shop of the heart." While in Yeats the transitory nature of the dream assumes nearly tragic proportions, in O'Hara the sense of self is far too tentative to be tragic. He belongs to the world of *Endgame* rather than of *Hamlet*.

Odes (1960) shows O'Hara at his closest to being a poet who deals with ideas about the human condition. ("In Memory of My Feelings," written just before O'Hara began work on the odes in the late fifties, does, however, already demonstrate this tendency.) Appropriately, the odes are also closer to formal structure than other poems at this stage in O'Hara's career; but the structure is less a recognizable, nameable form than a strong sense of discipline.

The "Ode to Willem de Kooning" is an example. It is a meditation on courage and genius, which in this poem amount to the same thing. It is also a meditation on the dawn and the renewal of courage that allows one to overcome "desperate conclusions of the dark." Reversing more traditional frames of reference in which the night is associated with the powers of imagination and the day with clear intellect, O'Hara sees the night as the home of specifically intellectual despair "where messages were intercepted/by an ignorant horde of thoughts," while the day renews hope and vision. While the traditional framework depends upon the outer world, especially the sun and moon, for its polarities, O'Hara's grows out of inner realities; his is the symbolism of a man who cannot sleep nights.

There is, however, complexity to O'Hara's imagery. The dawn brings renewed courage, it does not eliminate the source of anxiety. Daytime itself begins to be defined as a kind of night. "Only darkness lights our lives," O'Hara says near the poem's conclusion. We must depend upon ". . . imperishable courage and the gentle will/which is the individual dawn of genius rising from its bed."

Odes contains some of O'Hara's loveliest poetry, some of the clearest statements of his attitudes toward experience. It would not be surprising if poems from that volume were singled out as examples of his finest work. And yet, by and large, they do not communicate the perception of O'Hara's unique world. "The Day Lady Died," in *Lunch Poems* (1964), brings us back to his more idiosyncratic poetry. Paul Carroll has an interesting essay on the poem in *The Poem in Its Skin*. He uses it as an example of what he calls "impure poetry," that is, poetry that contains materials that are not poetically justifiable if we define poetry in New Critical terms. Carroll cites, for example, the reference early in the poem to Bastille Day as simply a way of fixing date, with none of the inevitable connotations of the holiday applicable. Carroll is probably correct in this reading, and it is significant that a poem of this sort is one of O'Hara's most effective performances. The question, of course, is what makes this an effective performance? If the elements of a poem will not submit to New Critical standards, how can we evaluate it? Carroll suggests that the poem is important because it is the first of its kind; but he himself admits this is unsatisfactory. A more interesting answer may be that, like Pound's *Cantos*, this poem operates not so much through the accidental details it contains but rather through the methodology that embeds them in the text.

O'Hara gets a shoeshine, plans to take a train, buys a paperback book, goes to the bank, buys a book by Verlaine, a bottle of Strega, a carton of Gauloises and one of Picayunes, and then, seeing Billie Holiday's picture on the *New York Post*, remembers hearing her sing at the "5 Spot." This recollection, which ends the poem, is its only reference to Billie Holiday, aside from the title. It is the description of a perfectly ordinary, possibly especially trivial day; and perhaps the juxtaposition of this triviality with the singer's death is an important part of the poem's mechanism. Although the day is ordinary, it is a particular kind of ordinariness.

"I don't know the people who will feed me," O'Hara remarks about his dinner engagement. Not world-shaking tragedy, maybe a bit uncomfortable. The day is muggy. Again uncomfortable. The paperback (*New World Writing*) is "ugly." There is irony in O'Hara's looking at it ". . . to see what the poets/in Ghana are doing these days." Trying to decide on gifts in the bookstore, he practically falls asleep with "quandariness." By the time he sees the dead singer's picture, he is sweating a lot. All in all, it is an oppressive picture, drawn in dull tones, which subtly prepares us for the conclusion, at the same time allowing it to stand out in sharp relief: O'Hara remembers

> . . . she whispered a song along the keyboard
> to Mal Waldron and everyone and I stopped breathing

In some of O'Hara's later work in *The Collected Poems*, dating from 1964, he seems to be reaching toward a new definition of his poetic line. Having experimented with strict meter, prosaic rhythms that sometimes actually turn into prose, endless variations on free verse, which are sometimes versions of Olson's breath-controlled lines, sometimes plays on barely perceptible meters, O'Hara now turns to something that bears striking resemblance to Williams' "variable foot." Williams generally admitted three of these variable feet to a line; O'Hara's basic unit contains two, with three as an occasional substitution. As was the case with Williams, O'Hara's foot is so variable that it provides a sense of discipline rather than any real constraint.

"Walking" begins:

> I get a cinder in my eye
>   it streams into
>   the sunlight
>   the air pushes it aside
>   and I drop my hot dog
>   into one of the Seagram Building's
>   fountains

The poem never moves far from its casual beginning. O'Hara records some more sensory impressions from his walk, and concludes with nothing more startling than a view of New York "rising . . . greater than the Rocky Mountains." Aside from a hint of the poet's preoccupation with the tension between the natural world and the city, which he invariably chooses, the poem has little point. It is not meant to. This brings us back to the start, to a poet who is more interested in capturing his experiences, in making them real, than in understanding them. O'Hara's reputation may not survive this limitation. Possibly it will consign him forever to the ranks of minor poets, although he will always be a particularly fascinating one. But it is also possible that O'Hara's works taken as a whole constitute a coherent vision of reality. In *Spring and All*, William Carlos Williams wrote that "poetry does not tamper with the world but moves it—. . . As birds' wings beat the solid air without which none could fly so words freed by the imagination affirm reality by their flight." By this definition, O'Hara is a considerable poet.

See also NEW YORK POETS and the Introduction, section V.

Selected Bibliography:
BY O'HARA:
A City Winter and Other Poems. New York: Tibor de Nagy Gallery, 1952.
Meditations in an Emergency. New York: Grove Press, 1957.
Jackson Pollack. [Art criticism.] New York: George Braziller, 1959.
Second Avenue. New York: Totem/Corinth, 1960.
Odes. New York: Tiber Press, 1960.
Lunch Poems. San Francisco: City Lights Books, 1964.
Love Poems (Tentative Title). New York: Tibor de Nagy Gallery, 1965.
In Memory of My Feelings. Edited by Bill Berkson. New York: The Museum of Modern Art, 1967.
The Collected Poems of Frank O'Hara. Edited by Donald Allen. New York: Alfred A. Knopf, 1971.

About O'Hara:
Carroll, Paul. "The Day Lady Died" in *The Poem in Its Skin.* Chicago: Follett Publishing Co., 1968. Pp. 154–68.
Howard, Richard. *Alone with America.* New York: Atheneum Publishers, 1969. Pp. 396–412.

OLSON, CHARLES (*b. Worcester, Mass., Dec. 27, 1910—d. Jan. 10, 1970*)

Six feet eight or nine. Appropriate stature for a man whose own career was to a large extent the history of one of the more important movements in contemporary American poetry. Heir to the Objectivist traditions of Ezra Pound and William Carlos Williams, Olson, almost before his poetry received widespread recognition, became an ancestor in his own right, particularly to such poets as Robert Duncan, Robert Creeley, Denise Levertov, Paul Blackburn, Edward Dorn, Joel Oppenheimer. He was also one of the most colorful, if not always the most comprehensible, spokesman for a much larger poetic sensibility, for open verse against tight forms, for unorthodoxy against the conservative academy.

Born in Worcester, Massachusetts, Olson grew up in Gloucester, locus of his major work, the *Maximus* poems. He was educated (or, as he said, "uneducated") at Wesleyan, Yale, and Harvard, receiving all his degrees from the latter. He held a variety of jobs, from fishing-boat hand to teacher at Clark University and Harvard. In 1947 Olson published *Call Me Ishmael*, a study of literary influences on Melville that bears the distinct imprint of its author's personality. The following year he replaced his friend Edward Dahlberg as instructor at Black Mountain College in North Carolina; the most significant phase of Olson's career had begun. Financially, the college was a shaky proposition from the very start. But with John Cage, Robert Duncan, Merce Cunningham, Franz Kline, and Robert Creeley on the faculty, and with Olson as rector from 1951 until 1956, the school became a center of cultural excitement. The *Black Mountain Review*, its seven issues edited by Robert Creeley, provided the group with its major outlet. Cid Corman's *Origin*, Paul Carroll's *Big Table*, LeRoi Jones's *Yugen*, and *Evergreen Review* were also sympathetic. By 1960 Donald M. Allen was able to put together a large, influential anthology, *The New American Poetry*, which consists exclusively of poets in the Projectivist tradition, "the true continuers of the modern movement in American poetry." Whether this poetry is new, whether it is, indeed, the most vital, the most promising now being written, is a matter of controversy, much of which centers on Olson.

In 1950 Olson's essay "Projective Verse" appeared in *Poetry New York*. It is a blatantly unacademic piece, in style as well as in content, a manifesto in the manner of Pound. To this essay in particular the critics have responded, and continue to respond, although over twenty years have passed and Olson and his followers have written a good deal since. Here, for example, is James Dickey, in *Babel to Byzantium* (1968):

> All the things he says are in various ways true enough, but "projective verse" has no claim on them; most of them are true of any poetry, or at least of any that is worth reading. Certainly, organic form —the poem growing naturally from its own materials and creating its own best internal relations and overall shape—is the form that all good poems must have: do have. What Olson's notion of "open" verse does is simply to provide creative irresponsibility with the semblance of a rationale which may be defended in heated and cloudy terms by its supposed practitioners. All "schools" theorize endlessly, it may be noted.

That is essentially the case against Olson. To many critics it has seemed self-evident enough to preclude further examination of Olson's principles. Some very effective poetry, however, has been written by poets (including Olson) who take them quite seriously. Even if, as many have contended, Projective verse at its best has little to do with its informing theory, the essay must be credited with remarkable catalytic powers.

Olson has said, "The harmony of the universe, and I include man, is not logical, or better, is post-logical, as is the order of any created thing" ("Human Universe"). Accordingly, "Projective Verse" is anything but a closely reasoned argument; it is, like the art it describes, post-logical. Or is it unlogical, meaningless? Its aphorisms might as easily be trite as profound;

its jargon blurs precise analogy. But it is filled with excitement. Olson describes the characteristics of open verse, or "composition by field," in the following way: (1) "Then the poem itself must, at all points, be a high energy-construct and, at all points, an energy discharge"; (2) "FORM IS NEVER MORE THAN AN EXTENSION OF CONTENT"; (3) "ONE PERCEPTION MUST IMMEDIATELY AND DIRECTLY LEAD TO A FURTHER PERCEPTION. . . . MOVE, INSTANTER, ON ANOTHER!"

Dickey's irritation is not difficult to comprehend: Olson's remarks seem to be either without precise meaning or applicable indiscriminately to all good poetry. However, while Olson's definitions viewed in isolation are hardly self-explanatory, they are not necessarily devoid of all significance when examined in the proper context, that is, as an outgrowth of Pound's IMAGISM and Williams' brand of OBJECTIVISM. Olson's definitions form part of the movement away from the discursive toward the imagistic—away from the notion that effective imagery consists of the accurate description of an object, toward the attempt to identify directly with that object and toward the corollary that the form and structure of a poem can somehow be derived from this identification.

"Don't be descriptive," Pound warned; the good poet does not describe, "he presents." At greater length, Williams, also, attacks the idea of poet as painter:

> Imagination is not to avoid reality, nor is it description nor an evocation of objects or situations, it is to say that poetry does not tamper with the world but moves it—It affirms reality most powerfully and therefore, since reality needs no personal support but exists free from human action, as proven by science in the indestructibility of matter and of force, it creates a new object, a play, a dance . . .
>
> (*Spring and All*)

This is precisely the tradition from which Olson's definitions have grown: "The descriptive functions generally have to be watched, every second, in projective verse, because of their easiness, and thus their drain on the energy which composition by field allows into a poem." All three poets seem to be getting at an aesthetic in which the poem is not simply an imitation of objective reality, but forms a reality in its own right, with its own set of laws and principles of coherence, whose relationship to the world of objects is less rationally knowable than it is intuitively mediated by the poet. If we take this seriously, Olson's remarks on composition by field seem not vague jargon but the most literal of metaphors; we are, after all, dealing with universes, and the laws that govern them. In the title essay of *Human Universe* (1965), Olson elaborates the metaphysic behind the aesthetic:

> [Description] does not come to grips with what really matters: that a thing, any thing, impinges on us by a more important fact, its self-existence, without reference to any other thing, in short, the very character of it which calls our attention to it, which wants us to know more about it, its particularity.

Again, the statement that form is no more than an extension of content becomes more than Dickey's "organic form"; in what Olson calls an "energy-discharge," the poet's share of the world is projected outward with predestined shape and tension. "Each man," says Olson in "Human Universe," "does make his own special selection from the phenomenal field and it is thus that we begin to speak of personality . . ." The projection of personality in this sense leads to a union of inner and outer worlds, of human and objective reality, which are here revealed to be thoroughly interdependent. This projection, this shaping of a universe, constitutes the poem. In this light, even the obvious exhortation that one perception follow another has special implications. The poet's perception is precisely his creation; only the tension between perceptions holds his poem together as a world in itself and frees it of the formulas that make poetry more logical and less in touch with experience.

The process of projection, the dynamics of this "energy-discharge," is tinged with the mystical even in its origins in Pound: "I said in the preface to my *Guido Cavalcanti* that I believed in absolute rhythm. I believe that every emotion and every phase of emotion has some toneless phrase, some rhythm-phrase to express it." Olson says it, or something like it, this way:

> the HEAD, by way of the EAR, to the SYLLABLE
> the HEART, by way of the BREATH, to the LINE

Olson does not deny the play of intellect (though, characteristically, it is the mind's *play* that interests him most), but most of his attention goes to those shaping forces, heart (or emotion) and corresponding breath, linking the form of the poem to both the poet's feelings and his biological rhythms. (In this, at least, Olson departs from Williams, who finally sought the "relative stability" of his "variable foot.") For Olson, reality cannot be described, it must be created:

> There is only one thing you can do about [the] kinetic, re-enact it. Which is why the man said, he who possesses rhythm possesses the universe. And why art is the only twin life has—its only valid metaphysic. Art does not seek to describe but to enact.
>
> ("Human Universe")

While he shares many general principles with Pound and Williams, Olson, if he has been successful, has carried still further their flight from the subjective to the objective, from the descriptive to the projective, from the ego to the universal, from the classical-representational to the primitive-abstract:

> Objectism is the getting rid of the lyrical interference of the individual ego, of the "subject" and his soul, that peculiar presumption by which western man has interposed himself between what he is as a creature of nature (with certain instructions to carry out) and those other creations of nature which we may, with no derogation, call objects. . . . If [man] sprawl, he shall find little to sing but himself,

and shall sing, nature has such paradoxical ways, by way of artificial forms outside himself. But if he stays inside himself, if he is contained within his nature as he is participant in the larger force, he will be able to listen, and his hearing through himself will give him secrets objects share.

("Projective Verse")

According to Olson, both Pound and Williams have failed to meet these goals, or at least to meet them completely. Pound transforms time into space (an important step toward entering the world of objects), but he does it by leveling all history by "the beak of his ego"; Williams escapes his ego, but he has not found an alternative, and so "lets time roll him under" (*Mayan Letters*). Olson's poetry embodies his search for this alternative, which seems for him to be the positive identification of the human universe with the natural universe and the avoidance of distortion by the individual ego: "projection is discrimination (of the object from the subject) and the unconscious is the universe flowing-in, inside" ("Pieces of Time," *Kulchur* 1 [Spring 1960]:19–21). To learn whether the distinctions Olson draws are valid, we must turn to his poetry.

"What does not change/is the will to change," Olson begins "The Kingfishers," probably his most well-known poem outside the *Maximus* sequence. The contrast, sometimes the conflict, between the illusion of stability and the reality of perpetual agitation is at the core, not only of this poem, but of most of Olson's work. "Into the same river no man steps twice," he later quotes Herakleitos. Flux is not simply the condition of the physical world, which is continuously decaying and renewing itself; the human universe as well as the objective one is subject to change. Collectively, civilizations rise and fall, conquered (like the Mayan) from without, or through revolution (like Mao's) from within; individually, personality is a conceit to provide the illusion of solidity upon shifting sands:

> Around an appearance, one common model, we grow up
> many. . . .

In a sense, "The Kingfishers" is simply another exercise on the Ozymandias theme. The kingfishers have lost the special significance given them by earlier civilizations; so has the mysterious E carved rudely in stone in the jungle. Mao rises in the East as other suns set. But what interests Olson most is not the historical inevitability of the ebb and flow of human affairs. The focus is rather on the strain of creating order out of chaos, form out of flux; it is epistemological rather than historiographical. Each civilization, like each individual personality, is an illusion, an act of will discovering possible patterns in experience, a temporary stay against confusion. Out of "a discrete or continuous sequence of measurable events distributed in time" the individual forges the illusion of personality, societies the illusion of purposes and values. The slightest relaxation of the imaginative will permits the reintroduction of chaos:

When the attentions change/the jungle
leaps in
                        even the stones are split   they rive

In "Projective Verse" Olson quotes Creeley: "Form is never more than an extension of content." True in all good poems, as Dickey said, but true in a
special way in Olson's. For the most significant instance of the discovery of
form in a shapeless universe is the poet, whose poems, twins to life, give
focus to experience. Now, when we speak of the poet's discovery of form
in flux, we must inevitably think of Pound; this is, after all, the major
theme of the *Cantos*. But there is a difference, a crucial one, which perhaps more
than anything else serves to distinguish modern from contemporary American
poetry. For Pound (as for Eliot, as for Yeats), order is the key, everything else subservient to it; in art, certainly, and in other aspects of experience
as well, for example, politics. For Pound and his contemporaries, the shock
of World War I, among other things, cast all standards in doubt, and
the recovery of form seemed essential to the continuance of civilized life.
In the time since World War II, the chaos has by no means disappeared,
though we are perhaps more accustomed to living with it; and now order
itself has terrifying implications. After the trenches, we try to reintegrate
a shattered world; after the concentration camps, we must confront the dark
formless side of experience in order that we not be overcome by it. Thus
Pound's fascism, sacrificing humanity to hierarchy; thus Olson's concern
for what is specifically human, even in the apparently rigid, inanimate universe. So the poet's search for order, clearly present in Olson's work,
is understandably modified. In his novel *Beautiful Losers*, Leonard
Cohen describes an attitude toward chaos probably very close to Olson's: "I do
not think that a saint dissolves the chaos even for himself, for there is something arrogant and warlike in the notion of a man setting the universe in
order. It is a kind of balance that is his glory." Discrete fragments, perceptions, observations are juxtaposed without transition; the tension among
these various parts, the balance that holds the poem together, is surely what
Olson means by the field of the poem, the energy-discharge. The interweaving of Mao's assertion that the light of the dawn is before us with a
vision of the kingfisher's flight into the setting sun forms a single picture joined
by the energy of rapid-fire montage. The permanence is both illusory
and real, in the poem as well as in Olson's vision of the human condition.

Still, whatever difference of philosophical emphasis serves to distinguish
Pound from Olson, it is not always easy to make similar distinctions of technique. Olson seems more comfortable with a longer line, his rhythms are
frequently more prosaic; he has picked up more of the purely musical possibilities of theme and motif from the archenemy, Eliot. But these are all reasonable variations of a single aesthetic and do not seem to fulfill the promise of a new approach heralded in Olson's manifestos. For this, we must
examine the *Maximus* poems, and discover in what ways, if any, they depart
from the *Cantos* and Williams' *Paterson*.

The indebtedness of the *Maximus* poems is too obvious to be belabored.

Maximus is a hero along the lines of Pound's Odysseus—"a Maximus song/the sirens sang:/he stopped his/ears with caulking"—journeying through history in search of significant form. In his association with a specific place, Gloucester, Massachusetts, he resembles even more closely Williams' Dr. Paterson. Like *Paterson*, the *Maximus* poems do not attempt to discover dogmatic patterns in political and economic experience but place the specifically human world within the context of larger natural cycles. Like *Paterson*, they contain (especially in *Maximus IV, V, VI*) a large proportion of intelligible excerpts from historical documents rather than the pastiche of brief allusions so often found in Pound, as if to carry to the fullest Williams' dictum: "No ideas but in things." Still of central importance is Olson's emphasis on the act of perception and the notion that the creation of a civilization is a collective version of the individual's selections from the phenomenological field:

> polis is
> eyes

he begins "Letter 6," and ends it with:

There are no hierarchies, no infinite, no such many as mass, there are only
eyes in all heads
to be looked out of

Seeing is the prototype of all creation; it is the first abstraction as well. The artist must at all times be on guard against succumbing to the illusion that his vision can be absolute. In "Letter 9," in a passage that sounds very much as if it might have been written by Williams or, even more likely, Stevens, Olson says:

> . . . one discovers
> there is no other issue than
> the moment of
>   the pleasure of
>   this plum,
>
>   these things
>   which don't carry their end any further than
>   their reality in
>   themselves

It is precisely from the world of things real in themselves that civilizations, ours in particular, tend to alienate their members. We live in a "pejorocracy," Olson constantly informs his fellow citizens of Gloucester, we have been corrupted by materialistic progress. So cut off are we from our own experience of the world by the superficial triumphs of technology that the poet, in "The Songs of Maximus," is brought to the point in song 3 of counting ". . . the blessing/that difficulties are once more"; "In the face of sweetness," Olson says, "piss"; "In the land of plenty, have/nothing to do with it." There is throughout his work a longing for the primitive—in civilizations as well as in art. But for Olson, who in fact spent a good part of his post–Black Mountain days studying Mayan culture, the emphasis is less on the reformation of society than on cleansing the doors of perception (though the two may be connected). In "Maximus to Gloucester, Letter 19 (A Pastoral Letter)," Olson describes his daughter, singing naked, who ". . . wears her own face/as we do not." So often, Olson's vision is pastoral, a juxtaposition of simple and complex approaches to experience, with advantage to the former. But "Letter 20" is specifically "not a pastoral letter," as Olson retreats from the easy generalization that drains energy from the struggle to experience the here and now.

At the time of Olson's death, the *Maximus* poems had been collected in two volumes: *The Maximus Poems* and *Maximus Poems IV, V, VI.* The poems quoted so far all appear in the first volume; the second book, basically more of the same, nonetheless shows some shifts in emphasis. An even greater proportion of the work than before consists of transcriptions of historical documents, journals, inventories, almanacs; and to a far greater extent than before, classical mythologies are drawn upon to give greater depth to Olson's treatment of the Gloucestermen.

> The sea was born of the earth without sweet union of love Hesiod says
>
> But that then she lay for heaven and she bare the thing which encloses every thing, Okeanos the one which all things are and by which nothing is anything but itself, measured so
>
> screwing earth, in whom love lies which unnerves the limbs and by its heat floods the mind and all gods and men into further nature
>
> (from "MAXIMUS, FROM DOGTOWN—I")

Curiously, these apparently contradictory shifts, one toward the particular, one toward the universal, achieve unity of purpose. The goal in each case is the elimination of ego: by seizing on the most concrete of details, the most objective form of experience, on the one hand; by burrowing deep within the ego to arrive at a kind of collective unconscious, a storehouse of racial memory in which Greek, Norse, Indian mythologies blend together, on the other.

The tension of opposites that holds together Olson's world, and his poetry, is here predominantly sexual, man uniting with woman, ocean with earth. The traditional Christian framework, which has formed the backbone of so much modern American poetry, is here rejected for a mythos linked to the birth of human civilization, incorporated by Olson into his vision of contemporary man. Here, too, the poet finds his most powerful symbology for the breaking down of barriers between subjective and objective realities:

> They said she went off fucking every Sunday.
> Only she said she walked straight through
> the mountain, and who fucked her was the spirit
> of that mountain

The old analytical-logical order is broken down; in its place is one of synthesis and feeling.

> No Greek will be able
>
> to discriminate my body.
>
> An American
> is a complex of occasions,
>
> themselves a geometry
> of spatial nature.
>
> I have this sense,
> that I am one
>
> with my skin.

> (from "*Maximus to Gloucester, Letter 27*")

While there is surely much in the *Maximus* sequence that would qualify as superior poetry by anyone's standards, the work, for the time being at least, stands as a monument to the inadequacy of our critical dicta. Olson, however, would almost certainly have insisted that he was trying to do, not something new, but something very old indeed: to see the world as it is, to see in concrete reality the secret signatures of things. The last lines in *Maximus Poems IV, V, VI* bring Olson's career back to its beginnings in Melville: "I set out now/in a box upon the sea." The allusion is to Queequeg's coffin; Maximus becomes Ishmael as well as Odysseus. He is in any case the archetypal voyager, seeking to penetrate the veil of his existence, descending into the underworld in order to work out his salvation.

See also BLACK MOUNTAIN POETS and the Introduction, sections II and III.

Selected Bibliography:
By OLSON:
Call Me Ishmael [Criticism]. New York: Reynal & Hitchcock (Harcourt Brace Jovanovich), 1947; New York: Grove Press, 1958.
Y & X. Washington: Black Son, 1950.
Apollonius of Tyana [Prose]. Black Mountain, N.C.: Black Mountain College Press, 1951.
Mayan Letters [Prose]. Palma de Mallorca: Divers Press, 1953.
In Cold Hell, In Thicket. Dorchester, Mass.: Origin, 1953.
The Maximus Poems. New York: Jargon/Corinth, 1960.
The Distances. New York: Grove Press, 1960.
Human Universe [Essays]. San Francisco: Auerhahn Society, 1965.
Selected Writings of Charles Olson. Edited by Robert Creeley. New York: New Directions Publishing Corp., 1966.

Maximus Poems IV, V, VI. London: Cape Golliard Press, 1968; New York: Grossman Publishers, 1968.
Archaelogist of Morning. New York: Grossman Publishers, 1971.

About Olson:
Creeley, Robert. Introduction to *Selected Writings of Charles Olson.* New York: New Directions Publishing Corp., 1966.
Dickey, James. *Babel to Byzantium: Poets & Poetry Now.* New York: Farrar, Straus & Giroux, 1968. Pp. 136–39.
Dorn, Edward. "What I See in The Maximus Poems," *Kulchur 4* (1961), 31–44.
Duberman, Martin B. *Black Mountain: An Experiment in Community.* New York: E. P. Dutton & Co., 1972.
Duncan, Robert. "Notes on Poetics Regarding Olson's 'Maximus,'" *Review,* #10 (January 1964), 36–42; original version appeared in *Black Mountain Review,* 6 (1956).
Rosenthal, M. L. *The New Poets: American and British Poetry Since World War II.* New York: Oxford University Press, 1967. Pp. 139–48.
Stepanchev, Stefan. *American Poetry Since 1945.* New York: Harper & Row Publishers, 1965. Pp. 124–45.

OPPENHEIMER, JOEL *(b. Yonkers, N.Y., Feb. 18, 1930—   )*

Associated from the very beginning of his career with the BLACK MOUNTAIN POETS, Joel Oppenheimer shares with Robert Creeley the distinction of being—within that group—the most concerned with interpersonal relations. Nonetheless, Oppenheimer's connection with the Projectivists is perfectly evident in his attention to perfecting open verse forms, to finding the appropriate breath-determined rhythms. Even his concern with relationships tends to be archetypal rather than individualized, bodily (generally sexual) rather than cerebral, as if he is trying to ground those relationships at a level deeper than the ego.

Joel Oppenheimer was born in Yonkers and lived there until 1947. He studied at Cornell, the University of Chicago, and Black Mountain College. After 1953, he worked as a "printer-typographer-advertising production man," but since 1971 he has conducted writing workshops in the Creative Writing Program at the City College of New York. He has been a regular contributor to the *Village Voice.*

"The Torn Nightgown" in *The Love Bit* is typical of Oppenheimer's poetry. Seeing his wife's body covered by a torn nightgown, he universalizes the perception, wondering "if all wives had such badges." He even goes beyond the specifically human, as he thinks of all the men and women making love at night,

> . . . of the heart
> which ponderously grasps its
> way back, great sea creature caught
> far up on the beach, a monstrous polyp or
> jellyfish. . . .

The poem concludes with a clear affirmation of the importance, perhaps the centrality, of sexual experience, but at least implicitly casts some doubt on whether the relation of bodies has anything to do with love:

> the cat makes it in the alley meanwhile,
> the neighbor makes it next door, heaving and
> grunting and shaking the springs.
> panting in the dark night, lusting
> again and again for warmth, for
> a semblance of love.   when day comes
> the cock rises and crows he crows.
> but the night is the day of my cock.

Occasionally, Oppenheimer seems almost interested in rhythm simply as a matter of technique, as in the interesting experiment of "Triplets" (also in *The Love Bit*), which repeats the same sentence three times: first, the sentence has one or two words per line; then, it is divided into three lines; and finally, it is divided into five lines. That there is a difference between each version as a result of the juxtaposition suggests that technique is never simply technique. But Oppenheimer is more often obviously involved in specifically human problems. He is aware of the essential oneness of life, in which he can participate biologically. He is also aware—often painfully so —of his existence as a separate human being and of the need to feel a powerful bond with others *as* a separate human being.

In "Leave It to Me Blues" (also from *The Love Bit*), he is typically hopeful but far from triumphant:

> . . . we turn our
> backs on each other so often,
> we destroy any community of
> interest.   yet our hearts are
> seeded with love and care sticks
> out of our ears. . . .

Although we are separate, there is at least the potential of community. But we persist in cutting each other off. There may be, the poet speculates, hope for his children. Maybe they will make it. Even so, he is aware that he is dealing with a paradox rather than a problem, and our separateness may well be incompatible with our oneness.

> . . . on the other
> hand, even with answers, where
> would we be, out in the cold, with
> an old torn blanket, and no one
> around us to cry

It is precisely in his willingness to confront this paradox directly that Joel Oppenheimer's chief strength as a poet lies.

Selected Bibliography:
BY OPPENHEIMER:
The Dancer. Highlands, North Carolina: Jargon Books, 1952.
The Dutiful Son. Highlands, North Carolina: Jargon Books, 1957.
The Love Bit and Other Poems. New York: Totem/Corinth, 1962.
The Great American Desert. [Play.] New York: Grove Press, 1965.
In Time: Poems 1962–1968. Indianapolis: Bobbs-Merrill Co., 1969.

PLATH, SYLVIA (*b. Boston, Mass., Oct. 27, 1932—
d. Feb. 11, 1963*)

At the heart of the legend that has grown up around the work of Sylvia Plath is the theory that she risked her life in the interest of her art, that her deep delving into her own psyche for poetic materials caused her ultimate destruction. It is easy enough to quarrel with this theory. The word "risk" implies a conscious decision to explore depths of the mind that would otherwise lie dormant; yet it seems all too likely that the "depths" were rising all around Sylvia Plath, without invitation, and that the last brilliant poems were part of her finally unsuccessful efforts to subdue self-destructive impulses rather than a disastrous attempt to invoke them. The logical conclusion of the risk theory—that she might not have committed suicide if she had forsaken poetry—is especially dubious. The real fallacy of the legend, however, is not that it may be psychoanalytically invalid—there is no sure way of knowing this—but that it misplaces critical emphasis.

For some years after her death, the life of this beautiful and sensitive girl, which interwove periodic attempts at suicide with the winning of writing prizes, studying under Robert Lowell, marriage to British poet Ted Hughes, and which ended one cold London morning with her head in the oven and her two children in the next room, quite naturally interposed itself between the reader and the poetry. In fact, the life seemed to justify the poetry, to give it legitimacy, as if it were somehow dishonest to write about suicidal impulses unless the writer was willing to go through with it. When the life and the art are unraveled, the poems are left to stand on their own. Like novae, they are perhaps somewhat diminished after the light of the initial explosion, but they unmistakably constitute a respectable achievement; some of them are remarkable.

Sylvia Plath acknowledged poetic debts to Robert Lowell, Theodore Roethke, Anne Sexton, and Elizabeth Bishop. Like the first three, she has been linked with the school of CONFESSIONAL POETRY, because, as M. L. Rosenthal puts it in *The New Poets,* her work places "the speaker himself at the center of the poem in such a way as to make his psychological vulnerability and shame an embodiment of his civilization."

The idea of some sort of identity between the poet's mind and the society in which it operates encompasses a broad range: at one extreme, the poet, completely conscious of his own separate existence may see himself as mi-

crocosm of what surrounds him, or the world as macrocosm of what is inside him; at the other extreme, the boundaries between inner and outer
worlds may be so eroded that they can no longer be distinguished. A great
deal of literature falls into the first category, while few works successfully
express the second, for they tend to be self-enclosed fantasies rather than
art. Sylvia Plath's strength lay in the ability to achieve a balance of the two
extremes; allowing her mind to explore beyond all customary limits the
boundaries of the self, she retained enough control to give her intensely
personal experience recognizable form.

It is a delicate balance. In her finest work, Plath makes it look easy;
however, in *The Bell Jar* (1963) she also demonstrates how difficult it can
be to maintain. This autobiographical novel deals with the breakdown and
attempted suicide that occurred shortly after the author had been guest editor of *Mademoiselle* in the summer and fall of 1953, representing Smith
College. The book is generally well written, and often moving. Although it
is more purely Confessional than any of the poetry, it is not in the least
self-indulgent or self-pitying; the irony is far too sharp to allow that. The
Confessional element nonetheless is not successfully resolved into art. The
price of detachment is here a journalistic descriptiveness that does not
probe deeply enough, that fails to provide an adequate context for the
many deeply felt passages scattered through the work. The overall result is
a novel that is at the same time so localized as to have little relevance to
the "normal" world from which the author is estranged and yet so general
as to seem interchangeable with any number of case histories. Plath herself
had sufficient reservations about the novel to make use of a pseudonym,
Victoria Lucas.

By the time of the publication of *The Bell Jar*, Sylvia Plath had already
found the mode most suited to her vision of reality. At work from an early
age perfecting her art—her first poem was published when she was eight—
she was in her mid-twenties when she saw the areas of experience with
which she was most concerned opened to poetry by two fellow New En-
glanders, Robert Lowell and Anne Sexton. To Sylvia Plath, the exploration
of previously "private and taboo subjects," such as nervous breakdowns and
experiences in mental hospitals, revealed "a kind of emotional and psychological depth which I think is something perhaps quite new and exciting." If
Lowell and Sexton provided the genre, it was Theodore Roethke who provided the method. As familiar with the inside of asylums as the other three
poets, Roethke very rarely chose to deal directly with the extreme emotional states of his illness; instead, by immersing himself in the purely sensuous, prerational world of the child, he emerged with a coherent symbolism for the adult's psychological and spiritual struggle. And it was Roethke
who matched the rhythms of his poetry to the rhythms of his experience in
a way most congenial to Plath.

The Colossus (1960), although it is a far more mature performance than
readers overwhelmed by *Ariel* (1965) realize, shows frequent evidence of
Roethke's influence. In "Mushrooms," for example, the plants, like Roethke's
"Cuttings," force their way to the surface: "The small grains make room."

As in the work of the older poet, there is identification with the inanimate natural world, and the sense of dynamic, even desperate, energy in what most people would regard as inert. What distinguished Plath's poem (although Roethke's greenhouse poems have a terror of their own) is the sinister note interjected at the end, where the mushrooms predict

> We shall by morning
> Inherit the earth.
> Our foot's in the door.

All in all, *The Colossus* has its share of fine moments, of especially effective lines: the pears that "fatten like little buddhas" ("The Manor Garden"); "the snail-nosed babies" in their jars ("Two Views of a Cadaver Room"); "Horses fluent in the wind" ("The Eye-mote"), anticipating "Ariel"; "The long wait for the angel,/For that rare random descent" ("Black Rook in Rainy Weather," in the British edition of *The Colossus*, reprinted in *Crossing the Water*, 1971); the "Stars grinding, crumb by crumb,/Our own grist down to its bony face" ("All the Dead Dears"); the impassioned wish "Stone, stone, ferry me down there" ("Lorelei"), looking ahead to the intense, repetitive pleas, commands, curses of *Ariel*. If the poems are not always even in quality, at their best they are of a piece with her better-known work.

Already present throughout the volume is the Keatsian sense of the sweetness of death, the longing to be swallowed up by something greater than oneself, to become part of the permanent, the eternal; "Lorelei" is the descendant of "Ode to a Nightingale," "The Manor Garden" of "To Autumn." Lacking, however, is the pure joy in sensuous experience that helped root Keats firmly in this world whatever his immortal longings. The stage is fully set for the poems of *Ariel*, poured out at a white heat the reader feels, in which Sylvia Plath incorporated her influences into a voice unmistakably hers, one that was capable of dealing with the terror of her existence.

"Lady Lazarus," which deals with experiences similar to those of *The Bell Jar*, is a fine illustration of how Sylvia Plath had learned to handle her materials. The title proposes an archetypal frame of reference; but, in a tradition that goes back through Eliot, Pound, and Joyce, the pattern is used ironically. Lazarus was raised from unwanted death, while the protagonist here speaks of frustrated attempts at suicide. And if the original story is a parable of immortality, the reworked myth is an ambivalent courting of the self's extinction. The modern world with its tawdry cheapness, its senselessness, has replaced the early Christian era. Rising from the dead is a spectacular performed every ten years. The poet is "A sort of walking miracle" eagerly watched by a "peanut-crunching crowd"; she performs, in effect, a "big strip tease," a "theatrical/Comeback in broad day." The world is callous and petty, responding to a drama of life and death as if it were a vaudeville act. At the same time that the poet mocks the world that is oblivious to the significance of her experience, she also mocks herself, speaking as her own agent, selling her act to a public that responds only to the sensational.

"Dying," she insists, "Is an art, like everything else./I do it exceptionally well." These lines are ambiguous. In a sense, they are meant literally: there is a kind of unity of art and death; beyond mutability, both are states of perfection. And so close has the poet been to death, she claims the right to speak as one who has died. But the irony is insistent. Although she is so good at dying, the poet is not dead; her survival becomes embarrassing, her continued existence must be a "miracle."

Art is, among other things, artifice. Sylvia Plath does not try to evade the charge that attempted suicide is theatrical, a dramatized call for help. She also knows, however, that it is a deadly serious business, that no matter how complex the intentions, the result is often simply death. And so the poet penetrates irony with a vision of external holocaust embedded in the inner world. She speaks of her skin as "a Nazi lampshade," her foot "A paperweight," her face "a featureless, fine/Jew linen." Her world contains a bitter antagonist, referred to variously as Herr Doktor, Herr Enemy, Herr God, Herr Lucifer, representing psychiatrist, father, husband, death itself, all responded to with love and hate. The shock treatments in which "I turn and burn" become associated with the crematorium; all that is left is soap, a ring, a gold filling. Persecuted by an unfeeling world, to which she appropriately speaks only with sarcasm ("Do not think I underestimate your great concern"), she becomes the archetypal victim.

But she is more than that. She does, after all, return with regularity from the grave, exacting payment for what she has been forced to endure: "There is a charge/For the eyeing of my scars. . . ." Like the phoenix, she rises from the ashes, "I rise with my red hair/And I eat men like air." If the poet is victim, she is also torturer; if she has been consumed by a hostile fire, she becomes herself a deadly flame.

The poem moves on this wave of ironic tension: the protagonist is both exploiter and exploited, destroyer and destroyed. Along with the sense of having been violated by the outer world goes the uneasy possibility of having created it. External reality has been so swallowed up, it can no longer be blamed; it scarcely seems to exist apart from the poet's mind. Then this tension is at least temporarily resolved in the spectacular manipulation of tone at the poem's center. After thirty-six lines of blustering sarcasm, Plath puts to use lessons learned from Roethke:

> The second time I meant
> To last it out and not come back at all.
> I rocked shut
>
> As a sea shell.
> They had to call and call
> And pick the worms off me like sticky pearls.

After this dead stop, the poem quickly picks up momentum and rushes headlong to its conclusion. The possibility of death ceases to be an abstraction in a dialectical process. Having died is experienced concretely and physically. The embryonic sensation of rocking shut, the reluctance to return made tangible in worms "like sticky pearls," these anchor the entire poem; the extreme pitch of emotion at which it operates is earned in a moment of terrible quiet.

In poem after poem, Plath pushes, or is pushed, beyond the boundaries we usually accept as safe. In "Daddy" she confronts her highly ambivalent feelings toward her father, who died when she was eight (although she says "ten" in the poem), leaving her with a weighty burden of guilt, and a tangle of unresolved emotions. He is envisioned as a Nazi, while she, thinking of possible ancestry, is "a bit of a Jew." She is, then, afraid of him, she hates him; but

> Every woman adores a Fascist,
> The boot in the face, the brute
> Brute heart of a brute like you.

She has tried to get back to him by dying. When this fails, and she is brought back ("they stuck me together with glue"), she makes a model of him—"A man in black with a Meinkampf look"—her husband. The poem ends with a stake in the heart of the vampire father-husband; the poet declares her freedom: "Daddy, daddy, you bastard, I'm through." Yet it is precisely through the intensity of this last line, and the quick violent rhythms that dominate the poem, that the reader senses she is not through at all. Indeed, a large number of the poems in this volume end not in quiet resolution, but rather in near hysteria: "Will you marry it, marry it, marry it" ("The Applicant"); ". . . These are the isolate, slow faults / That kill, that kill, that kill" ("Elm"); "Somebody's done for" ("Death & Co.").

As a kind of counterpoint to the darkness of *Ariel* is the theme of the child, usually characterized as "pure," and quite naturally associated with birth and life in their struggle with death. Even here, maybe especially here, the terror encroaches. The purity that dogs these children is often connected with a cry; it sometimes seems possible it is the purity of death. The poem "Balloons," which is potentially tender, builds increasing anxiety, finally ending with the child

> Contemplating a world clear as water.
> A red
> Shred in his little fist.

It is hard to say what builds the anxiety; it may in fact be possible to bring an entirely different tone to the poem. The terror is there, however, and it derives from the innocence of the child, and of the balloons, "Guileless and clear, / Oval soul-animals." The innocence invites destruction; and in spite of the traditional sweetness of a child playing with a balloon, the words' connotations suggest something grimmer: "shriek," "attacked," "trembling," "queer moons," "dead furniture," "squeak," "bites," "shred." This purity is murderous.

A word should be said about Plath's bee poems, the first of which, "The Beekeeper's Daughter," appears in *The Colossus*, the others—"The Bee Meeting," "The Arrival of the Bee Box," "Stings," "The Swarm,"

"Wintering"—in *Ariel*. Otto Plath, the poet's father, kept bees, not only providing her with an intimate knowledge of bee-tending, but charging the subject with unexpected intensity as well. In this area Sylvia Plath is able to confront those aspects of her experience that concern her most; the natural history of the bee colony, and its relation to the human world, provide symbols of her feelings toward father, husband, and men in general, of sexuality, of freedom and restraint, of power and impotence. Perhaps most significant of all, the bees are associated with the formless darkness within and without; in "The Arrival of the Bee Box" the world of undifferentiated being with which Sylvia Plath so often seemed anxious to unite becomes a source of horror: "It is the noise that appals me most of all, / The unintelligible syllables." Like the caves of Forster's *Passage to India* that reduce all sounds to BOUM, like the giant, foul-smelling insects of Sartre's *The Flies* on the other, Plath's bees provide some of the most powerful images in her work. They represent the terrors that are more than human sanity can tolerate. Similarly, when Sylvia Plath accosts the public world for objective correlatives to her inner life, as she so frequently does, she seizes precisely on the intolerable—the concentration camps, Hiroshima. Although she probably would have been the last to deny what she owed her mentors, Sylvia Plath time and time again goes further than Roethke, Lowell, and Sexton in giving herself up to her anxieties, in naming the unnameable. If we sometimes feel that courage or terror step in where cool literary talent ought to be in control, we should remember that even "Dying is an art." The artistry of Sylvia Plath's death lies in the concrete imagination that must have provided both the special intensity of her terror and the source of her poetry.

Since *Ariel*, two posthumous volumes of Sylvia Plath's poetry have appeared. While neither book contains any surprises or makes necessary a reconsideration of the poet's themes or methods, the poems are not simply of interest to a student of Plath's craft but deserve publication in their own right; and if they disappointed some readers because they did not have the original impact—nor could they have had—of such poems as "Daddy," "Lady Lazarus," and "Ariel," they can ultimately only add to Plath's stature by providing it with a more substantial base.

Crossing the Water (1971), comprised mostly of poems written between *The Colossus* and *Ariel*, can be said to fill in gaps. Nine of the poems, in fact, appeared in the British edition of the earlier book. Most effective are poems like "In Plaster" and "Mirror," which look forward toward the special intensity of the *Ariel* poems. On the whole, the volume is a good supplement to *The Colossus*.

Winter Trees (1972), however, is another matter. In an introductory note, Ted Hughes asserts that the poems come from the same batch as the *Ariel* poems, written the last year of Plath's life, and that the earlier selection was arbitrary. While this is not totally believable, since some of the poems in *Ariel* must have jumped off the pages, the poems in *Winter Trees* are clearly not rejects. They are taut and exciting, characterized by the same sharp imagery and energetic rhythmic patterns as the previously published work.

These lines from "Brasília," for example, echo, without slavishly imitating, parts of "Morning Song," "Lady Lazarus," and "Fever 103°":

> And my baby a nail
> Driven in, driven in.
> He shrieks in his grease,
>
> Bones nosing for distances.

Winter Trees also contains "Three Women: A Poem for Three Voices," written earlier than the other poems as a radio play for the British Broadcasting Corporation. Inspired by Ingmar Bergman's film *Brink of Life* (1959), it illustrates the development of Plath's style as she approached what was to be the last year of her life. The women experience the terrors of their own lives and the terrors of bringing new life into the world. But the play's final line is an image of rebirth: "The little grasses/Crack through stone, and they are green with life." This is the struggle to be reborn in which Sylvia Plath was involved metaphorically throughout her life, almost literally after each of her attempts at suicide. That final winter morning, the struggle ended.

See also the Introduction, section VI.

Selected Bibliography:
By SYLVIA PLATH:
The Colossus and Other Poems. London: William Heinemann, 1960. New York: Alfred A. Knopf, 1962. London: Faber & Faber, 1967.
The Bell Jar. [Novel.] London: William Heinemann, 1963 (under pseudonym Victoria Lucas). London: Faber & Faber, 1966. New York: Harper & Row Publishers, 1971.
Ariel. London: Faber & Faber, 1965. New York: Harper & Row Publishers, 1966.
Crossing the Water. New York: Harper & Row Publishers, 1971.
Winter Trees. New York: Harper & Row Publishers, 1972.
See also Sylvia Plath's statements in "Context," *London Magazine* 1 (n.s.) (Feb. 1962), 45–46.

About Sylvia Plath:
Alvarez, A. "Sylvia Plath," *Tri-Quarterly,* #7 (Fall 1966), 65–74.
———. *The Savage God: A Study of Suicide.* New York: Random House, 1972.
Ames, Lois. "Notes toward a Bibliography," *Tri-Quarterly,* #7 (Fall 1966), 95–107.
Cox, C. B. and A. R. Jones. "After the Tranquilized Fifties," Critical Quarterly, VI (Summer 1964), 107–22.
Dyson, A. E. "Sylvia Plath," *Tri-Quarterly,* #7 (Fall 1966), 75–80.
Howard, Richard. *Alone with America.* New York: Atheneum Publishers, 1969. Pp. 413–22.
Hughes, Red. "Notes on the Chronological Order of Sylvia Plath's Poems," *Tri-Quarterly,* #7 (Fall 1966), 81–88.
Jones, A. R. "Necessity and Freedom: The Poetry of Robert Lowell, Sylvia Plath and Anne Sexton," *Critical Quarterly,* VII (Spring 1965), 11–30.
Newman, Charles. "Candor Is the Only Wile," *Tri-Quarterly,* #7 (Fall 1966), 39–64.

———. *The Art of Sylvia Plath*. (Editor) Bloomington: University of Indiana Press, 1970.

Oberg, A. K. "Sylvia Plath and the New Decadence," *Chicago Review*, XX (1968), 66–73.

Rosenthal, M. L. *The New Poets: American & British Poetry Since World War II*. New York: Oxford University Press, 1967. Pp. 79–89.

Sexton, Anne. "The Barfly Ought to Sing," *Tri-Quarterly*, #7 (Fall 1966), 89–94.

Steiner, G. "Dying is an Art," *Reporter*, XXXIII (Oct. 7, 1965), 51–54.

Steiner, Nancy Hutger. *A Closer Look at Ariel: A Memory of Sylvia Plath*. New York: Harper's Magazine Press, 1973.

PROJECTIVE VERSE

In 1950 CHARLES OLSON's essay "Projective Verse" was published in *Poetry New York*. It served as manifesto for Olson's own poetry and for that of the BLACK MOUNTAIN POETS, a school that had begun to take shape around him, and which included ROBERT CREELEY and ROBERT DUNCAN. But the essay almost immediately had a far broader appeal. In the thirties and forties, the NEW CRITICISM had taken over the academic world; and while this criticism was perfectly suited to handle the ironies and intricate intellectual structure of a poet like T. S. Eliot, it took relatively little interest in the very lively poetic tradition that included the Ezra Pound of the *Cantos* and William Carlos Williams. While Pound was not ignored, and Williams received some attention, the younger poets influenced by them were given almost no consideration. Then Olson's manifesto, antiacademic, antirationalist, embracing open rather than closed forms, became a rallying point for many independently developing groups of poets who had been excluded from the mainstream of American poetry. By 1960, when Donald M. Allen's *The New American Poetry*—the first comprehensive anthology of projective verse—was published, the editor was able to include work of the Black Mountain poets, the SAN FRANCISCO RENAISSANCE, the BEAT GENERATION, the NEW YORK POETS, and a miscellaneous group with no particular affiliation.

Olson identifies closed verse as the poetry bred by print; his own movement is a revolution of the ear, a revolution that had been started by Pound and Williams. Olson first insists on "composition by field," that is, by juxtaposition of fragments rather than logical analysis. Second, he quotes Robert Creeley's phrasing, "Form is never more than an extension of content." While this is in a sense true of all good poetry, the particular point being made here is that form is not simply something against which content is played off, but is the original expression of that content and takes its shape according to the dynamics of the experience communicated. Finally, Olson argues that each perception must "move, instanter, on another!" There are to be no transitions, no discursive analysis, simply the rapid juxtapositions of perceptions creating their own field of energy.

The crucial unit of composition, according to Olson, is the line, the ground within which intellect and emotion are merged:

the HEAD, by way of the EAR, to the SYLLABLE
the HEART, by way of the BREATH, to the LINE

The determination of the line by breath is probably the practical implication of Olson principles that has received most attention. It is the most easily recognizable common denominator of the Projectivist poets, whose general allegiance to Olson has not in the least smothered their individuality. Robert Duncan has elaborated Olson's remarks about breath, rooting the shape and structure of the poem in basic biological rhythms. In other words, as Stanley Burnshaw has pointed out in *The Seamless Web* (1970), the poem is the expression not simply of man's consciousness but of the entire organism.

This notion is already implicit in Olson's "Projective Verse." "Objectism," he says, using a term that will include not only Williams' Objectivism but his own Projectivism as well, "is the getting rid of the lyrical interference of the individual as ego, of the 'subject' and his soul, that peculiar presumption by which western man has interposed himself between what he is as a creature of nature . . . and those other creations of nature which we may, with no derogation, call objects."

There remains the question of why Olson used the term *Projective* to refer to his verse. According to Olson, it is precisely by getting rid of the ego and understanding the essential harmony with the "objective" universe man contains within him that he can honestly encounter his reality; if man tries to reach the outer world through his intellect, he is simply turned in on himself:

If he sprawl, he shall find little to sing but himself, and shall sing, nature has such paradoxical ways, by way of artificial forms outside himself. But if he stays inside himself, if he is contained within his nature as he is participant in the larger force, he will be able to listen, and his hearing through himself will give him secrets objects share.

See also IMAGISM, OBJECTIVISM, and the Introduction, section II.

RICH, ADRIENNE CECILE   (*b. Baltimore, Md., May 16, 1929—   *)

For critics struggling with that old controversy brought once more to life— is a poet's primary obligation to the social and political reality of which he is part or is it purely and simply to the demands of his craft?—the poetry of Adrienne Rich provides welcome relief. No poet writing today is more responsive to our shared nightmares, to pointless, devastating wars, to shattering racial and class tensions, to the general dehumanization to which we are all prey and the selective dehumanization of particular groups, like blacks or women; and yet few contemporary poets are more obviously or successfully concerned with the formal problems of creating an art that is disciplined but not restrictive. Most remarkable of all, perhaps, is her ability to take passionate stands on specific issues without in the least denying, or failing to come to terms with, the complexities of experience.

Educated at Radcliffe and Oxford, Adrienne Rich's first book of poetry, *A Change of World* (1951), was selected for the Yale Series of Younger Poets while she was still an undergraduate at Radcliffe. She has traveled extensively abroad, has been the recipient of numerous prizes, and more recently has been assistant professor of English at the City College of New York, where most of her time and energy have been devoted to the SEEK (Seek Education, Elevation, and Knowledge) and Open Admissions programs.

The possible conflict between the needs of the artist and the needs of the total human being captured Adrienne Rich's attention at the very start of her career. "At a Bach Concert," from *A Change of World,* explores the proposition that "art is out of love with life." The importance of art to human love is reaffirmed: "This antique discipline"—Bach, in the context of the poem, but by implication all good art—"Renews belief in love yet masters feeling."

T. S. Eliot in "Tradition and the Individual Talent" defined poetry as an escape from personality and emotion, remarking that "only those who have personality and emotions know what it means to want to escape from these things." Similarly, Rich's need for discipline is a logical consequence of the intensity of her emotion, which without form would be overwhelming:

> Form is the ultimate gift that love can offer—
> The vital union of necessity
> With all that we desire, all that we suffer.
>
> (from "At a Bach Concert")

It is love itself that is the source of restraint. Art is not seen as the interaction between love and some alien force, like intellect; love and art feed each other directly.

Adrienne Rich's poetry has in recent years been associated with the women's liberation movement. Like all of the movements to which Rich has given her energy, her commitment is not the result of adopting an attractive abstraction but rather the outgrowth of her own experience, of intense self-examination. "Living in Sin," from *The Diamond Cutters* (1955), anticipates by at least ten years the now general reexamination of a woman's place in our society.

The poem operates through concrete perceptions rather than abstractions. The poet is living with a man while the precise nature of the relationship is never spelled out more thoroughly than in the title, the nature of the experience is nonetheless perfectly clear: dust on the furniture, grime on the windows; a cat stalking a mouse; "a pair of beetle-eyes" peering at her from the kitchen shelf; a piano out of tune. Most revealing of all, however, is the room itself, the place where she stays while the man comes and goes. The fact that it is disordered is important, but not quite as important as the fact that it confines her.

The room has emerged as the dominant symbol of modern woman's predicament (in the fiction of Doris Lessing, for example). It is both womb-like and protective, a tempting refuge from the world—although that particular aspect of the room is minimized in Rich's poem—and severely limiting. The room has also, with some differences, become a more general symbol of humanity's predicament, as in "The Metamorphosis" by Franz Kafka and in the plays of Harold Pinter. "Living in Sin," while focusing specifically on the persona's situation, and on that of women, is easily accessible to anyone who can share the sense of the human condition as being at least partially a trap. And it is characteristic of Rich's commitments that she approaches them from a perspective that is inclusive rather than exclusive.

The room, then, holds the poem together. But it does so in careful conjunction with another set of images: that of light and dark, day and night. Conventionally, night is the time of terror, day the time of hope. For very good reasons, the poet has reversed those associations in this poem. The cold light of day reveals the ugliness of the room, of her situation. Indeed, one of the chief distinctions between herself and the man is that he can, to her wonder, take the day for granted. Dawn announces a man's world, when he will leave and she will stay. Then, each night, she is again in love,

> Though not so wholly but throughout the night
> she woke sometimes to feel the daylight coming
> like a relentless milkman up the stairs.

The coming of light is associated with a man. And it is perhaps significant that he is a *milk*man, suggesting obliquely that women have been alienated from their natural condition.

The title poem of *Snapshots of a Daughter-in-Law* (1963) is one of the most successful in that book, certainly one that contributes to a study of the development of Adrienne Rich's poetry. Dated 1958–60, it forms a kind of transition between her earlier and later styles. The more formal stanzas are there, recalling the rhyme schemes of poems like "At a Bach Concert," the blank verse of "Living in Sin." But several sections—there are ten in all—are written in the carefully controlled "free" verse that increasingly dominates her work.

More important, perhaps, is the poem's focus on the photographic method so characteristic of her verse, a method which should from the start be distinguished from most varieties of Imagism. In another poem, "Merely to Know," Rich writes:

> Let me take you by the hair
> and drag you backward to the light,
> there spongelike press my gaze
> patiently upon your eyes,
> hold like a photographic plate
> against you my enormous question.

This passage could well function as a metaphor for Rich's poetics. The poet is a kind of photographic plate, a camera; but she is a "spongelike" camera, one that absorbs what it sees, incorporates it into itself. And it does not pretend to be an objective camera; it is rather a questioning one, with a particular perspective.

In "Snapshots of a Daughter-in-Law," the camera focuses on different women, including Emily Dickinson and Simone de Beauvoir, but they are all personae for Adrienne Rich, just as she is persona for them. In section 3, she concludes by rephrasing Baudelaire: "*ma semblable, ma soeur!*" This is, in short, a variety of Confessional poetry that looks outward rather than inward for its materials.

The theme of "Snapshots" is that nature has revealed secrets to women, to her daughters-in-law, that "her sons never saw," placing women in a privileged but terrifying position. Although male and female sensibilities are distinguished, a mode of apprehending reality is defined in which both men and women, in varying degrees, perhaps, participate. It is a way of knowing the world in touch with natural rhythms and harmonies, with the terrors and joys of emotions, with the unconscious. Rich rejects, however, the familiar dichotomy that associates these qualities with women and the forming intellect with men. This way of responding to experience is not nonintellectual; though it goes beyond reason, it is not at odds with it, except in the sense that it contains perceptions that reason cannot contain, as in section 3:

> A thinking woman sleeps with monsters.
> The beak that grips her, she becomes. And Nature
> that sprung-lidded, still commodious
> steamer-trunk of *tempora* and *mores*
> gets stuffed with it all: the mildewed orange-flowers,
> the female pills, the terrible breasts
> of Boadicea beneath flat foxes' heads and orchids.

If there is any single theme that binds together most of the original poems of *Necessities of Life* (1966), it is a very powerful sense of time, of the transience of experience. It is important to realize that although a good deal of Adrienne Rich's poetry is of a particular time and place, it is almost always firmly rooted in the inexorable realities of man's existential condition. A good deal of the terror of "Snapshots," for example, is the result of being in tune with a kind of primal chaos, the formless world that we attempt to dominate, but of which we are inevitably part. In "Moth Hour," after contemplating the million insects that die at twilight—"no one even finds their corpses"—Rich concludes: "When you put out your hand to touch me/you are already reaching toward an empty place."

In these poems, that nothingness, never far off, is only rarely associated with the dark; the moths meet their destruction in the flame. Sun, moon, red-hot lights, conflagrations of all sorts dominate. They consume. The sources of this almost apocalyptic imagery are sometimes topical: Hiroshima; the ghettos; oblique references to Vietnam. The particular world, however, appears as a manifestation of a universal process, as, for example, in the last stanza of "The Trees":

> Listen. The glass is breaking.
> The trees are stumbling forward
> into the night. Winds rush to meet them.
> The moon is broken like a mirror,
> its pieces flash now in the crown
> of the tallest oak.

More than before, many of the poems in *Necessities of Life* are truly Confessional: poems about her husband, her children. And yet, this is not really "another side" of Rich. It is the same vision—except that much that was before implicit here appears on the surface.

Many of the themes of *Necessities of Life* are picked up in *Leaflets* (1969), often with significant differences. The fires that pervaded the earlier volume are still present, but they seem to have gone cold. In "Orion," Rich speculates: ". . . the stars in it are dim/ and maybe have stopped burning." In "Picnic" she asks: "What kind of sunlight is it/ that leaves the rocks so cold?" "Leaflets" begins by evoking a vision of

> . . . endless night
> the Coal Sack gaping
> black veins of ice on the pane

The threat of a cold and dying world abounds.

These poems are in many ways visions of Hell. Like Dante, Rich has found the imagery of fire perfectly appropriate to that condition of the soul. "If," says the girl in section 3 of "Leaflets," "I do not go into the fire/ I will not be able to live with my soul." And also like Dante, Rich finds the very depths of Hell a kind of frozen lake, symbolic of the absence of love. There is, however, a source of heat and energy, potentially destructive in its own right, nonetheless a sign of life and maybe hope. This heat does not come from the sun or moon or stars; it comes from within, sometimes from within the very bowels of the earth, as it does for the woman "Completely protected on all sides/ by volcanoes" in "The Observer." That the volcanoes are probably a metaphor for a source of energy within the human body is supported by these lines in "Night in the Kitchen":

> The thickness budging forward in these veins
> is surely something other
> than blood:
> say, molten lava.

In fact, the poems of *Leaflets* are filled with images of blood and skin. The book becomes an attempt to understand the sources and limits of human energy, an exploration that can reach no clear conclusions. At times there is only what she calls in "Orion" the emptiness behind the eyes, and at times, as in "The Demon Lover," sexual experience and art combine to forge at least a momentary triumph:

> Only where there is language is there world.
> In the harp of my hair, compose me
> a song. Death's in the air,
> we all know that. Still, for an hour,
> I'd like to be gay. How could a gay song go?
> Why that's your secret, and it shall be mine.
> We are our words, and black and bruised and blue.
> Under our skins, we're laughing.

Leaflets ends with a sequence of *ghazals* (poems of at least five couplets modeled after the nineteenth-century Urdu poet Mirza Ghalib). The couplets do not rhyme, nor do they possess strict meters, but the organization of thought into two-line units and the emphasis on images as a unifying principle provide a discipline perfectly suited to Rich's craft. The themes are familiar ones. In the poem dated 7/16/68:ii, when the fields are mowed, she sees ". . . the world reformed/as if by snow, or fire, or physical desire." And she begins to examine the death of the city by snow.

In the *ghazal* dated 7/23/68, the earlier idea of the poet as a "sponge-like" photographic plate, a possible metaphor for her poetic methods, appears in a totally different but nonetheless recognizable form. The poem begins:

> When your sperm enters me, it is altered;
> when my thought absorbs yours, a world begins.

The point is clear. It is impossible to divide the world into discrete parts; everything impinges on everything else. The process of perception alters the nature of the world that is perceived. Thus, the act of perception itself, and the recording of it in a poem, becomes an act of love:

> If the mind of the teacher is not in love with the mind of the student,
> he is simply practising rape, and deserves at best our pity.

Here is probably the key to understanding how Adrienne Rich's poetry can be so personal, occasionally private, and so involved in the world of action around her. She does not recognize the difference as being significant; outer reality has become part of her inner reality.

In the poem dated 7/26/68:ii, this integration becomes even more evident, (and the relation is described by means of the photographic metaphor. She calls on LeRoi Jones and Eldridge Cleaver to listen to the ghosts, the whites, "condemned to haunt the cities where you want to be at home."

> The white children turn black on the negative.
> The summer clouds blacken inside the camera-skull.

Spirit and matter, black and white, inner and outer, all linked inseparably together, each version of reality dependent on its opposite for its existence, each altering the nature of the other and altered in turn.

The title of *The Will to Change* (1971) is taken from the opening lines of

Charles Olson's "The Kingfishers": "What does not change/is the will to change." An assertion of the transience of experience and of the paradox that flux contains within itself the principle of permanence, this idea also attempts to define the role of the artist, to understand the act of creation. The artist has traditionally been thought of as the one who creates form out of flux, permanence out of mutability. Although it can be said that in her poetry Adrienne Rich has striven to give shape to chaos, it is clear that she has given much more importance to the effort than to the result; her answers are almost always tentative and fluid. If the ordering of experience is a question of drawing lines, of defining boundaries, then her poems are continually discovering that lines are necessarily blurred, that boundaries inevitably shift. In "Images for Godard," she says, "the mind of the poet is changing/the moment of change is the only poem."

So powerful is "the will to change" throughout this volume that it threatens to undermine poetry itself. At the least there is an acute awareness of the difficulties of locating poetry in the world of change rather than in illusory permanence, of writing a language that is alive rather than dead. In "The Will to Change," Rich writes of "the artists talking of freedom/in their chains." And the chains are ironically forged of words, of the very medium poets must use to free themselves. In "Our Whole Life," our experience of reality is seen as "permissible fibs," "a knot of lies." It is expressed in ". . . dead letters/rendered into the oppressor's language."

The "oppressor's language" is a theme running through the book; it is the enemy of change, the enemy, therefore, of true poetry, which can only exist at the moment of change. In "The Burning of Paper Instead of Children," Adrienne Rich responds to a neighbor who has been outraged that her child and his have burned a mathematics textbook in the school's backyard. "The burning of a book," she quotes him, "arouses terrible sensations in me, memories of Hitler; there are few things that upset me so much as the idea of burning a book." The title itself expresses Rich's attitude. To be sure, she is ambivalent: "this is the oppressor's language/yet I need it to talk to you." Language is needed to communicate; but it is a language that binds—the language of war, colonialism, racism, the repression of passion. Rich is not, of course, sympathetic with Nazi book-burning. But now language has become the instrument of chains. It is the enemy:

> (the fracture of order
> the repair of speech
> to overcome this suffering)

In the end, Adrienne Rich—in agreement with many of her contemporaries—has reversed the formula governing poetry between the two world wars: for Rich, poetry is not the ally of order but of anarchy. In lines reminiscent of Blake's assertion that Milton in *Paradise Lost* was of the Devil's party though he knew it not, she calls Wallace Stevens "our poet of revolution all along." Dedicating the *ghazal* dated 9/28/68:ii to Stevens, she writes:

A man isn't what he seems but what he desires:
gaieties of anarchy drumming at the base of the skull.

Selected Bibliography:
By Rich:
A Change of World. New Haven: Yale University Press, 1951.
The Diamond Cutters. New York: Harper & Row Publishers, 1955.
Snapshots of a Daughter-in-Law: Poems 1954–1962. New York: Harper & Row Publishers, 1963.
Necessities of Life: Poems 1962–1965. New York: W. W. Norton & Co., 1966.
Leaflets: Poems 1965–1968. New York: W. W. Norton & Co., 1969.
The Will to Change: Poems 1968–1970. New York: W. W. Norton & Co., 1971.
Diving Into the Wreck: Poems 1971–1972. New York: W. W. Norton & Co., 1973.

About Rich:
Howard, Richard. Alone with America. New York: Atheneum Publishers, 1969. Pp. 423–41.

ROETHKE, THEODORE   (b. Saginaw, Mich., May 25, 1908— d. Aug. 1, 1963)

With great pride, Theodore Roethke thought of himself as a mad poet. He would not mind being institutionalized in heaven, he wrote late in his career, if allowed to ". . . eat and swear/With the likes of Blake,/And Christopher Smart,/And that sweet man, John Clare" ("Heard in a Violent Ward"). Elsewhere he asked, "What's madness but nobility of soul/At odds with circumstance?" ("In a Dark Time"). In the forefront of human consciousness, the company of great mad writers, among whom Roethke numbered himself, is in a privileged position to bring news of the human condition. Their greatness consists in using madness to intensify rather than distort their common humanity. Roethke's own tenuous sense of self led not to a formless shriek of pain but to controlled exploration of the nature of existence. There is agony in his art, but ultimately the agony is not pathological but existential. That is the core of Roethke's genius.

Roethke was born in Saginaw, Michigan, in 1908. The most significant material fact of his childhood was the twenty-five acre complex of greenhouses owned by his father, Otto, and his uncle. Here Theodore Roethke grew up; here he learned the greenhouse world's emotional vocabulary, which was to become the basic unit of his finest poetry; Roethke responded to all of his crucial experience in terms of this vegetable kingdom. The greenhouse, an enclosed area in which things grew, was an obvious symbol of the womb, of everything fertile, maternal, and protective. It was also a made thing, a masculine symbol of man's domination of nature, of Roethke's father, giver of life and order.

If the greenhouse itself was the most important physical reality in Roethke's world, the death of his father of cancer a month before the poet became fifteen was certainly the most overwhelming emotional reality. Otto Roethke was a stern Prussian who, Theodore revealed in "The Saginaw Song," never used a stick, but slapped him with his hand. Whatever admiration and love Roethke must have felt for his father—and the awe-filled respect for the master of the greenhouses is present in nearly every reference to Otto—was clearly tempered by fear and, undoubtedly, hatred. The death of such a father, a terrible, lingering death, just when the son is entering adolescence, is sufficient to account for an intolerable burden of guilt. An ugly family quarrel between father and uncle, ended by the suicide of Theodore's uncle shortly before his father's own death, must have added to this burden and contributed to the obsessive, unresolved allusions to his father, which appear throughout Roethke's verse.

Young Roethke's distrust of the adult world emerged from his sense of hypocrisy in middle-class Saginaw (he seemed to prize only the bootleggers and gamblers, though his association with them was largely fantasy). It extended to all the schools at which he was educated: the local high school, the University of Michigan (where he received his bachelor's (1929) and master's (1936) degrees), and Harvard. Much of this distrust, however justified, probably emerged from a lack of satisfaction with himself. After seriously considering becoming a lawyer or an advertising copy writer, he finally, with no small encouragement from Robert Hillyer at Harvard, decided to become a poet—and to earn his living teaching English.

From 1931 to 1935 he taught at Lafayette College in Easton, Pa., from 1936 to 1943 at Pennsylvania State College, in both instances doubling as tennis coach. The academic world presented special problems for Roethke. He was for most of his life a disturbed man, subject to periodic manic highs and schizophrenic dissociations of personality that seemed to increase in frequency as his life proceeded. Survival in the academic community depended on his repressing or masking his illness, a necessity he found as humiliating as the illness itself. (A brief stay at Michigan State was cut short by a nervous collapse in November 1935.) It was only when he had achieved some measure of success as a poet that his illness was accepted, tolerated, more or less incorporated into his life style.

Roethke's first collection of poems, *Open House*, was published in 1941. The title poem establishes his claim as one of the first of the avowedly Confessional poets. In it, he proclaims himself "naked to the bone," his heart open, his secrets crying aloud. Strangely enough, the revelation of self is one of the things Roethke accomplishes least effectively in this volume; the intention is there, but the tools necessary to put it into practice are lacking. These are well-wrought, witty poems, in the neometaphysical manner so prevalent at the time. Their orientation is largely intellectual, and Roethke ends by talking about talking about himself rather than putting the reader in direct contact with his private experience. Nonetheless, the preoccupations that shape so much of his later work are already in evidence: the tension between inner and outer reality, between being and nonbeing; the emphasis on vision, both as a poetic mode and a means of experiencing the world.

In "Epidermal Macabre," Roethke proclaims the indelicacy of ". . . he who loathes / The aspect of his fleshy clothes," but concludes with his willingness to dispense with "epidermal dress" and the "savage blood's obscenity," to be ". . . a most / Incarnadine and carnal ghost." Always uncomfortable with the purely physical, Roethke is also uncomfortable without it. Though he repudiates flesh as a superficial covering of his essential spirit, he is still a *carnal* ghost; if he is spirit, he is spirit bound—albeit awkwardly—to body, and much of his poetic career is devoted to a working out of the antagonism between these two essential aspects of his being.

"The Premonition," presumably dealing with young Roethke's foreboding of his father's death, is in a more general way devoted to the tenuousness of existence. His father dips his hand in the water, which then runs over the "narrow wrist bone," itself an intimation of mortality. A reflection appears in the water, until, ". . . when he stood up, that face / Was lost in a maze of water." It is this sense of inevitable dissolution, which haunts so much of Roethke's verse, that explains his mistrust of the material universe. As the extravagant wit of "Epidermal Macabre" makes clear, however, the impulse to escape the physical leads to the grotesque; Roethke's efforts must go toward forging links.

It is through a system of correspondences between inner and outer worlds—in the tradition of Hermes Trismegistus and the Theosophists, Baudelaire and the French Symbolists, or Emerson and the American Transcendentalists (all are appropriate)—that Roethke chiefly hopes to find unity of being. "The Light Comes Brighter" is an early, obvious, and not entirely ineffective instance of this effort. After several images of the coming light of day, and the advent of spring, Roethke turns to the real business of the poem.

> The leafy mind, that long was tightly furled,
> Will turn its private substance into green,
> And young shoots spread upon our inner world.

The rebirth experienced through the senses becomes inextricably associated with spiritual rebirth, the coming of the light with a new clarity of vision.

In *Open House* the problem of poetic means is still unresolved. One of the finest poems in the book, "The Adamant," talks of the core of truth no hammer can crush, no tool can chip. In other words, the tools of analysis are helpless before the total complexity of experience, which must be felt, not formulated. But with all of the high craftsmanship of so much of this volume, with all of its metaphysical wit and sometimes striking effects, Roethke has not yet succeeded in touching the core of his own experience. Ironically, *Open House* received far less adverse criticism than any of his greater, more controversial, achievements.

In the spring of 1943 he began his brief but momentous teaching career at Bennington. His amorous adventures are apparently legendary at the all-girl school. More significant, though it could hardly have seemed so at the time, was the fact that one of his students was a pretty art major, Beatrice Heath O'Connell, whom he later remet and, in 1953, married. Most significant of all were the poetic breakthroughs accomplished during the years at Bennington. In 1947 Roethke went to the University of Washington at Seattle, where he became full professor in 1948, and where he taught until his death. By that time he had written the poems that revealed his own poetic voice, and which established him as an important American poet.

The Lost Son and Other Poems (1948) is probably Roethke's most strikingly original performance. The book is divided into four sections, the second and third of which are relatively conventional, not very different from the poems of *Open House;* the first and fourth sections, however, open new worlds. Section 1 contains the "greenhouse poems." There are thirteen of these poems (a fourteenth, "Frau Bauman, Frau Schmidt, and Frau Schwartze" was added when the section was reprinted in *The Waking* in 1953). Superficially arranged in haphazard order, actually the sequence is crucial. The poems move from images of birth and childhood to the approach of adolescence and an awareness of mortality.

The attempt to enter the world of the child is not original in Roethke; but much about his way of doing it is. Roethke does not try to reproduce the infant's mind, he tries to approximate his perceptual system. He has shifted emphasis from the intellectual to the sensuous, and within the sensuous universe itself from the visual to the close-order senses. And whatever else may be going on in the poem, Roethke still assumes his world of correspondences. The perceptual reality of the child is closely related to the psychological or spiritual reality of the adult.

"*Cuttings (later)*" is a good example of Roethke's method, and deserves close examination:

> This urge, wrestle, resurrection of dry sticks,
> Cut stems struggling to put down feet,
> What saint strained so much,
> Rose on such lopped limbs to a new life?
>
> I can hear, underground, that sucking and sobbing,
> In my veins, in my bones I feel it,—
> The small waters seeping upward,
> The tight grains parting at last.
> When sprouts break out,
> Slippery as fish,
> I quail, lean to beginnings, sheath-wet.

If there is such a thing as a genre of "flower poems," Roethke's work is surely atypical. Flower poems are generally visual; here we have no idea at all what the plants look like. Sound and touch are the dominant senses, not sight. More important still, the one characteristic of plants we generally take for granted is that they stay put, they lack movement. Here, instead,

the reader's attention is drawn to the dynamic quality of vegetable existence: the fierce struggle to stay alive, the tremendous tension of restrained
energy—these are the poem's subjects.

The first stanza puts the cuttings in a specifically human, probably theological context: "resurrection," "saint," "new life." But the strain is essentially physical, the struggle of "feet" and "lopped limbs," with the sexual
overtones of "urge." The tension produced by this conflict is alive in the
poem's rhythm as well as its paraphrasable content:

> Cút stéms strúggling to pút dówn féet

Alliteration ("stems struggling," "saint strained so," "lopped limbs . . . life"),
assonance and consonance ("urge . . . resurrection," "cut . . . struggling
. . . put," "saint strained"), tend to increase the emphasis on stressed syllables, resulting in a forceful, choppy line not at all unrelated to the strain of
lopped limbs.

The rhythm of the second stanza, however, is quicker and smoother; any
choppiness that remains is a result of excitement rather than strain. Here
anapests reign in place of spondees:

> . . . súcking and sóbbing,
> In my véins, in my bónes I féel it,—

As the waters seep upward, and the lines grow shorter, the poem moves toward its climax; the ". . . sprouts break out,/Slippery as fish," with the last
line slow, exhausted, longer, as the poet leans ". . . to beginnings, sheath-
wet." Sooner or later, the reader becomes aware that he has been reading
about a male ejaculation, and it is generally the rhythm rather than the
sense of the poem that communicates this, although in this poem about
"sucking and sobbing," "bones," "small waters seeping upward," "tight
grains parting" and sprouts breaking out "Slippery as fish," there should be
little question as to the concerns of the "sheath-wet" poet.

The sexual preoccupations do not in the least deny the poem's spiritual
implications. It is, after all, about birth and rebirth, of plants and men,
sperm and saints. And the work's sexuality is not erotic but intuitive. The
poet, in the second stanza, has become part of the natural world, has lost
his sense of the separateness of creation in a feeling of sensuous unity. Per-
ceptually, if not "intellectually," the poet is participating in the universe of
the unborn, or just born, fetus. The symbolism Roethke uses to describe the
struggle toward spiritual awareness has its roots in a physical universe of
prelogical reality.

The greenhouse poems are extraordinarily successful, though their possibilities are limited. By their own nature confined to the perceptual instant,
they cannot—in spite of the fine resonance of meaning that accompanies
each one—encompass a total view of experience. Roethke was in need of a
framework that would hold together his moments of insight, and for this
purpose the more traditional, logical means of organization were inade-

quate; he sought a system of the unconscious rather than the conscious. In Jung, or, more likely, in Jung as seen through the literary eyes of critic Maud Bodkin, or his friend at Bennington, Kenneth Burke, he found what he was looking for.

Archetypal patterns stir responses deep within the reader; they correspond to universal experiences, to a collectively held unconscious. Of all psychological systems, Jung's is surely one of the least materialistic; it is spiritual rather than biological in its orientation. Roethke thus had in his hands a framework that would contain in a single vision man's psychological and spiritual development, that would allow him to approach the conscious world in terms of the prerational. And Jung's precept that a man must go backward in order to go forward, that he must sink into the slime in order to transcend the sensual, provided a source of dramatic tension all but essential in a longer poem. (That Roethke derived all of this from Jung, rather than coming upon it intuitively is, of course, conjecture. But it is difficult to believe that the aesthetics of "Open Letter," in which he explains his new method, bear no direct relation to some expression of Jung's thought.)

The result of this mixture of the techniques of the greenhouse poems and the Jungian aesthetic is the final section of *The Lost Son*, a series of long, developmental poems that express man's psychological struggle to be, his spiritual struggle to be something significant. These four poems were published a few years later as part of a still larger sequence of similar poems in *Praise to the End!* (1951), and it is in this context that they should be studied.

The movement of *Praise to the End!* as a whole, and of most of the individual poems in it, is from darkness to light; the night journey under the sea and the child-hero conquering darkness are the dominant archetypes, representing spiritual rebirth and man's coming to consciousness as a race and as an individual. The progress of the protagonist (though to assume there is throughout a single protagonist is to make a statement about the nature of human personality for which there is no positive basis in the poems) is intentionally uneven, a rocking back and forth. Some advances are followed by regressions so complete (as in the conclusion of the poem "Praise to the End!") that annihilation is threatened. In the end the child brings forth light, Jonah emerges from the deep, even though the permanence of these victories is seriously in doubt. For Roethke, the possession of a single stable identity was never to be taken for granted.

Praise to the End! is divided into two sections that are technically related but not identical. The first six poems deal with earlier years and emphasize psychological development, the last eight are generally concerned with the approach of adulthood and with a more spiritual kind of quest, although this division is certainly not absolute. A good way of pointing out the distinction between sections, as well as to illustrate the general methods of the poem, is to examine two passages which deal with the same experience from different perspectives:

His ears haven't time.
Sing me a sleep-song, please.
A real hurt is soft.

Once upon a tree
I came across a time,
It wasn't even as
A ghoulie in a dream.

There was a mooly man
Who had a rubber hat
The funnier than that,—
He kept it in a can.

(from "Where Knock Is Open Wide")

Rock me to sleep, the weather's wrong.
Speak to me, frosty beard.
Sing to me, sweet.

Mips and ma the mooly moo,
The likes of him is biting who,
A cow's a care and who's a coo?—
What footie does is final.

My dearest dear my fairest fair,
Your father tossed a cat in air,
Though neither you nor I was there,—
What footie does is final.

Be large as an owl, be slick as a frog,
Be good as a goose, be big as a dog,
Be sleek as a heifer, be long as a hog,—
What footie will do will be final.

(from "Praise to the End!")

Each passage begins with a request for a "sleep-song" or story, though what follows is filtered through the child's consciousness rather than objectively reported. There is a "mooly man," apparently a combination of father and milk-giving mother, in the first selection, "Mips" and a "mooly moo" in the second. Biting and cats appear in "Praise to the End!" as well as cows; "Where Knock Is Open Wide" begins (in a passage not quoted above) with a kitten "biting" with its claws, Papa and Mamma having more teeth, and some sexual confusion as cows have puppies. This complex of images in each case clearly relates to sexual behavior, particularly the sexual behavior of the child's parents. Lovemaking looks to him like a violent business; "A real hurt is soft" is an attempt to rationalize the threatening implications.

Closely linked to the dreamlike spatial distortions, the confusions of per-

son and action, are the temporal problems. The "time" described in the
first poem ". . . wasn't even as/A ghoulie in a dream." In the second
poem, the protagonist tells a part of himself, "Though neither you nor I was
there." It is the poet's own conception, linked with his parents' current sexual activities and his own potential sexual activities, that is the subject here.
"What footie does is final" is proven by his own existence. He speaks with
confidence that his own "footie" will be equally final, and insures this with
a kind of incantatory charm to promote its growth and development. As is
appropriate to the difference in perspective, the sexuality of "Praise to the
End!" is more phallic, more conscious than the distorted vision of "Where
Knock Is Open Wide."

Roethke here owes as much to James Joyce's *Finnegans Wake* as to any
poet. Distortion and telescoping of action and image penetrate the surface
of commonplace reality in both writers, though Joyce, of course, packs
much more into individual words than Roethke, while the latter depends
upon complete images and rhythmic patterns for his effects. Organization
by juxtaposition, association, and theme and variation falls into the tradition
of Pound and Eliot; but although this is difficult, private verse, it is never
perversely allusive. The passages quoted give no idea of the full rhythmic
range of *Praise to the End!*, but they are typical enough in their use of
quick, nursery rhyme movement to convey a sense of sexual excitement.

As the protagonist proceeds on his arduous journey, the prevalent rhythm
changes, as does the direction of the poems' preoccupations. Earlier in the
sequence, the poet struggles with the difficulties of separating himself from
nature's undifferentiated being. Having achieved at last something of an
identity, albeit a tenuous one, that has to be fought for fiercely, Roethke
then confronts an often terrifying sense of aloneness, and actually seeks to
be reunited with the world from which he has so painfully emerged. Nor is
this simply an instance of regression according to Jung's formula. What
Roethke wants is the best of both worlds: a simultaneous feeling of confidence in the self and unity with all being. In short, he begins to lean toward the mystical, following not the tradition of those who would isolate
themselves from the material world in order to find within the universal
self, but rather of those whose very love of sensuous reality led them to participate in it totally. In "Unfold! Unfold!" Roethke calls upon his forest of
symbols to sing:

> A house for wisdom; a field for revelation
> Speak to the stones, and the stars answer.
> At first the visible obscures:
> Go where the light is.

Roethke is at his best, however, when he is less specific, when the delicate
balance of his relation to the natural world emerges not as philosophy but
as experience:

> To stare into the after-light, the glitter left on the lake's surface,
> When the sun has fallen behind a wooded island;

To follow the drops sliding from a lifted oar,
Held up, while the rower breathes, and the small boat drifts
   quietly shoreward;
To know that light falls and fills, often without our knowing,
As an opaque vase fills to the brim from a quick pouring,
Fills and trembles at the edge yet does not flow over,
Still holding and feeding the stem of the contained flower.

(from "The Shape of the Fire")

Although *The Lost Son* made a sizable impact on the community of poets, it was not until 1953, the year of the publication of *The Waking*, and, incidentally, the year of his marriage to Beatrice O'Connell, that Roethke received the widespread recognition that meant so much to him. The volume, a selection of poems from *Open House, The Lost Son,* and the finally complete *Praise to the End!* sequence, as well as some new poems, received the Pulitzer Prize the following year. The new poems were of particular interest, since they announced a new direction in Roethke's verse: "I take this cadence from a man named Yeats," Roethke announced in "The Dance," a poem he insisted was dictated to him by Yeats's spirit, "I take it, and I give it back again." It was probably poor judgment to have made this confession; for while almost everyone was willing to concede that Roethke had borrowed much from Yeats, once it was pointed out to them, relatively few were willing to admit that he had given anything back. As Roethke himself suggested, it is the sixteenth-century poet Sir John Davies ("The Dance" is the first part of "Four for Sir John Davies") rather than Yeats who supplies the rhythm; the iambic pentameter lines are end-stopped rather than run-on, there is a feeling of music and the dance that Yeats generally mutes in more conversational cadences. The stanzaic pattern (a b a b c c), a modification of the one used in Davies' *Orchestra*, does bring Yeats to mind, but it is in pose rather than in technique that Roethke really began to resemble Yeats at this point in his career; Yeats is in this century the master of the philosophical lyric, and it is toward this mode that Roethke began increasingly to turn.

Until now, the threat to the self had been in the past: the danger of being swallowed up by the unconscious, the fear of regression to a vanishing point. Forty-five in 1953 and a sick man, Roethke turned to face imminent nonbeing, his death. "Great Nature has another thing to do/To you and me," Roethke declares in his great villanelle "The Waking"; at the very height of his powers, the poet began his preparations for the end. He began to read mystics, both Eastern and Christian, and the existential theologians, like Kierkegaard, Buber, Tillich. The results of these readings appeared in his very next book.

It is not difficult to make a case for *Words for the Wind* (1958) as the consummation of Roethke's career. Not that his last poems are necessarily inferior, but this book, composed of a reprinting of *The Waking* and an almost equally long section of new poems, forms a coherent whole, a spiritual autobiography of the artist.

The largest section of new work is entitled "Love Poems"; a quick reading of these poems suggests that the label is not entirely appropriate. Two
are concerned with specifically sexual love ("I Knew a Woman," "The Sen-
sualists"); several are celebrations of a more idealized, though decidedly
physical, relationship to the beloved ("Words for the Wind," "All the Earth,
All the Air," "The Swan," and others); then there is a distinct group of
poems, including "The Pure Fury," "The Renewal," "Plaint," that seem
only peripherally, or not at all, concerned with love. They are, in fact, visions of the abyss, of the emptiness of eternity. Not too long before the
American publication of *Words for the Wind* (an English edition had come
out in 1957, the only book of Roethke's to have been printed first in Britain), Roethke had gone through one of the deep depressions of his life. The
poems that came out of this period were added to the American edition
(they include the last three mentioned above, as well as "The Exorcism,"
one of Roethke's most terrifying poems). Rather than awkward intrusions,
these poems supply a crucial need; they place the love the poet feels for his
beloved in its proper context, without which the very nature of the emotional energy involved is distorted. In "Four for Sir John Davies," Roethke
saw himself and his "Beatrice" dancing while "Behind, before,/Lay all the
lonely pastures of the dead." Here again Roethke's love takes its shape and
its meaning from a vast dark backdrop. In the same sense as faith for Kierkegaard had no reality except as it emerged from despair, so love for
Roethke was born of aloneness.

Although these poems are filled with allusions to mystics and philosophers, to those who transcend or confront death, Roethke's intensity derives
from his juxtaposition of private and public worlds; love and anxiety give
concrete form to metaphysical speculation, a Yeatsian strategy if ever there
was one. As a matter of fact, the poems are held together by the tension between the conscious, intellectual, form the poet tries to give his experience
and the anxiety beneath the surface—not too far beneath—that threatens to
overwhelm all structure. The form of these poems reflects this tension. The
regular stanzaic patterns remain, champions of stability, witnesses to some ultimate harmony; within the stanza, excitement often verges on frenzy, as
Roethke, not satisfied with the insistent motion of his end-stopped lines,
breaks the line down into still smaller, nearly breathless units:

> We did not fly the flesh. Who does, when young?
> A fire leaps on itself: I know that flame.
> Some rages save us. Did I rage too long?
> The spirit knows the flesh it must consume.

> (from "The Sententious Man")

The last line, the longest sentence of the quatrain, brings a positive sense of
relief, of reintegration. At this effect, Roethke is a master.

Roethke did not turn his back on the rich sources of image and metaphor
he had exploited in the greenhouse poems and *Praise to the End!* This too
was adapted to new demands of rhythm and pattern:

The breath of a long root,
The shy perimeter
Of the unfolding rose,
The green, the altered leaf,
The oyster's weeping foot,
And the incipient star—
Are part of what she is.
She wakes the ends of life.

(from "Words for the Wind")

Words for the Wind concludes with two five-poem sequences of very different kinds. "The Dying Man" is a tribute to Yeats, written in formal lyrics, employing much of Yeats's vocabulary, though the sensibility is Roethke's. If the Dying Man is Yeats, he is also Roethke's father, and he is Roethke himself as well, entering "this last place of light," no longer a bird yet beating his wings "Against the immense immeasurable emptiness of things." The last sequence in the book, "Meditations of an Old Woman," goes back to many of the principles of organization and techniques of *Praise to the End!* This time, since the protagonist is an old woman (essentially the poet's mother or his own *anima*), the language is more discursive, the free verse smoother and less fragmentary, although there are moments of great excitement that resemble the earlier developmental poems, or even the terse, clipped speech of the metaphysical lyrics. Most important of all is the fact that the narrator is not seeking to forge her identity but preparing to relinquish it; the movement is not into time, but above and away from it. The "Meditations" are ultimately linked most closely not to *Praise to the End!* but to "The Dying Man." Just as the latter proclaims himself ". . . that final thing,/A man learning to sing," the old woman prays "O to be delivered from the rational into the realm of pure song." Both dying man and dying woman are Roethke, pitting his art against death with uncertain success.

At the swimming pool of a friend's house on the Puget Sound, Theodore Roethke, a sick man in body as well as mind, died of a heart attack, August 1, 1963. He had finally begun to achieve the recognition he sought. *Words for the Wind* had been awarded Bollingen and National Book awards; his readings were tremendously successful and soon became legendary; he had transformed the University of Washington into a center of creativity.

His posthumous volume of poems, *The Far Field*, appeared in 1964 and also won a National Book Award. It represents a curious accomplishment: although it contains some of Roethke's finest verse, the poet is working in forms he has already mastered, and the excitement of the breakthrough is lost.

The Far Field contains Roethke's last sequence of long, meditative poems, the "North American Sequence." In tone and method, these poems very closely resemble "Meditations of an Old Woman," except that poet and protagonist come as close to having a single identity as they ever do in Roethke's work and that instead of an old woman's back yard the entire

North American continent supplies the material setting. As in *Praise to the End!* and the "Meditations," an archetypal journey gives shape to the poetry, a similar goal motivating the quest: "How to transcend this sensual emptiness?" Rhythms resemble those of "Meditations," though they are in general smoother, the periods of choppy excitement more rare. Principles of organization are also similar, based on association and theme and variation, very much like Eliot's *Four Quartets* (although Roethke would have shuddered to acknowledge this influence); new, perhaps, is a Whitmanesque urge to catalog, for Roethke has learned well the lesson that the human mind approaches the spiritual through the concrete. The movement toward mysticism, the mysticism that embraces the senses as outlets of the soul, is more explicit than ever; again, it is most effective when least doctrinaire:

> As a blind man, lifting a curtain, knows it is morning,
> I know this change:
> On one side of silence there is no smile;
> But when I breathe with the birds,
> The spirit of wrath becomes the spirit of blessing,
> And the dead begin from their dark to sing in my sleep.

> (from "Journey to the Interior")

The final section of this final book is, in fact, devoted to final things. Entitled "Sequence, Sometimes Metaphysical," it focuses on the mystic's way of knowing the world. It begins with a description of a mystical experience (in "In a Dark Time"), and then explores the implications of this experience. Whether Roethke actually had any mystical experience himself is debatable, although he was certain of it. No consistent discipline, at any rate, was used in attaining it. Whatever its origins or implications, the nature of the experience is clear to Roethke. It involves above all the loss of the self and the participation in a greater unity, a greater unity that is devoid of personality, devoid of any trace of the individual existence Roethke so fiercely wrung from life. The last stanza of "In a Dark Time" tells it all:

> Dark, dark my light, and darker my desire.
> My soul, like some heat-maddened summer fly,
> Keeps buzzing at the sill. Which I is *I?*
> A fallen man, I climb out of my fear.
> The mind enters itself, and God the mind,
> And one is One, free in the tearing wind.

The comparison of the soul to a "heat-maddened summer fly" reveals the extent to which the "mystical experience," so much sought after by the poet, evokes in him responses of fear and even revulsion. "Which I is *I?*" he desperately asks; for whether this is mysticism or schizophrenic dissociation of personality (possibly the kind described in "The Exorcism"), Roethke feels his identity slipping away. Although the next line suggests a triumph over fear, the last couplet is ambiguous. Along with the joy of union is the terror it provokes:

In the Platonic sense, the one becomes the many, in this moment. But also—and this is what terrified me—the one not merely makes his peace with God . . . he—if we read One as the Godhead theologically placed above God—transcends God: he becomes the Godhead itself, not only the veritable creator of the universe but the creator of the revealed God. This is no jump for the timid, no flick from the occult, no moment in the rose garden. Instead it is a cry from the mire, and maybe the devil's own.

Roethke, from Anthony Ostroff's
"A Symposium on 'In a Dark Time' ")

What it amounts to is this: mystical experience for Roethke clearly brings news of the universe; but the experience itself takes man out of his humanity and does not offer salvation in strictly human terms. For this, man is thrown upon his own resources. He is essentially alone.

It is no accident that the joyous mysticism of "North American Sequence" is expressed in free verse, the torments of "Sequence, Sometimes Metaphysical" in relatively tight forms. The former is an opening up, a turning out; the latter a withdrawal inward, a gesture toward annihilation. The end-stopped lines, and even shorter groupings, that Roethke had so thoroughly mastered by the end of his career, are appropriate to the fiercely imposed control the poet tries to maintain over himself. The tendency toward aphorism that had always been present in Roethke's writing is given special power by the terse rhythm, the oracular manner in which he yoked together apparently unrelated images; he had above all learned about final things, about communicating a sense of finality, as in these last lines of the poems of "Sequence, Sometimes Metaphysical":

> I teach my eyes to hear, my ears to see
> How body from spirit slowly does unwind
> Until we are pure spirit at the end.

(from "Infirmity")

> I bleed my bones, their marrow to bestow
> Upon that God who knows what I would know.

(from "The Marrow")

Theodore Roethke is certainly a good poet, an important poet, maybe the first poet of his generation in America. To achieve this stature, however, he has had to weather several lines of criticism.

First, he has been accused of being derivative. There is, of course, his debt to Yeats. This has probably been exaggerated, and in any case only applies to the formal lyrics. Eliot's influence has been noted in the free verse sequences—and here Roethke himself protested vehemently, so that we may assume a certain amount of validity to the suggestion in this case (or is it simply that no one minds being compared to Yeats?). But this is probably no more than the vague, general influence of Eliot felt by most

poets of recent years. Except in his very earliest work, when he was learning his trade, Roethke is not an exceptionally derivative poet. In fact, if he
has done nothing else, he created one of the truly unique poet voices of his
time, and he is one of the few poets in recent years whose work is generally
recognizable at once.

Second, in his later years, some of his verse became aphoristic, almost
platitudinous; worse, perhaps, it seemed to lack its previous organic unity, a
possible result of Roethke's method of composition—the keeping of notebooks of isolated fragments which were then worked together into completed
poems. Much of this criticism is problematical. The line between aptness
and triteness is often difficult to draw. What is it that makes "I learn by
going where I have to go" ("The Waking") acceptable, while "The right
thing happens to the happy man" ("The Right Thing"), from his last book,
seems a cliché? It is impossible to answer this question without going into
the poems they come from; a cliché in the appropriate context is trans-
figured. So although it is possible that the reader's increased awareness of the
aphorisms is indicative of real weaknesses, what these weaknesses are has
not really been articulated. As for the fragmentary structure, we have
learned enough from Pound and Joyce to be cautious about limiting too
strictly principles of unity. In any case, these criticisms apply only to portions of Roethke's last work; it seems probable that his major achievement
preceded it.

One final charge is most serious: in some respects, Roethke's range is limited. Certain areas of experience were inaccessible to his art. Social and political awareness are almost completely absent from his collected works, and
with good reason. The few poems he attempted on these themes were not
impressive. In general, Roethke focused on the world of his own private experience. The question of his greatness must ultimately hang on the extent
to which he was able to make universal his own personal concerns. In this
he was not completely unsuccessful.

Roethke was not a consistent philosopher; it is easy to pick holes in the
intellectual framework around which many of his works were constructed.
But he did accurately record the flux of human experience; in his world,
ideas were emotional constructs. All of reality was seen by Roethke in terms
of tensions: between subjective and objective, inner and outer, spiritual and
fleshly. Psychology and metaphysics come together, charged with added
significance by their encounter. If the sense of correspondences is the flesh
of his poetry, his mastery of rhythms is the blood. More than fifty years ago,
Ezra Pound asserted his belief in "absolute rhythm," rhythms that would
precisely fit the experience communicated by the poem. If anyone has been
able to make the case for the existence of these rhythms seem convincing, it
has been Theodore Roethke.

Selected Bibliography:
By Roethke:
Open House. New York: Alfred A. Knopf, 1941.
The Lost Son and Other Poems. Garden City, N.Y.: Doubleday & Co., 1948.

Praise to the End! Garden City, N.Y.: Doubleday & Co., 1951.

The Waking: Poems 1933–1953. Garden City, N.Y.: Doubleday & Co., 1953.

Words for the Wind: The Collected Verse of Theodore Roethke. Garden City, N.Y.: Doubleday & Co., 1958.

I Am! Says the Lamb. Garden City, N.Y.: Doubleday & Co., 1961.

The Far Field. Garden City, N.Y.: Doubleday & Co., 1964.

The Collected Poems of Theodore Roethke. Garden City, N.Y.: Doubleday & Co., 1966.

On the Poet and His Craft: Selected Prose of Theodore Roethke. Edited by Ralph J. Mills, Jr. Seattle: University of Washington Press, 1965.

Straw for the Fire: From the Notebooks of Theodore Roethke 1943–63. Edited by David Wagoner. Garden City, N.Y.: Doubleday & Co., 1972.

About Roethke:

Burke, Kenneth. "The Vegetal Radicalism of Theodore Roethke," *Sewanee Review,* LVIII (Winter 1950), 68–108.

Heilman, Robert. "Theodore Roethke: Personal Notes," *Shenandoah,* XVI (Autumn 1964), 55–64.

Kramer, Hilton. "The Poetry of Theodore Roethke," *Western Review,* XVIII (Winter 1954), 131–54.

Kunitz, Stanley. "News of the Root," *Poetry,* LXXIII (January 1949), 222–25.

———. "Roethke: Poet of Transformations," *New Republic,* CLII (January 23, 1965), 23–29.

Lee, Charlotte. "The Line as a Rhythmic Unit in the Poetry of Theodore Roethke," *Speech Monographs,* XXX (March 1963), 15–25.

Malkoff, Karl. *Theodore Roethke: An Introduction to the Poetry.* New York: Columbia University Press, 1966.

Matheson, John William. *Theodore Roethke: A Bibliography.* University of Washington masters thesis, 1958.

McMichael, James. "The Poetry of Theodore Roethke," *Southern Review,* V (Winter 1969), 4–25.

Meredith, William. "A Steady Stream of Correspondences: Theodore Roethke's Long Journey Out of the Self," *Shenandoah,* XVI (Autumn 1964), 41–54.

Mills, Ralph J., Jr. "Theodore Roethke: The Lyric of the Self," in *Poets in Progress.* Edited by Edward Hungerford. Evanston, Ill.: Northwestern University Press, 1967. Pp. 3–23.

———. *Theodore Roethke.* Minneapolis: University of Minnesota Press, 1963.

———. *Selected Letters of Theodore Roethke.* Seattle: University of Washington Press, 1968.

Ostroff, Anthony. A Symposium on "In a Dark Time" in *The Contemporary Poet as Artist and Critic: Eight Symposia.* Boston: Little, Brown & Co., 1965. (Essays by John Crowe Ransom, Babette Deutsch, Stanley Kunitz, and Theodore Roethke) Pp. 23–53.

Rosenthal, M. L. *The New Poets: American & British Poetry Since World War II.* New York: Oxford University Press, 1967. Pp. 112–18.

Seager, Allan. *The Glass House: The Life of Theodore Roethke.* New York: McGraw-Hill Book Co., 1968.

Staples, Hugh. "Rose in the Sea-Wind: A Reading of Theodore Roethke's 'North American Sequence,'" *American Literature,* VI (May 1964), 189–203.

Stein, Arnold, (ed.). *Theodore Roethke: Essays on the Poetry.* Seattle: University of Washington Press, 1965.

ROTHENBERG, JEROME   (*b. Bronx, N.Y., Dec. 11,*
1931—   )

In *Poems for the Game of Silence* (1971), Jerome Rothenberg, whom Robert Kelly has credited with originating the term *deep image,* analyzes his
poetics by dividing his work into three "programs." The first, which remains
at the heart of all that follows, contains five definitions:

> The poem is the record of a movement from perception to vision.
> Poetic form is the pattern of that movement through space &
> time.
> The deep image is the content of vision emerging in the poem.
> The vehicle of movement is imagination.
> The condition of movement is freedom.

The second program specifies poetry's primary function as the breaking
down of stock responses to reality. The third, asserting that the Western vision of the world represents a failure of perception, announces an interest in
primitive and archaic cultures, in American Indian poetry and Jewish mysticism.

Rothenberg received his bachelor's degree from the City College of New
York and his master's from the University of Michigan. A frequent translator
of German literature, as well as an original poet, he is the founder of the
Hawk's Well Press.

Having its sources in the unconscious, and thereby linking worlds underneath and outside of the conscious self, the deep image is central to Rothenberg's poetry. The underlying assumption is that man is "deeply" in tune
with the universe from which his logical constructs alienate him. The first
of "Three Landscapes" (from *White Sun Black Sun*) begins: "The dark bull
quartered in my eye/turns slowly from his herd"; the last begins: "White
monks are climbing hills/inside her skull." In each case, it is impossible to
tell whether the images originate in the objective world or are archetypal
patterns sprung from the unconscious and therefore subjective in nature.
The real point may be that the question is meaningless, that experience is a
unity, and that the distinction between inner and outer worlds, which creates the problem, is artificial.

In redefining the perceptual process, Rothenberg utilizes a variety of
techniques, ranging from relatively conventional free-verse forms with
breath-determined units of rhythm (very much in the manner of the Projectivists, who are indeed an important technical influence), to more obviously
ritualistic and incantatory rhythms, to a breaking down of the distinctions
between poetry and prose, and finally to Concrete poetry, in which the arrangement of letters on the page is at least as significant as their content,
and the rhythmic use of apparently nonsense syllables. But the approach is
always in the interest of what Blake called cleansing the doors of perception.

See also DEEP IMAGISM and the Introduction, section VIII.

Selected Bibliography:
BY ROTHENBERG:
White Sun Black Sun. New York: Hawk's Well Press, 1960.
The Seven Hells of the Jigoku Zoshi. New York: Trobar Press, 1962.
Sightings I-IX. New York: Hawk's Well Press, 1964.
The Gorky Poems. Mexico: El Corno Emplumado Press, 1966.
Conversations. Los Angeles: Black Sparrow Press, 1968.
Poems 1964–1967. Los Angeles: Black Sparrow Press, 1968.
Poland / 1931. Santa Barbara, California: Unicorn Press, 1969.
Poems for the Game of Silence 1960–1970. New York: Dial Press, 1971.

SANCHEZ, SONIA (*b. Birmingham, Ala., 1935—*   )

Sonia Sanchez is an angry poet. She is chiefly angry at the white America that has attempted to strip blacks of their humanity, sometimes through physical force, sometimes through economic traps, sometimes through drugs. And she is angry at Blacks who exchange their blackness to become part of white America. Sonia Sanchez is also a love poet, but even her love is angry. It is angry in its insistence that black men and women be men and women politically as well as sexually, that they be themselves rather than the white man's image of what they should be.

Sonia Sanchez went to college in New York, at New York University and at Hunter College, where she received her B.A. in 1955. She has taught creative writing at San Francisco State College, and more recently at various schools in New York. She gives frequent readings of her work, readings that are part poetic performance, part exhortation to her audience to affirm the ideals that her poetry expresses.

The readings are not incidental to Sanchez's work. Her poetry is both oral and communal. Even on paper, the poems are marked with the inflections of oral presentation, as, for example, in *Home Coming* in the poem "the final solution":

>   the leaders speak
>   america.
>   land of free/
>   dom
>   land of im/mi/grant
>   whites
>   and slave/
>   blacks. . . .

Sometimes she uses black dialect. In "blk/chant" (from *We A BaddDDD People*), she writes of white men planning the deaths of blacks:

>   with   short / bread
>   for short / sighted / minds
>   with junk to paralyze our

blk/limbs from leapen on the
wite / mutha / fucka /

But she can also work with a more traditional "literary" language, as she
does in *Home Coming*'s "malcolm."

do not speak to me of living.
life is obscene with crowds
of white on black.
death is my pulse.
what might have been
is not for him/or me
but what could have been
floods the womb until i drown.

In fact, Sonia Sanchez is quite familiar with the white literary tradition and
seems to have learned a great deal from e. e. cummings in particular. Generally she rejects that tradition, not because she cannot handle it, or because she cannot express herself in those terms, but rather because the part
of herself she is most interested in expressing must be juxtaposed to anything
white in order to exist. And perhaps most important, she is less concerned
with unraveling the intricacies of her own psyche than in communicating a
few relevant truths to her audience. Again and again she makes the same
points: the assertion of blackness, freedom from white culture and especially
from drugs. The following lines from *We A BaddDDD People* (in the poem
"—answer to yo/question/of am i not yo : woman : even if u went on
shit again—") could very well stand as an epigraph to her entire work:

blk/
lovers   cannot   live
in wite powder that removes
them from they blk/selves

See also NEW BLACK AESTHETIC and the Introduction, section VII.

Selected Bibliography:
BY SANCHEZ:
Home Coming. Detroit: Broadside Press, 1969.
We A BaddDDD People. Detroit: Broadside Press, 1970.
It's a New Day (*poems for young brothas and sistuhs*). Detroit: Broadside Press,
1971.

SAN FRANCISCO RENAISSANCE

Aesthetically an offshoot of Projectivism and the BEAT GENERATION, the San
Francisco Renaissance locates in time and place the coalescence of existing
energies rather than the birth of a new poetic movement. Nonetheless, its

importance as the first major breakthrough of nonacademic poets committed to open rather than closed poetic forms should not be underestimated.

In the early fifties, Kenneth Rexroth, Kenneth Patchen, Brother Antoninus (William Everson), and ROBERT DUNCAN were all in San Francisco. But the most significant addition to the group, as far as the Renaissance was concerned, was LAWRENCE FERLINGHETTI. Along with Jack Kerouac and ALLEN GINSBERG, original founders of the Beat Generation, Ferlinghetti moved from New York to San Francisco in the early fifties. In 1953 he opened the City Lights Bookshop, which soon became the publishing center for City Lights Books. Poets such as Gary Snyder and Michael McClure were drawn into the fold. When Ginsberg's *Howl* was published in 1956, leading to a widely publicized obscenity trial and financial success, the movement was well under way.

See also BLACK MOUNTAIN POETS, PROJECTIVE VERSE, and the Introduction, section IV.

SCHUYLER, JAMES   (*b. Chicago, Ill., Nov. 9, 1923—   *)

Schuyler's concern with modern art, his friendship with the group of writers clustered around FRANK O'HARA, JOHN ASHBERY, and KENNETH KOCH, his use of what may be roughly described as PROJECTIVE VERSE principles in the composition of his poetry, serve to place James Schuyler as one of the NEW YORK POETS. Like the others in the "school," Schuyler brings to his poetry his own perspective, his own voice.

Born in Chicago, Schuyler grew up in Washington, D.C., New York State, and West Virginia. He attended Bethany College in West Virginia, and, after a few years in Italy, came to live in New York City. Like Frank O'Hara, he has been associated with both the Museum of Modern Art and *Art News*.

Most of Schuyler's poetry is devoted to the recording of perceptions rather than to any conscious attempt to give them order. The poem "3/23/66," in *Freely Espousing*, is typical:

> It's funny early spring weather, mild and washy
> the color of a head cold.
> The air rushes. Branches
> are going nowhere, like the ocean,
> spring salt unstopping sinuses. Winter salt doesn't.
> Everything just sitting around: a barn without eaves,
> a dumpy cottage set catty-corner
> on its lot, a field with a horse in it.

The poem's chief interest lies in the relationship between the scene perceived and the poet perceiving it. The poet is, of course, at least implicitly present throughout, locating the scene in time and space. He only appears once explicitly, however, as one of the "us" looked at by the fire as they read *Great Expectations* aloud. Just as the poet fixes each item in his landscape, the landscape reciprocally locates him.

This interchangeability between perceiver and perceived, which has the effect of including the poet in the objective universe rather than separating him from it, is important also in the section of the poem quoted above. The image of spring coming as a "head cold" is difficult to categorize. The reader's impulse is to try to determine whether this is a metaphor describing spring, or whether spring itself has become a metaphor for the physical condition of the poet. The poem frustrates this impulse, however, by refusing to make the usual distinctions between inner and outer realities. Schuyler seems in fact to be precisely illustrating Charles Olson's dictum that it is only by recognizing oneself as an object in a universe of objects, and by probing that part of the objective universe within oneself, that one can encounter the world as it is.

See also the Introduction, section V.

Selected Bibliography:
By Schuyler:
Alfred and Guinevere. [Novel.] New York: Harcourt Brace Jovanovich, 1958.
Salute. New York: Tiber Press, 1960.
May 24th or so. New York: Tibor de Nagy Gallery, 1966.
Freely Espousing. New York: Paris Review Editions, 1969.
The Crystal Lithium. New York: Random House, 1972.

SEXTON, ANNE   (*b. Newton, Mass., Nov. 9, 1928—*   )

A student of Robert Lowell, a close friend of Sylvia Plath, Anne Sexton is at the core of what M. L. Rosenthal and others have named the Confessional school of poetry. She certainly seems to draw her materials from the worlds of private torment, seeking the deep secrets of the self, even if the implications of these secrets are potentially destructive. However, if these are tendencies that serve to define a school, another fact is equally true: Confessional poetry does not necessarily amount to biography, perhaps cannot be biography. Like Lowell, Plath, Theodore Roethke, and John Berryman, she selects and distorts her experience, creates a myth of the self. Further, she introduces many personae, the events of whose lives have nothing to do with her own, while refusing to distinguish them from the reasonably consistent voice that runs through her verse or even from her own person. The assumption of early critics that "Unknown Girl in the Maternity Ward" implies an illegitimate child in Sexton's own life has apparently been dropped, but there is still controversy as to whether or not she had a brother who was killed in the war ("For Johnny Pole on the Forgotten Beach"). The poet has not involved herself in clarifying such confusions. Her point, perhaps, is that these considerations have nothing to do with her poetry, which, whatever its ultimate origins in the poet's own psyche, moves toward a universality of form and feeling.

As if in support of this thesis, the facts of Anne Sexton's life, certainly of her younger years, are not especially clear. In 1947–48 she attended Garland Junior College, but she has listed her education (in a questionnaire for *Poetry* magazine) as "none." She worked as a fashion model in Boston in the early fifties, married, and had two children. Her significant education took place in 1958–59, when she audited Robert Lowell's course in the writing of verse at Boston University, where she met Sylvia Plath. The mental breakdowns and suicide attempts recorded in her poetry are apparently true in essence, even if specific circumstances may be distorted. It is this particular area of experience that forms the subject, directly or indirectly, of most of Anne Sexton's first book of poems, *To Bedlam and Part Way Back* (1960).

The epigraph to this volume is often cited by Sexton's critics:

> It is the courage to make a clean breast of it in the face of every question that makes the philosopher. He must be like Sophocles's Oedipus, who, seeking enlightenment concerning his terrible fate, pursues his indefatigable enquiry, even when he divines that appalling horror awaits him in the answer. But most of us carry in our heart the Jocasta who begs Oedipus for God's sake not to inquire further. . . .

> (Schopenhauer, in a letter to Goethe)

This is relatively straightforward; but there are nevertheless some ambiguities that can only be resolved in the context of Sexton's poetry, and even then imperfectly. Does the poet identify with Oedipus alone, or with Jocasta, or with both? The poem "For John, Who Begs Me Not to Enquire Further," a response to poet John Holmes's objection that "The Double Image" revealed too much intimate experience, clearly alludes to the epigraph of the book, and seems to resolve the question in favor of Oedipus. But this is misleading; Sexton did not write the poem in search of truth, which she already had, but in search of form, which the truth lacked. "Not that it was beautiful,/but that I found some order there." The poet here is neither Oedipus nor Jocasta; she is perhaps Sophocles, giving shape to destructive chaos. In the quotation from Schopenhauer, Oedipus is likened to "the philosopher," while all the evidence suggests that Sexton thinks of herself as a poet rather than a philosopher. The poet's shaping impulses take her beyond the individual, beyond creating poetry for therapy. Final obligations are not to the healthiness of the self, but to the vision of reality the self has experienced.

The poem "Said the Poet to the Analyst" differentiates the business of poetry from the business of analysis, revealing at the same time important affinities. "Words are like labels," says the poet, "or coins, or better, like swarming bees." There is a distance between word and event, the poet is "only broken by the sources of things"; the words take on a reality of their own, one that is not necessarily inferior to the one the poet had in mind.

> I must always forget how one word is able to pick
> out another, to manner another, until I have got
> something I might have said . . .
> but did not.

The analyst's business, in this case at least, is "watching" the poet's words. The poet says she is at her best praising a nickel machine in Nevada; if the analyst says "this is something it is not," the poet grows weak,

> . . . remembering how my hands felt funny
> and ridiculous and crowded with all
> the believing money.

The slot machine coins, "the believing money," are the poet's words, which, when subjected to the analyst's scrutiny—and the analyst here seems to be both psychoanalyst and professional critic—leave the poet feeling uncomfortable. ". . . But I/admit nothing," is a crucial statement, highly self-protective. The imagination must be defended from the analytic eye, but the poet, almost alienated from her own experience, is on the defensive.

Two images appear in this poem that are central to the book as a whole: first, the association with bees, later an important subject for Sylvia Plath, which seem for Sexton to carry implications of time, sexuality, imprisonment, and death; second, the male antagonist, analyst, father, God, on whom the poet depends, from whom she must be freed. Both images are introduced in the book's first poem, "You, Doctor Martin." The doctor is seen walking "from breakfast to madness"; the poet, resenting, perhaps, the doctor's intermittent presence in the "antiseptic tunnel" to which she is indefinitely confined, is ". . . queen of this summer hotel / or the laughing bee on a stalk / of death." Almost casually, Sexton remarks: ". . . There are no knives / for cutting your throat." However, her feelings toward the man upon whom salvation depends cannot be wholly negative: "Of course, I love you." The doctor, like Tiresias in the Oedipus myth, holds the key to the truth, however threatening that truth might be; he is " . . . an oracular / eye in our nest." Making moccasins (surely a pun, since she is ". . . queen of all my sins / forgotten"), the poet gropes for something solid, taking the first long step toward reintegration of a fragmented psyche. Working against the threat of chaos, against an unpredictable world of charms and incantations, is the form of the poem, the rigid stanzaic pattern ($a^3b^4c^5a^3b^4c^5a^3$), the firm, cyclical structure.

The dominant images weave in and out of the poems, pulling the book together, and varying in form and context to avoid monotony. In "Ringing the Bells," the women inmates of Bedlam are described as being "like bees caught in the wrong hive, / we are the circle of the crazy ladies." In "The Moss of His Skin," Sexton's imagination is captured by the old Arabian custom of burying young girls alive next to their dead fathers as a sacrifice to tribal goddesses. The poem, rich in sexual connotation, moves into a dark room that is "like a cave or a mouth/or an indoor belly"; it ends with the doomed child pretending

> that Allah will not see
> how I hold my daddy
> like an old stone tree.

"The Double Image," Anne Sexton's long poem to her own daughter, appears in the section of the book concerned with "part way back" from Bedlam. Almost surely influenced by W. D. Snodgrass's "Heart's Needle," this poem (actually a sequence of seven poems) is the poet's account of what has happened to her in the recent past, as told to her younger daughter. (Of "Heart's Needle," Sexton told an interviewer: "I had written about half of my first book when I read that poem, and it moved me to such an extent . . . that I ran up to my mother-in-law's where she [her own daughter] was living and got her back.") The materials of the poem are powerful, so powerful they threaten to overwhelm the poet's powers of imagination, her mind as a whole. The poet herself has been in and out of institutions; twice she has tried to kill herself. As she struggles to regain the strength to deal with her experience and to regain her daughter, her own mother lies dying of cancer. Sexton's voice is surprisingly calm; she has her emotions firmly under control. But there is no mistaking the caldron of feeling not very far from the surface. If she relaxes one instant, she will drown. The mirror images, both reflecting and distorting, of grandmother, mother, and daughter, form the poem's dominant conceit. With pride and love and especially guilt, the poet's final remark to her daughter is: "I made you to find me." She has also made this poem, if not to find herself—though that is in a way true—at least to contain and give shape to the energies within. As in "You, Doctor Martin," the poet depends on a rigid stanzaic form, different within each poem, to help control and dominate explosive experience, as in this stanza from the sixth poem:

> And this was the cave of the mirror,
> that double woman who stares
> at herself, as if she were petrified
> in time—two ladies sitting in umber chairs.
> You kissed your grandmother
> and she cried.

As its title (taken from Macduff's outcry on hearing of the destruction of his family) suggests, *All My Pretty Ones* (1962) is devoted largely to images of guilt and terror at the human condition. There are moments of joy—Sexton does not exclude them—but they are few. They are generally connected with her daughters, as in "The Fortress," but even here joy is defensive: "We laugh and we touch./I promise you love. Time will not take that away."

The book begins with poems for her mother and father, who died within

four months of each other. The title poem, on the death of the father, concludes:

> Only in this hoarded span will love persevere.
> Whether you are pretty or not, I outlive you,
> bend down my strange face to yours and forgive you.

It is a dismal universe the poet inhabits; its only affirmative value seems to
be love. Sexton calls on love to help her bear the unbearable almost as a
deus ex machina. Love does not really invite examination; when the poet
does investigate, doubts are not dispelled. In "Old Dwarf Heart," we learn
that whenever the poet lies down to love, the dwarf heart negates the act.
"She knows the decay we're made of." The heart, this inmost self, links love
with the strange and corrupt, with terrible knowledge and terrible pain.
". . . Old ornament, old naked fist," exclaims the poet, almost with affec-
tion, unwilling, as well as unable, to give up her well-spring of emotion,

> even if I put on seventy coats I could not cover you . . .
> mother, father, I'm made of.

At this stage of her development, poems for Sexton explore the darker recesses of the imagination, reveal the ugliness and the decay that lurk behind even images of beauty. Sexton enters the world of Christ crucified,
who wakes in his tomb to find himself being eaten by rats, the performers
of the miracle ("In the Deep Museum"), and the world of Van Gogh, mad,
of starry night, as "The night boils with eleven stars" ("The Starry Night").
The purpose of poetry is, in fact, defined at the end of "With Mercy for the
Greedy":

> . . . This is what poems are:
> with mercy
> for the greedy,
> they are the tongue's wrangle,
> the world's pottage, the rat's star.

All My Pretty Ones must, in short, join the company of those works of art
whose affirmation lies not in their philosophy, but in the very fact that they
exist at all.

Live or Die (1966), winner of the Pulitzer Prize, contains some of Anne
Sexton's finest poetry. The epigraph this time is from a draft of Saul Bel-
low's *Herzog:* "With one long breath, caught and held in his chest, he
fought his sadness over his solitary life. Don't cry, you idiot! Live or die,
but don't poison everything . . ." In an author's note, Sexton apologizes
for, or at least attempts to justify, the gloominess of her work by quoting
Gide: "Despite every resolution of optimism, melancholy occasionally wins
out: man has decidedly botched up the planet." However, in comparison
with earlier work, the tone of this book is practically sunny. Forcing herself
to make a choice between nihilism and affirmation (or at least acceptance)
as a poet, literally between death and life as a human being, Sexton's decision is in the title of the book's last poem: "Live."

This decision is reached, however, only with misgivings, with unresolved doubts. The chronological order of the poems suggests a randomness that renders affirmation accidental; what if the book had ended elsewhere, at, for example, "Sylvia's Death"? "Thief!" Sexton accuses Sylvia Plath,

> how did you crawl into,
>
> crawl down alone
> into the death I wanted so badly and for so long

What if it had ended at "Pain for a Daughter," in which the poet hears her daughter, whose foot has been injured by a horse, cry out for God rather than for her mother. Sexton sees her daughter's life "stretch out":

> I saw her torn in childbirth,
> and I saw her, at that moment,
> in her own death and I knew that she
> knew.

What differentiates the visions of despair in this book from those of earlier ones is that Sexton has found a language for her love, made it a believable force in the universe rather than a desperate, scarcely credited hope. Look, for example, at the conclusion to "A Little Uncomplicated Hymn," written for her daughter Joy:

> I wanted to write such a poem
> with such musics, such guitars going;
> I tried at the teeth of sound
> to draw up such legions of noise;
> I tried at the breakwater
> to catch the star off each ship;
> and at the closing of hands
> I looked for their houses
> and silences.
> I found just one.
>
> you were mine
> and I lent you out.
>
> I look for uncomplicated hymns
> but love has none.

For the first time, a predominance of Anne Sexton's poems are written in free verse, rather than in exacting, if personally derived, forms. This is important, for now the discipline and control that prevent the poems from becoming undifferentiated shrieks of terror—to use a phrase applied by Stanley Kunitz to a poem by Theodore Roethke—reside in the language itself rather than in stanzaic patterns. Whether a sign of greater emotional health or increased poetic mastery, the result is the same: a stronger voice. Anne

Sexton is not through with tighter forms; she uses them here and she will use them again. But she is less dependent on them.

One would have thought by the mid-sixties that the Confessional poets had opened as much new ground to the poetic imagination as they were going to. But *Love Poems* (1969) makes it clear that although sexual behavior was already a commonplace theme, a certain amount of restraint had been operative. Titles such as "The Breast," "In Celebration of My Uterus," "The Ballad of the Lonely Masturbator," suggest a new range of possibility. In these poems Anne Sexton is writing of what is normally considered the spiritual side of love as an expression of the total organism:

> . . . in celebration of the woman I am
> and of the soul of the woman I am
> and of the central creature and its delight
> I sing for you. I dare to live.
> Hello, spirit. Hello, cup.
>
> (from "In Celebration of My Uterus")

Celebrating her uterus, she celebrates herself, her womanhood. One does not stand for the other; it is the other. *Love Poems* continues a journey begun in Bedlam; it furthers the reintegration of the self. Love is experienced as a tangible reality. There is a good deal of pain involved, but there is also joy; there is anxiety, but there is also the strength to endure.

Having led the way for Sylvia Plath many times in the past, it is now Anne Sexton's turn to be influenced by her. She has learned from the *Ariel* poems the ability to isolate the sharp, piercing image, which emerges with a clarity so brilliant it gives pleasure even when the subject is painful, as in the last lines of "For My Lover Returning to His Wife." The poet is sending her lover back to his solid, substantial wife: "As for me, I am a watercolor./I wash off." Or the last line of "The Breast": "I burn the way money burns." Or the beginning of "The Kiss": "My mouth blooms like a cut."

The book's first poem is appropriately entitled "The Touch," for it is this sense that is emphasized throughout, to a far greater extent than in previous volumes. While contact is not always unequivocally ecstatic, it is always evidence of life, evidence that Anne Sexton has followed the exhortation of the final poem of her previous book: "Live."

In *Transformations* (1971), Anne Sexton explores a new mode of plumbing the depths of the self. The book contains the retelling of seventeen Grimm fairy tales, each preceded by an introductory section that generally makes connections between the stories in particular and the human psyche in general. "Rumpelstiltskin," for example, begins "Inside many of us/is a small old man/who wants to get out"; "The Gold Key" opens with "The speaker in this case/is a middle-aged witch, me—" Fairy tales can be thought of as collective dreams, or parables, that reveal the world as perceived by the child who still lives in all of us. And these perceptions, concerning our loves and fears, are precisely those we are most likely to have suppressed in the interest of a less disturbing sense of reality.

It would seem, then, that in these poems, which deal with archetypal rather than personal experience, Sexton is abandoning the Confessional mode. This is only superficially true, for, as she demonstrates in this book, the insights made available to us through myths lie not in the myths themselves but in our relation to the myths. Sexton relates to the tales with a kind of sardonic wit that does not eliminate terror but does win at least a temporary victory over it. The wolf in "Red Riding Hood," for example, is ". . . dressed in frills,/a kind of transvestite." The ball dropped in the well by the princess in "The Frog Prince" is a moon, a butter calf, a yellow moth, a Hindu hare. "Balls such as these are not/for sale in Au Bon Marché." Finally, it is not simply by tone and interpretation but by imagery as well that a poet masters his material, as can be seen in this passage near the conclusion of "Briar Rose (Sleeping Beauty)":

> Daddy?
> That's another kind of prison.
> It's not the prince at all,
> but my father
> drunkenly bent over my bed,
> circling the abyss like a shark,
> my father thick upon me
> like some sleeping jellyfish.

In "The Hoarder," from *The Book of Folly* (1972), Anne Sexton writes: ". . . I am a hoarder of words/I hold them in though they are/dung." Since *The Book of Folly* is her third book in four years, it is difficult to take these lines too seriously. Many of the poems could have appeared in earlier volumes, but even in these her continuing development is evident in lines that seem shorter, often breathless rhythms, sharper imagery. In addition, there are now formal sequences of poems: "The Death of the Fathers," "Angels of the Love Affair," and "The Jesus Papers." And there are three short stories, which may not be prose poems, but in which language overwhelms event. Anne Sexton is reaching out to broaden the possibilities of her art. Her dominant theme has not been altered, however; as at the beginning of her career, it is still Oedipus' search for the truth—at all costs.

See also the Introduction, section VI.

Selected Bibliography:
BY SEXTON:
To Bedlam and Part Way Back. Boston: Houghton Mifflin Co., 1960.
All My Pretty Ones. Boston: Houghton Mifflin Co., 1962.
Live or Die. Boston: Houghton Mifflin Co., 1966.
Love Poems. Boston: Houghton Mifflin Co., 1969.
Transformations. Boston: Houghton Mifflin Co., 1971.
The Book of Folly. Boston: Houghton Mifflin Co., 1972.

About Sexton:
Fields, Beverly. "The Poetry of Anne Sexton" in *Poets in Progress*. Edited by Edward Hungerford. Evanston, Ill.: Northwestern University Press, 1967. Pp. 251–85.
Howard, Richard. *Alone with America*. New York: Atheneum Publishers, 1969. Pp. 442–50.
Jones, A. R. "Necessity and Freedom: The Poetry of Robert Lowell, Sylvia Plath and Anne Sexton," *Critical Quarterly*, VII (Spring 1965), 11–30.
Marx, Patricia. "Interview with Anne Sexton," *Hudson Review*, XVIII (Autumn 1965), 560–70.
Mills, Ralph J., Jr. *Contemporary American Poetry*. New York: Random House, 1965. Pp. 218–34.
Rosenthal, M. L. *The New Poets: American & British Poetry Since World War II*. New York: Oxford University Press, 1967. Pp. 130–38.

SHAPIRO, KARL (*b. Baltimore, Md., Nov. 10, 1913—   *)

No less a theme than the integrity of the perceiving self has turned out to be the dominant preoccupation of Karl Shapiro's poetry. Once taken for granted, secure in its position at the center of experience, the Western version of the ego has come to seem less and less inevitably the obvious vantage point from which to view reality. And if, as many suspect, stability in poetic form is a function of the stability of the consciousness that determines form, the significance of the development of Shapiro's technique from rigid to free structures takes on increased interest. Shapiro shares this particular pattern of development with most of the major figures in contemporary American poetry: Theodore Roethke, Robert Lowell, W. S. Merwin, Anne Sexton, for a start. But while for these poets the loosening of traditional control led to a new definition of poetic discipline, for Shapiro, at least temporarily, the very possibility of poetry existing was called into serious question. It is not that Shapiro's questioning of the self is more insistent; it is rather that, for him, so much more depends upon the self's coherence.

A Jew and a Southerner, Shapiro was born with ready-made crises of identity. He attended the University of Virginia and Johns Hopkins University, and, his bitter satire of "University" notwithstanding, he has generally been associated with the academic world since, teaching at Johns Hopkins and at the universities of Nebraska, Illinois, and California (at Davis). As editor of *Poetry* magazine from 1950 to 1956, he was at the height of his capacity to influence the lines along which contemporary American verse was developing.

Shapiro's first full book of poems, *Person, Place and Thing* (1942), is as thoroughly "classical" a book of poetry as one would expect of the times, with clear, sometimes intricate, stanzaic patterns and explicit meter shaping almost every poem in the volume. Yeats's influence can be felt, in the predominantly intellectual content of the lyrics, in the use of prosaic rhythms, run-on lines, and frequent near rhymes as a means of attaining maximum flexibility within static patterns. A good proportion of the poems are satirical, with the institutions, artifacts, and myths of contemporary, middle-class industrial society generally the objects of Shapiro's satire, as suggested by the titles "Drug Store," "University," "Waitress," "Auto Wreck," "Buick," "Terminal," "Hollywood," "The Snob." At no point in his career does Shapiro demonstrate greater confidence in the perspective of his poems; satire presupposes a coherent point of view from which experience can be evaluated. In "Drug Store," ". . . the attractive symbols/Watch over puberty and leer/Like rubber bottles waiting for sick-use"; in "University," "To hurt the Negro and avoid the Jew/Is the curriculum." Again and again Shapiro creates visions of a world that dehumanizes, and again and again he implies a faith that the qualities of humanness are worth preserving, and, in a better world perhaps, capable of being preserved.

V-Letter and Other Poems (1944), which won the Pulitzer Prize, maintains a tone similar to Person, Place and Thing. The poems disclose the ugliness of a wartime world that has replaced the merely tawdry cheapness of prewar America. But the naturally increased bitterness resulting from the war may conceal a change not only in what the poet sees but in the perspective from which he sees it as well.

"The Synagogue" illustrates in theme and method Shapiro's art at this stage of his development. The Jew is a frequent point of focus, his fate an intensification of the human condition, his place of worship a metaphor for human limitations. The synagogue "is the adumbration of the Wall." The "Wall" is not only a reference to the Wailing Wall in Jerusalem; it also becomes generalized as all boundaries that take man's measure. In a cathedral, "The soul moves upward" to meet the saints; in contrast, the synagogue is a "house," a place, it is committed to this world. Judaism, non-transcendant, becomes a skeptic's way of coming to terms with God:

> Our wine is wine, our bread is harvest bread
> That feeds the body and is not the body.

The poem almost achieves the form of a dialogue between the otherworldliness of Christianity and the thisworldliness of Judaism; but here, and elsewhere throughout V-Letter, the last ambiguous word is given to Judaism. Shapiro is suspicious of any vision of reality that provides access to the absolute. At any rate, he insists on a hard look at the possibility that this earth is all we will know of paradise.

For several reasons, "The Leg" is probably the most significant poem in V-Letter. One of the finest poems Shapiro has ever written, both thematically and formally, it is a kind of epitome of the first half of his career. Most important, perhaps, is that it is one of the first times Shapiro plunges into paradox so dark that the integrity of the self perceiving this paradox is threatened.

It is a poem devoted to the exploration of pain, with the unproven promise that on the other side of pain is solace, and maybe salvation. At the soldier's first consciousness of the fact that he has lost a leg, he begins to cry like a child "Whose puppy is mangled under a screaming wheel." However, not by avoiding his loss, but rather by confronting it as directly as possible, by endlessly fingering and learning the measure of the stump, the soldier learns to smile "to the wall" (again that symbol of human limits) and "The amputation becomes an acquisition." This vision of creation out of annihilation is the poem's dominant theme; it concludes:

> That if Thou take me angrily in hand
> And hurl me to the shark, I shall not die!

"The Leg" explicitly places Shapiro within that poetic tradition in which Donne pleads with God to break him that he may be whole, ravish him that he may be chaste, in which Gerard Manley Hopkins convinces his readers (in "The Wreck of the *Deutschland*") of God's greatness, not in spite of his having decreed the drowning of five nuns but because of it. It is at the same time a manifestation of the existential imagination, which founds its hope in despair, its inkling of meaning in the conviction of meaninglessness. And, finally, this plea for immersion in the destructive element becomes a way of reexamining relationships between body and spirit; it is only in loss that the self can be fathomed. The poem's finest moments come in the fourth stanza, where the leg is seen wondering where the man is, the man seen as the leg's injury, challenging the entire concept of consciousness as the irreducible core of identity.

The poems of *Trial of a Poet* (1947) continue Shapiro's explorations of inner and outer darkness. "The Progress of Faust" is evidence of his increasing discomfort at the distorted perception of reality produced by isolating faculties rather than insisting upon unity of being. Faust, who seems here to represent the passion for intellectual knowledge, for knowledge that binds and controls, begins in Cracow with black magic and ends in an American desert with the atom bomb. But Faust, from another perspective, is neither more nor less than the self—that is, the Western conception of the self, separate from and at odds with the natural world—carried to its logical conclusion; the highest form of self-assertion is dominion over natural forces. In depicting Hiroshima and Nagasaki as inevitable nightmares of romanticism, Shapiro is well on his way to rejecting that tradition. We are back to the paradoxical world of "The Leg"; it is only by giving up the self that a meaningful sense of self can be found.

"The Dirty Word" is one of the earliest examples of a prose poem by Shapiro, a method developed later in *The Bourgeois Poet*. The word—represented in the poem by a frightening black bird, a vulture perhaps—may be an offensive term for Jew. (The reprinting of the poem in 1958, in *Poems of a Jew*, reinforces this supposition.) The bird also functions as a more generalized symbol of fear, shame, and self-hatred, a .malignancy forced upon a young boy by the society in which he lives, a malignancy finally nurtured and even, in a perverse way, loved by the boy.

The third paragraph consists of a single sentence: "And the bird outlives the man, being freed at the man's death-funeral by a word from the rabbi." In spite of this promise of longevity, the poem's persona claims in the last paragraph not only to have outlived the bird, but to have murdered it. And here is what is most effective in the poem. The bird is clearly evil and filthy; yet it is taken in by the boy and cherished, its destruction is described as a murder. The word, the ostracism, that so terrifies the small child becomes a source of comfort, a protector, so that stepping out from behind the obscenity becomes an act of high courage. The simplistic self that has provided the perspective for almost all of Shapiro's previous poems is here replaced by a vision of complexity, in which consciousness is just one of many ways of perceiving the world. It seems more than coincidence that Shapiro abandons strict meter (present in his other poems even when rhyme is not) in precisely that poem in which the perceiving self experiences ambivalence, in which the ego is forced to share its triumphs with forces from beneath the surface of consciousness.

Poems 1940–1953 (1953) temporarily abandons *Trial of a Poet's* embryonic movement toward prose (in "The New Ring" as well as "The Dirty Word"). Formal structure, with possibly more emphatic rhyme schemes than before, is still dominant, and so, it would seem, is the poet's confidence in the ego as the prime arbiter of experience. "Adam and Eve," a seven-poem sequence, retells the Genesis myth, emphasizing the expulsion from Eden as the creation of the ego. Thinking creates its own garden, an inner world apart from Adam's external environment; banishment from this outer garden is not the disease from which Adam suffers but the cure for that disease: once out of Eden, the self is free to grow. As in "The Leg," pain and despair are the foundation of salvation. Even so, Shapiro is ambivalent. Human consciousness is consciousness of pain and loss, and although an autumnal beauty does indeed attend the beginning of man's exile, it is a terrible beauty. "Death is the mother of beauty," wrote Wallace Stevens. Shapiro here seems to agree. But unlike Stevens, Shapiro has no religion of aesthetics, no humanistic pieties, to satisfy the need for some imperishable bliss. Imagination is no longer at odds with chaos: it depends upon it for its existence.

If it is possible for a single book of poetry to be at the same time the height of a poet's achievement and evidence of the bankruptcy of his vision, that description would fit Karl Shapiro's *The Bourgeois Poet* (1964). The only human triumph in its pages, if any, is a triumph forced from the heart of human darkness.

There are several noticeable shifts in Shapiro's poetic stance. Where in the past Shapiro did not exempt himself as target of his satire, he now appears to be its principal mark. It is not a self-hating book; it is cynical enough to make the reader feel that Shapiro is no worse than anyone else. It is not self-pitying. It does not especially resemble Confessional poetry— certainly not the manner of Robert Lowell, Anne Sexton, or Sylvia Plath. But *The Bourgeois Poet* may go farther than their work in its deliberate undercutting of the poet as poet, its serious questioning of the role of poet.

The very notion of a "bourgeois" poet is intended by Shapiro to be a contradiction in terms. Bourgeois existence precludes the intensity and spontaneity of emotion essential to the business of being a poet. In the title poem,

> ". . . The bourgeois poet sits down at his inoffensive desk—a door with
> legs, a door turned table—and almost approves the careful disar-
> ray of books, papers, magazines and such artifacts as thumbtacks.
> The bourgeois poet is already out of matches and gets up. It is
> too early in the morning for any definite emotion and the B.P.
> smokes."

The desk is "inoffensive," the disarray is "careful," feelings are relegated to routine. In the land of the commonplace, perhaps even poets must be com-monplace. This is the question implicit throughout the book: has Shapiro failed his vocation, or has the vocation, that is, its possibility failed Shapiro? It is probably an unanswerable question; as definitive an answer as Shapiro is prepared to give concludes a poem with an appropriately paradoxical title, "I am an atheist who says his prayers":

> This is the camera with the built-in lie. This is the lens that defies the
> truth. There's nothing for it but to write the large bad poem in
> middle-class magic. Poem condemned to wear black, be quoted in
> churches, versatile as Greek. Condemned to remain unsung by
> criminals.

Why there is "nothing for it" is not clear; it may be the fault of either the poet or the world, most likely both.

The book is, among other things, a catalog of the circumstances that have led to the creation of the bourgeois poet: a dehumanizing world that reduces people to identifiable functions, the standardization of responses to experience, the insistence on categorization as the essential mode of appre-hending reality—all enemies of the wish to be human, all enemies of the wish to be a poet.

The form of these "poems" reflects the moral and metaphysical difficulties that make up their themes. They may even be said to constitute those themes. These are prose poems, without even the vague metrical justifica-tions of free verse; they are simply paragraphs of prose. Without rhythmic or metrical patterns, rhyme scheme, stanzaic form, or even a noticeable condensation of language, what possible basis could one have to call this poetry? That is the peculiar thing. They are poems. And while it is possible to argue that they are not great poems, that the ultimate achievements of this form are limited, the very fact that they succeed in becoming poems at all is evidence of Shapiro's craft and the suggestion that by a double irony the bourgeois poet may be a true poet after all.

What makes them poems? First, while there is no vestige of meter and rarely a rhythm that by its repetition becomes "poetic," Shapiro skillfully manipulates conversational rhythms; occasionally the staccato of short sim-ple sentences escapes from the prosaic almost in spite of itself. Second, the paragraphing is carefully handled and becomes a structural equivalent to the stanza; most of the poems of *The Bourgeois Poet* give the impression of tight control rather than limitless freedom. Finally, perhaps in place of the greater density of conventionally poetic language, Shapiro charges his words by removing them from comfortable contexts. Non sequiturs abound, images are placed in montage, the reader is presented with a world that must be understood intuitively rather than in terms of discursive prose.

In recent years, Shapiro has returned to more formal poetic modes. Here, for example, is a stanza from "Ballade," part of the twenty-nine-poem sequence published as *White-Haired Lover* (1968):

> Or bastard that I am and poet and Jew
> As you grow quiet and strong I cause you grief,
> Fighting what I desire, the group of two,
> And thieve your beauty like a sickly thief,
> Possessing you in phantasy—in brief
> Betraying all this joy for poetry,
> So terrified our love will not be safe,
> That you will not be with me till I die.

Thematically, this is familiar enough. But it possesses neither the chaotic energy of *Bourgeois Poet* nor the tough, almost cynical wit of his earlier work. Again it forces the question: after *The Bourgeois Poet*, what ground can the poet effectively occupy?

Excluding *White-Haired Lover*, Shapiro's career can—by the process of oversimplification that is second nature to the critical mind—be seen as cut into two complementary parts. The first achieves what is probably its finest expression in *Poems of a Jew* (1958), which is mainly a collection of earlier verse; not so much intended to define Jewishness as to describe the human condition, using the Jew as the most appropriate symbol of that condition in the twentieth century, the book becomes an exploration of the possibilities of humanism: the victories of the specifically human tend to be existential and absurd, the threat of failure never far from the surface. The second part is totally realized in *The Bourgeois Poet*, which attempts to take a step beyond humanism. Its triumphs are the triumphs of Kafka, that greater chronicler of the bourgeois nightmare, who also saw that man's struggle with God might well take the form of mean and petty experience.

Selected Bibliography:
BY SHAPIRO:
Person, Place and Thing. New York: Reynal & Hitchcock (Harcourt Brace Jovanovich), 1942.
V-Letter and Other Poems. New York: Reynal & Hitchcock (Harcourt Brace Jovanovich), 1944.
Essay on Rime. New York: Reynal & Hitchcock (Harcourt Brace Jovanovich), 1945.
Trial of a Poet. New York: Reynal & Hitchock (Harcourt Brace Jovanovich), 1947.
Poems 1940–1953. New York: Random House, 1953.

Beyond Criticism. [Criticism.] Lincoln, Neb.: University of Nebraska Press, 1953.
Poems of a Jew. New York: Random House, 1958.
In Defense of Ignorance. [Criticism.] New York: Random House, 1960.
The Bourgeois Poet. New York: Random House, 1964.
Karl Shapiro: Selected Poems. New York: Random House, 1968.
To Abolish Children & Other Essays. New York: Quadrangle Books, 1968.
White-Haired Lover. New York, Random House, 1968.
Edsel. [Novel.] New York: Bernard Geis, 1971.

About Shapiro:
Eckman, Frederick. "Karl Shapiro's 'Adam and Eve,'" *Texas Studies in English*, 35 (1956), Pp. 1–10.
Mills, Ralph J., Jr. *Contemporary American Poetry.* New York: Random House, 1965. Pp. 101–21.
Slotkin, Richard. "The Contextual Symbol: Karl Shapiro's Image of the Jew," *American Quarterly*, 18 (1966), 220–26.
Southworth, James. "The Poetry of Karl Shapiro," *English Journal*, 51 (1962), 159–66.
Stepanchev, Stephen. *American Poetry since 1945.* New York: Harper & Row Publishers, 1965. Pp. 53–68.
White, William. *Karl Shapiro: A Bibliography.* Detroit: Wayne State University Press, 1960.

SIMPSON, LOUIS (*b. Jamaica, British West Indies, Mar. 27, 1923—   *)

So involved in the American writer's traditional search for a specifically American mode of experience is Louis Simpson that it is hard to remember that he was in fact born in Jamaica. Simpson, the author of "Walt Whitman at Bear Mountain" and "Lines Written Near San Francisco," did not come to live in the United States until 1940 and did not become an American citizen until after he had earned a Bronze Star and two Purple Hearts serving with the 101st Airborne Division in World War II. Simpson is the son of a lawyer who had "a passion for facts" and a Polish actress whose nursery stories "gave my mind a turn for fantasy I have never been able to overcome." His entire poetic personality seems to focus on the mediation of conflicting tendencies, between a tough-minded irony and a sympathy for the romantic posture; between the sense of being outside of, yet of feeling very much at home in, an adopted literary tradition; even between the conviction that the poet is inevitably alienated from his society and acceptance of the conventional academic life (which has taken Simpson from Columbia University to Berkeley and back across country to Stony Brook, Long Island).

Simpson has been associated with *The Fifties* and *The Sixties* magazine, with poets such as Robert Bly, James Dickey, James Wright, and William Stafford. Even more than the others, he has been seen as guardian of relatively strict formal values in a period dominated, theoretically, by varieties of free verse. He is certainly connected with that poetic approach called the "deep image" by Robert Kelly, the "subjective image" by Stephen Stepanchev, and the "emotive imagination" by Ronald Moran and George Lensing.

Most well known of the poems in Simpson's first volume, *The Arrivistes* (1949), and one of only three from that book reprinted in *Selected Poems* (1965), is "Carentan O Carentan." Approximating traditional ballad form, the poem begins with the image of lovers of old walking hand in hand where now the soldiers walk "at combat-interval." The violent triumphs over the peaceful as the soldiers are ambushed, and here the inadequacy of the form Simpson is using to deal with what he has experienced is pointed up:

> Everything's all right, Mother,
> Everyone gets the same
> At one time or another.
> It's all in the game.

The ballad is a form well acquainted with the terrifying and the brutal, but it generally depends on a sense of simple, undiminished human dignity to mitigate the continuing tragedy of human experience. Attempts to assert courage, as in the stanza quoted above, turn into painful absurdity. The ballad's frequent indirection of statement is here inappropriate; it becomes euphemism incapable of confronting experience, as, for example, when the dead lieutenant is described as ". . . a sleeping beauty/Charmed by that strange tune." The dehumanizing aspects of modern warfare turn the romantic tradition, in which the individual could assert himself even in the most extreme of circumstances, into a parody of itself. A virtuoso piece to be sure, Simpson's poem nonetheless is a negative achievement. Lacking the authenticity of "A Story about Chicken Soup," or even "The Battle," it describes what experience is not, not what it is.

"The Battle" appears in Simpson's next collection, *Good News of Death* (1955), in which the poet is well on his way to forging his mature style: ". . . Like the circle of a throat/The night on every side was turning red." The soldiers arrive to dig in as the artillery barrage begins. The battle lasts for many days, until the snow turns black and the corpses stiffen. The narrator remembers most clearly

> . . . how hands looked thin
> Around a cigarette, and the bright ember
> Would pulse with all the life there was within.

Simpson has again kept to traditional forms; the poem, like "Carentan O Carentan," is composed of quatrains rhyming *a b a b*. But the rhythms are far more irregular, far more interesting. And the poem stands or falls primarily by its system of grotesque imagery. The night reddening "like the circle of a throat" looks forward to the bright embers clutched by the thin hands. More sinister still is the suggestion of an agonizing scream revealing the circle of the throat, and the anticipation of corpses "in their scarlet hoods." It is significant that what the poet remembers best is not the objective details of the battle, the disposition of the men, acts of heroism and cowardice; not only do we have no clear idea of the nature of the enemy, we do not even know who won. Military results are irrelevant. What matters is the nightmarish struggle to hang on to tenuous life, the spirit's desperate effort to survive dying flesh. The notion of the subjective image can be pushed too far, at least at this stage of Simpson's career. To be sure, the poem as a whole has a kind of hallucinatory effect, but a fidelity to sensuous impression is maintained, and the last lines, quoted above, could quite easily have come out of the Objectivist tradition. After all, both kinds of poet are trying to link subject and object; they simply start at opposite ends of reality.

In 1959, Simpson received his Ph.D. from Columbia and published his third book of poems, A Dream of Governors. With this work, Simpson has mastered the techniques of "timing, leaps, and muted shock." He can spectacularly begin a poem—"There are designs in curtains that can kill,/Insidious intentions in a chair" ("The Flight to Cytherea")—or end a poem with the voice of an oracle:

> The violence of waking life disrupts
> The order of our death. Strange dreams occur,
> For dreams are licensed as they never were.
>
> (from "I Dreamed that in a City Dark as Paris")

If there is anything lacking, it is perhaps the full release of passion without which the poem can easily seem to exist for its own sake rather than for the sake of the experience to which it corresponds and which it is trying to communicate. "Hot Night on Water Street," for example, is a fine poem (it brings to mind Robert Lowell's Life Studies), yet it somehow falls short of what it promises to be. It is a satire of small-town America—in fact, a vision of all of America as a small town. But just when he has us—as, for example, with the witchlike old woman vanishing on a bus "With hissing air brakes, like an incubus"—he presses too hard, too explicitly; he talks to us instead of making us feel:

> Some day, when this uncertain continent
> Is marble, and men ask what was the good
> We lived by, dust may whisper "Hollywood."

Simpson is perhaps at his best in handling the tone of a poem like "The Green Shepherd," in which a pastoral afternoon of shepherd and shepherdess coincides with the rise and fall of civilizations from ancient times to the present:

> The shepherd yawns and puts his flute away.
> It's time, she murmurs, we were going back.
> He offers certain reasons she should stay—
> But neither sees the dragon on their track.

More than once in this witty reworking of an old theme, Marvell comes to mind. But in the long poem "The Runner," another return to Simpson's World War II experiences, the reader is forced to wonder whether blank verse can effectively encounter the grotesquely chaotic, and to wonder further whether Simpson had not to this point been hampered by his reluctance to abandon traditional forms, albeit his use of them had frequently been brilliant. It is in fact hard to believe that the *relative* freedom of Simpson's next book did not have something to do with its success.

At the End of the Open Road was published in 1963 and received the Pulitzer Prize the following year; it is generally agreed that it contains much of Simpson's best work. The greater freedom of form is only part of its success, maybe the smaller part; Simpson has found his theme, or rather he has found the tone and perspective with which to handle it. The theme is the sense of loss and limitation in human experience, the tone and perspective are provided by the American vision, which Simpson had touched before. But he had touched it as an outsider; something of himself he held back. He was like the narrator of "A Hot Night on Water Street," who concludes, "I was a stranger here myself . . ./And bought the *New York Times,* and went to bed." Now Simpson writes, in "Lines Written Near San Fransicso":

> . . . The land is within.
> At the end of the open road we come to ourselves.

Simpson has become part of the "we." His criticism is no less biting, but he is more fully committed than ever to face its implications.

Like Lowell, Simpson is sensitive to the corruption of power; and like Lowell he finds analogs in the fall of Rome. After America won the First World War and became a world power, he writes in "The Inner Part":

> Priests, examining the entrails of birds,
> Found the heart misplaced, and seeds
> As black as death, emitting a strange odor.

Ironically, we had barely arrived before our fall was under way. Largely the product of its own actions, the failure of America is also the failure of the romantic imagination, as inevitable as the passage of time. "How sad it is, the end of America!" Simpson remarks ambiguously in the San Francisco poem, alluding both to the physical end of the continent where it meets the Pacific, and to the demise of the American Dream. Even in its former sense the irony is sharp, for surely this student of Keats must have thought of Cortez, "Silent, upon a peak in Darien." The sense of infinite possibility is gone; the sense of limitation is constantly with us: "For we are the colonists of Death—/Not, as some think, of the English" ("Lines Written Near San Francisco"); "And here's the same old city-planner, death" ("In California"); "You were born to waste your life" ("In the Suburbs"); "All that grave weight of America/Cancelled! Like Greece and Rome" ("Walt Whitman at Bear Mountain").

Finally it is brought home to us that Simpson's American landscapes are also landscapes of the mind; "We too are all for reducing/The universe to human dimensions" ("Moving the Walls"). Simpson has reconstructed the romantic myth of the conflict between innocence and experience, between the infinite possibilities of childhood and the narrow confines of adulthood, between romantic optimism and existential despair. For Simpson's preoccupation with limits extends to microcosm as well as macrocosm. The poem beginning "My father in the night commanding No/Has work to do" locates principles of negativity in the world of the poet's childhood, and implications are metaphysical as well as psychological. The capitalized "No" —which seems to demand something much weightier than he "Has work to do"—becomes the symbol for all nonbeing. Caught between his father's aloofness and his mother's fantasies, the child escapes with the wind to Thule, at once proof of his own imaginative powers and of their boundaries. Ultima Thule, a final place at the end of the open road, is surely another landscape of the mind, another version of America.

The sense of loss that informs so much of *At the End of the Open Road* finds what is perhaps its most effective expression, not in one of the "American poems," but in a piece returning Simpson again to the events of World War II, "A Story about Chicken Soup." The first section describes the home of the narrator's grandmother, where ". . . there was always chicken soup/And talk of the old country." Now, however, the family is gone: "The Germans killed them all." The second section finds the narrator among the ruins of Berchtesgaden, where a "German girl-child" runs out of a doorway, "Cuckoo, all skin and bones—/Not even enough to make chicken soup." The soldiers, having killed her "mechanical brothers," forgive her. In the final section, the poet's ancestors, the lovers of former times, make demands upon him, want him "to be more serious than I want to be,"

> Not to walk in the painted sunshine
> To a summer house,
> But to live in the tragic world forever.

Ironically, the poem's visual focus is the starving German girl; the poet, haunted by the past, hardly knows whether to feel guiltier for having revenged his family upon the Germans, or (at least in the case of the girl) for having forgiven them. Simpson has here learned to encounter the full complexity of his wartime experiences, which are clearly crucial to the unlocking of his emotions; he has moved from the generalized responses of "Carentan O Carentan" to a world of ambiguous feelings and responsibilities.

In 1965, Simpson published *Selected Poems*, which included twelve new poems. In no way startling, they reveal Simpson in the process of refining his art. A stanzaic form emerges in three of these poems: four triplets and a couplet, all unrhymed, with three or five of these sonnets to a poem. However chaotic the world about which Simpson writes, he still feels he can express his reactions to it best against the background of consistent form. This categorization is deceptive, for if nothing else, Simpson has learned to handle his forms flexibly. By now, Simpson's treatment of themes seems consistent, even, one is sometimes tempted to say, predictable. "Stumpfoot on 42nd Street" illustrates his method. He begins with a vivid image, "A Negro sprouts from the pavement like an asparagus," develops it through a series of related introspections, and concludes in aphoristic generalization: "It seems that a man exists/Only to say, Here I am in person." Technically, Simpson is one of the finest poets writing today; his imaginative use of extremes of imagery is bold and sure. But the technique is sometimes too visible, the touch a bit too sure.

See also DEEP IMAGISM and the Introduction, sections VIII and IX.

Selected Bibliography:
BY SIMPSON:
The Arrivistes: Poems 1940–1949. New York: Fine Editions, 1949.
Good News of Death and Other Poems, in *Poets of Today II.* New York: Charles Scribner's Sons, 1955.
A Dream of Governors. Middletown, Conn.: Wesleyan University Press, 1959.
Riverside Drive. [Novel.] New York: Atheneum Publishers, 1962.
James Hogg: A Critical Study. New York: St. Martin's Press, 1962.
At the End of the Open Road. Middletown, Conn.: Wesleyan University Press, 1963.
Selected Poems. New York: Harcourt Brace Jovanovich, 1965.
Adventures of the Letter I. New York: Harper & Row Publishers, 1971.
See also Louis Simpson, "Confessions of an American Poet," *New York Times Magazine* (May 2, 1965), Pp. 30–31, 108–10.

About Simpson:
Cox, C. B. "The Poetry of Louis Simpson," *Critical Quarterly,* 8 (Spring, 1966), 72–83.
Friedman, Norman. "The Wesleyan Poets—II: The Formal Poets—2," *Chicago Review,* XIX (1966), 66–72.
Gray, Yohma. "The Poetry of Louis Simpson" in *Poets in Progress.* Edited by Edward Hungerford. Evanston, Ill.: Northwestern University Press, 1967.
Howard, Richard. *Alone with America.* New York: Atheneum Publishers, 1969. Pp. 451–70.
Lensing, George, and Moran, Ronald. "The Emotive Imagination: A New Departure in American Poetry," *Southern Review,* III (Winter 1967), 51–67.
Rosenthal, M. L. *The New Poets: American & British Poetry Since World War II.* New York: Oxford University Press, 1967. Pp. 323–24.

SNODGRASS, W[ILLIAM] D[EWITT]   *(b. Wilkinsburg, Pa., Jan. 5, 1926—   )*

Anne Sexton once remarked that it was not Robert Lowell but W. D. Snodgrass who first opened up for her the possibilities of a searingly personal kind of poetry, which was later to be labeled "confessional." Whether CONFESSIONAL POETRY in fact exists as a school, whether, if it does, it contains materials never before used, is open to debate. But Snodgrass's influence on Sexton and other poets is a phenomenological fact, in itself a reason for assigning him an important place in any literary history of his time.

Born and raised in Pennsylvania, Snodgrass obtained his B.A. from Geneva College. After serving in the Navy during the Second World War, he attended the State University of Iowa, receiving the degrees of M.A. and M.F.A. Since then, he has taught creative writing at Cornell, the University of Rochester, Wayne State, and Syracuse University.

There is little question that Snodgrass' most impressive work is the title sequence of *Heart's Needle* (1959), a book that won a Pulitzer Prize in 1960. Consisting of ten separate poems closely linked by imagery, theme, and a kind of narrative, the "Heart's Needle" sequence is the story of a divorce told in terms of the poet's relationship to the daughter of his first marriage. The significance this choice of subject has for Snodgrass is worth a comment. In a piece written about the sequence for *Partisan Review* (Spring 1959), Snodgrass said:

> . . . I believe that the only reality which a man can ever surely know is that self he cannot help being, though he will only know that self through its interactions with the world around it. If he pretties it up, if he changes its meaning, if he gives it the voice of any borrowed authority, if in short he rejects this reality, his mind will be less than alive.

Taken together with a couplet from " 'After Experience Taught Me . . . ' " (from *After Experience*, 1968)—

> No virtue can be thought to have priority
> Over this endeavor to preserve one's being.

—this constitutes a clear, if simple, aesthetic. The writing of poetry is the assertion of one's being. It is further a means of obtaining knowledge of that being. The justification of the poem, then, lies not in the poem but in the man. And it follows that the poem's success for the poet must be judged by its perceptiveness and its honesty and that its success for the reader must be judged by its ability to communicate effectively the sense of honesty and accurate perception. This is not to say that the poem's formal elements are insignificant, but they are placed at the service of what the poem has to reveal. This analysis is probably exaggerated—Snodgrass has spent much time studying his craft—but it serves to point out the orientation of his poetry.

The title of "Heart's Needle" is derived from an Irish folktale: "And an only daughter is the needle of the heart." In the tale, the daughter is dead; for Snodgrass, separation is a kind of death, less final, but more complicated. The seasonally organized poem begins in winter. The poet's daughter is a "Child of my winter." He is referring, of course, not to his age but to a condition of the spirit. That spirit is itself complex. Snow is a recurrent image in the poem: the child is born "When new fallen soldiers froze / In Asia's steep ravines and fouled the snows" and the child's mind is "a landscape of new snow." It is associated both with brutality, death, and despair and with the protectiveness that will make possible new birth when winter is gone; it is compared to quilts on a bed of "birth or pain." The conceit in which the father is a "tenant-farmer" and his child the snow-covered farm is the first expression of a relationship that will change; that he is a *tenant-farmer* anticipates the nature of that change. The language captures not only a precise sense of physical surroundings, but also the crisp coldness of the poet's dark, though hopeful, winter mind and of the child's purity.

The second poem takes place in late April—spring. While the poet attempts to protect his daughter's garden from "Strange dogs at night and the moles tunneling," she herself is the first one to trample the fence down. Again using the natural world as metaphor, the poet communicates his uneasiness. He is beginning to learn the limits of his power to protect his daughter. Even at three, she is beginning to take on the responsibility for her life. A shadow falls across the garden bed. In addition to the usual separations involved in a child's growing up, there is the more dramatic reality of Snodgrass' departure. He tells his daughter to look at the flowers each day, "Because when they come to full flower / I will be away."

The third poem brings us to the "demented summer" that Snodgrass had hoped to "restrain" at the sequence's start. On the street he sees a child hanging between his parents, held up by their hands, and this becomes an image of his own daughter, suspended emotionally between her parents. The Korean War, alluded to in the winter poem, returns to the poet's mind. As before, farms are referred to, but now they are farms burned out by war. The thought of prisoners returned seems appropriate to him now; his daughter is a kind of prisoner, so is he. The prisoner imagery and the child dangling between parents converge on a recollection: he remembers the time he tugged his daughter's hand in play and dislocated her wrist:

> Love's wishbone, child, although I've gone
> As men must and let you be drawn
>   Off to appease another

Again, only the language of war can encompass this experience. As in so much Confessional poetry, boundaries between public and private worlds are blurred. The section ends with Snodgrass balancing the guilt he feels at having let his daughter go with the thought that Solomon would judge him the "real mother" for having relinquished the child rather than rip her in two like a wishbone.

The next autumnal poem begins with the poet's memory of telling his daughter he was leaving and how she cried long into the night. Images of dying plant life follow, and he takes a flower "with some late buds that might still bloom" into his daughter's room. It is a futile gesture and the poem ends with Snodgrass recalling how a friend's child cried because a familiar cricket had died.

The fifth poem returns to winter. The poet's child is growing; she already begins to seem strange to him. Again the outer world echoes the inner. A fox looses his paw in a trap. Snodgrass' method can possibly be described as an invocation of the pathetic fallacy. And yet it seems to go further. Nature is not simply sympathetic to human emotions; it seems to *be* the ground on which human emotions are made manifest.

In poem 6, beginning at the season of Easter rebirth, Snodgrass thinks of the year of his daughter's birth. The imagery of memory is painful. A blackbird had dived at the poet's head, and that summer chain saws had whirred like "iron locusts," hacking away at the torn limbs of trees. A pigeon had been caught, flapping fearfully in his hands. That fall his daughter had been sick and gasping for breath. Only at the poem's conclusion do we understand the underlying reason for all this anxiety. Another kind of renewal, toward which Snodgrass is quite ambivalent, has taken place: ". . . Child, I have another wife,/another child. We try to choose our life."

In July, in poem 7, the land is fecund; "fat goldfinches fly." The poet pushes his daughter in a swing, the pendulum motion a symbol of his relation with her. The swing is also a symbol of time. We realize here, if we have not before, that time is not simply an important factor in the sequence; it is, in a sense, its underlying subject. Snodgrass' relationship with his daughter keeps him constantly aware of his existence in time and adds poignancy to his longing for permanence.

The second half of poem 8 takes place at Hallowe'en, when the poet's daughter visits him. As they go trick-or-treating, the neighbors wonder whose child she is. Then,

> The time's up. Now our pumpkin sees
> me bringing your suitcase.
> He holds his grin;
> the forehead shrivels, sinking in.

The final image is even more striking. After his daughter leaves, Snodgrass craves sweets. ". . . Indeed our sweet/foods leave us cavities." What we love most leaves us empty; our love can, in fact, be destructive.

Winter and snow are back in poem 9, the longest in the sequence. It is the dead season with a vengeance. Snodgrass visits a natural history museum and walks through galleries of stuffed animals. At a tableau of polar bears and seals, he thinks of Napoleon's troops in the snow, bringing together the imagery of winter, snow, war, and death. The museum has worse to offer him—unborn children in jars of alcohol, deformed animal embryos, exhibits of malignant growths: "The world moves like a diseased heart/packed with ice and snow." As in previous poems, the conclusion explains the origins of the feelings we have been experiencing. It has been three months since he has seen his daughter, although they are only a mile apart. ". . . I cannot fight/or let you go."

In poem 10, "The vicious winter finally yields/the green winter wheat." Spring arrives, the plant and animal worlds are conspicuously alive. There is more talk of arrivals and departures, more decisions for the poet to make. Snodgrass at no point suggests that his pain has come to an end or that there are any real resolutions to his conflicts. The poem is full of life, however, and out of it emerges a vision of permanence, albeit one that fully participates in the world of flux. A zoo replaces the museum. The poet and his child are at least for the moment together. "And you are still my daughter."

Much of the power of the sequence comes directly from the intensity of Snodgrass' emotions—brooding, complex, but never falling into self-pity. The sharp imagery, drawn from an external world that seems an extension of the poet's mind, the seasonal framework, combining change with cyclical certainty, give the ten poems remarkable coherence.

Formally, Snodgrass skillfully uses a variety of simple, almost ballad-like, stanzas, with iambic lines that range in length from trimeter to hexameter. Against this strictness is the poet's ability to work variations on his meter, his running on of lines and stanzas, his conversational diction. Taken all together, the formal elements are perfectly suited to the poem's tensions.

To match the extraordinary power of "Heart's Needle" was a formidable task. Snodgrass' later work contains both freer forms and a broader range of subject. His wit, honesty, and technical mastery are still evident, but he has not yet been able to bring to his poetry the intensity of his first book.

Selected Bibliography:
By SNODGRASS:
Heart's Needle. New York: Alfred A. Knopf, 1959.
Gallows Songs. [Translations, with Lore Segal, of poems by Christian Morgenstern.] Ann Arbor, Mich.: University of Michigan Press, 1967.
After Experience: Poems and Translations. New York: Harper & Row Publishers, 1968.

About Snodgrass:
Carroll, Paul. "April Inventory" in *The Poem in Its Skin.* Chicago: Follett Publishing Co., 1968. Pp. 171–87.
Howard, Richard. *Alone with America.* New York: Atheneum Publishers, 1969. Pp. 471–84.
Torchiana, Donald T. "Heart's Needle: Snodgrass Strides through the Universe" in *Poets in Progress.* Edited by Edward B. Hungerford. Evanston, Ill.: Northwestern University Press, 1967. Pp. 92–115.

SNYDER, GARY (*b. San Francisco, Calif., May 8, 1930—*   )

In his influential essay, "Projective Verse," Charles Olson wrote: "Objectism is the getting rid of the lyrical interference of the individual as ego, of the 'subject' and his soul, that peculiar presumption by which western man has interposed himself between what he is as a creature of nature (with certain instructions to carry out) and those other creations of nature which we may, with no derogation, call objects." Gary Snyder, who suggests that "the rhythms of my poems follow the rhythm of the physical work I'm doing and life I'm leading at any given time," fits comfortably within the tradition for which Olson was principal spokesman. This is true of the forms of his work, which emerge from his physical or objective presence in the world, and its content, which so often consists of direct sensory experience or finds its roots in the "non-western" cultures of the American Indian, Japan, and China.

Gary Snyder was born in San Francisco and raised in Washington and Oregon. He received his bachelor's degree from Reed College in 1951, later studied linguistics at Indiana University and Japanese and Chinese culture at the University of California at Berkeley, and was associated with the poets of the San Francisco Renaissance. He has worked as logger, forester, carpenter, and seaman and spent nearly ten years in Japan. Most of these experiences are directly reflected in his work.

Snyder's first collection was entitled *Riprap* (1959). The poems, he tells us in a note in *The New American Poetry* (ed. Donald M. Allen, 1960), were written "under the influence of the geology of the Sierra Nevada and the daily trail-crew work of picking up and placing granite stones in tight cobble patterns on hard slab." (This defines the activity of "riprapping.") The title poem makes explicit the connection between riprapping and poetry:

> Lay down these words
> Before your mind like rocks.
> placed solid, by hands
> In choice of place, set
> Before the body of the mind
> in space and time:

"The body of the mind" is a crucial phrase. The greater part of the poems in *Riprap* are imagistic, sensory perceptions of the objective world, usually without any commentary beyond the simple recording of the perception. In a way, these poems are mental landscapes, but not in the traditional sense of the term, not, that is, objective correlatives of the conscious mind. They correspond to man's objective rather than subjective existence, to the rhythms of his body, to the complex of sensory patterns, even to the archetypal patterns of his unconscious, which are objective in the sense that they are located outside the center of consciousness. Thus, these poems demonstrate Olson's assertion of man's affinity with the rest of being, of the superficiality of the ego. In "Piute Creek," for example, Snyder writes:

> Hill beyond hill, folded and twisted
> Tough trees crammed
> In thin stone fractures
> A huge moon on it all, is too much.
> . . . .
> All the junk that goes with being human
> Drops away . . .

The title of *Myths and Texts* (1960), as well as the poetry in it, further underlines the basis of Snyder's aesthetics: "The title comes from the happy collections Sapir, Boas, Swanton, and others made of American Indian folk-tales early in this century; it also means the two sources of human knowledge—symbols and sense-impressions." Symbolic archetypal patterns and sensory perceptions—these are for Snyder the significant modes of apprehending reality. Buddhism and Indian ritual are central to *Myths and Texts*, each tradition having in common with the other the sense of a reality in which man can participate beyond the rational, beyond the grasp of the conscious mind. In the section entitled "Burning," Snyder writes:

> One moves continually with the consciousness
> Of that other, totally alien, non-human:
> Humming inside like a taut drum,
> Carefully avoiding any direct thought of it,
> Attentive to the real-world flesh and stone.

The Back Country (1968) covers the considerable range of Gary Snyder's experience—logging in the northwest, visits to Japan, China, and India (including translations of the Japanese poet Miyazawa Kenji), his return to the United States. What would be curious about these poems, if we were not aware of Snyder's particular perspective, is the fact that although he details within them his own experiences, there is not enough psychological insight for us to form a clear idea of his personality. We know where he has been, what he has done. We know, then, the things that interest him, but not, generally, his attitude toward those things. There is little or no introspection. It is true that this book in particular is highly charged sexually, but that can be considered an attitude of body as easily as of mind. The point is that Snyder is telling us what he considers most important about himself: the world as he physically experiences it, the images that evoke responses in him. The few glimpses of his conscious mind we are given are generally emotional reactions, arising from some concrete instance; they are almost never analyzed. Nonetheless, we come away from the book with a remarkably full sense of Snyder as a human being. The conclusion we must reach—undoubtedly this is Snyder's intention—is not that he has not revealed his personality, but that we may have to redefine, or at least seriously question, our notion of what personality is.

In his statement for *The New American Poetry*, Gary Snyder wrote he had been working on a long poem, *Mountains and Rivers without End*, since 1956. Like Ezra Pound's *Cantos*, William Carlos Williams's *Paterson*, and Charles Olson's *Maximus* poems, it is an open-ended work, which almost by definition cannot be brought to a conclusion. *Mountains and Rivers* is stylistically like its antecedents in its breath-determined rhythms, its juxtaposition of discrete fragments, its emphasis on concrete experience rather than abstract analysis. It is also like them—especially the *Maximus* poems—in its emphasis on space, for it is essentially a poem about journeys, journeys that are at once ordinary and archetypal. Sometimes they are literally dream journeys:

> . . . We walked down a dim-lighted stairway
> holding hands, walking more and more swiftly

> through an enormous maze, all underground.
> Occasionally we touched surface, and redescended.

Some are openly ritualistic. All are attempts to describe man's experience of the world in spatial rather than temporal terms, through concrete perceptions rather than analysis. That is the heart of Gary Snyder's poetry.

Selected Bibliography:
BY SNYDER:
Riprap. New York: Origin Press, 1959.
Myths and Texts. New York: Totem Press / Corinth Books, 1960.
A Range of Poems. London: Fulcrum, 1966.
The Back Country. New York: New Directions Publishing Corp., 1968.
Riprap & Cold Mountain Poems. San Francisco: Four Seasons Foundation, 1969.
Six Sections from Mountains and Rivers without End: Plus One. San Francisco: Four Seasons Foundation, 1970.
Regarding War. New York: New Directions Publishing Corp., 1970.

About Snyder:
Howard, Richard. *Alone with America*. New York: Atheneum Publishers, 1969. Pp. 485–98.

STAFFORD, WILLIAM   (*b. Hutchinson, Kans., Jan. 17, 1914—   *)

There is in the poetry of William Stafford a continual dialog between the natural world and man's impact on it. Nature is rugged, not idealized; and the poet sees himself as part of civilization; he does not express any romantic longing to abandon it. Yet one senses an almost apocalyptic longing for a time when civilization and nature might in some way coincide.

William Stafford was born and educated in the Midwest. He received his B.A. and M.A. from the University of Kansas, his Ph.D. from the University of Iowa. During the Second World War, he was a conscientious objector and has since been involved with pacifist organizations. He has taught at Manchester College in Indiana, San Jose State College, and at Lewis and Clark College in Oregon. In 1963, he received the National Book Award for *Traveling through the Dark*.

The title poem of his prizewinning volume makes his stance as clear as its ambiguities allow. Driving through the night, he comes upon a deer, "a recent killing," at the edge of the road. It is expedient, since the road is narrow, to roll the carcass into the river canyon below. When he touches the body, he discovers there is a live fawn within:

> around our group I could hear the wilderness listen.

> I thought hard for us all—my only swerving—,
> then pushed her over the edge into the river.

Stafford's sympathies are with nature, but he acts in behalf of civilization. Our attitudes toward the experience are difficult to define. (Are we comfortable with what he has done? If not, what should he have done instead?) Stafford seems to have entered a no-man's land between nature and civilization, making available to him, and us, a rarely used perspective.

That perspective is again at work in "At the Bomb Testing Site" (in *West of Your City*) where ". . . a panting lizard/waited for history." Stafford does not explicitly condemn the bomb test (although because of his political philosophy one might expect him to do so). Man's attempt to impose history on nature is finally doomed to failure, possibly a comforting thought. From the point of view of the lizard, perhaps, the change will indeed be cataclysmic. But men are simply "little selves," like the lizard, living on ". . . a continent without much on it/under a sky that never cared less."

In nature, things are what they are; human consciousness is double-edged, both probing and deceptive. In "At Cove on the Crooked River" (in *Traveling through the Dark*), Stafford writes that

> . . . the river there meant something
> always coming from snow and flashing around boulders
> after shadow-fish lurking below the mesa.

He is not suggesting that the river has a "message," a moral, except perhaps one in the very fact that it manifests itself unambiguously. This is his wish for the world of men:

> Oh civilization, I want to carve you like this,
> decisively outward the way evening comes
> over that kind of twist in the scenery.

William Stafford writes discursively, anecdotally, but his verse usually re-creates situations not easily resolved. He moves from free verse with shadows of formal structure to rhyme, meter, and stanzaic patterns very flexibly handled. As with the content of his poems, his techniques reveal an ambiguity that emerges from understanding rather than confusion.

In "In Dear Detail, By Ideal Light," he envisions going to some

> . . . imagined place
>
> Where finally the way the world feels
> really means how things are

—that is, a place in which man and nature are finally merged; it is also the place where Stafford's poetry exists.

Selected Bibliography:
By STAFFORD:
West of Your City. Georgetown, Calif.: Talisman Press, 1960.
Traveling through the Dark. New York: Harper & Row Publishers, 1962.
The Rescued Year. New York: Harper & Row Publishers, 1966.

Eleven Untitled Poems. Mount Hored, Wisc.: Perishable Press, 1968.
Allegiances. New York: Harper & Row Publishers, 1970.

About Stafford:
Howard, Richard. *Alone with America.* New York: Atheneum Publishers, 1969,
   Pp. 499–506.

STRAND, MARK   (*b. Summerside, Prince Edward Island, Canada,
Apr. 11, 1934—   )*

The epigraph to Mark Strand's *Reasons for Moving* (1968) is taken from
Jorge Luis Borges: "—while we sleep here, we are awake elsewhere and
that in this way every man is two men." The allusion to Borges prepares us
for something of the surreal, for a sense of the absurd in human experience;
even more, it prepares for the grounding of these attitudes in epistemology,
in the difficulties involved in apprehending reality and locating the self in
relation to that reality.

Although born in Canada, Mark Strand is an American citizen. He was
educated in America, receiving his B.A. from Antioch, his B.F.A. from Yale,
his M.F.A. from the University of Iowa. He has taught at such schools as
the University of Brazil, the University of Washington, Columbia University, and Yale.

The poem that most accurately sets the tone for Strand's work is "Keeping Things Whole," from *Reasons for Moving* (1968)—a poem that originally appeared in *Sleeping With One Eye Open* (1964) under the title "A
Reason for Moving":

> In a field
> I am the absence
> of field.
> This is
> always the case.
> Wherever I am
> I am what is missing.

This is a kind of poetic equivalent of the graphic work of M. C. Escher, in
whose drawings the spaces between forms are themselves forms, so that
each set of forms can be defined as the absence of the other. The dichotomy between the Self and the Other haunts Strand's poetry. But as in most
dichotomies, the opposite poles are dependent on each other for their very
existence. (Strand ends the poem by suggesting that his reason for moving
is "to keep things whole.") It is a strong attack against the absolute integrity
of the Self. Certainly it questions the Self's capacity to define reality, since
it is equally reasonable to assert that reality defines the Self.

It is only a short step from this to the difficulty of locating the Self. Do
we dream the world, or are we dreamed by it? From this point of view, it

is easy to think of the Self as the Other. This is precisely the theme of "The Man in the Mirror." Looking in the mirror, the poet recalls a day when

> . . . we used to stand,
> wishing the glass
> would dissolve between us
> . . . .
> But that was another life.

That was a time when the poet perceived his wholeness, which could not be actually demonstrated, but which seemed within reach. Since then, the man in the mirror departed, and then returned,

> dreamlike and obscene,
> your face lost
> under layers of heavy skin

The split between the Self and the Other is nearly total.

> It will always be this way.
> I stand here scared
> that you will disappear,
> scared that you will stay.

Here, and in many of his poems, Strand echoes the terrifying question of Theodore Roethke's "In a Dark Time": "Which I is *I*?" While Roethke's question emerges from a mystical experience, Strand's is rooted in everyday reality and may be all the more awesome for that.

Mark Strand's poetic methods are simple, but highly effective. His poems are stripped of inessential verbiage; he tries for the bare statement of the condition in which he is involved. In this context, however, the powerful images that spring from the unconscious become even stronger, as in "The Man in the Mirror":

> You drift in a pool
> of silver air
>
> where wounds and dreams of wounds
> rise from the deep
> humus of sleep
> to bloom like flowers against the glass.

Strand usually employs stanzas, but not rhyme and not regular meter. The feeling of control in his verse, in spite of its evident flexibility, is probably a consequence of the care with which Strand manipulates his rhythms to reinforce his meaning.

Strand has been characterized as a gloomy poet. To a point, that is true. He explores the darker recesses of the self, even threatens to undermine it altogether. But the energy of his poetry, without contradicting its gloom, overwhelms the darkness. In "Eating Poetry," the librarian is shocked at the ink running from the poet's mouth, at the voraciousness with which he devours the poems. And the intense joy he describes as a result of reading is clearly the same joy he has experienced in writing his poems:

> I am a new man.
> I snarl at her and bark.
> I romp with joy in the bookish dark.

Selected Bibliography:
By STRAND:
Sleeping With One Eye Open. Iowa City, Iowa: Stonewall Press, 1964.
Reasons for Moving. New York: Atheneum Publishers, 1968.
Darker. New York: Atheneum Publishers, 1970.

About Strand:
Bloom, Harold. "Dark and Radiant Peripheries: Mark Strand and A. R. Ammons," *Southern Review,* 8 n.s. (January 1972), 133–49.
Howard, Richard. *Alone with America.* New York: Atheneum Publishers, 1969. Pp. 507–16.

SWENSON, MAY (*b. Logan, Utah, May 28, 1919—   *)

While it is generally true of poets that they are involved in seeing the world freshly, in the case of May Swenson's poetry the reader is usually very much aware that this is precisely what she is doing. She turns a cold eye on the perceptual universe, and often seems to be recording rather than ordering. But that eye preserves its humanness through its endless curiosity, as Swenson experiments with perspectives and rhythms, as if searching for an alternative to conventional subjectivity.

Born in Utah of Swedish parents, May Swenson, who has translated poetry from Swedish, graduated from Utah State University. She has spent the better part of the subsequent time in New York and in Europe. She has been an editor at New Directions, the recipient of a Guggenheim Fellowship, and writer-in-residence at Purdue University.

In "Any Object," which appeared in May Swenson's first book of poems, *Another Animal* (in *Poets of Today I,* 1954), she wrote:

> any Object before the Eye
> can fill the space can occupy
> the supple frame of eternity

She seems to echo Emily Dickinson, but while Dickinson's eternity is one of the spirit, Swenson's is one of "anamolecular atoms" that "fly . . . through ether." It is the eternity of matter that allows for endless metamorphosis of form and has little sympathy with individual permanence. In a much later poem, "The Kite" (from *Half Sun Half Sleep,* 1967), she speculates " 'Perhaps all things are inanimate/and it is the void that lives.' " Although she is not generally grouped with the poets of PROJECTIVE VERSE—and indeed her rhythms, though not metered, create self-imposed patterns rather than following the Projectivist dictates of breath and other biological measures—Swenson's orientation resembles that of Charles Olson, who insists that we see man as an object in a universe of objects and that the word "object" itself be stripped of its pejorative connotations.

In "Why We Die" in *Another Animal*, Swenson suggests that man dies because he chooses to, because he voluntarily wishes to return to the relative peace of the inanimate world. In much of her poetry, however, this sense of kinship with the void has the paradoxical effect of endowing the inanimate with what we would normally call the qualities of life. The main point seems to be that the distinction between animate and inanimate is difficult to make. "Spring in the Square" is typical. It is a straightforward account of the subject, "objective," without explicit interpolations made by a consciousness, although we are aware of the poet's prerogative to select and arrange. The poem ends:

> This is the moment of released leaves
> Innumerable green hands uncurl their puckered palms
> Irrepressible grass bristles
> from the city's horny hide

The trees are human; the city itself is an animal. The importance denied the individual is replaced by a collective vitality in which the individual may participate.

The role of observer in May Swenson's poetry should be clarified. The poet does generally emerge as a recorder of perceptions—but not as a passive recorder. If reality can be defined as the result of the interchange between the randomness of atoms and the arbitrary order imposed by an instrument of observation, then the shifting of focus and direction of that instrument can produce continually new perceptions. "Water Picture," from *A Cage of Spines* (1958), is an example. The poem begins: "In the pond in the park/all things are doubled." This is hardly an original perception. What distinguishes Swenson, however, is that she takes the perception quite seriously, using it not as the basis of metaphor or of a play on illusion and reality, but as a perfectly literal rendering of the world. The poem ends with a twin-necked swan kissing herself,

> and all the scene is troubled:
> water-windows splinter,
> tree-limbs tangle, the bridge
> folds like a fan.

The use of an anxiety-ridden external landscape as the projection of the poet's inner anxieties is fairly common in contemporary poetry. One senses, however, that that is not precisely what is happening here. The anxiety does not reside so much in the poet, or her unconscious, as it does in the perception itself, in the tenuous nature of what we call reality, in the continual threat of chaos that becomes evident whenever we refuse to impose prefabricated systems upon our observations.

The first section of *To Mix With Time* (1963) makes explicit the principles a reader could derive from Swenson's techniques in earlier poems. "The Universe" explores the tension between human systems and reality's disregard of them. Concepts of cause and effect are seen as human impositions upon a universe (the "it" of the first line quoted below) that cares little for either cause and effect or the human intellects that invent such relations.

> Must it have laws? And what
> > if the universe
> > is *not about*
> us? Then what?
> > What
> > is it about
> > and what
> > > about
> > > > *us?*

The confusions of syntax in the poem are characteristic of Swenson's attempts to mirror in her language the difficulties of pinning down reality, especially in poems that are relatively devoid of concrete images.

In "God," divinity is described simply as man's response to the deficiencies of his logic, which cannot come to terms with infinity and eternity. "Out of My Head" attacks the notion that there is such a thing as a discrete consciousness confined within the boundaries of one's head. In "The Wish to Escape into Inner Space," "all expands, explodes / and scampers out and speeds apart." The inner world finally

> > is dragged
> > through galactic vapors;
> > the cold pain of unwanted growth.

The explosion is no less than the explosion of the coherent self. In Yeats's words, "the centre cannot hold." This is the thrust of most of *To Mix With Time*'s first section, establishing Swenson as one of the poets most explicitly responsive to the challenges of contemporary science and philosophy.

Many of the subsequent poems of *To Mix With Time* involve the working out of the implications of the resulting fluidity of perspective. In "Distance and a Certain Light," the distance of an airplane transforms the ugliness of the city into orderly pattern; seen through the microscope, "a gob of spit" is ". . . fastidious / in structure as a crystal." This is obvious enough. What is most interesting in the poem, however, is Swenson's extension of spatial distortion to temporal observations:

> > In any random, sprawling, decomposing thing
> > is the charming string
> > of its history—and what it will be next.

As in "Why We Die," there is a sense of relief at the prospect of escaping specifically human perspectives of space and time, the betraying agonies of the human condition that Swenson rarely encounters directly.

In *Half Sun Half Sleep* Swenson continues her perceptual experiments. In poems such as "The Kite," "A Basin of Eggs," and "In the Hair of the Night," the surfaces, patterns, and textures of the natural world suggest the human body. Often, as in "On Handling Some Small Shells from the Windward Islands," the inanimate world is eroticized, a final confirmation of its vitality. Here, seashells are

> . . . Peculiar fossil-
> fruits that suck through rubbed
>
>   lips and gaping sutures
>   into secret clefts

Thus, although there is indeed something potentially tragic in what amounts to a loss of the integrity of the individual self, the dominant tone struck by May Swenson in her encounters with atomic reality is one of joy. She says in "Spectrum Analysis":

> When I taste
>   *I*
>   I taste something akin
> to suprafruit or neutronic
>   flower
> a solar heart engorged with life's rich
>   juice
>   infrared.

Ultimately, this mode of relating to the insensate world has application to the more specifically human universe. This is clear in *Iconographs* (1970), a book that has been noted chiefly for its typographical arrangements (although Swenson, in an afterword, insists that language rather than shape is the main thing) but which develops further the poet's characteristic themes. In "Feel Me," she writes:

> "Lie down with me, and hold me, tight.   Touch   me.   Be
>   with me.   Feel with me.   *Feel* me,   to do right."

If the traditional self has been lost, human relationships have not; but they must be redefined. The tragic sense is stronger than ever. (The words "Feel me, to do right" were spoken by Swenson's father on his deathbed; the lines quoted above are what the poet finally suggests he meant.) When individual consciousness, acutely aware of its separation from the rest of being in the presence of death, cannot cope with reality, physical contact reestablishes lost connections.

Selected Bibliography:
By Swenson:
Another Animal in *Poets of Today I*. New York: Charles Scribner's Sons, 1954.
A Cage of Spines. New York: Holt, Rinehart & Winston, 1958.
To Mix With Time: New and Selected Poems. New York: Charles Scribner's Sons, 1963.
Half Sun Half Sleep. New York: Charles Scribner's Sons, 1967.
Iconographs. New York: Charles Scribner's Sons, 1970.
See also Swenson's essay "The Experience of Poetry in a Scientific Age" in *Poets on Poetry*. Edited by Howard Nemerov. New York: Basic Books, 1966. Pp. 147–59.

About Swenson:
Howard, Richard. *Alone with America*. New York: Atheneum Publishers, 1969. Pp. 517–32.

VORTICISM

Ezra Pound described Vorticism as a movement in the arts which included Cubism and expressionism in painting and IMAGISM in poetry. A Vorticist journal, *BLAST*, appeared twice (1914 and 1915), but the movement's most comprehensive manifesto is probably Pound's essay "Vorticism," written for the *Fortnightly Review* in 1914. Intended as a clarification of Pound's Imagism, this essay also enabled Pound to push his theories forward, with a view toward dissociating himself from the Imagist movement, which had been appropriated by Amy Lowell.

See also the Introduction, section II.

WAGONER, DAVID   (*b. Massillon, Ohio, June 5, 1926—   *)

Having begun his poetic career as a disciple of THEODORE ROETHKE, it is perhaps not the least of David Wagoner's achievements that he has managed to forge a style that is distinctly his own without abandoning the sympathies that drew him to Roethke in the first place. While, like Roethke, engaged in defining the boundaries of the self in relation to the external world, Wagoner maintains a tough-minded, often witty control of a reality that always seems threatening to dissolve into chaos.

Born in Ohio, educated at Pennsylvania State College and Indiana University, Wagoner studied with Roethke at Penn State and also at the University of Washington, where, through Roethke, he got a job teaching and later became professor of English. A successful novelist as well as a poet, Wagoner can be said to have taken Roethke's place at the center of creative activity in the Pacific Northwest.

It is probably not coincidental that when Wagoner issued a selected edition of his poetry in 1969, he included no poems from his first book, *Dry Sun, Dry Wind* (1953), a book that shows Roethke's influence. *In a Place to Stand* (1958), however, is written in Wagoner's own voice, and "The Feast" is a good showcase for his poetic powers. "Maimed and enormous in the air," the poem begins, "The bird fell down to us and died." With its echoes of Yeats's "The Second Coming," "The Feast" is apocalyptic in tone. But while Yeats deals with his disquiet from a public and historical perspective, Wagoner's emphasis is characteristically private; the poem's attention is on "us."

The poem can be interpreted in a specifically Christian context. The bird coming down to us and dying may itself be an emblem of Christ. "Fire was pouring from its side," like blood from Christ's wound; "It floundered like a dying fish," a traditional symbol of Christ. Winter is seen as the holy ghost. And the poem concludes with the witnesses to the event kneeling to the body and eating, so that the "feast" is a version of the Eucharist. To fall back too confidently on the Christian frame of reference, however, is to miss much that is important in the poem. The tone is in many ways more pagan than Christian. The poem is, after all, on a literal level, probably about hunters, and the guilt experienced is less significantly over a betrayal of Christ than the sense of having broken the natural order of things. The order is partially restored when, "like animals," the hunters partake of the feast. Even so, "all of the staring eyes were false." Jaws unhinge themselves, an image that is neither human nor natural.

Wagoner's strength, as shown in "The Feast," lies in the ability to render accurately complex emotional responses to experience. He is always in tight control of his materials, rooting his perception of the tension between ritual and chaos in the tension between the conventional form (rhyming quatrains of iambic tetrameter lines) and surreal imagery. Wagoner has a broad technical range. In "A Guide to Dungeness Spit," from *The Nesting Ground* (1963), he reverses the methods of "The Feast" by employing free verse and matter-of-fact imagery. The poem operates effectively out of the contrast between the narrator's explicit assumption that he is simply pointing out what happens to be there and the implication in the poem that he is attempting to put the universe in order. While pointing out the flora, fauna, and landscape of Dungeness Spit, the narrator tells his companion she must decide

> . . . whether all birds are the young of other creatures
> Or their own young ones,
> Or simply their old selves because they die. . . .

And the poem ends:

> Those are called ships. We are called lovers.
> There lie the mountains.

This is in the end a poem about poetry—the process of naming and selecting, the act of perception as a creative attempt to define one's relation to reality.

The title poem of *Staying Alive* (1966) is another example of the same technique. The poem pretends to be a guide to survival in the woods—and in a sense that is precisely what it is—but it is also a commentary on the human condition in general. At times, the poem's broader concerns are in the open:

> . . . There may even come, on some uncanny evening,
> A time when you're warm and dry, well fed, not thirsty,
> Uninjured, without fear,
> When nothing, either good or bad, is happening.
> This is called staying alive. It's temporary.
> What occurs after
> Is doubtful. . . .

One of the poem's assets is that it is not allegorical; the problems of survival in the woods and the problems of quotidian experience do not correspond systematically. There are, however, emotional correspondences. Wagoner is thus able to keep his eye fixed directly on his subject without narrowing his range.

Wagoner is probably at his best when the connection between what he is observing and its larger resonances is least explicit, as in "The Osprey's Nest," also from *Staying Alive:*

> They saw the world was bones and curtain-rods,
> Hay-wire and cornstalks—rubble put to bed
> And glued into meaning by large appetites.
> Living on top of everything that mattered,
> The fledglings held it in the air with their eyes,
> With awkward claws groping the ghosts of fish.

While maintaining a specifically human perspective, Wagoner subtly affirms man's connections with the natural world.

One of the finest of the new poems of Wagoner's *New and Selected Poems* (1969) is "In the Open Season." Because of its thematic resemblance to "The Feast," it offers us an opportunity to determine the extent to which Wagoner's attitudes and techniques have shifted and the extent to which they have remained the same in the intervening years. Like "The Feast," "In the Open Season" is about hunting, but, as is increasingly true of Wagoner's work, the literal surface of the poem is less difficult to penetrate. There are sounds of shotguns and rifles, animals come "spilling out of hiding." Light breaks out of everything the hunters touch "in bristling spectrums," recalling the fire of the earlier poem; the deer are "bleeding toward sundown." And like "The Feast," "In the Open Season" concludes with a kind of communion:

> We touched each other's wounds
> Like star-crossed, stir-crazed lovers
> Dying again and again.

We become aware why hunting, to which Wagoner has such ambivalent reactions, is one of the dominant obsessions of his work. It represents a life-and-death relationship with nature, reaffirming man's ties to the natural world as well as his own special identity in that world. Chiefly, however, the act of hunting is a reassertion of the self through the perception of the self's fundamental unity with the outer world. It could not be simply coincidental that the traditional pun on dying as orgasm, which Wagoner unquestionably intended in these final lines, brings to the poem another mode of experience in which the self is both lost and affirmed at the same time.

"In the Open Season" has a simpler texture than the earlier poem "The Feast," but its approach to experience is at least as complex, shifting its emphasis to the human implications of man's relation to nature. Although the strict formal structure is gone, the poet's control is always evident. While the imagery is less spectacularly surreal, there are surreal touches. And this is a reasonably accurate summary of the development of Wagoner's poetic methods.

David Wagoner is not among the most widely known American poets writing today, certainly not in the sense that Robert Lowell, Sylvia Plath, John Berryman, and Allen Ginsberg, for example, are known. But his work has earned for him respect in the community of poets. He is at the very least a superior craftsman, one who does not fit neatly into any school or movement but one who has succeeded in powerfully and uniquely communicating his vision of reality.

Selected Bibliography:
By WAGONER:
Dry Sun, Dry Wind. Bloomington, Ind.: Indiana University Press, 1953.
The Man in the Middle. [Novel.] New York: Harcourt Brace Jovanovich, 1954.
Money Money Money. [Novel.] New York: Harcourt Brace Jovanovich, 1955.
A Place to Stand. Bloomington, Ind.: Indiana University Press, 1958.
Rock. [Novel.] New York: Viking Press, 1958.
The Nesting Ground. Bloomington, Ind.: Indiana University Press, 1963.
The Escape Artist. [Novel.] New York: Farrar, Straus & Giroux, 1965.
Staying Alive. Bloomington, Ind.: Indiana University Press, 1966.
New and Selected Poems. Bloomington, Ind.: Indiana University Press, 1969.
Straw for the Fire: From the Notebooks of Theodore Roethke 1943–63. [Editor.]
     Garden City, N.Y.: Doubleday & Co., 1972.

About Wagoner:
Howard, Richard. *Alone with America.* New York: Atheneum Publishers, 1969.
     Pp. 533–51.

WAKOSKI, DIANE   (*b. Whittier, Calif., Aug. 3, 1937—*   )

One of the group known as "deep imagists," Diane Wakoski could also be located among the Confessional poets, since private and painful experiences —the death of a young brother, the sense of inevitable betrayal in love—are indeed the areas from which she has derived her most powerful poetry.

Born and raised in California, a graduate of the University of California at Berkeley, Diane Wakoski has taught and given frequent readings. In a brief biographical statement prepared for Leary and Kelly's *A Controversy of Poets* (1965), she herself underscores the Confessional bias of her poetry, although she does not use that precise term: "I feel that poetry is the completely personal expression of someone about his feelings and reactions to the world. I think it is *only interesting* in proportion to how interesting the person who writes it is."

In Diane Wakoski's poetry, "interesting" and "painful" often seem synonymous. It would be unfair to suggest that she revels in self-pity, or that she is attracted to mere sensation. The preoccupations of her work are simply assertions of the fact that man must define his being in terms of its limitations, that beauty has meaning only in relation to ugliness, love only in relation to loneliness. This is in fact the theme of a relatively early poem, "Justice Is Reason Enough" (from *Coins and Coffins,* 1961).

The poem begins with the flat announcement, "He, who was once my brother, is dead by his own hand." Each day, for over a year, the mother asks the poet, ". . . in her whining way, why it had to happen . . ." The mother's response, pathetic in an Aristotelian sense, is clearly an alternative open to the poet as well. It is the response of the conscious intellect, confronted with experience it cannot order, unable to accept the disparity between the world as it is and the world as it ought to be. Rejecting this, the poet moves beyond the rational; and here, as a craftsman, Wakoski's predilection for the "deep image," the particularly evocative symbol derived from the poet's unconscious, stands her in good stead.

She recalls her brother's dream, in which a gull beats its wings together until they draw blood, and her own dream of giant wings swooping over her that brings her

> brother to my room that night and pushed his whole taut body
> right over mine until I yielded, and together we yielded to the dark tension.

The mother's endless questioning, which has lasted a year, is now replaced by "Over a thousand passing years" in which the poet will not forget her brother; the restricted vision of the individual consciousness has been replaced by the broader perspectives of myth and the unconscious, without sacrificing the particularity of the loss. It is a way of breaking through the boundaries of the self without denying the pain that has served to define it.

The conclusion of the poem is crucial to an understanding of Wakoski's poetic stance:

> Mother asked me why
> every day for a year; and I told her justice. Justice is
> reason enough for anything ugly. It balances the beauty in the world.

What is remarkable about these lines is that the poem has provided for them a context in which they are at the same time terribly ironic and completely straightforward. David's death is still manifestly unjust, which the mother knew all along. But the release of tensions in the dream, the affirmation of beauty against death, of sexual pleasure against pain, result in a kind of balance that might be called justice, though still not in its conventional sense.

The materials of which Diane Wakoski makes her poetry have not significantly shifted in more recent volumes. Pain, loss, loneliness still dominate. Her language, however, has undergone if not change then at least refinement. In "Justice Is Reason Enough," a relatively flat voice is brought to life by several striking images and by the intensity of the subject itself. In *Discrepancies and Apparitions* (1965) and *Inside the Blood Factory* (1968) the language itself is charged, consistently at a high pitch. An example is "In Gratitude To Beethoven" in *Inside the Blood Factory*. Of roses she is carrying, Wakoski writes:

> they seem to have come out of my skin
> on this hot fragrant night,
> and I imagine the inside of my body
> glowing, phosphorescent, with strange flower faces
> looking out from the duodenum
> or the soft liver,
> white as my belly, the eyes always disbelieving
> the ugly processes that make a living body.

As in the earlier poem, Wakoski has entered the world of myth; but while previously the myth, a variation on Leda and the Swan, was prefabricated, here it is of the poet's own invention. It is a myth of metamorphosis, of turning the body inside out, of attempting to delineate modes of being. The consequent fluidity of the imagery is very much at the core of the poem. The poet finds herself "admittedly a strange combination of images;/yet constantly myself." Somewhere, she speculates, there must be ". . . a consistency,/perhaps the thread of destruction."

The tenuous sense of self leaves her open, vulnerable; she seeks comfort in the music of Beethoven, one in a series of surrogate fathers who parade through her poetry. She is unloved or, worse, she is ripped apart by those who pretend to love her:

> I am like the guerilla fighter
> who must sleep with one eye open for attack . . .

The poetry verges on the edge of self-pity, but it does not go over. As is often the case in the poetry by Sylvia Plath, it is saved by anger, not simply anger of attitude, which could easily seem a pose, but anger firmly rooted in the violence of the imagery, the energy of the language; that is, finally, the hallmark of Diane Wakoski's poetry. A sensitivity—almost hypersensitivity—to experience is embodied in acutely sensuous imagery. It is as if nerve endings are stripped bare, as if all sensory data are magnified. Even lying in the sun can become a battle to the death against a malignant universe, as it is in another poem in *Inside the Blood Factory:*

> Today I did battle with huge black-green flies
> that sucked at me in the sun along the shore
> leaving yellow lumps under my tanning legs.

(from "To The Man in the Silver Ferrari")

Diane Wakoski is a poet who takes risks—in her language, in her sensibility. She is not uniformly successful. But when she is on the mark, she is a powerful, even a terrifying, poet.

See also CONFESSIONAL POETRY; DEEP IMAGISM.

Selected Bibliography:
BY WAKOSKI:
Coins and Coffins. New York: Hawk's Well Press, 1961.
Discrepancies and Apparitions. Garden City, N.Y.: Doubleday & Company, 1965.
The George Washington Poems. New York: Riverrun Press, 1967.
Inside the Blood Factory. Garden City, N.Y.: Doubleday & Company, 1968.
The Motorcycle Betrayal Poems. New York: Simon & Schuster, 1972.
See also Wakoski's statement in *A Controversy of Poets.* Edited by Paris Leary
    and Robert Kelly (Garden City, N.Y.: Doubleday & Company, 1965).

WALKER, MARGARET (*b. Birmingham, Ala., July 7, 1915—   )*

Margaret Walker's *For My People* (1942), a winner of Yale Series of Younger Poets award, is probably one of the two or three most important books by a black poet in America since the start of World War II. It was the sole basis of its author's considerable reputation until the publication of her novel *Jubilee*, in 1966, and her second collection of poems in 1970. The fact that Yale University Press decided to reissue the book in 1968 attests to its being more than a historical document; its particular expression of the black experience is still relevant.

The daughter of a Methodist preacher, Margaret Walker was born in Birmingham, raised there and in Mississippi and Louisiana. After receiving her B.A. from Northwestern in 1935 and her M.A. from the University of Iowa in 1940, she worked as a social worker, newspaper reporter, magazine editor, and has taught English at various colleges, including Jackson State. She received her Ph.D. from the University of Iowa in 1965.

For My People is divided into three parts: the first contains two varieties of free verse; the second, ballads; the third, sonnets. Thus, within the confines of this single volume she displays the range of her craft. Probably the best known of her poems is the opening "For My People." She uses the long flowing sentences used before her by Whitman and Sandburg, later by Allen Ginsberg. This form, which looks prosaic on the page, is actually perfectly suited to the development of the poem's energetic rhythms:

> For the cramped bewildered years we went to school to learn to know
> the reasons why and the answers to and the people who and the
> places where and the days when, in memory of the bitter hours
> when we discovered we were black and poor and small and
> different and nobody cared and nobody wondered and nobody
> understood;

The poem moves from childhood to adulthood, from the South to the North, from slavery to confusion. But it ends on a note that puts Walker years ahead of her time. She is not content simply to document the plight of the black man in America. Her vision is apocalyptic; it is the vision of someone who cannot wait for slow change. And so the poem concludes:

> Let a new earth rise. Let another world be born. Let a bloody peace
> be written in the sky. Let a second generation of courage issue
> forth; let a people loving freedom come to growth. Let a
> beauty full of healing and a strength of final clenching be the
> pulsing in our spirits and our blood. Let the martial songs be
> written, let the dirges disppear. Let a race of men now rise and
> take control.

Walker's technical abilities are very much in evidence here. Most of the poem has presented a dark picture; here, she sees hope, and that hope takes the form of an incantatory call to arms. The rhythms approach formal meter, most spectacularly in the anapests accompanying the pulsing martial songs.

Other poems in the first part of the book are written in the more usual kind of free verse; that is, with line lengths determined by breath rather than sentence. Here, too, Walker uses repetition as a dominant principle of organization, often achieving a biblical effect:

> Then with a longing dearer than breathing
> love for the valley arises within us
> love to possess and thrive in this valley
> love to possess our vineyards and pastures
> our orchards and cattle

(from "Delta")

Again, although the poem as a whole would have to be classified as free verse, there are frequent passages, like the one cited above, in which meter becomes crucial. "Delta" is, after all, an attempt to reaffirm man's essential harmony with the natural world.

Most of the ballads in part two are written in quatrains, very much part of the folk tradition. The interweaving of sound and sense of "Molly Means," however, expands the possibilities of the conventional form. (Although the poem is written in eight-line stanzas, each stanza could be broken down into four quatrains.)

> Sometimes at night through the shadowy trees
> She rides along on a winter breeze.
> You can hear her holler and whine and cry.
> Her voice is thin and her moan is high,
> And her cackling laugh or her barking cold
> Bring terror to the young and old.
> O Molly, Molly, Molly Means
> Lean is the ghost of Molly Means.

The sonnets of part three are the least well-known poems of *For My People*. They are not impressive in the ways that sonnets generally are: they lack the intricacy of structure, the density of language, that can be found in the sonnets of Gwendolyn Brooks, for example. They are rather simple and direct, held together by Walker's familiar use of repetition and parallel structure more than by the patterns inherent in sonnet form. And they are about the black man's struggle to survive:

> Out of this blackness we must struggle forth;
> from want of bread, of pride, of dignity.

> (from "The Struggle Staggers Us")

In spite of the twenty-eight years that separated it from *For My People*, *Prophets for a New Day* (1970) contains no serious departures in tone or style. The titles do indeed reflect the events of the fifties and sixties: "Street Demonstration," "Girl Held Without Bail," "For Malcolm X," "For Andy Goodman—Michael Schwerner—and James Chaney." And it is probably quite significant that Walker now deals with events, rather than simply stating a condition, affirming a vague hope. But there is ample precedent in her earlier work for the apocalyptic mood, for the rhetorical structures that organize the poems, and never before have the biblical underpinnings of her verse been more clearly revealed. Here, for example, is the beginning of the third section of the book's title poem:

> A beast is among us.
> His mark is on the land.
> His horns and his hands and his lips are gory with our blood.
> He is War and Famine and Pestilence
> He is Death and Destruction and Trouble
> And he walks in our houses at noonday
> And devours our defenders at midnight.

In the end, what is remarkable about Margaret Walker's new collection is not that her style and perspective have not greatly altered, but rather that they fit in so well with the new black poetry. Her verse has always been deeply rooted in a sense of community; it has always had an aggressive rather than a passive vision of how that community must assert its fundamental dignity.

Selected Bibliography:
By WALKER:
For My People. New Haven: Yale University Press, 1942.
Jubilee. [Novel.] Boston: Houghton Mifflin Co., 1966.
Prophets for a New Day. Detroit: Broadside Press, 1970.

WEISS, THEODORE (b. Reading, Pa., Dec. 16, 1916—   )

In a statement made for *A Controversy of Poets,* Theodore Weiss distinguishes himself from those poets involved with the "merely personal and lyrical and happily fragmented. It is easy to go with the time or to cry out against it; but to do something with it, to take it by surprise, to make more of it (as poets usually have) than it can do itself—might that not still occupy poets? And let it be poetry, rather than the poor poet and his predicaments." Whether or not the distinction Weiss makes between himself and many of his contemporaries is as absolute as he suggests—whether they have not transformed experience into art, whether he himself is totally removed from personal and lyric tradition—he does belong with those poets who have felt that what art has in common with life is the quality of being real. The emphasis then falls on craft in the creation of poetry that comments on our world, not necessarily through direct statement but rather through the simple fact of its existence.

Born in Reading, Pennsylvania, Theodore Weiss received his bachelor's degree from Muhlenberg College in 1938, his master's from Columbia University in 1940. A few years later, he and his wife founded *Quarterly Review of Literature.* Weiss has taught at the University of North Carolina, Yale, the New School, M.I.T., Bard College, and Princeton.

"Barracks Apt. 14" from *Outlanders* contains one of Weiss's clearest statements of poetic theory. "All must be used," the poem begins; later it goes on:

> all are parts hopeful, possible,
> expecting their place in the song;
> more appealing because parts
> that must harmonize into something
> that rewards them for being, rewards
> with what they are.

The poet is a celebrant of being. He harmonizes fragments, finds connections in the face of divisiveness. Nothing must be excluded from the contin-

uous web that defines reality, that defines the poem. In "Preface," a young
poet searches for the words that will " 'get those old weeds through.' " The
weeds also have their place. We are, Weiss suggests, like a dream trying to
recall the dreamer, separate parts of reality trying to regain a sense of
wholeness. But unlike the Projectivist poets, who do share Weiss's vision of
connections, he insists on the power of the separate, conscious self to perceive that wholeness.

There is consequently a tragic dimension to Weiss's verse, a sense of the
transience of the shaping powers that hold the universe together. In a poem
in *The Medium*, "The Web," he thinks "of someone stitched into a
complex/tapestry." By means of art, the individual becomes part of the
whole. Then the poem ends by evoking a vision of precisely the destruction
that art momentarily conquers; there is a wind that

> . . . would, blowing,
> blast the web—torn also by the tatter
> crows, fled far beyond their thread-
> bare wings—and, last, its instruments.

Weiss's poetry, though filled with the imagery of dissolution, also contains the emblems of renewal. "The Fire at Alexandria" from *Outlanders*
imagines the destruction of masterpieces, but in this poem the manuscripts
rise from the ashes like the phoenix. And "House of Fire," a meditation on
Job, on destruction by wind and fire, sees that

> . . . in the abandoned field
> below, through this intense decaying
> and its acrid breath, a freshness wells
> as if an April, some forgotten day of,
> starting up out of the time's debris,
> looked round amazedly.

The "fathering first desire" of sea and fire endures.

Selected Bibliography:
By WEISS:
The Catch. New York: Twayne Publishers, 1951.
Outlanders. New York: Macmillan Co., 1960.
Gunsight. New York: New York University Press, 1962.
The Medium. New York: Macmillan Co., 1965.
The Last Day and the First. New York: Macmillan Co., 1968.
The World Before Us: Poems 1950–70. New York: Macmillan Co., 1970.
See also Weiss's essay "Toward a Classical Modernity and a Modern Classicism"
    in *Poets on Poetry*. Edited by Howard Nemerov (New York: Basic Books,
    1966; pp. 212–24), and his statement in *A Controversy of Poets*, eds. Paris
    Leary and Robert Kelly (Garden City, N.Y.: Doubleday & Co., 1965).

About Weiss:
Howard, Richard. *Alone with America*. New York: Atheneum Publishers, 1969.
    Pp. 522–74.

WHITTEMORE, REED (*b. New Haven, Conn., Sept. 11,*
*1919—   *)

Reed Whittemore's most successful poetry is characterized by fine wit and
irony. While these qualities are certainly present in the work of other contemporary American poets, Whittemore's work is distinguished by his apparent faith in the capacity of intellect to apprehend, if not to resolve, the
absurdities of human experience. Although his language is not especially
dense and he is relatively easy to read, he frequently creates resonant images that transcend the rational surfaces of his poems.

Whittemore attended Yale University in his native New Haven, Connecticut. He has taught at Carleton College in Minnesota and the University of
Maryland, and has been senior program associate at the National Institute
of Public Affairs in Washington.

One of Whittemore's most often anthologized poems is "A Day with the
Foreign Legion" (a revised version is included in *Poems: New and Selected*), in which his talents are particularly well suited to handle the tensions between illusion and reality. The heroic tableaux created in countless
Foreign Legion movies are played off against the reality of the actual legionnaires "Cursing the food and the bugs." The point of the poem is not,
of course, that movies are generally unrealistic in portraying the Foreign
Legion. What Whittemore does is to merge movie and reality, so that the
metaphor of the film breaking down because the legionnaires cannot go
through their romanticized paces becomes a commentary on the nature of
modern reality. It was not the film, nor the projector, Wittemore says.
It was

> . . . some other darker cause having to do
> With the script perhaps, or the art,
>
> Or simply the time,
> The time and the place, and how could one blame them?

The illusions that previously sustained men are no longer effective; as the
lights go on, "The enemy roamed the desert, and everyone itched."

"Still Life" explores a similar theme. At night, the poet sits on his couch,
with a stillness bred of devotion and fright. His world of inanimate objects
comes to life, and he finds himself wishing that he might "Bring into day-
light the eloquence, say, of a doorknob." He cannot, however, because
everyone in the waking world draws back ". . . from the tossing
turbulence/Of a cough, a creaking stair." The understanding of the nature
of reality earned at night is rooted in fear, among other emotions, and hard
to face; the imagination is rejected in favor of the quotidian. Yet it is the
imagination that penetrates to the core of things, to the secrets objects
share. In one sense, the poem simply plays with paradox, with the clarity
and intelligence of a vision shrouded in darkness, with the heightened vi-
vacity of the inanimate. But, as is the case in most of Whittemore's poetry,

the play has serious foundations, dealing with the most serious problems art can pose: those that concern themselves with the question of what is real and what is no more than an illusion of reality.

Selected Bibliography:
By WHITTEMORE:
An American Takes a Walk. Minneapolis: University of Minnesota Press, 1956.
The Self-Made Man. New York: Macmillan Co., 1959.
The Boy from Iowa: Poems and Essays. New York: Macmillan Co., 1962.
The Fascination of the Abomination. New York: Macmillan Co., 1963.
Poems: New and Selected. Minneapolis: University of Minnesota Press, 1967.
From Zero to the Absolute. New York: Crown Publishers, 1967.
Fifty Poems Fifty. Minneapolis: University of Minnesota Press, 1970.
See also Whittemore's essay "Poetry as Discovery" in *Poets on Poetry.* Edited by
   Howard Nemerov. New York: Basic Books, 1966. Pp. 198–211.

WILBUR, RICHARD (*b. New York City, Mar. 1, 1921*—   )

Of those contemporary American poets who have found it possible to work effectively within traditional poetic disciplines, few have been more consistent in their commitment than Richard Wilbur. Although he has certainly developed in diction, moving from the relatively ornate to the relatively bare, and although the range of perspectives through which he can accost the real world has broadened, Wilbur's use of demanding stanzaic patterns and meters has not in the least diminished. The tension that led poets like Theodore Roethke and Robert Lowell to vacillate between strictly controlled and free verse, and frequently to transform the very conventions they adopted into completely new instruments of communication, is missing from Wilbur's work. Since rhyme and meter in recurrent patterns seems to imply agreement, correspondence, harmony, it is easy in these times to understand why Wilbur finds himself in the minority. The sense of agreement that he embodies in his view of reality, however, is not a simplistic faith in the rightness of things; it is rather what Wilbur has called "the proper relation between the tangible world and the intuitions of the spirit." To the tentative establishment of such an ordering of experience his poetry has been chiefly devoted.

After graduating from Amherst College in 1942, Wilbur served in the infantry until the end of World War II. He received his master's degree from Harvard in 1947, the same year his first volume of poetry was published, and was a Junior Fellow and teacher at Harvard until 1954. He subsequently taught at Wellesley, and at Wesleyan, where he became professor of English in 1957. In that same year, he received both the National Book Award and the Pulitzer Prize for *Things of This World,* one of the few books of poetry in recent years to receive both awards.

Of his earliest work, Richard Wilbur wrote in "On My Own Work": "My first poems were written in answer to the inner and outer disorders of the second World War and they helped me, as poems should, to take ahold of raw events and convert them, provisionally, into experience." It is interesting that Wilbur sees his art as a response to disorder, with the further implication that only the formally contained event qualifies as experience; raw events are potentially chaotic. Wilbur's statement notwithstanding, the most effective poems in his 1947 collection, *The Beautiful Changes*—with the possible exception of "Mined Country," a description of a serene pasture in postwar Europe in which "cows in mid-munch" are "splattered over the sky" when they step on buried mines—are not the ones that concern themselves with the war. As critics have often observed of Wilbur's work, the emphasis is on vision, on seeing; the goal is the transfiguration of the commonplace. "In a Bird Sanctuary" ends with the lines:

> In order's name let's not turn down our thumbs
> on routine visions; we must figure out
> what all's about.

A possible gloss on this appears at the end of "On My Own Work": "What poetry does with ideas is to redeem them from abstraction and submerge them in sensibility; it embodies them in persons and things and surrounds them with a weather of feeling; it thereby tests the ability of any ideas to consort with human nature in its contemporary condition."

The focus for Wilbur is, then, the object itself, never the abstraction alone. But always, or nearly always, the object draws the poet toward another level of being. In the poem "Objects," he sees himself voyaging in a world

> . . . where in every tangible tree
> I see afloat among the leaves, all calm and curled,
> The Cheshire smile which sets me fearfully free.

Both this poem and "A Dutch Courtyard" allude to a painting by Pieter de Hooch. It is a painting whose dominant characteristics are sunlight and order (". . .What surprising strict/Propriety!" the poet exclaims), a celebration of the benignity of the material universe. Wilbur, however, is not without a sense of irony about man's relation to this vision. In "A Dutch Courtyard," he pictures "Old Andrew Mellon," "Consumed with greedy ire," so disturbed by the painting that he cannot rest until he buys "the thing entire." Of course, purchasing the canvas is not necessarily to possess its vision. And the moment captured by de Hooch, in which the servant girl tirelessly and eternally smiles at the motionless cavalier, both totally beyond the influence of the observer, is, like the figures on Keats's urn, a frozen moment, out of time, out of the human condition. From the very start, Wilbur refuses to oversimplify the ordering of experience.

The complexity of this ordering forms at least part of the poet's concern in "The Beautiful Changes." (One is frequently reminded in Wilbur of Wallace Stevens' description of the "supreme fiction": It Must Be Abstract; It Must Change; It Must Give Pleasure.) The beautiful is seen to change in at least two ways in this poem. Implicit throughout, since the beauty the poet has chosen to confront is natural, temporal beauty, is the idea that the permanence man finds in the beautiful is illusory. Explicitly, however, he addresses himself to the idea that essences of objects are not absolute, but can only be known in relation to other objects; the mantis on the green leaf ". . . makes the leaf leafier, and proves / Any greenness is deeper than anyone knows." Rather than finding definite symbolic meanings in the natural world, Wilbur moves back toward a state of original wonder.

There are, of course, pitfalls in a poetry of ideas, even when the ideas are grounded in the concrete, even when the ideas are carefully qualified. Some of Wilbur's finest poems come perilously close to denying raw events in the interest of a general truth. "The Death of a Toad," in his second book, *Ceremony and Other Poems* (1950), threatens on the one hand to sentimentalize the dying toad, whose leg has been clipped by the power mower, on the other hand to reduce the toad totally to an object existing mainly to provide a powerful, almost mythological, image for the poet. Nonetheless, the poem is for most readers extremely powerful, a classic of what is practically a genre of dead-animal poems in contemporary American poetry (William Stafford's "Traveling through the Dark," Howard Nemerov's "The Goose Fish," for example), and in this case at least, Wilbur walks a thin line with reasonable success.

Although Wilbur's images are drawn frequently from the natural world and from the world of art, he does not completely avoid the specifically human universe. Even here, the human beings tend to be figures in literary history (often characters), or themselves artists or performers, like Nijinsky or like the central figure of "Juggler." In that poem, the audience applauds the juggler, "Who has won for once over the world's weight." The performance, then, becomes symbolic, or at least emblematic; the juggler is the hero who defeats the earth, the pull of the material universe on his five red balls, "Swinging a small heaven about his ears," that is, affirming the spiritual. Wilbur's avoidance of most everyday human experience is not owing to his lack of interest in it—it is probably his main interest—but through metaphor and symbol, he ranges far in the perceptual world in search of models.

There is a potential monotony in Wilbur's dominant theme, the relation between the spiritual and the material; the real business of his poems, however, is structural rather than thematic. The pattern of the juggler's art finds its equivalent in the poem's stanzaic pattern: $a^5b^5c^5b^3a^3c^5$, a relatively strict form, although not as demanding as many employed by Wilbur. What stands out in the reader's mind is not the rigidity of the poem's structure, but rather the fluidity of the poet's touch. The careful intermingling of end-stopped and run-on lines, the repetitions—alliteration, internal rhyme, as well as simple repetition of words or cognates—serve not only to capture the changing cycle of the juggler's act, but to create within a contained world one that seems infinite.

In " 'A World Without Objects Is a Sensible Emptiness,' " whose title is taken from the work of the seventeenth-century British poet Thomas Traherne, Wilbur's virtuosity, still certainly in evidence, shows great variation. The "camels of the spirit" search their desert for Traherne's *"sensible emptiness"*; they ". . . long to learn to drink/Of pure mirage." Wilbur reminds these beasts of his soul that "all shinings need to be shaped and borne." Again, he is testing connections between the tangible and the abstract. The stanzaic pattern is different: $a^3b^5a^6b^3$. But even this representation of the pattern, which reveals an expansion and contraction of metrical units, suggests that the real interest in this poem is rhythmic. As opposed to the iambs of "Juggler," the anapestic substitutions here, especially in the middle, longer lines, are insistent enough to challenge the lines' identity. Wilbur seems to have gone to school with Dylan Thomas and Gerard Manley Hopkins here, certainly in such phrases as "Lampshine blurred in the steam of beasts." Just as the expansion of line length returns to the three beats of the first and last of each stanza, similarly the wilder anapestic lines are framed by the relatively sedate iambs and trochees of these same lines. And the whole process corresponds to the expansion of spirit that occurs within the poem itself, only to be returned and linked again to the world of objects as a necessary condition of its existence. Wilbur is closer than might be expected to less rigidly formal poets who feel that each experience has its own distinct rhythm; in his case it is simply that each experience has its appropriate formal pattern.

Wilbur's most critically acclaimed volume of poems to date has been *Things of This World* (1956), in which there are more palpable shifts in method than have to this point been easily discernible. The poem from which the book takes its title, " 'Love Calls Us to the Things of This World,' " is in the tradition of "The Beautiful Changes" and " 'A World Without Objects Is a Sensible Emptiness.' " In "On My Own Work," Wilbur himself described " 'Love Calls Us to the Things of This World' " and some of his other poems as a test of these two questions: "Is it possible . . . to speak of angels in the modern world? Will the psyche of the modern reader consent to be called a soul?" Thus, Wilbur is again exploring the relation between the spiritual and the material, albeit from a different perspective. (It must not be supposed that Wilbur is incapable of writing successful poems on other subjects; he has. It is a measure either of the poet or his audience that these are the poems most anthologized, most often read, most commonly referred to.)

The title of " 'Love Calls Us to the Things of This World' " is a quotation from Saint Augustine; Wilbur proposes to test its applicability to the contemporary experience. The persona of the poem opens his eyes to the sound of pulleys; looking out the window, he finds "The morning air is all awash with angels." The pun is soon revealed; it is the clotheslines billowing in the wind. The sleepy observer resists the loss of his vision: "The soul shrinks/From all that it is about to remember." Finally, however, ". . . the sun acknowledges . . . the world's hunks and colors." The persona sees the angels now as the clothing of thieves, lovers, and "the heaviest nuns . . . keeping their difficult balance."

The testing of experience implicit in this poem yields highly ambiguous results. Angels and souls seem able to exist only in a sleepy morning world that refuses to remember the deadliness of raw events. The speaker's final words, however, are witty as well as ironic, and the fellowship of thieves, lovers, and nuns, who, after all, ". . . walk in a pure floating/Of dark habits," may be neither so strange nor so pessimistic as it first seems. The soul has descended ". . . in bitter love/To accept the waking body"; still it is love whatever its qualification; and we must never forget that the very possibility of angels has been suggested, almost incarnated in, the scorned world of physical objects.

The poem's techniques mirror, and in part create, the uncertainty of its conclusions. Wilbur does not employ a recurring rhyme scheme—less frequently used in this volume than in those preceding it—although the shadows of rhymes still lurk, producing an uneasiness that might not be present if the rhymes and off-rhymes were totally gone. Untypically, the stanzaic pattern is not instantly obvious; the five-line stanzas—a line of rough iambic tetrameter followed by four of pentameter—are typographically broken in the middle. The poem, then, produces a tension between form and chaos that is rare in Wilbur's work.

Advice to a Prophet (1961) is the fourth of the books included in Wilbur's first collected volume, *The Poems of Richard Wilbur* (1963). It contains new translations, "Pangloss's Song" from *Candide* (the comic opera Wilbur wrote in collaboration with Lillian Hellman and Leonard Bernstein), and new and original poetry, much of which confirms the hints of the subtly changing style of his previous book. His reading in and translations of other languages begins to show more definite fruit in his own work, as in the poem "Junk," a description of a trash can in the manner of Anglo-Saxon alliterative verse. (Wilbur, with W. H. Auden, is one of the few contemporaries to be not only influenced metrically by the Anglo-Saxon poets, but to directly transpose their methods as well.) "Two Voices in a Meadow," however, is the poem that Wilbur himself points to as evidence of new directions. It is a dramatic poem, as opposed to what Wilbur calls the "ironic meditative poem." Wilbur is apparently concerned about the distancing effects of irony, which reflects the complexities of experience, but mutes emotional impact. The two voices in the meadow are that of a milkweed and a stone; the dichotomy of above and below, lightness and heaviness, persists. Linked by the phrase "the crib of God," above which the milkweed is, under which the stone, each is triumphant by submission to its own nature.

A similar dramatic poem, "The Aspen and the Stream," is more ambitious, certainly more complex. The opposites here embody affirmation of experience (aspen) and deep gloominess (stream); they also embody the individuated self and world of undifferentiated being respectively. The aspen seeks unity of being, wishes to ". . . ensnare/With roots the earth, with branches all the air." A Yeatsian symbol, the tree may not really have the last word; or at any rate that last word may be an ironic one, since all this noble strain may succeed in achieving no more than a few more aspen leaves. In any case, the stream, rushing to ". . . repossess my soul / In blackness and in fall," provides a darker view than Wilbur, a poet of light and clarity, usually is willing to confront.

In *Walking to Sleep* (1969) Wilbur develops predictably, although the dramatic poem seems to have been at least temporarily abandoned. This time an entire section is given over to translation, principally of Borges, Voznesensky, and Villon. There is another Anglo-Saxon—inspired poem, "The Lilacs," which is ultimately concerned with "The depth and dumbness / of death's kingdom." Wilbur is remarkably successful in wedding the alliterative pattern to reasonably straightforward language, but few poets can accomplish this kind of imitation without giving the impression that the emotions are second-hand. (When Ezra Pound succeeds, as in "The Seafarer," it is because a good part of his intention is to evoke another age; if W. H. Auden succeeds in *Age of Anxiety*, he owes much to the parallels implicit between the English at war and the Anglo-Saxons; Wilbur's poems lack comparable context.)

Wit is as much as ever at the center of Wilbur's approach, along with his sharpness of vision. Sometimes it is in the service of dark humor, as in "Matthew VIII, 28 ff.," in which the Gadarenes, described as lovers of the material world frequently subject to possession by devils, conclude their re-marks to Christ: "If you cannot cure us without destroying our swine, / We had rather you shoved off." Sometimes it is in the service of what approxi-mates a metaphysical conceit, as in "On the Marginal Way," in which a beach "rubbled with strange rock" is compared to a shore in Spain at which ". . . George Borrow saw / A hundred women basking in the raw," and then, as the light shifts, to the scene of a massacre. Here wit and vision work closely together, are almost indistinguishable, as Wilbur continues his joy in correspondences between animate and inanimate worlds, in finding "the manhood of this stone."

The book's title poem, and another entitled "The Agent," represent the chief technical innovations, if they can be called that. They are slightly longer than the poems Wilbur has been accustomed to writing, and they are in blank verse. But it is a blank verse so infused with the spirit of An-glo-Saxon verse that Wilbur can be credited with having transformed it into a personal instrument.

Richard Wilbur's insistence on adhering to traditional forms has often raised reservations in even his admirers. Nonetheless, his handling of these forms is so skillful, his range of technique so wide, perhaps this criticism is really a response to the rarity of Wilbur's encounters with the darker sides of the human condition. He is a poet of affirmation, of celebration; and there is nothing at all naive in his understanding of the complexities of ex-perience. But he has not yet wanted, or perhaps not yet been able, to en-counter face to face the terror that poets like Roethke, Lowell, Berryman, Plath, so often faced. At its best, however, Wilbur's poetry is like the pool, by whose side Vishnu sleeps in "Walking to Sleep," "On whose calm face all images whatever / Lay clear, unfathomed, taken as they came."

See also the Introduction, section IX.

Selected Bibliography:

BY WILBUR:

The Beautiful Changes and Other Poems. New York: Reynal & Hitchcock (Harcourt Brace Jovanovich), 1947.

Ceremony and Other Poems. New York: Harcourt Brace Jovanovich, 1950.

Molière's The Misanthrope [Translation.] New York: Harcourt Brace Jovanovich, 1955.

Things of This World. New York: Harcourt Brace Jovanovich, 1956.

Candide: A Comic Opera (with Lillian Hellman and others). New York: Random House, 1957.

Advice to a Prophet and Other Poems. New York: Harcourt Brace Jovanovich, 1961.

Tartuffe [Translation.] New York: Harcourt Brace Jovanovich, 1963.

The Poems of Richard Wilbur. New York: Harcourt Brace Jovanovich, 1963.

Walking to Sleep: New Poems and Translations. New York: Harcourt Brace Jovanovich, 1969.

Digging for China. New York: Doubleday & Co., 1970.

See also Wilbur's essay "On My Own Work" in *Poets on Poetry*. Edited by Howard Nemerov. New York: Basic Books, 1966. Pp. 160–71.

About Wilbur:

Cambon, Glauco. *Recent American Poetry*. Minneapolis: University of Minnesota Press, 1962. Pp. 8–16.

Dickey, James. *Babel to Byzantium: Poets & Poetry Now*. Farrar, Straus & Giroux, 1968. Pp. 170–72.

Faverty, Frederic E. "Well-Open Eyes: or, The Poetry of Richard Wilbur" in *Poets in Progress*. Edited by Edward Hungerford. Evanston, Ill.: Northwestern University Press, 1967. Pp. 59–72.

Hill, Donald L. *Richard Wilbur*. New York: Twayne Publishers, 1967.

Mills, Ralph, Jr. *Contemporary American Poetry*. New York: Random House, 1965. Pp. 160–75.

Stepanchev, Stephen. *American Poetry since 1945*. New York: Harper & Row Publishers, 1967. Pp. 93–106.

WRIGHT, JAMES *(b. Martins Ferry, Ohio, Dec. 13, 1927—   )*

Wright has earned his recently acquired status as one of the more significant contemporary American poets by abandoning traditional forms in order to make accessible to his verse areas of experience too painful or chaotic to be contained by orderly structures. His growth in poetic technique has been accompanied by a shift in his conception of the artist's relation to reality, from confidence in the poet's ability to perceive reality from a coherent and consistent point of view to acceptance of a multiplicity of perspectives that he can no longer order. It is not a question of ideas—they remain more or less constant; it is a question of vision.

Educated at Kenyon College, the University of Vienna, and the University of Washington, Wright has become firmly entrenched in the academic world, since 1966 in the English Department of Hunter College in New

York City. He is closely associated with that group of writers that includes Robert Bly, Louis Simpson, and William Duffy, who have published regularly in the magazine now known as *The Seventies*. If there is any characteristic that unites this group, it is their interest in what has been called the "deep" or "subjective" image. Wright's concern with something resembling surreal imagery—the relationship between the deep image and the surreal image itself being unclear—seems evident. So does the fact that he has learned much from contemporaries and from his translations. But the drama formed by tensions present within his own work from the very start is probably of far greater interest and critical usefulness than his place in any movement.

The Green Wall (1957) is, not surprisingly, filled with echoes, most obviously of Frost, E. A. Robinson, and Roethke. The poems have the flavor of the American Midwest; the Garnie Braxton poems of later years are not at this point even a remote possibility, so removed from the urban imagination is Wright's voice. There is the continual effort to work man into a comforting natural framework. The effort is rarely successful, probably by design, for at no point in his poetic career is Wright simple-mindedly benign. But sentimentality is never very far away, as in the concluding lines of "Mutterings over the Crib of a Deaf Child": the poet will ". . . lift him into my arms and sing/Whether he hears my song or not." At its best the verse is skillfully wrought, but ethereal, in spite of its obvious commitment to the concrete:

> . . . I rose, lay back
> In trees, and died again. The spiders care
> For trellises they hold against the sky,
> Except for walls of air the houses die
> And fall; and only for my flesh of air
> Your flesh of earth would lean and drift away;
>
> (from "The Assignation")

But even in *The Green Wall*, Wright has leanings that move counter to these. "A Poem about George Doty in the Death House" is not totally free from the threat of sentimentality, but it also holds the key to the kind of toughness that ultimately pervades his work; it is a toughness that grows from his identification with the outcasts and failures of his first book. Wright began by trying to resolve Robinson's bleak and lonely vision with the humanized natural world of Frost. His essential problem was to work out the conflicts with his own perceptions, his own voice.

Saint Judas (1959) is closer in subject and method to *The Green Wall* than any of Wright's later volumes of poetry. If anything, Robinson's presence is more strongly felt, and the regular meters and stanzaic patterns are even more polished. New chords are struck, however, even though they are shifts in emphasis rather than totally new directions. "In Shame and Humiliation," bearing an epigraph from Dostoevski's *Notes from Underground*, suggests that evil and ugliness are not simply qualities to be endured but possibly the only means of salvation. In "At the Executed Murderer's Grave," Wright returns to George Doty. Seen with a strange compassion in the earlier book, but still seen from the outside, Doty becomes more and more Wright's double: ". . . Doty, killer, imbecile, and thief:/Dirt of my flesh, defeated, underground." The last word refers, of course, to the buried murderer; at the same time it also may allude to Dostoevski's protagonist. Doty here is not only a murderer; he has himself been murdered. He is a criminal-victim, he is invoked as well as exorcized. He is Saint Judas, whose ambiguity haunts the book. The title seems to indicate Judas, the loyal Apostle. But the title poem reveals that Wright has in mind Judas Iscariot; and *he* is the saint.

Wright's identification with the outcast, his understanding that the term "common humanity" may include much that is horrifying, seems to extend to the natural world as well. There are moments in *Saint Judas* when the conventional boundaries of the self begin to dissolve, as in "Evening," where Wright says of a boy:

> I saw his hair turn leaf,
> His dancing toes divide
> To hooves on either side,
> One hand become a bird.

Surreal this may be. But it is not simply the temporary victory of the unconscious. It seems rather a result of the perception that the world deeply within and the world without are ultimately reconcilable.

The Branch Will Not Break (1963) begins with "As I Step Over a Puddle at the End of Winter, I Think of an Ancient Chinese Governor," a poem for which Wright's previous volumes scarcely prepare us. Most obviously, the careful meters and stanzaic patterns of earlier poems have been abandoned. Parallel to this new freedom, and maybe in some way related to it, is a new tone, a new perspective, that the poet brings to bear upon his materials. Po Chu-i seems at first in the tradition of Robinsonian failures, outcasts, or lonely men that fill *The Green Wall* and *Saint Judas*. And the poem is certainly characteristic in Wright's immediate impulse to identify with his subject, to break down the distinctions between them. Here the word "identify" takes on new implications. What was before an act of imaginative sympathy now approaches merger. Widely separated periods of time and areas of space are juxtaposed: ninth-century China with twentieth-century America. But this is merely the context for a similarity not so much of personality as of predicament, that of the poet involved in politics, which leads Wright to conclude the poem with "Or have you been holding the end of a frayed rope/For a thousand years?"

The tone of "As I Step Over a Puddle . . ." is so great an expansion of Wright's previous range that Paul Carroll devotes an entire essay in *The Poem in Its Skin* to exploring the poem's comic dimensions, an approach unlikely to suggest itself in Wright's earlier poetry. The change is possibly Wright's greater detachment from the self, which allows him more room for irony, and which encourages him to take risks.

"Fear Is What Quickens Me" catches up all of these strands. Wright begins with the animals "our fathers killed in America"; "they stared about wildly." Images of an encroaching civilization, and then more mysterious images of woman, rabbits and doves, lead to the poem's brief final section: "I look about wildly." It is again the reversal of killer and victim, the man here identifying with the animals. But the poet does not tell us he feels like a frightened animal; he becomes one. The center of consciousness of the poem is still the poet, but the boundaries of that center are no longer clearly defined. While the poem is very carefully bound together by the wild looks at its beginning and its end, there is the unexpectedness of a non sequitur about the poem's conclusion, and a kind of self-mocking that is here more closely related to terror than to wit.

The structure of "Fear Is What Quickens Me" is similar to that of "Lying in a Hammock at William Duffy's Farm in Pine Island, Minnesota." The circular movement is provided by the bronze butterfly at the poem's start and the chicken hawk at its conclusion. Here, however, there is no preparation at all for the final line: "I have wasted my life." What has taken place in the poem is most accessible if the reader understands the relation of the "objective" description of Duffy's Farm to Wright's inner world. To call it an inner landscape would be pointless; its interest lies precisely in the fact that it is outer. The relation between inner and outer here seems closely to resemble William Carlos Williams' distinction between art and reality:

> Nature is the hint to composition not because it is familiar to us and therefore the terms we apply to it have a least common denominator quality which gives them currency—but because it possesses the quality of independent existence, of reality which we feel in ourselves. It is not opposed to art but apposed to it.

> *(Spring and All)*

As it was for Williams, the outcome of this aesthetic in Wright's poetry is a mode of perceiving the world that allows an open flow between consciousness and objective reality, that refuses to recognize as firmly fixed the boundaries of the self.

Perhaps the clearest illustration of the principle of apposition rather than opposition is in "Beginning." Early in the poem "The dark wheat listens"; toward the end, the persona declares, "I listen." In the final lines, "The wheat leans back toward its own darkness,/And I lean toward mine." The poet both is and is not the wheat; the reality of each is a comment on the other.

The Branch Will Not Break, while never far from the specifically human world, is probably the furthest Wright has gone in his wish to explore the relationship between man and nature. In *Shall We Gather at the River* (1968), Wright continues to use the techniques of apposition developed in the previous volume; but now it is the human rather than the natural landscape upon which he relies. An overwhelming majority of the poems are concerned with death and loneliness; old age becomes a dominant symbol for the human condition.

The poems of *Shall We Gather at the River* are more difficult to categorize in terms of method than most of Wright's earlier work. The lessons possibly learned from Williams, and the unmistakable echoes of Roethke, have been fully absorbed into a now distinctive voice. "Old Age Compensation," for example, begins with autumn or winter images of death and desolation: frost, "haggard" pumpkins, dying ants. To this point, the poem is relatively straightforward; it is almost, but not quite, naturalistic. Then Wright asserts: "All creatures who have died today of old age/Have gone more than ten miles already." The metaphor is ambiguous. The fact that the poet trails behind this ghostly procession ("All day I have slogged behind") does not help. Whether we are dealing with the dead or the dying, the terror of oblivion or of aging—distinctions the poem itself refuses to make—the poet's relation to his subject begins to emerge, to become the poem's subject. The candle, the old-age home, the night-herons, the river that must be crossed; again no clarity of reference, but a strong suggestion of a journey into the underworld. The tension of the poem comes out of the poet's strain to join the procession, because he sympathizes, because he wishes to be dead; the distinction is: "They don't need my candle./But I do." The techniques are identifiable: surreal imagery, apposition, confusion of the boundaries of the self. The special quality that Wright brings to these methods is a very strong sense of a "realistic" world of human suffering against which the imagery of the poem is played, very much the way free verse can be played off against iambic meters that are not really present but are somehow evoked by the poet's rhythms.

A more coherent unit than any of Wright's previous books, *Shall We Gather at the River* is woven together by threads of imagery. Dark waters abound, people drown, sometimes whole cities; "suckholes" are waiting to swallow them up. Shadows hover over the waters, Christian imagery is never far from the poems' surfaces. Most often, however, the anticipated resurrection cannot take place:

> The strange water, the
> Ohio river, that is no tomb to
> Rise from the dead
> From.

> (from "Three Sentences for a Dead Swan")

The despair, not always equally intense, sometimes interspersed with joy, is never totally dissipated. As he puts it in "The Lights in the Hallway": ". . . I float among/Lonely animals, longing/For the red spider who is God."

James Wright's *Collected Poems* (1971) contains a substantial selection of new work. At times, his vision is so dark it seems a hole in the darkness, and there are moments of Swiftian venom that make the blackness of earlier works seem but a gentle gloom:

> Man's heart is the rotten yolk of a blacksnake egg
> Corroding, as it is just born, in a pile of dead
> Horse dung.
> I have no use for the human creature.
> He subtly extracts pain awake in his own kind.
> I am born one, out of an accidental hump of chemistry.
> I have no use.

(from "A Secret Gratitude")

The lines are so absolute that their dramatic context does not serve totally to dissociate the poet's own position from the persona's. It is nonetheless clear that this poem represents *a* vision of reality, not *the* vision. The new poems often demonstrate a lighter touch than those of the previous volume —lighter in the sense both of being witty and more detached and of penetrating the murkiness. Sexual love is more insistent here, more nearly a balance for the dark, destroying waters.

In "A Moral Poem Freely Accepted from Sappho," Wright merges lovers, deer, and the poem itself: "This poem is a deer with a dream in it." He plays with the pun on dying as orgasm; here, the dead rise in the "Brilliance of the sun that is / More gold than gold."

"Northern Pike," however, is probably most typical of Wright's stance in this book. Near the poem's start, Wright takes a position with which the readers of his poetry have become familiar:

> . . . Every body
> I know and care for,
> And every body
> Else is going
> To die in a loneliness
> I can't imagine and a pain
> I don't know. . . .

A fish is caught and slit open. Images of brutality are interspersed among perceptions of harmony with nature. There is, perhaps, no contradiction. The fish is eaten, and the poem concludes:

> There must be something very beautiful in my body,
> I am so happy.

How does Wright get from death, loneliness, and pain to happiness? By means of the fish. By means of the body. (The use of "every body" rather than "everybody" becomes significant here.) There is a strong temptation to see this as a Christian poem. "The body of this fish," we read. "We ate the fish." Since a fish is a traditional symbol of Christ, it is not difficult to see this poem as a version of the Eucharist. There is, however, a process unfolding through the poem that does not depend on any religious frame of reference for its significance. The killing of the fish seems almost a ceremonial act that unites man with nature, the living with the dead, good with evil. It breaks down the conventional distinctions to which human consciousness is accustomed and replaces them with a vision of simple being. This vision is not unrelated to the wish to be gathered into nature in Wright's earliest work. It is not, here, a question of mysticism, of losing one's identity to some vast oneness; it is a question of interpenetration of distinct realities.

This interpenetration is clearer in poems that present an alternative to the natural setting, for example, the poems involving Garnie Braxton, a young black friend of Wright's. "A Poem by Garnie Braxton" consists of a statement by Wright and a response by Garnie, apparently a literal transcription. Garnie's language is surreal; it is Garnie's voice that speaks, but his mode of apprehending reality is Wright's. There is no question here of "identification." There are rather interchangeable perspectives.

In "Many of Our Waters: Variations on a Poem by a Black Child," a much longer poem, the process is reversed. A "poem" by Garnie is followed by a sequence of poems by Wright. Garnie creates the image of the blind boy who drowns after riding a bicycle into water that seems to be acid. This poem combines the cluster of images Wright has already made his own, and the stage is set for a series of appositions: a city and country (New York and Ohio), black and white, art and nature, birth and death, images drawn from the life of Garnie and his family and images drawn from Wright's own life. There is even metrical apposition, with the more familiar, longer units of Wright's breath juxtaposed with the excited staccato of Garnie's.

The poem's voices are brought together in a couplet that sounds platitudinous in isolation but that works well enough in its proper context: "And how can I live my life/Unless you live yours?" It sounds something like the Robinsonian sympathy of the early works. Wright, however, has moved a great distance since then. He has moved from pity, the emotion of an observer, to love, the emotion of one who participates in the existence of others.

See also DEEP IMAGISM and the Introduction, section VIII.

Selected Bibliography:
BY WRIGHT:
The Green Wall. New Haven: Yale University Press, 1957.
Saint Judas. Middletown, Conn.: Wesleyan University Press, 1959.
The Branch Will Not Break. Middletown, Conn.: Wesleyan University Press, 1963.
Shall We Gather at the River. Middletown, Conn.: Wesleyan University Press, 1968.
Collected Poems. Middletown, Conn.: Wesleyan University Press, 1971.

About Wright:
Carroll, Paul. "As I Step Over a Puddle at the End of Winter, I Think of an Ancient Chinese Governor" in *The Poem in Its Skin.* Chicago: Follett Publishing Co., 1968. Pp. 189–202.

Howard, Richard. *Alone with America*. New York: Atheneum Publishers, 1969.
    Pp. 575–86.
Mills, Ralph J., Jr. *Contemporary American Poetry*. New York: Random House,
    1965. Pp. 197–217.
Stepanchev, Stephen. *American Poetry since 1945*. New York: Harper & Row
    Publishers, 1965. Pp. 180–85.